R
317.3

THE
OLD FARMER'S ALMANAC

Calculated on a new and improved plan for the year of our Lord

1993

Being 1st after LEAP YEAR and (until July 4)
217th year of American Independence

FITTED FOR BOSTON, AND THE NEW ENGLAND STATES, WITH SPECIAL
CORRECTIONS AND CALCULATIONS TO ANSWER FOR ALL THE UNITED STATES.

Containing, besides the large number of Astronomical Calculations
and the Farmer's Calendar for every month in the year, a variety of

NEW, USEFUL, AND ENTERTAINING MATTER.

ESTABLISHED IN 1792

BY ROBERT B. THOMAS

There was never any more inception than there is now,
Nor any more youth or age than there is now,
And will never be any more perfection than there is now,
Nor any more heaven or hell than there is now.

– WALT WHITMAN

COVER T.M. REGISTERED
IN U.S. PATENT OFFICE

ISSN 0078-4516

LIBRARY OF CONGRESS
CARD No. 56-29681

Address all editorial correspondence to
THE OLD FARMER'S ALMANAC, DUBLIN, NH 03444

83581

CONTENTS

The Old Farmer's Almanac • 1993

FEATURES

188

162

Anecdotes and Pleasantries **240**
Aphelion, Earth at **37**
Astrological Timetable **193**
Calendar Pages **56-83**
Calendars, 1992-1994 .... **256**
Chronological Cycles **36**
Church Holy Days **36, 57-83**
Classified Ads **235**
Conjunctions, Astronomical ... **37, 42, 57-83**
Dawn and Dark **35**
Day, Length of **35, 56-82**
Earthquakes **36**
Eclipses **44**
Eras **36**
Essay Contest **184**
Fishing, Best Days for **181**
Foreword, To Patrons **4**
Frosts and Growing Seasons **202**
Glossary **40**
Holidays **38**
How to Use This Almanac **34**
Key Letters **34, 198**
Measuring Units, Origin of Old-Time **216**
Meteor Showers **44**
Moon: Astrological Place **211**
    Astronomical Place **34, 56-82**
    Full, 1993-1997 .... **44**
    Gardening by **210, 211**
    Phases of **56-82**
    Rise and Set **34, 56-82**
Perihelion, Earth at **37**
Planets: Rise and Set **35, 42**
    Symbols for **37**
Planting Tables **210, 211**
Puzzles **170**
    Answers to **174**
Recipe Contest **182**

Seasons **36**
Stars, Bright **45**
Sun: Astrological Signs **194**
    Declination **56-82**
    Rise and Set **34, 56-82**
Sun Fast **35, 56-82**
Sundials **35**
Tidal Glossary **205**
Tides, Boston **34, 56-83**
Tides, Correction Tables ... **204**
Time Correction Tables **198**
Twilight, Length of **35**
Wind Speeds, Beaufort's Scale of **120**
Zodiac **211, 192-197**

Weather:

Forecast Methods **38**
General U.S. Forecast **128**
Map of U.S. Regions **129**
Regional Forecasts **130-156**
1. New England **130**
2. Greater N.Y.-N.J. **132**
3. Middle Atlantic Coast .. **134**
4. Piedmont & S.E. Coast **136**
5. Florida **138**
6. Upstate N.Y.-Toronto-Montreal **140**
7. Greater Ohio Valley **142**
8. Deep South **144**
9. Chicago-S. Great Lakes **146**
10. N. Great Plains-Great Lakes **148**
11. Central Great Plains **150**
12. Texas-Oklahoma **152**
13. Rocky Mountains **153**
14. Southwest Desert **154**
15. Pacific Northwest **155**
16. California **156**

TO PATRONS

Whew. The party's over. But we sure did have a wonderful 200th birthday year. What made it particularly fun was the fact that, in one way or another, so many members of the Almanac family participated. We have boxes of congratulatory messages — including one from the president of the United States. One from the prime minister of Canada, too. More than 700 readers submitted "names" for the Earth and the Moon. (See page 186 for a full report.) Equally as many entered the essay, recipe, and cookbook contests. Puzzle contributors were twice the number of a normal year.

Many wrote to say, "Happy birthday," and then ask a question they'd "always been meaning to ask." Like why did we write, "Beware the Pogonip," last December 16 on the Right-Hand Calendar Page? (Pogonip is an American Indian term for icy fog, considered bad for the lungs.) Why aren't the Moon signs consistent throughout the Almanac? (Astrological and astronomical signs are not the same, and while we have one annual astrological Moon signs table — page 211 — all other calculations are based on astronomy.) When's the best time to plant potatoes, catch fish, castrate my bull? (When the Moon's on the wane, the hours before or after high tide, and between the last quarter and new Moon, respectively.)

So now, with this 201st consecutive annual edition, we're beginning our third century, 99 years away from our next centenary. None of us will be around to celebrate it, but this 1993 edition will surely still exist — somewhere. Probably in some attics and stacked on the dusty shelves of a few antique shops. For certain it'll be at the Smithsonian Institution in Washington, D.C. They maintain a complete set of Almanacs.

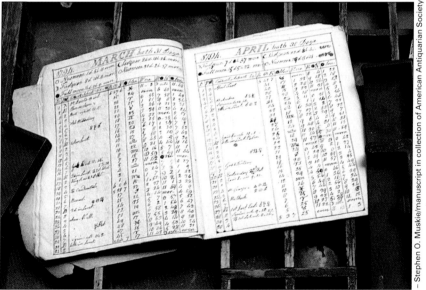

Handwritten draft of the 1794 edition, prepared by founder Robert B. Thomas in the summer of 1793.

Someone in 2092 will likely read these words. Someone as yet unborn . . .

Hello, there. We've just completed our 200th birthday celebration. It was a big time. But, of course, in all honesty we can't say it was the most important event of the year. We experienced economic hard times, the collapse of something we called Communism, a quick little war in the Middle East (we were still dependent on oil as fuel, you see), and lots of fickle weather caused, we think, by a cyclical shift in a Pacific Ocean current known as El Niño. Our worries included a gap in the Earth's ozone layer, the horrendous size of the national debt, the strong possibility of global warming, and a terrible disease we called AIDS. By now you know how well we succeeded in coping with these concerns. Maybe just by the fact that you're reading this century-old greeting, we can say we muddled through all right. If readers are still querying the Almanac about gardening matters, when dog days begin, and why the Moon looks bigger on the horizon than overhead (it's an optical illusion), then it's likely your problems will eventually be solved, too! The human coping mechanism is always underrated.

Good luck. And think of us once in a while . . .

Well, enough talking to strangers. We want to thank you, our present-day readers, for your extra support and friendship over this past anniversary year. Our hope now, however, is that you'll feel that this edition, the first of our third century, is the best one of them all . . . so far.   J.D.H.

However it is by our works and not our words that we would be judged. These, we hope, will sustain us in the humble though proud station we have so long held in the name of

Your ob'd servant,

June 1992

The 1993 Edition of
THE OLD FARMER'S ALMANAC
Established in 1792
and published every year thereafter
ROBERT B. THOMAS (*1766-1846*)
FOUNDER

EDITOR (*12th since 1792*): JUDSON D. HALE SR.
MANAGING EDITOR: SUSAN PEERY
EXECUTIVE EDITOR: TIM CLARK
ART DIRECTOR: MARGO LETOURNEAU
BUSINESS MANAGER, EDITORIAL: ANN DUFFY
WEATHER PROGNOSTICATOR:
DR. RICHARD HEAD
ASTRONOMER: DR. GEORGE GREENSTEIN
COPY EDITOR: LIDA STINCHFIELD
ASSISTANT EDITORS: ANNA LARSON, DEBRA
SANDERSON, JODY SAVILLE, MARY SHELDON
RESEARCH EDITOR: JAMIE KAGELEIRY
FACT CHECKER: MARE-ANNE JARVELA
ARCHIVIST: LORNA TROWBRIDGE
CONTRIBUTING EDITORS:
CASTLE FREEMAN JR., *Farmer's Calendar;*
FRED SCHAAF, *Astronomy*
PRODUCTION DIRECTOR: JAMIE TROWBRIDGE
PRODUCTION MANAGER: PAUL BELLIVEAU
PRODUCTION ARTISTS:
LUCILLE RINES, STEVE KUSNAROWIS
PRODUCTION SYSTEMS COORDINATOR:
STEVE MUSKIE

PUBLISHER (*22nd since 1792*): JOHN PIERCE
ASSOCIATE PUBLISHER: SHERIN WIGHT
ADVERTISING DIRECTOR: KEVIN SCULLY
MARKETING RESEARCH MANAGER:
MARTHA CAVANAUGH
ADVERTISING PRODUCTION:
RITA TROUBALOS, *Manager;*
STACY BERNSTEIN, LORI GRAY
NEWSSTAND CIRCULATION:
KEMCO PUBLISHERS SERVICES

ADVERTISING & PUBLISHING OFFICE:
MAIN STREET, DUBLIN, NH 03444
PHONE 603-563-8111

YANKEE PUBLISHING INC., DUBLIN, NH 03444

JOSEPH B. MEAGHER, *President;* JUDSON D. HALE SR.,
Senior Vice President; BRIAN PIANI, *Vice President* and *Chief
Financial Officer;* JAMES H. FISHMAN, JOHN PIERCE, AND
JOE TIMKO, *Vice Presidents.*

The Old Farmer's Almanac *Celebrates*

★☆★ Great Trad

The backbone of our nation has always been a deep and abiding belief in certain values. Many are spelled out in elegant detail in our Constitution and our Bill of Rights; others have been defined more laboriously through our legislatures and our courts. Still others are inherited from our families, our ancestors, or our religious preference. All, however, are important because they form the frame on which we as a people and as individuals can build our lives.

Just as these cultural values have shaped our society, a number of famous names in the world of business have influenced our approach to commerce. Through their commitment to producing products of consistent quality offered at a fair price, they have set standards in the world of business to which other companies must aspire if they wish to remain competitive. We have invited a number of them to join us in a special celebration of certain of those Great Traditional Values that define our lives in so many different ways. These values are the bedrock that underlies all our efforts to make progress toward a brighter future.

Historical information compiled by Mary W. Cornog

ional Values

COMMUNITY AND INDIVIDUALITY:

I believe that every right implies a responsibility, every opportunity an obligation, every possession a duty.
— J. D. Rockefeller Jr.

I've labored long and hard for bread,
For honor and for riches,
But on my corns too long you've tread,
You fair-haired sons of bitches.
— Charles E. "Black Bart" Boles, stagecoach robber (note attached to empty strongbox, Fort Ross, California, 1877)

★ The annals of America are full of individuals who insist on doing things their own way. The first pirate on the Atlantic coast, for instance, began his career in 1632. Dixie Bell had been robbed by a French pirate and decided the best way to exact revenge was by becoming a pirate himself. Piracy continued to be a nuisance along the coast and on the high seas for almost another 200 years.

★ In 1632 members of the Massachusetts Bay Colony instituted a property tax, which the town of Dorchester then chose in 1639 to use to support its public school.

★ Massachusetts declared education compulsory in 1642; each town was responsible for its own schools and taxed the property of its residents from then on.

★ The first local board of health was established in 1792 in Baltimore, Maryland. It consisted of one quarantine physician each for land and sea.

★ The first quarantine was proclaimed in 1793 in Philadelphia for yellow fever.

★ A public health service operated nationally by 1798, but concerned itself only with the health of merchant seamen entering the country's ports and taxed each as he came in.

★ Louisiana established the first state board of health to regulate quarantines in 1855.

⁕Great Traditional Values

COMPETITION AND COOPERATION:

The highest and best form of competition is the spontaneous cooperation of a free people.
– Woodrow Wilson, quoted by Bernard Baruch

Competition brings out the best in products and the worst in people.
— David Sarnoff in *Esquire*

★ Competition demands advertising. The first advertisement for patent medicine appeared in 1692 in Benjamin Harris's *Boston Almanack*: John Allen offered "That excellent Antidote against all manner of Gripings called Aqua anti torminales, which if timely taken, it not only cures the Griping of the Guts, and the Wind Cholick; but preventeth that woeful Distemper of the Dry Belly Ach; With printed directions for the use of it." It could be purchased for three shillings

the half-pint bottle at Harris's London Coffee House.

★ Automobile advertising began in 1898 in *Scientific American* with an ad for cars made by the Winton Motor Car Company of Cleveland, whose motto was, "Dispense with a horse."

★ Cooperative ventures have been less numerous than competitive ones, but important nonetheless. A cooperative cheese factory began operations in Cheshire, Massachusetts, in 1801. On July 20 of that year members pressed a cheese that weighed 1,235 pounds when cured one month later. This cheese arrived at President Jefferson's White House doorstep in a large horse-drawn wagon on January 1, 1802.

Great Traditional Values

CONFIDENCE AND HUMILITY:

Be always sure you are right — then go ahead. — Davy Crockett, *Autobiography*

It's just a job. Grass grows, birds fly, waves pound the sand. I beat people up. — Muhammad Ali in *The New York Times*

★ Confidence and humility seem to go hand in hand in American history. The colonies gave themselves the name United Colonies on June 7, 1775, and simultaneously decreed that the 20th of July "be observed throughout the Twelve United Colonies as a day of humility, fasting, and prayer." Only 12 colonies acted on these matters, because Georgia had sent no delegate to the meeting.

★ At the Second Continental Congress, held in September 1776, the colonies agreed to call themselves the United States, but forebore to decree any public celebration of humility.

★ The first road map designed for public use in navigating the colonies' highways appeared in *Tully's Almanac* in 1698; it depicted the area around Boston, and all towns, roads, and distances were calculated with Boston at the hub. Later editions also gave the names of local tavernkeepers.

☆Great Traditional Values

IDEALISM AND PRAGMATISM:

Imagination is more important than knowledge. – Albert Einstein in *On Science*

All you need for happiness is a good gun, a good horse, and a good wife.
– Daniel Boone, attributed

★ Some inventions have their start in the dreams of their inventors. New Haven was home to a planetarium and orrery from 1743 on.

★ The first typewriter was patented in 1829, the first typewriter that typed successfully in 1843, and the first typewriter to produce a line of type that could be seen as it was typed in 1893. The portable typewriter appeared in 1892, the electrical portable model in 1956.

★ The canning process was patented in 1825, but was not really successful until after the Civil War — until then at least 50 percent of everything canned spoiled because the art of hermetically sealing the cans had not been mastered.

★ The tintype camera was patented by H. L. Smith in 1856. The roll-film camera appeared in 1888, but at $8,500 it did not quickly replace earlier versions.

★ Computers began to appear on the scene in 1946. In 1958 Remington Rand Univac developed a solid-state version that weighed 3,500 pounds and took up 275 square feet. But that was less than a sixth of the weight and volume of its predecessors.

Link Between Citrus Fruit and Cancer Prevention Cited

As science brings the link between diet and disease prevention closer, the old adage "you are what you eat" is taking on a whole new meaning. For example, orange juice is rich in vitamin C, a powerful antioxidant. Vitamin C can help prevent oxidation of cells (a decaying process) and counter the damage done to cells by environmental stress.

More than a dozen classes of phytochemicals (the protective chemicals made by plants) are found in orange juice. As our bodies do not make or store these materials, we must consume these natural substances continually throughout our lives. By making them part of our daily diet, we can derive long-term benefits from their antioxidant and disease-preventive properties.

Dr. Herbert Pierson, founder and former director of the National Cancer Institute's "designer food" program, notes that chemical components of various fruits and vegetables have been shown to help prevent certain forms of cancer, including breast, colon, and oral cancers.

Dr. Pierson also notes that the best natural source of antioxidants and phytochemicals is citrus fruit. "Fresh citrus has practically every species of phytochemical studied thus far." However, Dr. Pierson adds that citrus fruit is only the agent, or "vehicle," that will help prevent disease. Overall diet and the environment play a crucial role in keeping healthy.

NEW STUDY LINKS VITAMIN C TO A DRAMATIC DROP IN HEART DISEASE

A 10-year government study conducted by the National Center for Health Statistics has examined the relationship between Vitamin C intake and mortality. 11,348 average American men and women participated. They ranged in age from 25 to 74. The results, analyzed by a research team at UCLA, were adjusted for disease history, smoking, exercise, and other differences.

What the researchers discovered was that Vitamin C can offer remarkable protection against heart disease, especially when consumed in amounts well above the government's recommended daily allowance of 60 mg. Consuming 300-400 mg each day seems to be far more beneficial. Based on the results of the study, it could help women extend their lives by a year and men up to six years.

100% Pure Florida Orange Juice can be a big help in getting more Vitamin C into your diet. It's one of the very best sources. With 300-400 mg as the goal, you could be halfway there with just two delicious 8-oz. glasses of orange juice per day.

The rest is easy. You can also get Vitamin C from foods like fresh oranges, grapefruit, cantaloupes, broccoli, tomatoes, and peppers.

The smart thing to do is to maintain a healthy, well-rounded diet and make orange juice a part of it every day.

100% PURE FLORIDA ORANGE JUICE

© State of Florida, Dept. of Citrus, 1992

☆Great Traditional Values

FRUGALITY AND LUXURY:

We never repent of having eaten too little.
                              – Thomas Jefferson

"Goodness, what beautiful diamonds."
"Goodness had nothing to do with it, dearie." — Mae West in *Night After Night*

★Frugal Americans always hated to waste anything, especially effort or food. Nathaniel Briggs of New Hampshire patented the first washing machine in 1797 — "an improvement in washing cloaths." The machine appeared with hand-cranked rotary motion in 1858.

★ The refrigerator began saving food in Baltimore kitchens in 1803, when Thomas More placed one box inside another with insulation between them and then kept ice and food in the inner box. He sold licenses to people to manufacture these, but gave permission to the poor for no charge.

★ Comfort arrived in various forms. Ben Franklin probably invented the rocking chair around 1760. The deck chair as we know it today appeared in 1891. It was designed and built by Heinrich Conried, impresario of the Metropolitan Opera Company, who produced thousands and rented them to steamships companies.

★ The famous Murphy bed, made by the Murphy Door Bed Company of San Francisco, arrived in crowded apartments in 1909.

★ And in 1858, a good year for frugality and luxury, bustles, baby carriages, and pencils with attached erasers were all patented.

Now We're Talkin' Horsepower.

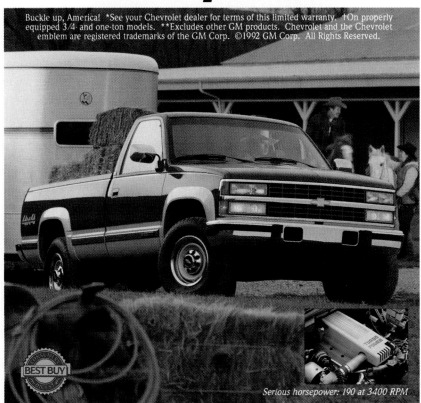

Serious horsepower: 190 at 3400 RPM

• *Towing capacity of up to 9500 lbs. 2WD, 9000 lbs. 4WD.†* • *Payload capacity of 3784 lbs. to 4764 lbs. 2WD, 3313 lbs. to 4355 lbs. 4WD.†* • *3-year/36,000-mile Bumper to Bumper Plus Warranty. No deductible.** • Winner of 1992 Consumers Digest "Best Buy" award.*

The most horsepower of any turbo-diesel pickup. Introducing the new 6.5 Liter, 190-HP HD Turbo-Diesel V8—and it's only available in Chevrolet full-size pickups for '92.** The latest in diesel technology, this turbo-diesel is engineered for quick response and smokeless performance. Chevrolet. The trucks you can depend on. The trucks that last.

The Heartbeat Of America Is Winning.™

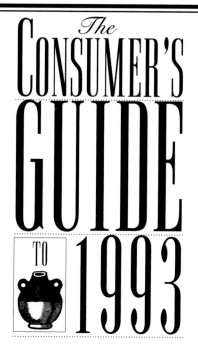

The CONSUMER'S GUIDE TO 1993

According to projections of current statistical trends, here's what you can expect will happen in 1993 . . . **by Kim Long**

The coming year has at least one predictable outcome — the traditional relief from the exaggeration of reality that accompanies every presidential year. Recovering from the hype, we are still left with the same problems

VITAL STATISTICS

	1983	1993 (est.)
Population:	234 mil.	256 mil.
Births:	3.6 mil.	4.1 mil.
Deaths:	2.1 mil.	2.4 mil.
Marriages:	2.4 mil.	2.0 mil.
Divorces:	1.2 mil.	1.0 mil.
Average Family Size:	3.26 pers.	2.95 pers.

as before. Worried about the cost of health care or the shape of the economy? In 1993 it is likely that the economy, at least, will have recovered enough on its own to avoid unnecessary tinkering by Washington. This is unlikely to happen with the health-care system, which is almost certainly due for major surgery.

Middle-Class Changes

In the remainder of the decade, some changes can be expected in the way the middle class lives and works. This part of the American population is generally considered to be those households with incomes of $15,000 to $50,000 a year — a total of about 36 million families in 1991. A few changes in life-style to look for include:

☞ **College** will become the high school of the 1990s. As part of this trend, school years will be thought of as grades 1 through 16 or at least 1 through 14. For those who really aspire to advancement, graduate school will become a new norm.

☞ **The office of the future** could be invisible. About one million people are now working full-time at home as part of their regular employment; more than 20 million households have some kind of income-generating business operating from home. These numbers will increase as telecommunication costs drop; however, even a decade from now, the majority of work will still be done in office and factory settings.

☞ **The gymnasium of the future** will be the outdoors. Although the majority of the adult population still does not exercise regularly, the number that does is gradually increasing. Because of costs and convenience, many of these exercisers are moving away from gyms and exercise clubs, instead using outdoor activities to burn off their calories.

Backyard Changes

Enthusiasm for composting is heating up. New composting activity includes the adaptation of large-scale commercial methods to divert biodegradable material from landfills. The first such operation in the United States was begun in Thornton, Colorado (near Denver), in 1976 by Jim McNelly, the founder of the Natursoil Company. On a smaller scale, backyard composting by homeowners is being widely adopted — sometimes because of local laws re-

stricting the dumping of grass clippings, leaves, or other organic yard wastes in landfills. Some super-enthusiastic fans of this ancient practice are even composting indoors, with carefully controlled, odor-free bins.

Another new twist is the growing interest in *vermicomposting* — the use of worms to turn kitchen scraps and yard trimmings into rich soil. One sign that this may become a new national pastime: schools, museums, and nature programs are encouraging kids to start indoor windowsill "worm gardens."

Another trend inspired by concern for the environment is the replacement of traditional lawns and ornamental gardens with "xeriscape" substitutes. *Xeriscaping* is the use of plants with low or no watering requirements, a concept developed in the water-scarce urban environments of the western states. Although a full-time concern in the West, "dry gardens" will be catching on in the East and South as well, spurred by recent droughts, increasing water bills, and new environmental awareness.

A related gardening development is being called *mesiscaping*, referring to plants that thrive in moderately moist climates. Both xeriscaping and mesiscaping provide gardeners with increased opportunity to enjoy a variety of vegetation without needless watering or protection from local climate conditions.

Health Trends

☞ **Super aspirin.** Chemists are working to perfect the next generation of aspirin-based products. In several major drug companies, research is underway to perfect a "super aspirin," with the ability to prevent blood clots during heart attacks. Regular aspirin has already proven effective, in small doses, at reducing the potential for blood clots to clog arteries; the new version is expected to be much more effective in emergency situations.

☞ **One-stop coping.** One of the latest trends in mental health is the practice of single-visit therapy programs. In certain kinds of cases — not including serious psychiatric conditions such as depression, psychosis, or schizophrenia — some specialized psychiatrists and psychologists are beginning to offer "quick fix" sessions with patients.

☞ **Prescription nags.** One of the biggest problems in modern medicine is "patient noncompliance," or patients who do not follow their doctors' orders, especially for prescribed medications. Solutions will include telephone reminder programs, electronically controlled medication dispensers, and a wider array of timed-release drugs.

☞ **Prescription yogurt.** A special type of yogurt with the capability of controlling diarrhea has been developed in Finland and is available in that country. The FDA is evaluating the product for eventual sale here.

☞ **Hangover medicine.** A new drug has

MILESTONES

300th ANNIVERSARY: In 1693 the last person was executed for witchcraft in the American colonies.

200th ANNIVERSARY: In 1793 the first balloon ascent in the United States took place. (See page 188.)

100th ANNIVERSARY: In 1893 the World Columbian Exposition (see page 162) attracted 12 million visitors to Chicago, Illinois. Also: Cracker Jacks were invented, aspirin was developed, and the first electric toaster was sold.

50th ANNIVERSARY: In 1943 the Jefferson Memorial was dedicated in Washington, D.C. (see page 250 about Jefferson); the Allies landed in Sicily and Tarawa; and the Chicago subway was opened.

25th ANNIVERSARY: In 1968 the Tet Offensive began in Vietnam, the Gateway Arch was dedicated in St. Louis, and Lake Erie was proclaimed dead.

been developed to eliminate hangover symptoms. This controversial "morning after" medication must first be approved by the FDA, a process that might take several years. Critics hope its use will be strictly controlled, lest it provide unintentional encouragement for excessive drinking.

Cooking Changes

The change to two-wage-earner households has helped push along another trend that has been quietly building for some time — the decline in cooking skills. In short, we are becoming a nation of cooking illiterates. *Less than half of all meals eaten at home now have dishes made from scratch.*

As a result, more cookbooks for beginners will be published in the next few years. In packaged foods, more step-by-step instructions are included, and the ingredients must have a greater tolerance for error.

Despite their ignorance in the kitchen, however, more consumers than ever have developed a taste for above-average food. The result is the birth of a new chapter in home cooking. The new trend is built on faster and more efficient ways of making meals, taking advantage of prepack-

aged ingredients and microwave ovens or simply buying prepared foods from restaurants or grocery stores for eating at home. In fact, in the last few years, dining at home has increased faster than dining out.

Based on "old-fashioned" cooking from scratch, the new "kit cooking" uses shortcuts — prepackaged "fresh" pasta, frozen sauces, premixed spices — to assemble meals. Those consumers satisfied to let the microwave be their chef might welcome new *microwave packaging* from the United Kingdom that will make their job even easier. The new food containers open automatically when done.

Food Trends

☞ **Crunchy raisins.** The clever farmers in California, who always seem to be trying to increase our hankering for more raisins, have discovered another marketing twist. This time, whole raisins are processed in a special way, turning them into dry, puffy fruit with a nontraditional crunch.

☞ **High-tech vegetables.** Through biotechnology, newly created forms of vegetables are on the way to market. Look for celery without strings, bell-

1 **Viva Italia Hybrid.** Tastes great fresh and in sauces.

2 **Big Girl® Hybrid VF.** Perfect for slicing or wedges.

3 **Supersteak Hybrid VFN.** Extra-meaty 1-2 lb. fruits.

4 **Super Sweet 100 Hybrid.** Long season, extra sweet.

5 **Early Girl Hybrid.** Produces fruit early and often.

6 **Delicious.** Its seed grew the world's largest tomato!

7 **Long-Keeper.** Keeps up to five months!

8 **Roma VF.** Recommended for sauces and catsup.

9 **Gardener's Delight.** An old time favorite.

10 **Pixie Hybrid II.** Our fastest-ripening tomato.

11 **Yellow Pear.** Mild and pleasing, great for salads.

12 **Celebrity Hybrid.** Great flavor, disease resistant.

12 Juicy Reasons to Send for a FREE 1993 Burpee Gardens Catalogue!

Tomatoes! Burpee's 1993 Garden Catalogue features 28 different tomato varieties! Early ones, late ones, big beauties and bite-sized gems. All packed full of garden-fresh flavor and *guaranteed* to satisfy. You will be able to choose from over 300 varieties of vegetables and over 400 varieties of flowers. Plus fruit trees, bulbs, shrubs, garden supplies. Your new catalogue will arrive in early January.

jalapeño pepper hybrids, and super-sweet carrots.

☞ **Domestic olive oil.** California olive growers, heartened by the marketing successes of the California wine industry, are beginning to impress gourmet cooks and upscale consumers with the quality of olive oil grown and produced in the United States.

☞ **More fat-free foods.** Among the upcoming arrivals in the low-calorie food department are a fat-free Eskimo Pie, full-flavor skim milk, and "skim" butter.

☞ **Gourmet heat.** Sometime in 1990, sales of salsas bypassed ketchup to become the number one condiment in the country. This new flush of popularity for hot pepper sauces is also creating a new market among gourmet restaurants and connoisseurs for premium chilis. Some gourmet hot sauces are being created in their traditional American home, the southwestern states; others are being imported from the Caribbean islands, Africa, Mexico, and southeast Asia.

☞ **Cheap sweet.** The patent on aspartame — brand name NutraSweet — expires at the end of 1992, allowing competing companies to produce this popular artificial sweetener, thus lowering prices on artificially sweetened products.

☞ **Breakfast snacks.** Consumption of convenience breakfast foods is going up, with much of the new demand coming from busy workers with less time to prepare traditional breakfast meals.

What-Will-They-Think-of-Next Department

Coming soon to a store near you — or already there if you live in a test market — are a host of strange new gizmos and gadgets.

☞ GREEN TIRES

No, rubber is not going to be dyed green. Green tires are a new generation of automotive treads that are designed to wear longer and increase gas mileage, thus helping the environment. As part of the process, tires are also getting smaller, requiring less material to make. The difference in size will not be accomplished by making the outside smaller, but by making the inside bigger — the wheels for these new "low-profile" tires will be larger in diameter to make up the difference.

☞ EDIBLE COTTON

Cottonseed has been a common product as a food filler, but until now, cotton itself has been of interest only to clothing manufacturers and boll weevils. A new process turns cotton fibers into an edible cellulose, making it a cheap — and thus desirable — additive for food products. Although the process is intended for newly farmed cotton, in the future it might be applied to discarded clothes, giving the human race its first opportunity to complete a recycling process under its own power.

☞ HIGH-TECH DRYERS

Within a few years, traditional gas and electric clothes dryers may have competition from a new design that uses microwaves to remove moisture.

☞ EXPANDING DIET PILLS

Many dieters may have fantasized about an ideal solution to their hunger pangs — a substance that expands in the stomach, but doesn't cost them extra calories. Modern science has now provided just such a solution — low-calorie tablets that expand up to five times their original size when exposed to gastric fluids in the stomach. The pills are made from edible forms of cellulose that swell up within 30 minutes after ingestion.

Order Your Special 1993 Hardcover Edition of

The Old Farmer's Almanac

The Hardcover Edition of the 1993 *Old Farmer's Almanac* is truly a Collector's Edition — one you'll be proud to display on your home library shelf.

Handsomely bound and protected by a full color, glossy dustjacket, the 1993 Edition is packed with all of the facts and fancy that millions of readers have enjoyed for over 200 years!

You'll delight in all of the regular Almanac features on science, amazingly accurate weather forecasts, gardening advice, planting tables, down-home humor, zesty recipes, incredible facts and oddities, sports and nature, handy household hints . . . *plus,* a special 32-page full-color section on Great Traditional Values . . . 280 pages in all!

☞ PLUS YOUR FREE GIFT

Act now, and you'll also receive the 1993 *Old Farmer's Almanac* Gardening Calendar. It sells for $4.95, but it's yours FREE with each copy of the Special Hardcover Edition of the 1993 *Old Farmer's Almanac* that you order! Newly redesigned for 1993, this beautifully illustrated full-color calendar features twelve seasonal gardening paintings; and you'll also discover wonderful bits of gardening wisdom to help insure a bumper crop for '93! It has 24 pages, opens to 11″ x 17″ so there's plenty of room for gardening notes, as well as moon phases, holidays, and seasonal events.

PLEASE DON'T MISS OUT! Mail the coupon below *OR* for fastest service, call **Toll-Free 1-800-234-6064.**

Unique Gifts and Collectible

*This fine assortment of gift ideas has been created especially fr
you . . . our loyal readers. We've carefully selected these items in
celebration of* **The Old Farmer's Almanac's** *200 years of
continuous publication. You'll find they are as delightful
to give as they are to receive.*

A true collectible.

The first in a planned series of tractor replicas for *The Old
Farmer's Almanac,* this Special Edition tractor has been
designed using the Massey-Harris Twin Power Challenger.
Die-cast metal, 1/16th scale.

**Massey-Harris Tractor,
#201TR $49.95**

Our most popular Ford.

A beautiful die-cast scale model replica of a 1913
Model T delivery truck, this commemorative coin
bank is sure to catch the fancy of any new or
seasoned collector on your gift list.

Model T, #204MT $19.95

Sure to appreciate in value.

Each replica model in this Collector's Edition
set is attractively detailed and marked with the
special *Old Farmer's Almanac* anniversary
dating 1792-1992. Each one doubles as a coin
bank with locking coin access and key. Includes
a Horse & Covered Wagon . . . a 1905 Ford
Delivery . . . and, a 1948 Diamond T Tractor Trailer.

Classic Banks Set, #202CS $74.95

> *Two 2-oz. coffee samples included*
> ——— **F R E E** ———
> *with each set of mugs.*

Useful and fun.

Colorful art and homespun advice from the pages of *The Old Farmer's Almanac* adorn
these 12-oz ceramic mugs. Each mug in this set of four features a sampling of old-time wit and wisdom
such as sure fire methods for predicting rain and the duties of a good daughter and son.

Set of 4 Mugs, #203MS $14.95

100% Satisfaction
Guaranteed Or Your
Money Back.

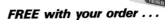

(continued from page 18)

Entertainment Trends

Leisure-minded Americans have been losing ground to the work ethic. Some studies have shown that the average amount of time spent working has increased — the opposite of what many pundits were expecting for the end of this century. The amount of leisure time has seemed to diminish mostly because of the great increase in families with both adults working.

One new trend for *family-oriented enter-tainment* is to replace major vacations with short breaks, such as visits to theme parks, campgrounds, rafting trips, educational museums, or other activity-intensive places.

More new leisure ac-

tivities will focus on family fun. Big companies are already spending big bucks. Major amusement parks are expanding, new entertainment centers are being planned, and existing adult entertainment destinations such as Las Vegas are rapidly remodeling to accommodate children and family activities.

Among the coming attractions are a Legoland theme park modeled after the original park in Europe, a 30-story pyramid in Las Vegas, a major expansion of Sea World in California, and an extension to the original Disneyland.

Fast-food chains now offer a variety of "eat-and-run" products. Expect to see a new category of finger foods created just for morning snacking, as well as more varieties of liquid breakfasts.

☞ **Hix Nix Organic Foodstuffs.** Commitment to organic foods may have reached saturation in the United States. After decades of growth, recent progress in sales of ingredients, fruits, and vegetables has stalled, leading to speculation that this trend will not hit the big time. However, the organic trend is also unlikely to shrink, having a dedicated audience of followers.

Gardening and Farming Trends

Heirloom vegeta-bles — varieties of familiar plants with historic roots — are becoming a hot item with many gardeners. Among the newly sought-after plants are wren's-egg shell beans, Maine yellow-eye beans, rattlesnake beans, black Aztec sweet corn, wild currant tomatoes, purple Peruvian potatoes, and Anasazi flour corn. These varieties generally date to before 1940, when hybridized vegetables began appearing nationwide.

Fans of the old, open-pollinated vegetables have established catalogs, newsletters, gardening clubs, and seed exchanges to resurrect, protect, and trade antique seeds. Another part of this trend is a new reverence for old flowers, particularly roses.

☞ **Designer grains.** Some agricultural seed companies are working with end users of grain — millers, bakers, cereal producers, and others — to create new specialty grains with unique proportions of protein, oil, moisture, or other components that directly affect the grain's use.

Miscellaneous Trends

☞ **Crackdown on pet collectors.** People who keep large populations of cats or dogs on their property (see page 104 for example) have been a continuous prob-

THE OLD FARMER'S ALMANAC

The first 200 years!

If you're one of the millions of readers who enjoys reading *The Old Farmer's Almanac* each year, here are some of the most interesting . . . most unusual . . . most humorous . . . and most useful stories, quotes, charts, and tidbits personally selected by Editor Jud Hale from the past 200 editions.

You'll delight in reading each of the 15 chapters which include over 200 historical photographs, woodcuts, and cartoons — 244 pages of pure reading pleasure!

In Part I: The First 200 Years, you'll read about the beginnings of *The Old Farmer's Almanac* in "Begun When Washington Was President" and about Robert B. Thomas, founder and first editor of *The Old Farmer's Almanac.*

In Part II: The Greatest Moments, you'll chuckle and be amazed when you read:

- ☛ **The Seeds Your Grandfather Used to Grow.**
- ☛ **The Secrets of Championship Vegetable Showing.**
- ☛ **Expert Advice on Catching, Keeping, Measuring, and Cooking Your Favorite Fish.**
- ☛ **The Real Reason Why the Week Has Seven Days!**
- ☛ **Was a Pig Really Responsible for Starting the War of 1812?**
- ☛ **How to Cook An Ostrich!**
- ☛ **Recipes From More Than 100 Years Ago.**
- ☛ **The Night Grandma Disappeared — *Completely!***

The Best of The Old Farmer's Almanac is handsomely bound in hard cover, large format (7½" x 9½"), printed on fine quality paper and contains 15 chapters plus index with a personal introduction by Jud Hale, the 12th editor of *The Old Farmer's Almanac.*

ORDER NOW and start enjoying this outstanding collection of American folklore, forecasts, and fun.

▼ **Complete the order form below *OR* call Toll-Free 1-800-234-6064 for fastest service!** ▼

- -

lem for humane societies and law-enforcement personnel for years. Because of pressure from them and from local health departments, many cities are beginning to consider new, tougher regulations to control these pet fanatics. And because a growing body of evidence indicates that the desire to keep large numbers of creatures may be linked to psychological disorders, there may soon be a new official psychiatric disorder named for this compulsion — collectors, when confronted, could then claim, "Guilty, but insane."

☞ **Factory outlet creep.** Now an established part of the American retail shopping scene, factory outlets are beginning to push into new territory. With generally flat sales elsewhere in the mall industry, shopping centers anchored by these establishments are beginning to interest developers, cities, and even owners of older, neglected traditional malls. This trend will ultimately result in some factory outlets leapfrogging the suburbs and establishing their own turf where shopping centers first began and then abandoned — inner cities.

☞ **Mouthwash malodor.** The next generation of public protests can be expected to develop over mouthwash poisonings. Thousands of cases of toxic alcohol poisoning in children have been reported over the past few years, the result of easily accessible, good-tasting products that are widely marketed without warnings about their contents. The major brands of mouthwashes contain high percentages of alcohol, as much as 50 percent, turning this oral-hygiene product into a potent poison in the wrong hands. Meanwhile, Spritz, a nonalcohol-based mouthwash now on the market, is finding new markets in hospitals, drug- and alcohol-rehabilitation centers, and among diabetics.

☞ Another product category about to get child-proofed is **disposable lighters.** At least two states will soon have rules requiring this new design feature; the Consumer Product Safety Commission may require it nationally by 1994.

The author: Kim Long has been researching and writing about consumer trends for the past ten years. He is the author of *The American Forecaster Almanac,* an annual book about the future.

WHAT A DIFFERENCE A DECADE CAN MAKE

	1983	1993 (est.)
Total ad spending	$76 bil.	$135 bil.
Ad spending per person	$324	$526
Number of franchised stores	442,000	620,000
Average movie ticket	$3.15	$5.40
Number of Boy Scouts	4.7 mil.	5.5 mil.
Number of Girl Scouts	2.9 mil.	3.2 mil.
Number of trips outside the U.S.	9.6 mil.	16 mil.
Number of foreign visitors to U.S.	7.9 mil.	16 mil.
Households with microwave ovens	35%	70%
Households with gas barbecue grills	18%	30%
Sales of electric toothbrushes	0.5 mil.	2.0 mil.
Sales of electric razors	5.9 mil.	9.1 mil.
Sales of electric popcorn poppers	3.6 mil.	6.5 mil.

If you love The Old Farmer's Almanac, you're sure o love these 1993 Old Farmer's Almanac Calendars!

1993 OLD FARMER'S ALMANAC GARDENING CALENDAR

Did you know . . . that the average American vegetable garden is 350 square feet? . . . that you should sow cabbage seeds in your nightclothes? . . . that for every fog in October there will be a storm in winter? You'll discover these and many more bits of wit and wisdom in the 1993 *Old Farmer's Almanac* Gardening Calendar. Redesigned for 1993 — beautiful full-color illustrations; ample room for gardening notes; Moon phases; holidays, seasonal events, and anniversaries. *Plus* — in the new feature "The Gardener's World," you'll learn about: growing horseradish; gardening in the woods; the "Carotene Routine;" how to test your soil; selecting just the right gardening tool, and much more. It's the calendar gardeners have relied on for fifteen years!

#3421-93 *8½" x 11" 24 pages, saddle-stitched* **$4.95**

1993 HEARTH & HOME CALENDAR

rand New for 1993 and chock full of wonderful recipes such as Gingered quash and Bean Soup, Swedish Cardamom Bread and Spiced Pear Muffins; time and money-saving hints from "The Frugal Housekeeper" ike removing rings from furniture, cleaning ivory piano keys, keeping ye glasses from steaming up in cold weather, and some innovative ses for onions, vinegar, and herbs; invaluable tips on quilting, hardaner embroidery, bargello and more in "The Sewing Basket;" and thought-rovoking quotes from the famous and the not-so-famous. Colorful drawngs and lively design make this an especially decorative wall calendar for our home.

#3430-93 *11" x 8½" 24 pages, saddle-stitched* **$5.95**

1993 OLD FARMER'S ALMANAC DIARY CALENDAR

For the person who has a busy schedule, this compact-size calendar goes along with you and fits easily into a jacket pocket or purse — always accessible. This weekly diary, with spacious format, allows plenty of space for daily appointments and reminders. It takes the best of *The Old Farmer's Almanac* — weather forecasts, astrological information, and unique tips and quotes — and brings them to you in this wonderful pocket calendar, richly wrapped in a *genuine* black leather cover and hot-foil stamped with *The Old Farmer's Almanac* trademark.

#3432-93 *3⅝" x 6⅛" 96 pages* **$14.95**

Just Who Is the American Farmer?

We asked researcher DEBORAH PAPIER to sketch a
statistical picture of the group for which this Almanac
was named, 201 years ago.

To lift a phrase from Mark Twain, the reports of the death of the family farm have been greatly exaggerated. It's true that over the last 100 years the number of American farmers has declined, and the percentage of the population that farms has plummeted. But the vast majority of America's farmland is still in the hands of American families, having eluded the grasp of the big corporations.

Those hands, however, are likely to be less callused than they once were. While farming is still a family business, it's an increasingly complicated one, requiring much more than a feeling for the soil. Today's farmer is likely to spend as much time feeding data into his (or her) computer as feeding the livestock.

"Farmers aren't rubes and hicks," says Calvin Beale, senior demographer for the Department of Agriculture in Washington. "Farming is a big business. People who don't want to be big can't make a living without other income." Many family farms are so large that they've incorporated, giving rise to the perception that corporations have squeezed out the family farmer.

Farmers today are also older, on the average, and they're overwhelmingly white. While a smattering of Hispanic and Asian immigrants have taken up farming, African Americans, once a significant part of the agricultural community, have largely abandoned the agrarian life. Women, however, are displaying increased interest in farming. More and more, according to Beale, they think of themselves as partners in the farm business and are also running farms independently.

1) NUMBER OF FARMS:
1991	2.14 million (preliminary)
1990	2.11 million
1940	6.1 million
1890	4.6 million

2) PERCENTAGE OF THE POPULATION THAT FARMED:
1990	2.3 percent of the population lived in households that contained a farm operator or that reported some "self-employment" income from farming
1940	23.2 percent
1890	39.3 percent

3) OF ALL FARMERS, THE PERCENTAGE THAT FARMED FULL-TIME:
1987	40.4 percent
1939	69 percent

4) STATE WITH THE MOST FARMS:
1990	Texas	186,000
1987	Texas	189,000
1940	Texas	418,000
1890	Ohio	251,000

5) AVERAGE SIZE OF FARMS:
1991	467 acres

1987	462 acres
1940	174 acres
1890	137 acres

6) DISTRIBUTION OF FARMS BY PRINCIPAL SPECIALTY, 1987:

- 34.3 percent beef cattle
- 22.0 percent cash grain
- 6.6 percent dairy
- 6.1 percent peanuts, potatoes, sugar, and other field crops
- 5.4 percent hogs
- 4.2 percent tobacco
- 4.2 percent fruits and nuts
- 4.2 percent animal specialties (horses, furs, aquaculture)
- 2.7 percent general farms, primarily crops
- 1.8 percent poultry
- 1.7 percent general livestock
- 1.5 percent horticulture (nursery and greenhouse crops)
- 1.5 percent sheep and goats
- 1.4 percent vegetables and melons
- 1.3 percent cotton
- 1.1 percent general farms, primarily livestock

DISTRIBUTION IN 1959:

- 25.5 percent livestock (excluding ranches)
- 17.3 percent dairy
- 16.5 percent cash grain
- 10.0 percent cotton
- 8.7 percent general farms
- 7.9 percent tobacco
- 4.3 percent poultry
- 2.8 percent livestock ranches
- 2.5 percent fruit and nuts
- 1.9 percent peanuts, potatoes, sugar, and other field crops
- 1.7 percent miscellaneous
- .9 percent vegetables

7) PERCENTAGE OF CROPS PRODUCED FOR EXPORT:

1989	25 percent
1940	3 percent
1890	19 percent

8) NUMBER OF PEOPLE FED BY EACH FARM WORKER:

1989	98 people
1940	10.7 people
1890	5.8 people

(continued on page 30)

My Feet Were Killing Me...Until
I Discovered the Miracle in Germany!

It was the European trip we had always dreamed about. We had the time and money to go where we wanted - see what we wanted. But I soon learned that money and time don't mean much when your feet hurt too much to walk. After a few days of sightseeing my feet were killing me.

Oh, my wife tried to keep me going. In Paris I limped through Notre Dame and along the Champs-Elysées. And I went up in the Eiffel Tower although I can't honestly say I remember the view. My feet were so tired

and sore my whole body ached. While everybody else was having a great time, I was in my hotel room. I didn't even feel like sitting in a sidewalk cafe.

The whole trip was like that until I got to Hamburg, Germany. There, by accident, I happened to hear about an *exciting breakthrough for anyone who suffers from sore, aching feet and legs.*

This wonderful invention was a custom formed foot support called Flexible Featherspring® Foot Supports. When I got a pair and slipped them into my shoes *my pain disappeared almost instantly.* The flexible shock absorbing support they gave my feet was like cradling them on a cushion of air. I could walk, stand, even run. The relief was truly a miracle.

And just one pair was all I needed. I learned that my wife also can wear them - even with sandals and open backed shoes. They're practically invisible.

Imagine how dumbfounded I was to discover that these miraculous devices were sold only in Europe. Right then I decided that I should bring my discovery to America.

In the last 15 years over a half million Americans of all ages - many with foot problems far more severe than mine -have experienced this blessed relief for themselves.

© Featherspring International, Inc.
712 N. 34th Street, Seattle WA 98103-8881

MADE FOR YOUR FEET ALONE

Here's why Feat'hersprings work for them and *why they can work for you.* These supports are like nothing you've ever seen before. They are custom formed and made for *your feet alone!* Unlike conventional devices, they actually imitate the youthful elastic support that nature originally intended your feet to have.

NO RISK OFFER

Whatever your problem - corns, calluses, pain in the balls of your feet, burning nerve ends, painful ankles, old injuries, backaches or just generally sore, aching feet, Flexible Feathersprings will bring you relief with every step you take or your money back. **Don't suffer pain and discomfort needlessly. If your feet hurt, the miracle of Germany can help you. Write for more detailed information. There is no obligation whatsoever. Just fill out the coupon below and mail it today. No salesman will call.**

What people say about the miracle:

"Wish I had believed your ad five years ago."
Mrs. W.C. Fayetteville, N.C.

" A number of my patients have ordered your Featherspring Foot Supports and have been very pleased with the relief and comfort."
Dr. C.J.S., Pittsburg, PA

(continued from page 27)

9) MEDIAN INCOME OF FARMING HOUSEHOLDS:
  1989 $33,338
  1986 $25,604

10) PERCENTAGE OF FARMERS THAT PARTICIPATE IN THE CROP-SUPPORT SYSTEM:
  1987   31 percent

11) PERCENTAGE OF FARMS OWNED BY CORPORATIONS:
  1987   3.2 percent

12) PERCENTAGE OF FARM CORPORATIONS THAT ARE FAMILY-OWNED:
  1987   90.7 percent

13) PERCENTAGE OF AGRICULTURAL LAND OWNED BY FOREIGN CORPORATIONS OR INDIVIDUALS:
  1990   1.1 percent

14) AVERAGE AGE OF FARMERS:
  1987   52
  1940   48

15) ETHNIC BREAKDOWN OF FARMERS:
  1987   97.2 percent white
         1.1 percent African American
         .8 percent Hispanic
         .3 percent Native American
         .3 percent Asian
         .3 percent other
  1940   88.2 percent white
         11.2 percent African American
         .6 percent other
  1900   86.6 percent white
         13 percent African American
         .4 percent other

16) NUMBER OF WOMEN FARMERS:
  1987   131,641 (6.3 percent)
  1978   112,799 (5 percent)

17) SIZE OF AVERAGE FARM FAMILY:
  1989   3.20 persons
  1940   4.25 persons
  1890   5.20 persons

18) EDUCATION OF FARMERS:
  1990   36.9 percent had one or more years of college and 81.8 were high school graduates
  1960   8.8 percent had some college and 27.9 percent were high school graduates
  1940   3.4 percent had some college and 10.2 percent were high school graduates

19) NUMBER OF YEARS FARMERS HAVE WORKED THEIR FARMS:
  1987   Average of 18.8 years
  1982   Average of 17.3 years
  1959   Average of 15.0 years

20) NET WORTH OF FARMS:
  Total farm assets in 1990, $834.6 billion; total debt, $136.5 billion; total equity, $698.1 billion; average net worth, $326,215 ($698.1 billion divided by 2,140,000 farms).

  Total farm assets in 1945 (earliest available statistic), $81.3 billion; total debt, $6.7 billion; total equity, $74.6 billion; average net worth, $12,502 ($74.6 billion divided by 5,967,000 farms).   ☐☐

N.B. The numbers above were obtained from the Economic Research division of the United States Department of Agriculture. The primary source of information about American farms is the Census of Agriculture, which is taken every five years. The last census year was 1987. Figures from the 1992 census will be available in 1994. The 1987 figures cited above are from the Census of Agriculture; later figures are from other, less comprehensive surveys that are done at varying intervals.

WHAT YOU DON'T KNOW ABOUT INSTALLMENT LOANS

Read the following before you consider refinancing or paying off a loan early . . .

BY JOHN MOLNAR

Considering repaying your car loan early? Tired of making monthly payments on your consumer loan? Plan to refinance at a lower interest rate? Don't even consider it after the first 14 months of a 48-month installment plan — by then you will have paid about 50 percent of the total interest due on the loan. After 24 months, the amount approaches 75 percent of the total interest. While each installment payment is the same, the sum does not consist of identical amounts of interest and principal for all installments. The interest decreases with time and the principal increases; the sum of the two always equals the monthly payment.

Creditors use the "Rule of 78" to determine the interest remaining (rebate) when the loan is repaid early. When you add all the digits from 1 through 12, the answer is 78, hence the name of the rule. Although the rule applies only to a 12-month installment plan, the same principle applies to plans of different lengths. A simple formula expresses the rule:

FORMULA FOR SUM OF DIGITS:

$\frac{N}{2}$ x **(N+1)** = Sum of Digits
where **N** = the number of installments

For a 12-month plan, the formula works out this way: $\frac{12}{2}$ x **(12+1) = 78**

For a 48-month plan: $\frac{48}{2}$ x **(48+1) = 1,176**

Example:

Calculate the rebate at 24 months of a 48-month installment plan with an interest charge of $3,000.

M = Remaining months
I = Total loan interest
S = Sum of the digits (calculated above)
R = Rebate (remaining interest)

FORMULA FOR REBATE:

$\frac{M}{2}$ x $\frac{(M+1)}{S}$ x I = R

$\frac{24}{2}$ x $\frac{(24+1)}{1,176}$ x $3,000 = $765

Thus, if you repay your 48-month car loan after 24 months, you would receive $765 rebate of the total $3,000 interest — not half the interest, as many consumers expect. Upon deducting $765 from the total interest of $3,000, you find that you paid $2,235 during the first 24 months. In other words, you paid 74.5 percent of the total interest during the first 50 percent of the installment plan.

Still thinking of refinancing or paying off the loan early? Before you do anything, ask your lender what you owe on the principal and what the balance (rebate) of the interest is.

The accompanying graph shows the relationship between interest rebates versus installment payments, using the figures given in the example above. The dollar amounts along the curve represent the rebate over time. ☐☐

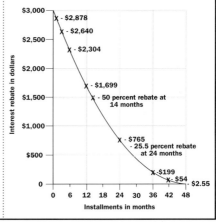

INTRODUCTION
Including How to Use This Almanac Anywhere in the U.S.A.

THE LEFT-HAND CALENDAR PAGES
(Pages 56-82)

THESE PAGES will provide you with the astronomical highlights and the phases of the Moon for each month; the hour and minute of the Sun's rising and setting for each day of the year and month; the length of each day; the times of high tides in Boston in the morning and evening ("11¼" under "Full Sea Boston, A.M." means that the high tide that morning will be at 11:15 A.M. — with the number of feet of high tide shown for some of the dates on the Right-Hand Calendar Pages); the hour and minute of the Moon's rising and setting (dashes indicate that moonrise or moonset has occurred on or after midnight and so is recorded on the next date); the declination of the Sun in degrees and minutes (angular distance from the celestial equator); the Moon's place in the heavens; and finally, in the far right column, the Moon's age.

The Moon's place given on the left-hand pages is its *astronomical* place in the heavens. (*All* calculations in this Almanac, except for the astrological information on pages 211 and 192-197, are based on astronomy, not astrology.) As well as the 12 constellations of the zodiac, three other abbreviations appear in this column: Ophiuchus (OPH) is a constellation primarily north of the zodiac, but with a small corner between Scorpius and Sagittarius. Sextans (SEX) lies south of the zodiac except for a corner that just touches it near Leo. Orion (ORI) is a constellation whose northern limit first reaches the zodiac between Taurus and Gemini.

Eastern Standard Time is used throughout this Almanac. (Be sure to add one hour for Daylight Saving Time between April 4 and October 31.) **All of the times on the Left-Hand Calendar Pages are calculated for Boston.** Key Letters accompany much of the data; they are provided for the correction of Boston times to other localities. Here's how . . .

SUNRISE, SUNSET

☞ Note the Key Letter to the right of each time for sunrise and sunset in the column entitled "Key." To find the time of sunrise or sunset for your area, consult the Time Correction Tables (pages 198-202). Find your city or the city nearest you and locate the figure, expressed in minutes, in the appropriate Key Letter column. Add, or subtract, that figure to the time given for Boston. The result will be accurate to within 5 minutes for latitudes north of 35°, 10 minutes for latitudes 30°-35°, and 15 minutes for latitudes 25°-30°.

Example: April 11 (Easter), 1993, sunrise in Boston is 5:10 A.M., EST, with Key Letter B (page 66). To find the time of sunrise in Little Rock, Arkansas, look on page 200. Key Letter B for Little Rock is +35 minutes, so sunrise in Little Rock is 5:45 A.M., CST. Use the same process for sunset. (For dates between April 4 and October 31, add one hour for Daylight Saving Time.)

MOONRISE, MOONSET

☞ Moonrise and moonset are figured the same way except that an additional correction factor (see table below) based on longitude should be used. For the longitude of your city, consult pages 198-202.

Longitude of city	Correction minutes
58°- 76°	0
77°- 89°	+1
90°-102°	+2
103°-115°	+3
116°-127°	+4
128°-141°	+5
142°-155°	+6

Example: To determine moonrise in Chicago, Illinois, for July 4, 1993, see page 72. Moonrise in Boston is 7:46 P.M., EST, with Key Letter E. For Chicago, Key Letter E (page 199) is +4 minutes, moving moonrise to 7:50 P.M. The longitude of Chicago is 87° 38', so the additional correction is +1 minute. Moonrise in Chicago is therefore 7:51 P.M., CST. (Add one hour for Daylight Saving Time between April 4 and October 31.) Follow the same procedure to determine moonset.

SUNDIALS

☞ Also in the Left-Hand Calendar Pages is a column headed "Sun Fast." This is for changing sundial time into local clock time. A sundial reads natural, or Sun, time, which is neither Standard nor Daylight time except by coincidence. Simply *subtract* Sun Fast time to get local clock time and use Key Letter C (pages 198-202) to correct the time for your city. (Add one hour for Daylight Saving Time April 4-October 31.)

Example:	**Boston**
Sundial reading, May 1	12:00
Subtract Sun Fast	−19
Clock time	11:41 EST

Example:	**Denver, CO**
Sundial reading, May 1	12:00
Subtract Sun Fast	−19
Use Key C (for Denver)	+15
Clock time	11:56 MST

RISING AND SETTING OF THE PLANETS

☞ The times of rising and setting of visible planets, with the exception of Mercury, are given for Boston on pages 42-43. To convert these times to those of other localities (pages 198-202), follow the same procedure as that given for finding the times of sunrise and sunset.

LENGTH OF DAY

☞ The "Length of Day" column for Boston (pages 56-82) tells how long the Sun will be above the horizon. Use the Time Correction Tables (pages 198-202) to determine sunrise and sunset times for your city. Add 12 hours to the time

of sunset, subtract the time of sunrise, and you will have the length of day.

LENGTH OF TWILIGHT

☞ Subtract from time of sunrise for dawn. Add to time of sunset for dark.

Latitude	25°N to 30°N	31°N to 36°N	37°N to 42°N
	h m	h m	h m
Jan. 1 to Apr. 10	1 20	1 26	1 33
Apr. 11 to May 2	1 23	1 28	1 39
May 3 to May 14	1 26	1 34	1 47
May 15 to May 25	1 29	1 38	1 52
May 26 to July 22	1 32	1 43	1 59
July 23 to Aug. 3	1 29	1 38	1 52
Aug. 4 to Aug. 14	1 26	1 34	1 47
Aug. 15 to Sept. 5	1 23	1 28	1 39
Sept. 6 to Dec. 31	1 20	1 26	1 33

Latitude	43°N to 47°N	48°N to 49°N
	h m	h m
Jan. 1 to Apr. 10	1 42	1 50
Apr. 11 to May 2	1 51	2 04
May 3 to May 14	2 02	2 22
May 15 to May 25	2 13	2 42
May 26 to July 22	2 27	—
July 23 to Aug. 3	2 13	2 42
Aug. 4 to Aug. 14	2 02	2 22
Aug. 15 to Sept. 5	1 51	2 04
Sept. 6 to Dec. 31	1 42	1 50

DAWN AND DARK

☞ The approximate times dawn will break and dark descend are found by applying the length of twilight taken from the table above to the times of sunrise and sunset at any specific place. The latitude of the place (see pages 198-202) determines the column from which the length of twilight is to be selected.

Boston (latitude 42° 22')

Sunrise, August 1	4:36 A.M.
Length of twilight	−1:52
Dawn breaks	2:44 A.M., EST
Sunset, August 1	7:04 P.M.
Length of twilight	+1:52
Dark descends	8:56 P.M., EST

Las Vegas, NV (latitude 36° 10')

Sunrise, August 1	4:52 A.M.
Length of twilight	−1:38
Dawn breaks	3:14 A.M., PST
Sunset, August 1	6:51 P.M.
Length of twilight	+1:38
Dark descends	8:29 P.M., PST

THE RIGHT-HAND CALENDAR PAGES

(Pages 57-83)

THESE PAGES are a combination of astronomical data; specific dates in mainly the Anglican church calendar, inclusion of which has always been traditional in American and English almanacs (though we also include some other religious dates); tide heights at Boston (the Left-Hand Calendar Pages include the daily times of high tides; the corrections for your locality are on pages 204-205); quotations; anniversary dates; appropriate seasonal activities; and a rhyming version of the weather forecasts for New England. (Detailed forecasts for the entire country are presented on pages 130-156.)

The following is a summary of the highlights from this year's Right-Hand Calendar Pages, the signs used, and a sample (the first part of November 1992) of a calendar page explained....

MOVABLE FEASTS AND FASTS FOR 1993

Septuagesima Sunday	Feb. 7
Shrove Tuesday	Feb. 23
Ash Wednesday	Feb. 24
Palm Sunday	Apr. 4
Good Friday	Apr. 9
Easter Day	Apr. 11
Low Sunday	Apr. 18
Rogation Sunday	May 16
Ascension Day	May 20
Whit Sunday-Pentecost	May 30
Trinity Sunday	June 6
Corpus Christi	June 10
1st Sunday in Advent	Nov. 28

THE SEASONS OF 1993

Winter 1992	Dec. 21, 9:43 A.M., EST (Sun enters Capricorn)
Spring 1993	Mar. 20, 9:41 A.M., EST (Sun enters Aries)
Summer 1993	June 21, 4:00 A.M., EST (Sun enters Cancer)
Fall 1993	Sept. 22, 7:22 P.M., EST (Sun enters Libra)
Winter 1993	Dec. 21, 3:26 P.M., EST (Sun enters Capricorn)

CHRONOLOGICAL CYCLES FOR 1993

Golden Number (Lunar Cycle)	18
Epact	6
Solar Cycle	14
Dominical Letter	C
Roman Indiction	1
Year of Julian Period	6706

ERA	Year	Begins
Byzantine	7502	Sept. 14
Jewish (A.M.)*	5754	Sept. 15
Roman (A.U.C.)	2746	Jan. 14
Nabonassar	2742	Apr. 25
Japanese	2653	Jan. 1
Grecian	2305	Sept. 14
(Seleucidae)		(or Oct. 14)
Indian (Saka)	1915	Mar. 22
Diocletian	1710	Sept. 11
Islamic (Hegira)*	1414	June 20
Chinese (Lunar)	4691	Jan. 23
(Rooster)		

*Year begins at sunset

DETERMINATION OF EARTHQUAKES

☞ Note, on right-hand pages 57-83, the dates when the Moon (☾) "rides high" or "runs low." The date of the high begins the most likely five-day period of earthquakes in the Northern Hemisphere; the date of the low indicates a similar five-day period in the Southern Hemisphere. You will also find on these pages a notation for Moon on the Equator ($\mathbb{C}$ on Eq.) twice each month. At this time, in both hemispheres, is a two-day earthquake period.

NAMES AND CHARACTERS OF THE PRINCIPAL PLANETS AND ASPECTS

☞ Every now and again on these Right-Hand Calendar Pages, you will see symbols conjoined in groups to tell you what is happening in the heavens. For example, ♂ ♂ $\mathbb{C}$ opposite December 12, 1992, on page 59 means that Mars ♂ and the Moon $\mathbb{C}$ are on that date in conjunction ♂ or apparently near each other.

Here are the symbols used ...

☉ The Sun   ○ ● $\mathbb{C}$ The Moon

☿ Mercury	♄ Saturn
♀ Venus	♅ Uranus
⊕ The Earth	♆ Neptune
♂ Mars	♇ Pluto
♃ Jupiter	

♂ Conjunction, or in the same degree
♂ Opposition, or 180 degrees
☊ Ascending Node
☋ Descending Node

EARTH AT APHELION AND PERIHELION 1993

☞ The Earth will be at Perihelion on January 3, 1993, when it will be 91,400,005 miles from the Sun. The Earth will be at Aphelion on July 4, 1993, when it will be 94,512,258 miles from the Sun.

SAMPLE PAGE
(from November 1992 — page 57)

Day of the month.   Day of the week.   For detailed regional forecasts, see pages 130-156.

The Dominical Letter for 1992 was E during January and February because the first Sunday of the year fell on the fifth day of January; after Leap Year Day the preceding letter D is used.

The Moon is at apogee, the point in its orbit farthest from the Earth.

22nd Sunday after Pentecost. (Events in the church calendar generally appear in this typeface.)

Morning tide at Boston, shown to be at midnight on the left-hand page, will be 9.5 feet. The noon tide will be 10.9 feet.

Conjunction — closest approach — of Pluto and the Sun.

St. Hilda, seventh-century British abbess, founder of the Whitby Monastery. Her wise counsel and advice were sought by rulers and commoners. (Certain religious feasts and civil holidays appear in this typeface.)

D.M.	D.W.	Dates, Feasts, Fasts, Aspects, Tide Heights	Weather ↓
1	D	21st $\mathbb{S}$. af. $\mathbb{P}$. • All Saints • Tides {8.7 {9.4	Farewell,
2	M.	♂♄$\mathbb{C}$ • All Souls • North and South Dakota statehood, 1889 •	summer!
3	Tu.	$\mathbb{C}$ at apo. • Politics makes strange postmasters. • {8.6 {8.9 •	Rain's a
4	W.	Mass. Bay Colony declared heresy punishable by death, 1646 •	drummer,
5	Th.	$\mathbb{C}$ on Eq. • Fawkes's Plot (it's never forgot) • Roy Rogers born, 1912 •	beating
6	Fr.	St. Leonard • First U.S. football game. Rutgers vs. Princeton, 1869 • {9.4 {9.0	retreat.
7	Sa.	Bolsheviks led by Lenin seized government, 1917 • Marie Curie born, 1867 • Tides {9.7 {9.2	Snow
8	D	22nd $\mathbb{S}$. af. $\mathbb{P}$. • 25" snow, northern Plains, 1986 • {10.1 {9.3	betrays
9	M.	The hole and the patch should be commensurate. • Boston in flames, 1872 •	the deer;
10	Tu.	Full Beaver ○ • Marine Corps created, 1775 • Tides {10.6 {9.5	days
11	W.	St. Martin • Veterans Day • ☿ stat. • Indian summer begins. •	warm
12	Th.	$\mathbb{C}$ at ☋ • $\mathbb{C}$ high. • rides Skunks hibernate. • Tides {10.6 {10.9	warm
13	Fr.	Holland Tunnel opened. N.Y.-N.J. 1927 • Louis Brandeis born, 1856 • {9.5 {10.9	and
14	Sa.	♂♇☉ • Sadie Hawkins Day • Ideas never work unless you do. •	clear.
15	D	23rd $\mathbb{S}$. af. $\mathbb{P}$. • ♂♂$\mathbb{C}$ • William Herschel born, 1738	Dark
16	M.	Oklahoma statehood, 1907 • Premiere of Sound of Music, N.Y.C., 1959 • Tides {9.4 {10.3	and
17	Tu.	St. Hilda • William Larimer founded Denver, 1858 • {9.6 {10.1	sopping,
18	W.	$\mathbb{C}$ on Eq. • $\mathbb{C}$ at perig. • Congress adopted std. time zones, 1883 •	mercury's

NOTE: The values of Key Letters are given in the Time Correction Tables. (See pages 198-202.)

HOLIDAYS, 1993

(*) Recommended as holidays with pay for all employees
(**) State observances only

Jan. 1 (*) New Year's Day
Jan. 6 Epiphany
Jan. 18 (*) Martin Luther King Jr.'s Birthday (observed)
Jan. 19 (**) Robert E. Lee's Birthday (Ark., Fla., S.C., Tenn.)
Feb. 2 Groundhog Day
Feb. 12 (**) Abraham Lincoln's Birthday
Feb. 14 Valentine's Day
Feb. 15 (*) Presidents Day
Feb. 22 George Washington's Birthday
Feb. 23 (**) Mardi Gras (Ala., La.)
Feb. 24 Ash Wednesday
Mar. 2 (**) Texas Independence Day
Mar. 15 (**) Andrew Jackson Day (Tenn.)
Mar. 17 (**) St. Patrick's Day; Evacuation Day (Boston and Suffolk Co., Mass.)
Mar. 29 (**) Seward's Day (Alaska)

HOW THE ALMANAC WEATHER FORECASTS ARE MADE

Our weather forecasts are determined both by the use of a secret formula devised by the founder of this Almanac in 1792 and by the most modern scientific calculations based on solar activity. We believe nothing in the universe occurs haphazardly; there is a cause-and-effect pattern to all phenomena, including weather. It follows, therefore, that we believe weather is predictable. It is obvious, however, that neither we nor anyone else has as yet gained sufficient insight into the mysteries of the universe to predict weather with anything resembling total accuracy.

Apr. 2 (**) Pascua Florida Day
Apr. 4 Palm Sunday
Apr. 6 Passover
Apr. 9 Good Friday
Apr. 11 Easter
Apr. 13 (**) Thomas Jefferson's Birthday (Okla.)
Apr. 18 Easter (Orthodox churches)
Apr. 19 (**) Patriots Day (Fla., Me., Mass.)
Apr. 30 Arbor Day (except Alaska, Georgia, Kansas, Virginia, Wyoming)
May 1 May Day
May 7 (**) Harry Truman Day (observed Mo.)
May 9 Mother's Day
May 15 Armed Forces Day
May 24 Victoria Day (Canada)
May 31 (*) Memorial Day (observed)
June 5 World Environment Day
June 11 (**) King Kamehameha Day (Hawaii)
June 14 Flag Day
June 17 (**) Bunker Hill Day (Boston and Suffolk Co., Mass.)
June 20 Father's Day; West Virginia Day
July 1 Canada Day
July 4 (*) Independence Day
July 24 (**) Pioneer Day (Utah)
Aug. 9 (**) Victory Day (R.I.)
Aug. 16 (**) Bennington Battle Day (observed Vt.)
Aug. 26 Women's Equality Day
Sept. 6 (*) Labor Day
Sept. 9 (**) Admissions Day (Calif.)
Sept. 12 Grandparents Day
Sept. 13 (**) Defenders Day (observed Md.)
Sept. 16 Rosh Hashanah
Sept. 25 Yom Kippur
Sept. 28 (**) Frances Willard Day (Minn., Wis.)
Oct. 11 (*) Columbus Day (observed); Thanksgiving (Canada)
Oct. 18 (**) Alaska Day
Oct. 24 United Nations Day
Oct. 31 Halloween; (**) Nevada Day
Nov. 2 Election Day
Nov. 4 (**) Will Rogers Day (Okla.)
Nov. 11 (*) Veterans Day
Nov. 19 Discovery Day (Puerto Rico)
Nov. 25 (*) Thanksgiving Day
Nov. 28 John F. Kennedy Day (Mass.)
Dec. 9 Chanukah
Dec. 10 (**) Wyoming Day
Dec. 15 Bill of Rights Day
Dec. 25 Christmas Day
Dec. 26 Boxing Day (Canada)

GLOSSARY

Aph. — Aphelion: Planet reaches point in its orbit farthest from the Sun.

Apo.— Apogee: Moon reaches point in its orbit farthest from the Earth.

Celestial Equator: The plane of the Earth's equator projected out into space.

Conj. — Conjunction: Time of apparent closest approach to each other of any two heavenly bodies. **Inf. — Inferior:** Conjunction in which the planet is between the Sun and the Earth. **Sup. — Superior:** Indicates that the Sun is between the planet and the Earth.

Declination: Measurement of angular distance of any celestial object perpendicularly north or south of celestial equator; analogous to terrestrial latitude. The Almanac gives the Sun's declination at noon EST.

Dominical Letter: Used for the ecclesiastical calendar and determined by the date on which the first Sunday of the year falls. If Jan. 1 is a Sunday, the Letter is A; if Jan. 2 is a Sunday, the Letter is B; and so to G when the first Sunday is Jan. 7. In leap year the Letter applies through February and then takes the Letter before.

Eclipse, Annular: An eclipse in which sunlight shows around the Moon.

Eclipse, Lunar: Opposition of the Sun and Moon with the Moon at or near node.

Eclipse, Solar: Conjunction of Sun and Moon with the Moon at or near node.

Epact: A number from 1 to 30 to harmonize the lunar year with the solar year, used for the ecclesiastical calendar. Indicates the Moon's age at the instant Jan. 1 begins at the meridian of Greenwich, England.

Eq. — Equator: A great circle of the Earth equidistant from the two poles.

Equinox, Autumnal: Sun passes from Northern to Southern Hemisphere: Sun enters Libra. **Vernal:** Sun passes from Southern to Northern Hemisphere: Sun enters Aries.

Evening Star: A planet that is above the horizon at sunset and less than 180 degrees east of the Sun.

Golden Number: The year in the 19-year cycle of the Moon. The Moon phases occur on the same dates every 19 years.

Greatest Elongation (Gr. El.): Greatest apparent angular distance of a planet from the Sun as seen from the Earth.

Julian Period: A period of 7,980 Julian years, being a period of agreement of solar and lunar cycles. Add 4,713 to year to find the Julian year.

Moon's Age: The number of days since the previous new Moon. First Quarter: Right half of Moon illuminated. Full Moon: Moon reaches opposition. Last Quarter: Left half of Moon illuminated. New Moon: Sun and Moon in conjunction.

Moon Rides High or Runs Low: Day of month Moon is highest or lowest above the south point of the observer's horizon.

Morning Star: A planet that is above the horizon at sunrise and less than 180 degrees west of the Sun in right ascension.

Node: Either of the two points where the Moon's orbit intersects the ecliptic.

Occultation: Eclipse of a star or planet by the Moon or another planet.

Opposition: Time when the Sun and Moon or planet appear on opposite sides of the sky (El. 180 degrees).

Perig. — Perigee: Moon reaches point in its orbit closest to the Earth.

Perih. — Perihelion: Planet reaches point in its orbit closest to the Sun.

R.A. — Right Ascension: The coordinate on the celestial sphere analogous to longitude on the Earth.

Roman Indiction: A cycle of 15 years established Jan. 1, A.D. 313, as a fiscal term. Add 3 to the number of years in the Christian era and divide by 15. The remainder of the year is Roman Indiction — no remainder is 15.

Solar Cycle: A period of 28 years, at the end of which the days of the month return to the same days of the week.

Solstice, Summer: Point at which the Sun is farthest north of the celestial equator: Sun enters Cancer. **Winter:** Point at which the Sun is farthest south of the celestial equator: Sun enters Capricorn.

Stat. — Stationary: Halt in the apparent movement of a planet against the background of the stars just before the planet comes to opposition.

Sun Fast: Subtract times given in this column from your sundial to arrive at the correct Standard Time.

Sunrise & Sunset: Visible rising and setting of the Sun's upper limb across the unobstructed horizon of an observer whose eyes are 15 feet above ground level.

Twilight: Begins or ends when stars of the sixth magnitude appear or disappear at the zenith; or when the Sun is about 18 degrees below the horizon.

THE VISIBLE PLANETS, 1993

The times of rising or setting of the planets Venus, Mars, Jupiter, and Saturn on the 1st, 11th, and 21st of each month are given below. The approximate time of rising or setting of these planets on other days may be found with sufficient accuracy by interpolation. For an explanation of Key Letters (used in adjusting the times given here for Boston to the time in your town), see page 34 and pages 198-202. Key Letters appear as capital letters beside the time of rising or setting. (For definitions of morning and evening stars, see page 40.)

VENUS is brilliant in the evening sky from the beginning of the year until the end of March, when it becomes too close to the Sun for observation. Early in April it reappears in the morning sky, where it can be seen until early December when it again becomes too close to the Sun for observation. Venus is in conjunction with Mercury on April 16 and November 14 and with Jupiter on November 8.

Boldface — P.M. Lightface — A.M.

Jan. 1	set **8:11**	B	May 1	rise 3:06	B	Sept. 1	rise 2:18	A
Jan. 11	" **8:30**	B	May 11	" 2:45	B	Sept. 11	" 2:39	B
Jan. 21	" **8:46**	B	May 21	" 2:28	B	Sept. 21	" 3:02	B
Feb. 1	set **8:58**	C	June 1	rise 2:10	B	Oct. 1	rise 3:25	B
Feb. 11	" **9:04**	D	June 11	" 1:56	B	Oct. 11	" 3:49	B
Feb. 21	" **9:03**	D	June 21	" 1:44	B	Oct. 21	" 4:13	C
Mar. 1	set **8:53**	D	July 1	rise 1:35	A	Nov. 1	rise 4:40	D
Mar. 11	" **8:25**	D	July 11	" 1:29	A	Nov. 11	" 5:05	D
Mar. 21	rise 5:44	B	July 21	" 1:28	A	Nov. 21	" 5:30	D
Apr. 1	rise 4:49	B	Aug. 1	rise 1:33	A	Dec. 1	rise 5:56	E
Apr. 11	" 4:05	B	Aug. 11	" 1:42	A	Dec. 11	" 6:21	E
Apr. 21	" 3:32	B	Aug. 21	" 1:57	A	Dec. 21	" 6:43	E
						Dec. 31	rise 7:00	E

MARS can be seen in Gemini from the beginning of the year. On January 7 it is at opposition, when it can be seen throughout the night. Its elongation gradually decreases, and by late April it passes into Cancer, when it can be seen only in the evening sky. It continues through Leo, Virgo, and Libra. From early November until the end of the year it is too close to the Sun for observation. Mars is in conjunction with Jupiter on September 6 and with Mercury on October 6 and 28.

Jan. 1	**rise 4:39**	A	May 1	set 12:53	E	Sept. 1	set **7:34**	B
Jan. 11	set 7:25	E	May 11	" 12:28	E	Sept. 11	" **7:09**	B
Jan. 21	" 6:32	E	May 21	" 12:03	E	Sept. 21	" **6:45**	B
Feb. 1	set 5:37	E	June 1	set **11:33**	D	Oct. 1	set 6:22	B
Feb. 11	" 4:51	E	June 11	" **11:07**	D	Oct. 11	" 5:59	B
Feb. 21	" 4:11	E	June 21	" **10:41**	D	Oct. 21	" 5:39	A
Mar. 1	set 3:42	E	July 1	set **10:15**	D	Nov. 1	set **5:18**	A
Mar. 11	" 3:10	E	July 11	" **9:49**	D	Nov. 11	" **5:01**	A
Mar. 21	" 2:40	E	July 21	" **9:23**	C	Nov. 21	" **4:46**	A
Apr. 1	set 2:10	E	Aug. 1	set **8:54**	C	Dec. 1	set **4:33**	A
Apr. 11	" 1:44	E	Aug. 11	" **8:28**	C	Dec. 11	" **4:23**	A
Apr. 21	" 1:18	E	Aug. 21	" **8:02**	C	Dec. 21	rise 7:21	E
						Dec. 31	rise 7:14	E

JUPITER

JUPITER is visible for more than half the night in Virgo from January on, reaching opposition on March 30. By the end of June it is visible only in the evening sky and from early October becomes too close to the Sun for observation. It reappears in the morning sky, still in Virgo, in early November until mid-December, when it passes into Libra. Jupiter is in conjunction with Mars on September 6, with Mercury on September 24, and with Venus on November 8.

Date				Date				Date			
Jan. 1	rise	12:04	C	May 1	set	3:31	C	Sept. 1	set	7:42	B
Jan. 11	rise	11:25	A	May 11	"	2:50	C	Sept. 11	"	7:07	B
Jan. 21	"	10:47	C	May 21	"	2:10	C	Sept. 21	"	6:33	B
Feb. 1	rise	10:04	C	June 1	set	1:26	C	Oct. 1	set	5:58	B
Feb. 11	"	9:23	C	June 11	"	12:46	C	Oct. 11	"	5:24	B
Feb. 21	"	8:41	C	June 21	"	12:08	C	Oct. 21	rise	5:51	D
Mar. 1	rise	8:06	C	July 1	set	11:26	C	Nov. 1	rise	5:20	D
Mar. 11	"	7:21	C	July 11	"	10:49	C	Nov. 11	"	4:52	D
Mar. 21	"	6:36	C	July 21	"	10:12	C	Nov. 21	"	4:23	D
Apr. 1	rise	5:45	C	Aug. 1	set	9:32	C	Dec. 1	rise	3:54	D
Apr. 11	set	4:55	C	Aug. 11	"	8:56	C	Dec. 11	"	3:24	D
Apr. 21	"	4:13	C	Aug. 21	"	8:21	B	Dec. 21	"	2:54	D
								Dec. 31	rise	2:23	D

SATURN

SATURN is visible in the evening sky in Capricorn until late January, when it becomes too close to the Sun for observation. It reappears in the morning sky in late February, passing into Aquarius in late March; it is at opposition on August 19, when it is visible throughout the night. Its eastward elongation gradually decreases as it passes back into Capricorn, until by mid-November it is visible only in the evening sky. By late December it returns to Aquarius.

Date				Date				Date			
Jan. 1	set	7:13	A	May 1	rise	1:59	D	Sept. 1	set	4:07	B
Jan. 11	"	6:40	B	May 11	"	1:21	D	Sept. 11	"	3:24	B
Jan. 21	"	6:06	B	May 21	"	12:43	D	Sept. 21	"	2:41	B
Feb. 1	set	5:30	B	June 1	rise	12:00	D	Oct. 1	set	1:55	B
Feb. 11	rise	6:48	D	June 11	rise	11:17	D	Oct. 11	"	1:14	B
Feb. 21	"	6:12	D	June 21	"	10:38	D	Oct. 21	"	12:34	B
Mar. 1	rise	5:43	D	July 1	rise	9:58	D	Nov. 1	set	11:50	B
Mar. 11	"	5:07	D	July 11	"	9:18	D	Nov. 11	"	11:12	B
Mar. 21	"	4:30	D	July 21	"	8:37	D	Nov. 21	"	10:35	B
Apr. 1	rise	3:50	D	Aug. 1	rise	7:52	D	Dec. 1	set	9:58	B
Apr. 11	"	3:13	D	Aug. 11	"	7:11	D	Dec. 11	"	9:22	B
Apr. 21	"	2:36	D	Aug. 21	set	4:54	B	Dec. 21	"	8:47	B
								Dec. 31	set	8:12	B

MERCURY

MERCURY can be seen only in the east before sunrise or low in the west after sunset. It is visible mornings between these approximate dates: January 1-8, March 16-May 8, July 24-August 21, and November 12-December 18. The planet is brighter at the end of each period (best viewing conditions in northern latitudes occur the second half of November). It is visible evenings between these approximate dates: February 5-March 2, May 24-July 6, and September 9-October 31. The planet is brighter at the beginning of each period (best viewing conditions in northern latitudes occur for a few days just after mid-February).

DO NOT CONFUSE 1) Jupiter with Mars from late August until mid-September, and with Mercury the third week of September, when Jupiter is the brighter object. 2) Mercury with Mars from the end of September until mid-October and during the last week of October, when Mercury is the brighter object. The reddish tint of Mars should assist in its identification. 3) Venus with Jupiter during the second week of November and with Mercury around mid-November and mid-December; on all occasions Venus is the brighter object.

ECLIPSES FOR 1993

There will be four eclipses in 1993, two of the Sun and two of the Moon. One of the solar eclipses will not be visible in the United States or Canada; the others will be seen in certain locations, as specified below. Lunar eclipses technically are visible from the entire night side of the Earth; solar eclipses are visible only in certain areas.

1. Partial eclipse of the Sun, May 21. The eclipse will be visible from North America except the eastern and southeastern regions. Along the West Coast, the eclipse will happen at sunrise (in San Francisco maximum eclipse will occur at 4:55 A.M., PST, and end at 5:40 A.M., PST). In central and western North America, the eclipse will begin at 7-8 A.M., EST (4-5 A.M., PST), and end at 8-9 A.M., EST (5-6 A.M., PST), depending on location.

2. Total eclipse of the Moon, June 4. The beginning of the umbral phase will be visible from the Hawaiian Islands, southern Alaska, extreme western Canada, and the western United States. The end will be visible from the Hawaiian and Aleutian Islands. The Moon enters penumbra at 5:11 A.M., EST (2:11 A.M., PST); totality begins at 7:12 A.M., EST (4:12 A.M., PST); the Moon leaves penumbra at 10:50 A.M., EST (7:50 A.M., PST).

3. Partial eclipse of the Sun, November 13. This eclipse will be visible only from northern Australia, Antarctica, and southern South America.

4. Total eclipse of the Moon, November 28-29. This eclipse will be visible throughout the United States and Canada. The Moon enters penumbra on November 28 at 10:27 P.M., EST (7:27 P.M., PST); totality begins on November 29 at 1:02 A.M., EST (10:02 P.M., PST, on November 28); the Moon leaves penumbra at 4:25 A.M., EST, on November 29 (1:25 A.M., PST).

FULL MOON DAYS

	1993	1994	1995	1996	1997
Jan.	8	27	16	5	23
Feb.	6	25	15	4	22
Mar.	8	27	16	5	23
Apr.	6	25	15	3	22
May	5	24	14	3	22
June	4	23	12	1/30	20
July	3	22	12	30	19
Aug.	2/31	21	10	28	18
Sept.	30	19	8	26	16
Oct.	30	19	8	26	15
Nov.	29	18	7	24	14
Dec.	28	17	6	24	13

PRINCIPAL METEOR SHOWERS

Shower	Best Hour (EST)	Radiant Direction*	Date of Maximum**	Approx. Peak Rate (/hr.)	Associated Comet
Quadrantid	5 A.M.	N.	Jan. 4	40-150	—
Lyrid	4 A.M.	S.	Apr. 21	10-15	1861 I
Eta Aquarid	4 A.M.	S.E.	May 4	10-40	Halley
Delta Aquarid	2 A.M.	S.	July 30	10-35	—
Perseid	4 A.M.	N.	Aug. 11-13	50-100	1862 III
Draconid	9 P.M.	N.W.	Oct. 9	10	Giacobini-Zinner
Orionid	4 A.M.	S.	Oct. 20	10-70	Halley
Taurid	midnight	S.	Nov. 9	5-15	Encke
Leonid	5 A.M.	S.	Nov. 16	5-20	1866 I
Andromedid	10 P.M.	S.	Nov. 25-27	10	Biela
Geminid	2 A.M.	S.	Dec. 13	50-80	—
Ursid	5 A.M.	N.	Dec. 22	10-15	—

* Direction from which the meteors appear to come.
** Date of actual maximum occurrence may vary by one or two days in either direction.

BRIGHT STARS, 1993

The upper table shows the Eastern Standard Time when each star transits the meridian of Boston (i.e., lies directly above the horizon's south point there) and its altitude above that point at transit on the dates shown. The time of transit on any other date differs from that on the nearest date listed by approximately four minutes of time for each day. For a place outside Boston the local time of the star's transit is found by correcting the time at Boston by the value of Key Letter "C" for the place. (See footnote.)

Time of Transit (EST)

Boldface — P.M. Lightface — A.M.

Star	Constellation	Magni-tude	Jan. 1	Mar. 1	May 1	July 1	Sept. 1	Nov. 1	Alt.
Altair	Aquila	0.8	**12:49**	8:57	4:57	12:57	**8:49**	**4:50**	56.3
Deneb	Cygnus	1.3	**1:40**	9:48	5:48	1:48	**9:40**	**5:40**	87.5
Fomalhaut	Psc. Austr.	1.2	**3:54**	12:02	8:02	4:03	**11:55**	**7:55**	17.8
Algol	Perseus	2.2	**8:05**	4:13	**12:13**	8:13	4:09	12:10	88.5
Aldebaran	Taurus	0.9	**9:32**	5:40	**1:40**	9:41	5:37	1:37	64.1
Rigel	Orion	0.1	**10:11**	6:19	**2:19**	10:19	6:15	2:15	39.4
Capella	Auriga	0.1	**10:12**	6:20	**2:21**	10:21	6:17	2:17	85.4
Bellatrix	Orion	1.6	**10:21**	6:29	**2:29**	10:30	6:26	2:26	54.0
Betelgeuse	Orion	var. 0.4	**10:51**	6:59	**2:59**	11:00	6:56	2:56	55.0
Sirius	Can. Maj.	−1.4	**11:41**	7:49	**3:49**	11:49	7:45	3:46	31.0
Procyon	Can. Min.	0.4	12:39	**8:43**	**4:43**	**12:43**	8:39	4:39	52.9
Pollux	Gemini	1.2	12:45	**8:49**	**4:49**	**12:49**	8:45	4:45	75.7
Regulus	Leo	1.4	3:08	**11:12**	**7:12**	**3:12**	11:08	7:08	59.7
Spica	Virgo	var. 1.0	6:24	2:32	**10:28**	**6:28**	**2:25**	10:25	36.6
Arcturus	Bootes	−0.1	7:15	3:23	**11:19**	**7:19**	**3:15**	11:16	66.9
Antares	Scorpius	var. 0.9	9:28	5:36	1:36	**9:32**	**5:28**	**1:28**	21.3
Vega	Lyra	0.0	11:35	7:43	3:43	**11:39**	**7:36**	**3:36**	86.4

RISINGS AND SETTINGS

The times of the star's rising and setting at Boston on any date are found by applying the interval shown to the time of the star's transit on that date. Subtract the interval for the star's rising; add it for its setting. The times for a place outside Boston are found by correcting the times found for Boston by the values of the Key Letters shown. (See footnote.) The directions in which the star rises and sets shown for Boston are generally useful throughout the United States. Deneb, Algol, Capella, and Vega are circumpolar stars — this means that they do not appear to rise or set, but are above the horizon.

Star	Int. hr.m.	Rising Key	Dir.	Setting Key	Dir.
Altair	6:36	B	EbN	D	WbN
Fomalhaut	3:59	E	SE	A	SW
Aldebaran	7:06	B	ENE	D	WNW
Rigel	5:33	D	EbS	B	WbS
Bellatrix	6:27	B	EbN	D	WbN
Betelgeuse	6:31	B	EbN	D	WbN
Sirius	5:00	D	ESE	B	WSW
Procyon	6:23	B	EbN	D	WbN
Pollux	8:01	A	NE	E	NW
Regulus	6:49	B	EbN	D	WbN
Spica	5:23	D	EbS	B	WbS
Arcturus	7:19	A	ENE	E	WNW
Antares	4:17	E	SEbE	A	SWbW

NOTE: The values of Key Letters are given in the Time Correction Tables (pages 198-202).

Natural Look
CAPLESS Stretch WIGS
Feels as light and cool as your own hair
"PERMANENTLY SET" • READY TO WEAR STYLES • NEVER NEED SETTING

Any
2 WIGS
FOR $**29**⁹⁰

(when you buy two!)

$15.95 ea. When Ordering One.

- Choice of 15 attractive colors or custom matched to your own hair
- Permanently set—wash and wear—the setting bounces back
- Made of miracle modacrylic fiber—has the luster, rich body and bounce of human hair—behaves better than real hair
- No costly settings at the beauty parlour
- Packs in your purse—crush resistant
- Looks and feels like real hair—you'll mistake it for your own

Style C-383

Style C-353

Style C-348

Style C-362

Style T-1035

Style C-340

Style C-303

Style C-347

Style T-390

Style T-300

Style TG-345

Style C-331

FREE 30 DAY TRIAL COUPON

Since 1960

FRANKLIN FASHIONS CORP., Dept. NP-636
103 E. Hawthorne Ave., Valley Stream, NY 11580

Rush my "Natural Look Capless Wig" style(s) checked. I must be absolutely satisfied or I can return my order within 30 days and my money will be refunded.

☐ **PREPAID:** SAVE $2.00. I enclose $29.90 for any 2 wigs plus $4.00 for shipping & handling. TOTAL $33.90

☐ **PREPAID:** I enclose $15.95 for one wig plus $2.00 for shipping & handling. TOTAL $17.95

Call TOLL FREE 1-800-556-0034

CHARGE IT: (Check One) ☐ VISA ☐ MasterCard

Acc't #_____ Exp. Date_____

Check Box of Style Number Desired

☐ C-383	☐ C-353	☐ C-348	☐ C-362
☐ T-1035	☐ C-340	☐ C-303	☐ C-347
☐ T-390	☐ T-300	☐ TG-345	☐ C-331

Check Box of Color Desired (or Send a sample of Your Hair for Expert Matching)

☐ Black
☐ Off Black
☐ Light Brown
☐ Medium Brown
☐ Dark Brown
☐ Light Blonde
☐ Medium Blonde

☐ Dark Blonde
☐ Ash Blonde
☐ Platinum
☐ Light Auburn
☐ Medium Auburn
☐ Dark Auburn
☐ Light Frosted

☐ Dark Frosted
☐ Mixed Black & Grey
☐ Mixed Brown & Grey

Name_____

Address_____

City_____State_____Zip_____

Park Seed
Flowers and Vegetables
1993

Yours
FREE!

The Big New Park Seed Catalog

Quarter Days and

This arcane knowledge comes in handy when you try to explain why June is the month of weddings, or how Groundhog Day got started, or why we have elections in the fall.

BY

ANDREW E.
ROTHOVIUS

he ancient Celtic peoples who first inhabited the British Isles divided the year into four major sections and then divided each of these in half to make an eight-part year that reflected the natural procession of the seasons. Long after the Anglo-Saxon culture became dominant and the 12-month Roman calendar was adopted for both civil and religious purposes, the old Celtic division of the year continued, especially in rural societies. It lingers on in the timing of some of our holidays, as noted in the Right-Hand Calendar Pages (57-83).

The days that marked the four major divisions of the year were called Quarter Days; they indicated the days of the solstices and equinoxes, on which the seasons begin. Gradually, to conform more closely with the liturgical year of the Christian church, they became identified with its high seasonal festivals, which occurred close to the astronomical dates. In the same way, the Cross-Quarter Days, which occurred roughly halfway between each pair of Quarter Days, came to be identified with other major religious festivals. They all became occasions for community gatherings and feasts.

The Quarter Days

These days, which originally marked the four seasons, fitted readily into the rhythm of the annual round of the farming year. March 25, Lady Day (in the church calendar the feast of the Angel Gabriel's annunciation to the Virgin Mary that she would be the mother of Christ), became the traditional day for hiring farm laborers for the planting and harvesting seasons ahead. Midsummer Day, June 24, seems to our modern way of thinking a misnomer — is it not the very beginning of the summer season? But to the farmer, it was the midpoint of the growing season, halfway between planting and harvest, and therefore an occasion for festivity. The English church celebrated the day as the birthday of John the Baptist, who foretold the birth of Jesus exactly six months later. Farm rents to the landowner came to be customarily paid on Michaelmas, September 29, the feast of the Archangel Michael (the slayer of that old dragon, the Devil) because by then the harvest was in, the surplus crops were sold, and the farmers had money to pay the rent.

Christmas, December 25, the fourth Quarter Day, was both the grand culmination of the old year and the first festival of the new. The day originated as a solstice festival and celebrated a time of resting and gathering fertility for a new round of sowing and reaping; this merged easily with the Christian celebration of the birth of Jesus. Farm workers, who were largely itinerant, were usually paid off for the year's labor at Christmas, giving them three months in which to look around for where they would work the next season. On Lady Day the great hir-

Cross-Quarter Days

ing fairs would come around again to mark the start of the agricultural year.

The Cross-Quarter Days

These days marked the midpoint of each season; the old Celts also invested them with gender characteristics. Candlemas, February 2, acquired its English name from the candles lighted that day in churches to celebrate the presentation of the Christ Child in the temple at Jerusalem; but originally it was called Imbolc (lambs' milk) because the lambing season began then. It was also called Brigantia for the Celtic female deity of light, calling attention to the Sun's being halfway on its advance from the winter solstice to the spring equinox. Yet it was

– illustration by Margo Letourneau and Sara Mintz Zwicker

Harvest traditionally began at the following Cross-Quarter Day, known to the Celts as Lughnasaid, August 1, the wedding of the Sun god Lugh to the Earth goddess.

not held as a good omen if the day itself was bright and sunny, for that betokened snow and frost to continue to the hiring of the laborers six weeks hence on Lady Day; whereas if it was cloudy and dark, warmth and rain would thaw out the fields and have them ready for planting. Our Groundhog Day is a remote survivor of that belief.

Beltane or May Day, May 1, was the halfway point between the beginning of spring and that of summer, a day for dance and song to hail the sown fields starting to sprout, a time of male fertility that in time would yield fecundity. It was the day for young couples' pairing, though not yet their wedding; that in the earlier ages would not come until the next Cross-Quarter Day, after three months of seeing how they suited each other. Impatience being already a common trait, the waiting period came to be shortened to a six-week span to Midsummer Day; whence our tradition of June bridals.

Harvest traditionally began at the following Cross-Quarter Day, known to the Celts as Lughnasaid, August 1, the wedding of the Sun god Lugh to the Earth goddess, now fecund with ripening crops (hence, despite its male name, this festival was held to be a female one). The church transformed it into an offering of the first fruits of the labor of the tillers of the land; on this day the first loaves baked from the new wheat were offered at the Loaf Mass, which became corrupted in pronunciation to Lammas.

The harvest, commenced at Lammas, would be completed by the Quarter Day of Michaelmas, September 29; at this point it was assumed that the farmer would have enough ready money from the sale of his crops to pay his yearly rent to the lord who owned the land. Great market fairs (connected in their own way to Harvest Home festivals) came to be held on the days immediately preceding the Quarter Day; it was also a time when it was convenient for people to gather and elect their mayors and magistrates. Therefore, from very early times came the custom of autumnal general elections, though they came to be shifted to November in the American climate where the harvest season was more stretched out.

So we come to the end of the eight-part year on October 31, Samhain, or Halloween. (The unequal intervals between Lammas, Michaelmas, and Halloween resulted from a complicated attempt to reconcile the ancient Celtic lunar year with the 12-month solar year.) Since Samhain was the death-night of the old year, it came to be associated with ghosts and ghouls and graveyards; but it has happier linkages too, such as apple bobbing, which was a form of telling fortunes for the new year commencing the next day.

– Sara Mintz Zwicker

It was also the day that the cattle were brought in from summer pasture, where they had grazed since the Cross-Quarter Day of Beltane, May 1; those needed for the winter's supply of meat would be slaughtered in ten days. This was a male task and hence this final Cross-Quarter Day was considered a masculine one.

□□

1992   NOVEMBER, The Eleventh Month

At mid evening, the bright constellations of the Summer Triangle are setting in the west; and even brighter Orion, Taurus, Auriga, and Gemini are rising in the east. A fairly dim section of Milky Way glow arches high across the north sky from Auriga to Cygnus, but along that stretch shine the bright stars of Perseus and Cassiopeia. High in the south is the Great Square of Pegasus and, extending from it to overhead, the stars and great naked-eye galaxy of Andromeda. Venus and Saturn are in the southwest in the early evening; Venus is breathtakingly near a fairly bright star (in binoculars) on the 18th. Brilliant Mars passes 5 degrees south of Pollux in Gemini on the 4th, then enters Cancer. Moonlight interferes with viewing many Leonid meteors on the 17th and 18th.

ASTRONOMICAL CALCULATIONS

☽	First Quarter	2nd day	4th hour	12th min.
○	Full Moon	10th day	4th hour	21st min.
☾	Last Quarter	17th day	6th hour	40th min.
●	New Moon	24th day	4th hour	12th min.

FOR POINTS OUTSIDE BOSTON SEE KEY LETTER CORRECTIONS — PAGES 198-202

Day of Year	Day of Month	Day of Week	☉ Rises h. m.	Key	☉ Sets h. m.	Key	Length of Days h. m.	Sun Fast m.	Full Sea Boston A.M.	Full Sea Boston P.M.	☽ Rises h. m.	Key	☽ Sets h. m.	Key	Declination of Sun ° '	☽ Place	☽ Age
306	1	**D**	6 17	D	4 38	B	10 21	32	$3\frac{3}{4}$	$3\frac{3}{4}$	$12^{P}_{M}17$	E	$10^{P}_{M}38$	B	14s.40	SAG	7
307	2	M.	6 19	D	4 37	B	10 18	32	$4\frac{1}{2}$	$4\frac{3}{4}$	12 45	D	$11^{P}_{M}43$	A	14 58	AQU	8
308	3	Tu.	6 20	D	4 35	B	10 15	32	$5\frac{1}{2}$	$5\frac{3}{4}$	1 11	D	— —	–	15 17	CAP	9
309	4	W.	6 21	D	4 34	B	10 13	32	$6\frac{1}{2}$	$6\frac{3}{4}$	1 35	D	$12^{A}_{M}36$	C	15 35	AQU	10
310	5	Th.	6 22	D	4 33	B	10 11	32	$7\frac{1}{4}$	$7\frac{1}{2}$	1 58	C	1 35	D	15 53	PSC	11
311	6	Fr.	6 24	D	4 32	A	10 08	32	8	$8\frac{1}{2}$	2 22	B	2 35	D	16 11	PSC	12
312	7	Sa.	6 25	D	4 31	A	10 06	32	$8\frac{3}{4}$	$9\frac{1}{4}$	2 47	B	3 36	E	16 29	PSC	13
313	8	**D**	6 26	D	4 30	A	10 04	32	$9\frac{1}{4}$	$9\frac{3}{4}$	3 16	B	4 39	E	16 47	PSC	14
314	9	M.	6 27	D	4 28	A	10 01	32	10	$10\frac{1}{2}$	3 49	B	5 43	E	17 04	ARI	15
315	10	Tu.	6 29	D	4 27	A	9 58	32	$10\frac{3}{4}$	$11\frac{1}{4}$	4 29	B	6 48	E	17 21	ARI	16
316	11	W.	6 30	D	4 26	A	9 56	32	$11\frac{1}{4}$	—	5 17	B	7 52	E	17 37	TAU	17
317	12	Th.	6 31	D	4 25	A	9 54	32	12	12	6 12	B	8 52	E	17 53	TAU	18
318	13	Fr.	6 32	D	4 24	A	9 52	32	$12\frac{3}{4}$	$12\frac{3}{4}$	7 16	B	9 46	E	18 09	TAU	19
319	14	Sa.	6 34	D	4 23	A	9 49	32	$1\frac{1}{2}$	$1\frac{1}{2}$	8 24	B	10 33	E	18 25	GEM	20
320	15	**D**	6 35	D	4 23	A	9 48	31	$2\frac{1}{4}$	$2\frac{1}{2}$	9 36	C	11 13	E	18 40	GEM	21
321	16	M.	6 36	D	4 22	A	9 46	31	$3\frac{1}{4}$	$3\frac{1}{2}$	$10^{P}_{M}48$	C	$11^{A}_{M}48$	D	18 54	CAN	22
322	17	Tu.	6 37	D	4 21	A	9 44	31	$4\frac{1}{4}$	$4\frac{1}{2}$	— —	–	$12^{P}_{M}19$	D	19 09	LEO	23
323	18	W.	6 38	D	4 20	A	9 42	31	$5\frac{1}{4}$	$5\frac{1}{2}$	$12^{A}_{M}00$	D	12 48	D	19 23	SEX	24
324	19	Th.	6 40	D	4 19	A	9 39	31	$6\frac{1}{4}$	$6\frac{1}{2}$	1 13	D	1 17	C	19 37	LEO	25
325	20	Fr.	6 41	D	4 19	A	9 38	30	7	$7\frac{1}{2}$	2 25	D	1 46	B	19 51	VIR	26
326	21	Sa.	6 42	D	4 18	A	9 36	30	8	$8\frac{1}{2}$	3 37	E	2 19	B	20 04	VIR	27
327	22	**D**	6 43	D	4 17	A	9 34	30	9	$9\frac{1}{2}$	4 49	E	2 56	B	20 17	VIR	28
328	23	M.	6 45	D	4 17	A	9 32	29	$9\frac{3}{4}$	$10\frac{1}{2}$	6 00	E	3 38	B	20 29	LIB	29
329	24	Tu.	6 46	D	4 16	A	9 30	29	$10\frac{1}{2}$	$11\frac{1}{4}$	7 06	E	4 26	B	20 41	SCO	0
330	25	W.	6 47	E	4 15	A	9 28	29	$11\frac{1}{4}$	—	8 04	E	5 21	B	20 53	OPH	1
331	26	Th.	6 48	E	4 15	A	9 27	29	12	12	8 56	E	6 20	B	21 04	SAG	2
332	27	Fr.	6 49	E	4 14	A	9 25	28	$12\frac{3}{4}$	$12\frac{3}{4}$	9 39	E	7 21	B	21 15	SAG	3
333	28	Sa.	6 50	E	4 14	A	9 24	28	$1\frac{1}{2}$	$1\frac{1}{2}$	10 15	E	8 23	B	21 26	SAG	4
334	29	**D**	6 51	E	4 14	A	9 23	28	$2\frac{1}{4}$	$2\frac{1}{2}$	10 45	D	9 24	C	21 36	CAP	5
335	30	M.	6 52	E	4 13	A	9 21	27	3	$3\frac{1}{4}$	$11^{A}_{M}12$	D	$10^{P}_{M}24$	C	21s.45	AQU	6

NOVEMBER hath 30 days. 1992

The wild gander leads his flock through the cool night,
Ya-honk! he says, and sounds it down to me like an invitation;
The pert may suppose it meaningless, but I listen closer,
I find its purpose and place up there toward the November sky.
— *Walt Whitman*

D.M.	D.W.	Dates, Feasts, Fasts, Aspects, Tide Heights	*Weather* ↓
1	D	21st S. af. P. • All Saints • Tides {8.7 / 9.4	*Farewell,*
2	M.	☌♄☾ • All Souls • North and South Dakota statehood, 1889 •	*summer!*
3	Tu.	☾ at apo. • *Politics makes strange postmasters.* • {8.6 / 8.9 •	*Rain's a*
4	W.	Mass. Bay Colony declared heresy punishable by death, 1646 •	*drummer,*
5	Th.	☾ on Eq. • Fawkes's Plot (it's never forgot) • Roy Rogers born, 1912 •	*beating*
6	Fr.	St. Leonard • First U.S. football game, Rutgers vs. Princeton, 1869 • {9.4 / 9.0	*retreat.*
7	Sa.	Bolsheviks led by Lenin seized government, 1917 • Marie Curie born, 1867 • Tides {9.7 / 9.2	*Snow*
8	D	22nd S. af. P. • 25" snow, northern Plains, 1986 • {10.1 / 9.3	*betrays*
9	M.	*The hole and the patch should be commensurate.* • Boston in flames, 1872 •	*the deer;*
10	Tu.	Full Beaver ○ • Marine Corps created, 1775 • Tides {10.6 / 9.5 •	*days*
11	W.	St. Martin • Veterans Day • ☿ stat. • Indian summer begins. •	
12	Th.	☾ at ☋ • ☾ rides high • Skunks hibernate. • Tides {9.5 / 10.9 •	*warm*
13	Fr.	Holland Tunnel opened, N.Y.-N.J., 1927 • Louis Brandeis born, 1856 • {9.5 / 10.9 •	*and*
14	Sa.	☌♇☉ • Sadie Hawkins Day • *Ideas never work unless you do.*	*clear.*
15	D	23rd S. af. P. • ☌♂☾ • William Herschel born, 1738	*Dark*
16	M.	Oklahoma statehood, 1907 • Premiere of *Sound of Music,* N.Y.C., 1959 • Tides {9.4 / 10.3	*and*
17	Tu.	St. Hilda • William Larimer founded Denver, 1858 • {9.6 / 10.1 •	*sopping,*
18	W.	☾ on Eq. • ☾ at perig. • Congress adopted std. time zones, 1883 •	*mercury's*
19	Th.	*Art is the elimination of the unnecessary.* • Tides {10.2 / 9.9 •	*dropping.*
20	Fr.	St. Edmund • ☌♃☾ • Indian summer ends. • {10.6 / 9.9	*Count*
21	Sa.	☿ at inf. ☌ • Mayflower Compact signed, Provincetown Harbor, 1620 • {11.0 / 10.0 •	*each*
22	D	24th S. af. P. • St. Cecilia • Prune grapevines • Tides {11.3 / 10.0	
23	M.	St. Clement • Franklin Pierce born, 1804 • {11.5 / 10.0	*snowflake*
24	Tu.	New ● • *The best way to study human nature is when nobody else is present.* • {11.5 / 9.9	*as a*
25	W.	☾ at ☊ • ☾ runs low • 28" snow, Pittsburgh; 108 mph winds on coast, 1950	*blessing;*
26	Th.	Thanksgiving Day • ☌♀⛢ • Draft lottery estab., 1969 •	*just like*
27	Fr.	☌♀♆ • ☌⛢☾ • ☌♆☾ • ☌♀☾ • {9.5 / 10.8	*turkey*
28	Sa.	*If there be ice in November that will bear a duck, There'll be nothing thereafter but sleet and muck.* •	*and*
29	D	1st S. in Advent • ♂ stat. • ☌♄☾ • {9.1 / 9.9	*walnut*
30	M.	St. Andrew • Winston Churchill born, 1874 • Tides {8.9 / 9.4	*dressing!*

November's sky is chill and drear,
November's leaf is red and sere. – Sir Walter Scott

Farmer's Calendar

Nights in late fall when the frost is hard and the air clear and sharp are best for looking at the sky. There is woodsmoke on the air. Overhead the sky bends over the earth like the top of a great circus tent, crowded with the familiar beasts: the bull, the ram, the winged horse. About halfway up the eastern sky is a very bright star, and just above it to the right is a fuzzy, vague patch in the sky. That patch, if you have a pair of binoculars, can give you a hint of the excitement of discovery.

The big star below the bright patch is Aldebaran, the patch itself is the Pleiades. The Pleiades is not a star but a so-called *open cluster* of stars. There are altogether something like 1,400 stars in the Pleiades, but only nine are bright enough to have been named. Simple binoculars resolve the cluster into a startling array of hundreds of stars, six of which form a brilliant hook, with the lesser stars scattered among them. The Pleiades fairly leap down at you from the haze of their great distance, and where you saw only a fog you find detail, complexity, and an intimation of the strangeness of the heavens.

Galileo in 1609 pointed his new telescope at the Pleiades one night and found 40 formerly invisible stars in one of the early steps in what was perhaps the richest period of discovery in history. In a way, it's a breakthrough that can still be made. Only in the sky can you come close to repeating the discovery of worlds. You can't return to New York Harbor in 1524 and find it as Verrazano did, and similarly for the source of the Nile and the Newfoundland Capes. The Pleiades endure. They have been found, but not changed. The Consolations of Astronomy.

1992   DECEMBER, The Twelfth Month

On December 9th, at least some of the total eclipse of the Moon is visible to all of North America except the extreme west, though only the east sees all of totality after sunset and moonrise; the total phase lasts 74 minutes. A partial solar eclipse on the 23rd is visible only in most of southern Alaska. Venus blazes higher in the southwest in early evening, standing near Saturn on the 21st. Mars retrogrades back into Gemini, going just 3 degrees south of Pollux on the 22nd. Sirius and Procyon rise soon after Gemini and Orion. A waning Moon hampers views of the Geminid meteors around the 14th. Winter begins at 9:43 A.M., EST, on the 21st.

ASTRONOMICAL CALCULATIONS

☽	First Quarter	2nd day	1st hour	18th min.
○	Full Moon	9th day	18th hour	41st min.
☾	Last Quarter	16th day	14th hour	15th min.
●	New Moon	23rd day	19th hour	43rd min.
☽	First Quarter	31st day	22nd hour	39th min.

FOR POINTS OUTSIDE BOSTON SEE KEY LETTER CORRECTIONS — PAGES 198-202

Day of Year	Day of Month	Day of Week	☉ Rises h. m.	Key	☉ Sets h. m.	Key	Length of Days h. m.	Sun Fast m.	Full Sea Boston A.M.	Full Sea Boston P.M.	☽ Rises h. m.	Key	☽ Sets h. m.	Key	Declination of Sun ° '	Place	Age
336	1	Tu.	6 54	E	4 13	A	9 19	27	4	4	11 ᴬᴍ 36	D	11 ᴾᴍ 23	D	21s.55	AQU	7
337	2	W.	6 55	E	4 13	A	9 18	26	4¾	5	12 ᴾᴍ 00	C	— —	-	22 03	AQU	8
338	3	Th.	6 56	E	4 12	A	9 16	26	5½	6	12 23	C	12 ᴬᴍ 22	D	22 11	PSC	9
339	4	Fr.	6 57	E	4 12	A	9 15	26	6½	6¾	12 47	B	1 22	D	22 19	PSC	10
340	5	Sa.	6 58	E	4 12	A	9 14	25	7¼	7¾	1 15	B	2 23	E	22 27	PSC	11
341	6	D	6 59	E	4 12	A	9 13	25	8	8½	1 46	B	3 26	E	22 34	PSC	12
342	7	M.	7 00	E	4 12	A	9 12	24	8¾	9¼	2 23	B	4 31	E	22 41	ARI	13
343	8	Tu.	7 01	E	4 12	A	9 11	24	9½	10	3 07	B	5 36	E	22 47	ARI	14
344	9	W.	7 01	E	4 12	A	9 11	23	10¼	10¾	4 00	B	6 39	E	22 53	TAU	15
345	10	Th.	7 02	E	4 12	A	9 10	23	11	11½	5 03	B	7 37	E	22 58	TAU	16
346	11	Fr.	7 03	E	4 12	A	9 09	23	11¾	—	6 11	B	8 28	E	23 03	GEM	17
347	12	Sa.	7 04	E	4 12	A	9 08	22	12¼	12½	7 24	B	9 12	E	23 07	GEM	18
348	13	D	7 05	E	4 12	A	9 07	22	1¼	1¼	8 38	C	9 50	D	23 11	CAN	19
349	14	M.	7 06	E	4 12	A	9 06	21	2	2¼	9 51	D	10 23	D	23 15	CAN	20
350	15	Tu.	7 06	E	4 12	A	9 06	21	2¾	3¼	11 ᴾᴍ 03	D	10 52	D	23 18	SEX	21
351	16	W.	7 07	E	4 13	A	9 06	20	3¾	4¼	— —	-	11 21	C	23 20	LEO	22
352	17	Th.	7 08	E	4 13	A	9 05	20	4¾	5¼	12 ᴬᴍ 15	E	11 ᴬᴍ 49	C	23 22	VIR	23
353	18	Fr.	7 08	E	4 13	A	9 05	19	5¾	6¼	1 26	E	12 ᴾᴍ 20	B	23 24	VIR	24
354	19	Sa.	7 08	E	4 14	A	9 06	19	6¾	7¼	2 37	E	12 54	B	23 25	VIR	25
355	20	D	7 10	E	4 14	A	9 04	18	7¾	8¼	3 47	E	1 33	B	23 26	LIB	26
356	21	M.	7 10	E	4 14	A	9 04	18	8½	9¼	4 53	E	2 18	B	23 26	LIB	27
357	22	Tu.	7 11	E	4 15	A	9 04	17	9½	10¼	5 54	E	3 09	B	23 26	OPH	28
358	23	W.	7 11	E	4 16	A	9 05	17	10¼	11	6 47	E	4 06	B	23 25	OPH	0
359	24	Th.	7 11	E	4 16	A	9 05	16	11	11¾	7 34	E	5 07	B	23 24	SAG	1
360	25	Fr.	7 12	E	4 17	A	9 05	16	11¾	—	8 12	E	6 09	B	23 22	SAG	2
361	26	Sa.	7 12	E	4 17	A	9 05	15	12½	12½	8 45	E	7 11	C	23 20	CAP	3
362	27	D	7 13	E	4 18	A	9 05	15	1	1¼	9 14	D	8 12	C	23 17	AQU	4
363	28	M.	7 13	E	4 19	A	9 06	14	1¾	2	9 39	D	9 11	C	23 14	AQU	5
364	29	Tu.	7 13	E	4 20	A	9 07	14	2½	2¾	10 02	D	10 10	D	23 11	AQU	6
365	30	W.	7 13	E	4 20	A	9 07	13	3¼	3½	10 26	C	11 ᴾᴍ 08	D	23 07	PSC	7
366	31	Th.	7 13	E	4 21	A	9 08	13	4	4¼	10 ᴬᴍ 49	C	— —	-	23s.02	PSC	8

DECEMBER hath 31 days. 1992

All things counter, original, spare, strange;
Whatever is fickle, freckled (who knows how?)
With swift, slow; sweet, sour; adazzle, dim;
He fathers forth whose beauty is past change:
Praise him.
— *Gerard Manley Hopkins*

D. M.	D. W.	Dates, Feasts, Fasts, Aspects, Tide Heights	*Weather* ↓
1	Tu.	☿ stat. • ☾ at apo. • Second Crusade began, 1145 • Tides 8.8 / 9.0	*Snow*
2	W.	☾ on Eq. • *No one ever forgets where he buried a hatchet.* • Tides 8.8 / 8.7	*and*
3	Th.	First U.S. flag raised aboard *Alfred*, 1775 • Charles Pillsbury born, 1842 • 8.9 / 8.5 •	*rain*
4	Fr.	Jacques Marquette built mission house at site of Chicago, 1674 •	*(freezin') —*
5	Sa.	Bessemer steel process patented, 1865 • P. K. Wrigley born, 1894 • Tides 9.3 / 8.5	*It's*
6	D	**2nd S. in Adv. • St. Nicholas** • Tides 9.7 / 8.7	*sneezin'*
7	M.	Ice formed in Los Angeles swimming pools, 1978 • Madame Tussaud born, 1760	*season.*
8	Tu.	**Concep. of V.M.** • U.S. declared war on Japan, 1941 • 10.4 / 9.1 •	*So*
9	W.	☿ Gr. Elong. W. (21°) • Full Hunting ○ • Eclipse of ☾ • 10.8 / 9.3	*cold*
10	Th.	☾ at ☋ • ☾ rides high • "Gift of the Magi" published, 1905 • 11.1 / 9.6 •	*it*
11	Fr.	*All things I thought I knew, but now confess, The more I know I know, I know the less.* •	*makes*
12	Sa.	☌♂☾ • First Bank of the United States opened, Philadelphia, 1792 • 9.7 / 11.3	*your*
13	D	**3rd S. in Adv. • St. Lucy** • ☾ at perig. •	*eyeballs*
14	M.	George Washington died, 1799 • Margaret Chase Smith born, 1897 • 10.0 / 10.9	*squeak;*
15	Tu.	Bill of Rights Day • Virginia approved Bill of Rights, completing ratification, 1792 •	*rainy*
16	W.	☾ on Eq. • Ember Day • Beware the Pogonip. • "Cold Wednesday," New England, 1835	*and*
17	Th.	First successful flight by Wright brothers, 1903 • Tides 10.3 / 9.7 •	*bleak.*
18	Fr.	☌♃☾ • Ember Day • Fell timber during the waning Moon. • 10.4 / 9.4	*Is*
19	Sa.	Ember Day • *Knowledge, like timber, must be seasoned before use.* • 10.6 / 9.3	*the*
20	D	**4th S. in Adv. • Chanukah** • Halcyon days; calm seas.	*climate*
21	M.	**St. Thomas** • Winter Solstice • ☌♀♄ • Pilgrims landed, Plymouth Rock, 1620	*out*
22	Tu.	☾ at ☊ • ☌☿☾ • 27" snow, Gettysburg, Pennsylvania, 1839 • Tides 10.9 / 9.3	*of*
23	W.	☾ runs low • New ● • Eclipse of ☉ • Tides 10.9 / 9.4	*sorts?*
24	Th.	Green Christmas, White Easter • Kit Carson born, 1809 • Tides 10.9 / 9.3	*Santa's*
25	Fr.	**Christmas Day** • *Peace on Earth, good will to men.* • 10.7 / — •	*in*
26	Sa.	**St. Stephen** • Boxing Day (Canada) • Tides 9.3 / 10.5	*Bermuda*
27	D	**1st S. af. C. • St. John** • ☌♄☾ • 9.3 / 10.2	*shorts!*
28	M.	**Holy Innocents** • ☌♀☾ • Chewing gum patented, 1869 • 9.2 / 9.8	*A*
29	Tu.	☾ at apo. • *Elbow grease makes wealth increase.* • Tides 9.1 / 9.4 •	*damp*
30	W.	☾ on Eq. • –13° F, New York City, 1917 • Sandy Koufax born, 1935 • 9.0 / 9.0	*adieu*
31	Th.	**St. Sylvester** • *End the old year square with every man.* – Robert B. Thomas	*to '92.*

Farmer's Calendar

It's possible we have gotten to know too much about the weather. Broadcast weather bulletins inundate us with information and half-understood principles. The forecasters tell us much more than we want or need to know, to the point that, with the weather as with politics, art, and the conduct of life, we are overcome with information and lose our way.

Consider a typical weather report on my radio. A *meteorologist* (note that he or she is not a weatherman or an announcer, but a scientist) clears his throat and carries on something like this: "A preponderant Arctic system originating east of Great Slave Lake is rapidly autorelocating southwesterly across the Laurentian Highlands, encountering a subsidiary low-pressure configuration emanating from the region of the Bay of Campeche, rendering it probable that should these two meteorological entities converge at high altitude over Churubusco the likelihood of solid or semisolid precipitation will be in the range of 22.1 to 37.4 percent, *whereas* should the Arctic superbarometric eventuality and the Oaxacan subbarometric abstraction fail to effect conjunction before reaching the latitude of the Fishkill Salient, the probability of such precipitation achieves the inverse of the range hypothecated immediately above. We'll keep you posted. Now back to you, Edgar."

OK, it's not really that bad. But you get the point: a blizzard of data driven by a hurricane of lingo, most of it only remotely relevant. What we need is this: "It's going to snow tonight, probably. Probably start about dark. Might snow a foot or so. If you have to go to town, go now. Back to you, Edgar."

JANUARY, THE FIRST MONTH

Mars reaches opposition on the night of January 7th-8th, with the full Moon passing south of it as both set at night's end. The ruddy planet greatly outshines Castor and Pollux, near it in Gemini, and is closest to Earth, about 58 million miles away, on the 3rd. Only Sirius (in the southeast at mid-evening) slightly outshines Mars. Venus reaches greatest elongation (47 degrees east) on January 19th. To the right of Mars and Sirius, Orion forms the most splendid of all star patterns. Jupiter rises in late evening. Just before dawn on the 3rd and 4th, watch for Quadrantid meteors from the northeast. Earth is at perihelion on the night of the 3rd.

ASTRONOMICAL CALCULATIONS

○ Full Moon	8th day	7th hour	38th min.
☾ Last Quarter	14th day	23rd hour	2nd min.
● New Moon	22nd day	13th hour	28th min.
☽ First Quarter	30th day	18th hour	20th min.

FOR POINTS OUTSIDE BOSTON SEE KEY LETTER CORRECTIONS — PAGES 198-202

Day of Year	Day of Month	Day of Week	☉ Rises h. m.	Key	☉ Sets h. m.	Key	Length of Days h. m.	Sun Fast m.	Full Sea Boston A.M.	Full Sea Boston P.M.	☽ Rises h. m.	Key	☽ Sets h. m.	Key	Declination of Sun ° '	☽ Place	☽ Age
1	1	Fr.	7 14	E	4 22	A	9 08	12	4¼	5¼	11 A.M. 14	B	12 A.M. 08	E	22s.57	PSC	9
2	2	Sa.	7 14	E	4 23	A	9 09	12	5½	6	11 A.M. 43	B	1 10	E	22 51	PSC	10
3	3	**C**	7 14	E	4 24	A	9 10	11	6½	7	12 P.M. 16	B	2 13	E	22 45	ARI	11
4	4	M.	7 14	E	4 25	A	9 11	11	7¼	8	12 56	B	3 16	E	22 39	ARI	12
5	5	Tu.	7 14	E	4 26	A	9 12	11	8	8¾	1 44	B	4 20	E	22 33	TAU	13
6	6	W.	7 14	E	4 27	A	9 13	10	9	9½	2 42	B	5 21	E	22 26	TAU	14
7	7	Th.	7 13	E	4 28	A	9 15	10	9¾	10½	3 49	B	6 15	E	22 18	GEM	15
8	8	Fr.	7 13	E	4 29	A	9 16	9	10½	11¼	5 02	B	7 04	E	22 10	GEM	16
9	9	Sa.	7 13	E	4 30	A	9 17	9	11½	—	6 18	C	7 46	E	22 01	CAN	17
10	10	**C**	7 13	E	4 31	A	9 18	8	12	12¼	7 35	C	8 22	D	21 52	CAN	18
11	11	M.	7 13	E	4 32	A	9 19	8	12¾	1	8 50	D	8 54	D	21 43	LEO	19
12	12	Tu.	7 12	E	4 33	A	9 21	8	1¾	2	10 04	D	9 24	C	21 33	LEO	20
13	13	W.	7 12	E	4 34	A	9 22	7	2½	2¾	11 P.M. 17	E	9 53	C	21 23	LEO	21
14	14	Th.	7 12	E	4 36	A	9 24	7	3½	3¾	— —	–	10 23	C	21 12	VIR	22
15	15	Fr.	7 11	E	4 37	A	9 26	7	4¼	4¾	12 A.M. 28	E	10 57	B	21 01	VIR	23
16	16	Sa.	7 11	E	4 38	A	9 27	6	5¼	6	1 38	E	11 A.M. 34	B	20 50	LIB	24
17	17	**C**	7 10	E	4 39	A	9 29	6	6¼	7	2 45	E	12 P.M. 16	B	20 38	LIB	25
18	18	M.	7 10	E	4 40	A	9 30	6	7½	8¼	3 47	E	1 05	B	20 26	SCO	26
19	19	Tu.	7 09	E	4 42	A	9 33	5	8¼	9	4 42	E	1 59	B	20 13	OPH	27
20	20	W.	7 08	E	4 43	A	9 35	5	9¼	10	5 30	E	2 57	B	20 00	SAG	28
21	21	Th.	7 08	E	4 44	A	9 36	5	10	10¾	6 12	E	3 58	B	19 47	SAG	29
22	22	Fr.	7 07	D	4 45	A	9 38	4	10¾	11½	6 46	E	5 00	B	19 33	SAG	0
23	23	Sa.	7 06	D	4 47	A	9 41	4	11½	—	7 16	D	6 01	C	19 19	CAP	1
24	24	**C**	7 05	D	4 48	A	9 43	4	12	12	7 43	D	7 01	C	19 05	CAP	2
25	25	M.	7 05	D	4 49	A	9 44	4	12½	12¾	8 06	D	8 00	D	18 52	AQU	3
26	26	Tu.	7 04	D	4 50	A	9 46	3	1¼	1½	8 30	C	8 58	D	18 35	PSC	4
27	27	W.	7 03	D	4 52	A	9 49	3	1¾	2	8 53	C	9 57	D	18 19	PSC	5
28	28	Th.	7 02	D	4 53	A	9 51	3	2½	2¾	9 17	B	10 57	E	18 03	PSC	6
29	29	Fr.	7 01	D	4 54	A	9 53	3	3¼	3½	9 44	B	11 P.M. 59	E	17 47	PSC	7
30	30	Sa.	7 00	D	4 56	A	9 56	3	4	4½	10 14	B	— —	–	17 30	ARI	8
31	31	**C**	6 59	D	4 57	A	9 58	3	4¾	5¼	10 A.M. 50	B	1 A.M. 00	E	17s.13	ARI	9

JANUARY hath 31 days. 1993

Winter for a moment takes the mind; the snow
Falls past the arc-light; icicles guard a wall;
The wind moans through a crack in the window;
A keen sparkle of frost is on the sill.
— Conrad Aiken

D. M.	D. W.	Dates, Feasts, Fasts, Aspects, Tide Heights	Weather ↓
1	Fr.	New Year's Day • Circumcision • Tides {9.0 / 8.3	*Rain*
2	Sa.	St. Gregory of Nazianzus • Tides {9.1 / 8.2 •	*departs,*
3	C	2nd S. af. Ch. • ♂ closest approach • ⊕ at perihelion	*wind*
4	M.	Sir Isaac Pitman, inventor of shorthand, born 1813 • Tides {9.6 / 8.4 •	*smarts.*
5	Tu.	Twelfth Night • –23° F, Yale University, New Haven, Conn., 1835 • Benj. Rush born, 1745	*Where*
6	W.	Epiphany • ☾ rides high • ☾ at ☋ • {10.5 / 9.1	*are*
7	Th.	♂ at ☍ • January fog means a wet spring. • Tides {11.0 / 9.6 •	*the*
8	Fr.	☌♅☉ • Full Wolf ○ • ☌♂☾ • ☌♆☾	*snows of*
9	Sa.	*Genius is talent provided with ideals.* • Joan Baez born, 1941 {11.7 / —	*yesteryear?*
10	C	1st S. af. Epiphany • ☾ at perig. • Tides {10.4 / 11.8	*Here!*
11	M.	Plough Monday • Great Lakes blizzard, 1918 • F. S. Key died, 1843 {10.7 / 11.6	*Heedless*
12	Tu.	☾ on Eq. • Sunshine today foretells much wind. •	*couch*
13	W.	St. Hilary • Sophie Tucker born, 1884 {10.9 / 10.7	*potatoes*
14	Th.	☌♃☾ • Propitious for birth of women. • Snowflakes, San Diego, Cal., 1882	*order*
15	Fr.	*To believe a thing impossible is to make it so.* {10.6 / 9.5	*seedless*
16	Sa.	Fell timber as Moon wanes. • Dizzy Dean born, 1911 • Tides {10.4 / 9.0	*new*
17	C	2nd S. af. Epiphany • Brink's robbery, Boston, 1950	*tomatoes.*
18	M.	Martin Luther King Jr.'s Birthday • Tides {10.2 / 8.7	*Dig*
19	Tu.	☾ runs low • ☾ at ☊ • ♀ Gr. Elong. (47° East) • Robert E. Lee born, 1807	*we*
20	W.	St. Fabian • Favorable for birth of men. • Tides {10.3 / 8.9 •	*must.*
21	Th.	St. Agnes • *Drive thy business, let it not drive thee.* • Tides {10.4 / 9.1	*Drivers*
22	Fr.	St. Vincent • New ● • Druid New Year • {10.4 / 9.2 •	*feel*
23	Sa.	☿ at sup. ☌ • National Handwriting Day; birthday of John Hancock, 1737 •	*like*
24	C	3rd S. af. Epiphany • Tides {9.3 / 10.2 •	*helpless*
25	M.	Conversion of Paul • ☌♅♆ • Raccoons mate. •	*klutzes*
26	Tu.	☾ on Eq. • ☾ at apo. • ☌♀☾ • Michigan statehood, 1837 {9.4 / 9.8	*as*
27	W.	Herring spawn, Norway • Vietnam War cease-fire signed in Paris, 1973 •	*their*
28	Th.	St. Thomas Aquinas • Alexander Mackenzie b., 1822 • {9.3 / 9.0 •	*cars*
29	Fr.	♃ stat. • *To err is human, to repent divine, to persist devilish.* •	*do*
30	Sa.	Charles I beheaded, 1649 • F. D. Roosevelt born, 1882 • Tides {9.2 / 8.3 •	*triple*
31	C	4th S. af. Epiphany • Nolan Ryan born, 1947 •	*lutzes!*

Farmer's Calendar

Since real snow has ceased to fall in the winter around here, we have had to make do with some pretty strange matter dropping from the sky. Do I exaggerate? The newspaper the other day said the state's average snowfall has been normal. I find I am no more reassured by that than the littlest kid on the team is reassured to learn that the team members' average height is six-three. He's five-eight, and the mathematical fact that his average height is seven inches taller than his real height doesn't comfort him one bit. Same for snow: whatever the weather bureau's calculators say, the fact is that in my backyard we haven't had a real snowstorm in three years. Instead we have this . . . stuff.

For the winter sky is never empty. There is always something making up overhead, and it still falls on the just and the unjust, only now it's seldom quite snow. Not long ago there came down on my house something that looked like beach sand except that it was sticky, as though the sand had fallen through a zone of atmospheric syrup. Then we had a storm of what might have been insulation: little pieces, round, kind of soft. It bounced when it hit, but not hard, not like good old hail, more like Silly Putty. The Eskimos, I have read, have 200 words that describe snow. Send me an Eskimo.

I hope the stuff I'm seeing isn't what I fear it is: low-cal snow, *nouvelle neige,* snow that doesn't clog your arteries, boost your blood pressure, give you cancer, put you under stress, or cause you to become overexcited. So many things already make life longer by making it thinner; only let us have our snow full strength again, and they can keep the beef, the cigarettes, and the black coffee.

1993   FEBRUARY, The Second Month

Four planets are prominent in the evening sky this month. Venus is a spectacle all month, attaining greatest brilliancy in the west on the 24th, when it lies close to the Moon. Mercury shines well below Venus for more than an hour after nightfall, achieving its best evening showing of the year for about two weeks before and one week after its greatest elongation on the 21st. Mars fades, but remains a captivating ruddy ornament in the south in the midst of the "Heavenly G" formed by bright stars Aldebaran, Capella, Castor, Pollux, Procyon, Sirius, Rigel, and Betelgeuse. Sirius, the Dog Star, marks the head or heart of Canis Major, the Large Dog, while Procyon lies in Canis Minor, the Small Dog. Jupiter rises a few hours after nightfall, near Spica in Virgo. Between Castor and Pollux in Gemini, and Jupiter and Spica in Virgo, dim Cancer the Crab and bright Leo the Lion shine. There is no first quarter Moon this month, but two next month.

ASTRONOMICAL CALCULATIONS

○	Full Moon	6th day	18th hour	56th min.
☽	Last Quarter	13th day	9th hour	58th min.
●	New Moon	21st day	8th hour	6th min.

FOR POINTS OUTSIDE BOSTON SEE KEY LETTER CORRECTIONS — PAGES 198-202

Day of Year	Day of Month	Day of Week	☉ Rises h. m.	Key	☉ Sets h. m.	Key	Length of Days h. m.	Sun Fast m.	Full Sea Boston A.M.	Full Sea Boston P.M.	☽ Rises h. m.	Key	☽ Sets h. m.	Key	Declination of Sun ° '	☽ Place	☽ Age
32	1	M.	6 58	D	4 58	A	10 00	2	5¾	6¼	11ᴬM33	A	2ᴬM02	E	16s.56	TAU	10
33	2	Tu.	6 57	D	4 59	A	10 02	2	6½	7¼	12ᴾM25	A	3 02	E	16 39	TAU	11
34	3	W.	6 56	D	5 01	A	10 05	2	7½	8¼	1 25	B	3 59	E	16 22	TAU	12
35	4	Th.	6 55	D	5 02	A	10 07	2	8½	9¼	2 34	B	4 51	E	16 04	GEM	13
36	5	Fr.	6 54	D	5 03	A	10 09	2	9¼	10	3 49	C	5 36	E	15 46	GEM	14
37	6	Sa.	6 53	D	5 05	A	10 12	2	10¼	10¾	5 06	C	6 15	E	15 27	CAN	15
38	7	C	6 52	D	5 06	B	10 14	2	11	11½	6 25	D	6 50	D	15 08	LEO	16
39	8	M.	6 50	D	5 07	B	10 17	2	—	12	7 42	D	7 23	D	14 49	SEX	17
40	9	Tu.	6 49	D	5 09	B	10 20	2	12½	12¾	8 59	E	7 53	C	14 30	LEO	18
41	10	W.	6 48	D	5 10	B	10 22	2	1¼	1¾	10 13	E	8 24	C	14 10	VIR	19
42	11	Th.	6 47	D	5 11	B	10 24	2	2	2½	11ᴾM26	E	8 58	B	13 50	VIR	20
43	12	Fr.	6 45	D	5 12	B	10 27	2	3	3½	— —	–	9 35	B	13 30	VIR	21
44	13	Sa.	6 44	D	5 14	B	10 30	2	4	4½	12ᴬM36	E	10 16	B	13 10	LIB	22
45	14	C	6 43	D	5 15	B	10 32	2	5	5½	1 40	E	11 03	B	12 50	SCO	23
46	15	M.	6 41	D	5 16	B	10 35	2	6	6¾	2 38	E	11ᴬM55	B	12 30	OPH	24
47	16	Tu.	6 40	D	5 18	B	10 38	2	7	7¾	3 28	E	12ᴾM52	B	12 09	SAG	25
48	17	W.	6 38	D	5 19	B	10 41	2	8	8¾	4 11	E	1 51	B	11 48	SAG	26
49	18	Th.	6 37	D	5 20	B	10 43	2	9	9½	4 48	E	2 52	B	11 27	SAG	27
50	19	Fr.	6 36	D	5 21	B	10 45	2	9¾	10¼	5 19	D	3 53	C	11 05	CAP	28
51	20	Sa.	6 34	D	5 23	B	10 49	2	10½	11	5 46	D	4 53	C	10 44	AQU	29
52	21	C	6 33	D	5 24	B	10 51	2	11¼	11½	6 11	D	5 52	D	10 22	AQU	0
53	22	M.	6 31	D	5 25	B	10 54	3	11¾	—	6 35	D	6 51	D	10 00	PSC	1
54	23	Tu.	6 30	D	5 26	B	10 56	3	12¼	12¼	6 58	C	7 49	D	9 38	PSC	2
55	24	W.	6 28	D	5 28	B	11 00	3	12¾	1	7 22	B	8 49	E	9 16	PSC	3
56	25	Th.	6 26	D	5 29	B	11 03	3	1¼	1¾	7 48	B	9 49	E	8 54	PSC	4
57	26	Fr.	6 25	D	5 30	B	11 05	3	2	2¼	8 17	B	10 49	E	8 31	PSC	5
58	27	Sa.	6 23	D	5 31	B	11 08	3	2½	3	8 50	B	11ᴬM50	E	8 08	ARI	6
59	28	C	6 22	D	5 33	B	11 11	3	3¼	3¾	9ᴬM29	A	— —	–	7s.46	TAU	7

FEBRUARY hath 28 days. 1993

The sky is low, the clouds are mean,
  A traveling flake of snow
Across a barn or through a rut
  Debates if it will go.
    — *Emily Dickinson*

D. M.	D. W.	Dates, Feasts, Fasts, Aspects, Tide Heights	Weather ↓
1	M	**St. Brigid** • –45° F, Pittsburg, New Hampshire, 1920 { 9.2 / 8.0	*Groundhogs*
2	Tu.	**Candlemas** • **Purif. of Mary** • Groundhog Day • { 9.5 / 8.2 •	*blink;*
3	W.	☾ rides high • Four Chaplains • Horace Greeley born, 1811 Tides { 9.9 / 8.7	*snow,*
4	Th.	☌♂☾ • Auspicious for marriage and repair of ships. • Rosa Lee Parks born, 1913	*we*
5	Fr.	**St. Agatha** • *Hunger is the best pickle.* • Tides { 11.0 / 9.9 •	*think.*
6	Sa.	Accession of Queen Elizabeth II, 1952 • Full Snow ○ • { 11.5 / 10.5 •	*Roses*
7	C	**Septuagesima** ☾ at perig. • Laura Ingalls Wilder born, 1867 { 11.9 / 11.1	*are*
8	M.	☾ on Eq. • Boy Scouts of America chartered, 1910 • –23° F, Seminole, Texas, 1933	*red*
9	Tu.	☌♄☉ • Mata Hari arrested as a German spy, 1917 • Tides { 11.4 / 11.8	*and*
10	W.	☌♃☾ • –39° F, Milligan, Ohio, 1899 • Jimmy Durante born, 1893 { 11.6 / 11.3	*violets*
11	Th.	A cat basking in the February sun will go to the stove again in March. • –15° F, Washington, D.C., 1899	*are*
12	Fr.	Abraham Lincoln born, 1809 • Charles Darwin born, 1809 • { 11.2 / 10.0	*swell;*
13	Sa.	By Valentine's Day both the good and bad goose will lay. • Tides { 10.7 / 9.3	*I'd*
14	C	**Sexagesima** • **St. Valentine** • **Sts. Cyril & Methodius** •	*love*
15	M.	**Presidents Day** • ☾ runs low • ☾ at ☊ • ♂ stat. • { 9.9 / 8.5	*to*
16	Tu.	Winter's back breaks. • *Toleration should spring from charity, not from indifference.*	*stay, but*
17	W.	☌♆☾ • ☌⛢☾ • Premiere of *Madame Butterfly*, Milan, 1904, •	*it's*
18	Th.	*A censor is a man who knows more than he thinks you ought to.* • { 9.8 / 8.8	*snowing*
19	Fr.	Marines invaded Iwo Jima, 1945 • Stan Kenton born, 1912 • { 9.9 / 9.1 •	*like*
20	Sa.	30" snow, Racine, Wisconsin, 1898 • Phil Esposito born, 1942 • { 10.0 / 9.3 •	*hell.*
21	C	**Quinquagesima** • ☿ Gr. Elong. (18° E.) • New ●	*Good*
22	M.	George Washington born, 1732 • ☾ on Eq. • ☾ at apo. • { 10.0 / —	*time to*
23	Tu.	**Shrove Tues.** • ☌☿☾ • *Well begun is half done.* •	*thaw'n a*
24	W.	**Ash Wed.** • **St. Matthias** • ♀ Gr. Bril. • Occult. ♀ by ☾	
25	Th.	*Religion is the best armour, but the worst cloak.* • Tides { 9.7 / 9.4	*sauna.*
26	Fr.	One-pound and two-pound bank notes first used in England, 1797 • Tides { 9.7 / 9.1	*Awake*
27	Sa.	☿ stat. • The Great Snow (36") of 1717, Boston, Mass. • { 9.6 / 8.7 •	*to*
28	C	**1st Sun. in Lent** • Bugsy Siegel born, 1906 • Tides { 9.4 / 8.4	*flakes.*

Life is full of miserableness,
loneliness, unhappiness, and suffering.
And it's over with all too quickly.
– Woody Allen

Farmer's Calendar

February 28. A hopeful day. Final day of the mind's winter, the end of the last fully winter month. I got in the car and headed northwest to Burlington, by the long way that comes down out of the mountains at Manchester and then runs north, through Poultney, past Bomoseen, and so on to Middlebury and Lake Champlain: say 150 miles. A journey to the edge.

My side of the state is a close country, narrow, wooded, but west of the mountains the land opens up, and you get into a country of broad valleys, real farmland, with flat, wide fields and blue silos the height of office buildings. I stopped to buy a doughnut in Whiting, a little village built up on top of a hill with plowed fields spreading down and away in all directions. Crows in flocks of 30 or 40 flapped over the fields. Pretty weather — cold, though. Ice in the fields and along the brooks, the lakes and ponds still frozen hard. Around here in 1775 old Ethan Allen organized his attack on the British at Fort Ticonderoga, an easy day's march due west. From Whiting you can look west and see, for the first time, the big mountains in New York, the Adirondacks, blue and gray in the distance; I ate my doughnut and admired them, not without misgivings. Somewhere between here and those peaks is a borderline. Over there is not New England. Beyond the Adirondacks there is an enormous country, a continent, a nation, and from this little hilltop it all seems at the same time very far off and very near, almost as though you could walk over to those mountains, climb up, and look out over the whole republic spread before you: the Great Lakes, the Plains, the Rockies, and the Golden Gate.

MARCH, THE THIRD MONTH

Full Moon on March 8th occurs within an hour of perigee — in fact, within an hour of the Moon's closest approach to us this year; the year's farthest Moon is on the 21st. Jupiter arrives at opposition on the 30th, when it shines brightly all night long. Venus gets closer to Earth each night, but shows more of its night side, displaying a crescent phase detectable even in binoculars. The last days of March and first of April offer the U.S. the best chance in the eight-year cycle of Venus appearances to see it as both Morning Star (just before sunrise) and Evening Star (just after sunset) on the same day. Vernal equinox is at 9:41 A.M.*, EST, on the 20th.*

ASTRONOMICAL CALCULATIONS

☽	First Quarter	1st day	10th hour	47th min.
○	Full Moon	8th day	4th hour	47th min.
☾	Last Quarter	14th day	23rd hour	17th min.
●	New Moon	23rd day	2nd hour	16th min.
☽	First Quarter	30th day	23rd hour	11th min.

FOR POINTS OUTSIDE BOSTON SEE KEY LETTER CORRECTIONS — PAGES 198-202

Day of Year	Day of Month	Day of Week	☉ Rises h. m.	Key	☉ Sets h. m.	Key	Length of Days h. m.	Sun Fast m.	Full Sea Boston A.M.	Full Sea Boston P.M.	☽ Rises h. m.	Key	☽ Sets h. m.	Key	Declination of Sun ° ′	☽ Place	☽ Age
60	1	M.	6 20	D	5 34	B	11 14	4	4	4¾	10 A.M. 16	B	12 A.M. 50	E	7 S. 23	TAU	8
61	2	Tu.	6 19	D	5 35	B	11 16	4	5	5¾	11 A.M. 10	B	1 46	E	7 00	TAU	9
62	3	W.	6 17	D	5 36	B	11 19	4	6	6¾	12 P.M. 13	B	2 38	E	6 37	GEM	10
63	4	Th.	6 15	D	5 38	B	11 23	4	7	7¾	1 23	B	3 25	E	6 14	GEM	11
64	5	Fr.	6 14	D	5 39	B	11 25	4	8	8¾	2 37	C	4 07	E	5 51	CAN	12
65	6	Sa.	6 12	D	5 40	B	11 28	5	9	9½	3 54	C	4 43	D	5 28	CAN	13
66	7	**C**	6 10	D	5 41	B	11 31	5	10	10½	5 12	D	5 16	D	5 04	LEO	14
67	8	M.	6 09	D	5 42	B	11 33	5	10¾	11¼	6 30	D	5 49	C	4 41	LEO	15
68	9	Tu.	6 07	D	5 43	B	11 36	5	11½	—	7 48	E	6 21	C	4 18	VIR	16
69	10	W.	6 05	D	5 45	B	11 40	6	12	12½	9 05	E	6 54	B	3 54	VIR	17
70	11	Th.	6 04	C	5 46	B	11 42	6	12¾	1¼	10 18	E	7 31	B	3 31	VIR	18
71	12	Fr.	6 02	C	5 47	B	11 45	6	1¾	2¼	11 P.M. 26	E	8 12	B	3 07	LIB	19
72	13	Sa.	6 00	C	5 48	B	11 48	7	2½	3¼	— —	–	8 58	B	2 43	SCO	20
73	14	**C**	5 58	C	5 49	B	11 51	7	3½	4¼	12 A.M. 30	E	9 50	B	2 20	OPH	21
74	15	M.	5 57	C	5 50	B	11 53	7	4½	5¼	1 23	E	10 47	B	1 56	SAG	22
75	16	Tu.	5 55	C	5 52	B	11 57	7	5½	6¼	2 09	E	11 A.M. 46	B	1 32	SAG	23
76	17	W.	5 53	C	5 53	B	12 00	8	6¾	7½	2 48	E	12 P.M. 46	B	1 08	SAG	24
77	18	Th.	5 52	C	5 54	B	12 02	8	7¾	8¼	3 21	E	1 47	C	0 45	CAP	25
78	19	Fr.	5 50	C	5 55	C	12 05	8	8½	9¼	3 50	D	2 47	C	0 S. 21	AQU	26
79	20	Sa.	5 48	C	5 56	C	12 08	9	9½	9¾	4 16	D	3 46	C	0 N. 01	AQU	27
80	21	**C**	5 46	C	5 57	C	12 11	9	10	10½	4 39	D	4 44	D	0 26	AQU	28
81	22	M.	5 45	C	5 59	C	12 14	9	10¾	11	5 03	C	5 43	D	0 50	PSC	29
82	23	Tu.	5 43	C	6 00	C	12 17	9	11¼	11½	5 27	C	6 42	D	1 13	PSC	0
83	24	W.	5 41	C	6 01	C	12 20	10	—	12	5 52	B	7 42	E	1 37	PSC	1
84	25	Th.	5 39	C	6 02	C	12 23	10	12¼	12½	6 21	B	8 42	E	2 00	PSC	2
85	26	Fr.	5 38	C	6 03	C	12 25	10	12¾	1¼	6 53	B	9 43	E	2 23	ARI	3
86	27	Sa.	5 36	C	6 04	C	12 28	11	1¼	2	7 30	B	10 42	E	2 47	ARI	4
87	28	**C**	5 34	C	6 05	C	12 31	11	2	2½	8 13	B	11 P.M. 39	E	3 11	TAU	5
88	29	M.	5 32	C	6 06	C	12 34	11	2¾	3½	9 03	B	— —	–	3 34	TAU	6
89	30	Tu.	5 31	C	6 08	C	12 37	12	3½	4¼	10 02	B	12 A.M. 31	E	3 58	TAU	7
90	31	W.	5 29	B	6 09	C	12 40	12	4½	5¼	11 A.M. 07	B	1 A.M. 19	E	4 N. 21	GEM	8

MARCH hath 31 days. 1993

The snow has left the cottage top;
The thatch moss grows in brighter green;
And eaves in quick succession drop,
Where grinning icicles have been.
— *John Clare*

D. M.	D. W.	Dates, Feasts, Fasts, Aspects, Tide Heights	Weather ↓
1	M.	**St. David** • ☾ at ☋ • ♇ stat. • Tides {9.4 / 8.2 •	*It's*
2	Tu.	**St. Chad** • ☾ rides high • Town Meeting Day, Vt. • {9.4 / 8.2 •	*lovely*
3	W.	☌♂☾ • Ember Day • Mass. set ten-hour workday for children under 12, 1842 •	*for*
4	Th.	FDR's first inaugural; Hoover says, "We have done all we can do," 1933 • Tides {9.9 / 8.9	*Lapps,*
5	Fr.	Skunks mate. • Ember Day • Five colonists killed at Boston Massacre, 1770 •	*who*
6	Sa.	Skunk cabbage bloomed, Lexington, Mass., 1964 • Ember Day • *Full cups must be held steady.*	*dig*
7	**C**	**2nd S. in Lent** • **St. Perpetua** • Tides {11.5 / 11.1	*cold*
8	M.	☾ on Eq. • ☾ at perig. • Full Worm ○ • ☿ in inf. ☌ {11.8 / 11.7	*snaps.*
9	Tu.	♀ stat. • ☌♃☾ • Town Meeting Day, N.H. • Tides {11.8 / —	*And*
10	W.	*Stick to your winter flannels 'til your flannels stick to you.* • Oscar Mayer born, 1888 {12.0 / 11.6	*a*
11	Th.	*A Raisin in the Sun,* first play on Broadway by a black woman, opened, 1959 {12.0 / 11.2	*smirk'll*
12	Fr.	**St. Gregory** • William Lyon Mackenzie born, 1795 • Blizzard of 1888 •	*grace*
13	Sa.	*Our first 40 years give the text, the next 30 supply the commentary.* • Tides {11.3 / 9.8 •	*the*
14	**C**	**3rd S. in Lent** • ☾ runs low • ☾ at ☊ • {10.7 / 9.2 •	*face*
15	M.	Cincinnati Red Stockings became first professional baseball team, 1869 • Harry James born, 1916	*of*
16	Tu.	Barnum and Bailey Circus debut in New York City, 1881 • Tides {9.6 / 8.4 •	*any*
17	W.	**St. Patrick** • ☌♆☾ • ☌♅☾ • −50° F, Snake R., Wyo., 1906	*race*
18	Th.	*Govern a small family as you would cook a small fish, very gently.* •	*that*
19	Fr.	**St. Joseph** • Swallows arrive, San Juan Capistrano, Cal. • Tides {9.4 / 8.9	*lives*
20	Sa.	☌♄☾ • Vernal Equinox • Chipmunks emerge • {9.5 / 9.2 •	*above*
21	**C**	**4th S. in Lent** • ☾ on Eq. • ☌☿☾ • ☿ stat. ☾ at apo.	*the*
22	M.	4" snow, Rome, Georgia, 1872 • German troops occupied Hungary, 1944 •	*Arctic*
23	Tu.	New ● • Robins, Dublin, N.H., 1953 • Fanny Farmer born, 1857 • {9.8 / 9.9	*Circle.*
24	W.	☌♀☾ • *No man is rich enough to buy back his past.* •	*But*
25	Th.	**Annunciation** • Clear today means a fertile year. •	*temperate*
26	Fr.	Britain required driving tests for car owners, 1934 • 19" snow, Chicago, 1930 {10.1 / 9.4	*dwellers*
27	Sa.	Earthquake, 8.4 Richter scale, Anchorage, Alaska, 1964 • Sara Vaughan born, 1924 •	*should*
28	**C**	**5th S. in Lent** • **Passion** • ☾ at ☋ • {9.9 / 8.9	*hide*
29	M.	☾ rides high • A bushel of March dust is worth a king's ransom. • Tides {9.8 / 8.7	*in*
30	Tu.	♃ at ☍ • U.S. bought Alaska from Russia for $7,200,000, 1867 •	*their*
31	W.	☌♂☾ • *An old friend is the best mirror.* • Tides {9.7 / 8.6 •	*cellars!*

Farmer's Calendar

"How's your mud?" people ask me. "How is it up there, pretty deep?" In the past I would have bragged. I would have said something like, "Don't know if it's deep; haven't found the bottom yet." Nowadays I make some noncommittal answer. "Not too bad," I say, or, "Yes, it's a little soft today." I have learned that my friends don't admire my mud. Many of them regard mud-encumbered Marches and Aprils with something near scorn.

The issue, after all, is not mud as mud, not mud *per se*. Mud is everywhere, and nobody cares. The earth itself is mostly mud, more or less dried up, when you think about it. Nobody objects. No, the issue is not mud; the issue is roads. Over most of the country, or as much of it as is subject to freezing and thawing, the civilizers have been at work for long enough so that today roads axle deep in spring mud are a part of remote history, like runaway teams. Even quiet country roads are usually paved — not well paved always, not recently paved, but still relatively black, relatively hard.

Not in my state. Here we like dirt roads. I have never been entirely sure why, but I hope the reason is a principled reluctance to squander the taxpayer's dollar on fripperies (and an inability as yet to figure out a way of getting the Feds to pick up the paving tab). Whatever the reason, my little town, typical of the state, contains about 70 miles of roads, of which some three-quarters are dirt. Roads that in any other state would glisten with asphalt here remain in their primeval innocence. It's not so bad, really. It's nowhere near the hardship they must believe it is who each spring ask, "How's your mud?" as they might ask the Ancient Mariner, "How's your albatross?"

1993 APRIL, THE FOURTH MONTH

Venus reaches inferior conjunction on the morning of the 1st, far enough north of the Sun to be glimpsed rising just minutes before it. On the 5th, Mercury reaches its maximum "greatest elongation" (28 degrees west) of the year. Look for it low in the east just before dawn. The occultation of Venus by the Moon will be visible across most of the United States, from Hawaii (early morning) to the Atlantic coast (midday), on the 19th. Mars is in the south at nightfall, still a little brighter than Pollux when it passes 5 degrees south of that star on the 14th. The Big Dipper wheels high in the north these evenings; a line extended from the arc of the handle leads to the brilliant orange star Arcturus. The Lyrid meteors stream out of the east around and after midnight on the 21st and 22nd. Daylight Saving Time begins at 2 A.M. on the 4th.

ASTRONOMICAL CALCULATIONS

○ Full Moon	6th day	13th hour	45th min.
☾ Last Quarter	13th day	14th hour	39th min.
● New Moon	21st day	18th hour	49th min.
☽ First Quarter	29th day	7th hour	42nd min.

ADD 1 hour for Daylight Saving Time after 2 A.M., April 4th.

FOR POINTS OUTSIDE BOSTON SEE KEY LETTER CORRECTIONS — PAGES 198-202

Day of Year	Day of Month	Day of Week	☉ Rises h. m.	Key	☉ Sets h. m.	Key	Length of Days h. m.	Sun Fast m.	Full Sea Boston A.M.	Full Sea Boston P.M.	☽ Rises h. m.	Key	☽ Sets h. m.	Key	Declination of Sun ° '	☽ Place	☽ Age
91	1	Th.	5 27	B	6 10	C	12 43	12	5½	6¼	12 P.M. 17	B	2 A.M. 01	E	4N.44	GEM	9
92	2	Fr.	5 26	B	6 11	C	12 45	12	6½	7¼	1 29	C	2 38	D	5 07	CAN	10
93	3	Sa.	5 24	B	6 12	C	12 48	13	7½	8¼	2 44	D	3 11	D	5 30	LEO	11
94	4	**C**	5 22	B	6 13	D	12 51	13	8½	9	4 01	D	3 44	D	5 53	SEX	12
95	5	M.	5 20	B	6 14	D	12 54	13	9½	10	5 18	D	4 15	C	6 15	LEO	13
96	6	Tu.	5 19	B	6 15	D	12 56	14	10½	10¾	6 35	E	4 48	C	6 38	VIR	14
97	7	W.	5 17	B	6 17	D	13 00	14	11¼	11½	7 52	E	5 23	B	7 01	VIR	15
98	8	Th.	5 15	B	6 18	D	13 03	14	—	12¼	9 05	E	6 03	B	7 23	VIR	16
99	9	Fr.	5 14	B	6 19	D	13 05	14	12½	1	10 13	E	6 48	B	7 45	LIB	17
100	10	Sa.	5 12	B	6 20	D	13 08	15	1¼	2	11 P.M. 12	E	7 39	B	8 07	SCO	18
101	11	**C**	5 10	B	6 21	D	13 11	15	2	2¾	— —	–	8 36	B	8 29	OPH	19
102	12	M.	5 09	B	6 22	D	13 13	15	3	3¾	12 A.M. 03	E	9 36	B	8 51	SAG	20
103	13	Tu.	5 07	B	6 23	D	13 16	15	4	4¾	12 46	E	10 37	B	9 13	SAG	21
104	14	W.	5 05	B	6 24	D	13 19	16	5	5¾	1 21	E	11 A.M. 38	B	9 34	SAG	22
105	15	Th.	5 04	B	6 26	D	13 22	16	6	6¾	1 52	D	12 P.M. 39	C	9 56	AQU	23
106	16	Fr.	5 02	B	6 27	D	13 25	16	7	7¾	2 19	D	1 38	C	10 17	AQU	24
107	17	Sa.	5 01	B	6 28	D	13 27	16	8	8½	2 43	D	2 37	D	10 38	AQU	25
108	18	**C**	4 59	B	6 29	D	13 30	17	8¾	9¼	3 07	C	3 35	D	10 59	PSC	26
109	19	M.	4 57	B	6 30	D	13 33	17	9½	9¾	3 31	C	4 34	D	11 20	PSC	27
110	20	Tu.	4 56	B	6 31	D	13 35	17	10¼	10½	3 56	B	5 34	E	11 41	PSC	28
111	21	W.	4 54	B	6 32	D	13 38	17	11	11	4 24	B	6 35	E	12 01	PSC	0
112	22	Th.	4 53	B	6 33	D	13 40	18	11½	11¾	4 55	B	7 36	E	12 22	ARI	1
113	23	Fr.	4 51	B	6 35	D	13 44	18	—	12¼	5 30	B	8 36	E	12 42	ARI	2
114	24	Sa.	4 50	B	6 36	D	13 46	18	12¼	12¾	6 12	B	9 34	E	13 01	TAU	3
115	25	**C**	4 48	B	6 37	D	13 49	18	1	1½	7 01	B	10 28	E	13 21	TAU	4
116	26	M.	4 47	B	6 38	D	13 51	18	1¾	2¼	7 57	B	11 P.M. 16	E	13 40	TAU	5
117	27	Tu.	4 45	B	6 39	D	13 54	18	2¼	3	8 59	B	— —	–	13 59	GEM	6
118	28	W.	4 44	B	6 40	D	13 56	19	3¼	4	10 06	B	12 A.M. 01	E	14 18	GEM	7
119	29	Th.	4 43	B	6 41	D	13 58	19	4¼	5	11 A.M. 16	C	12 37	D	14 37	CAN	8
120	30	Fr.	4 41	B	6 42	D	14 01	19	5¼	5¾	12 P.M. 27	D	1 A.M. 10	D	14N.55	LEO	9

APRIL hath 30 days. 1993

A flower is looking through the ground,
Blinking at the April weather;
Now a child has seen the flower:
Now they go and play together.
— Harold Monro

D. M.	D. W.	Dates, Feasts, Fasts, Aspects, Tide Heights	Weather ↓
1	Th.	♀ in inf. ☌ • **All Fools** • Wallace Beery born, 1886 • Tides {9.8 9.0 •	*Fools*
2	Fr.	The voice of the turtle-dove is heard in the land. • Blizzard, Chicago, 1975 •	*slush*
3	Sa.	*Love and scandal are the best sweeteners of tea.* • Doris Day born, 1924 • {10.4 10.2 •	*in.*
4	C	**Palm Sun.** • ☾ on Eq. • Daylight Saving Time begins. {10.8 10.9	*Warm*
5	M.	☿ Gr. Elong. (28° West). • ☾ at perig. • Spencer Tracy born, 1900 Tides {11.2 11.6	*and*
6	Tu.	**Passover** • ☌♃☾ • Full Pink ○ • {11.4 12.0 •	*sunny;*
7	W.	Alewives run, Cape Cod, Mass. • 21° F, Houston, Texas, 1857 • Tides {11.4 12.2	*dare*
8	Th.	Mary Pickford born, 1893 • Bald eagle protected as an endangered species, 1940 •	*we*
9	Fr.	**Good Friday** • *Whispered words are heard afar.* {12.1 10.8	*hope?*
10	Sa.	☾ at ☊ • A late spring is a great blessing. • Omar Sharif born, 1932 {11.8 10.3	*Nope!*
11	C	**Easter Day** • ☾ runs low • Napoleon banished to Elba, 1814 •	*Grab*
12	M.	**Easter Monday (Canada)** • Polio vaccine OK'ed for use, 1955 Tides {10.6 9.2	*your*
13	Tu.	☌♆☾ • ☌♅☾ • Thomas Jefferson born, 1743 •	*raincoats*
14	W.	Hepatica in bloom, Lexington, Mass., 1963 • 13" snow, Twin Cities, Minn., 1983 {9.4 8.6	*—man*
15	Th.	Dow Jones average hit record high of 1171.34, 1983 • *Titanic* sank, 1912 •	*the*
16	Fr.	☌☿♀ • ☌♄☾ Wilbur Wright born, 1867 Tides {9.0 8.8	*lifeboats!*
17	Sa.	*What is patriotism but the love of the good things we ate in our childhood?* •	*Dry*
18	C	**1st S. af. Easter** • ☾ on Eq. • ☾ at apo. • {9.2 9.4 •	*out;*
19	M.	Occult. ♀ by ☾ • ♀ stat. • ☌☿☾ •	*there's*
20	Tu.	A cold April the barn will fill. • 35" snow, Warren, Ohio, 1901 • Tides {9.4 10.0	*blue*
21	W.	**St. Anselm** • Birthday of Queen Elizabeth II • New ● {9.5 10.2	*sky*
22	Th.	♆ stat. • *Too much of a good thing is wonderful.* (Mae West) •	*out.*
23	Fr.	**St. George** • New Coke debuted, 1985 • Shakespeare born, 1564	*Vergin'*
24	Sa.	Physicists announce validation of Big Bang theory, 1992 • Library of Congress established, 1800	*on*
25	C	**2nd S. af. E.** • **St. Mark** • ☾ rides high • ☾ at ☋	*sub-*
26	M.	♅ stat. • Rain before seven, Clear by eleven. • Tides {10.3 9.1 •	*mergin!*
27	Tu.	Rogers Hornsby born, 1896 • Coretta Scott King born, 1927 •	*There's a*
28	W.	☌♂☾ • Flora's Day, or Floralia • Mutiny on *Bounty*, 1789 • {10.1 9.6	*shower*
29	Th.	Duke Ellington born, 1899 • First condor egg laid in captivity hatched, San Diego, 1988	*every*
30	Fr.	Willie Nelson born, 1933 • Washington's first inaugural, 1789 • {10.0 9.6 •	*hour.*

Experience is what enables you to recognize a mistake when you make it again.

Farmer's Calendar

For three days, four days, the hillsides faintly blush. You can't see the transformation well up close, but if you look out across a hollow or beyond a river, you'll find the wooded flanks of the ridges gently suffused with a red or pink haze. It's not spring. The trees are bare and the woods may be full of snow. But the top branches of the hardwoods hold briefly a soft scarlet nimbus almost like red smoke.

The fleeting red haze that comes in early April and is among spring's earliest precursors is produced by the rock maple trees. Find a maple that has a low branch and examine the ends of the twigs. The last couple of inches, last year's new growth, have turned red. At the tips of the twigs the scales covering the tree's flower buds have taken on the same color. It's a dark, dusky red with a bit of purple in it, approaching a color artists call alizarin or Turkey red. The maple's flowers themselves will come in another few days. They are little russet sprigs not much bigger than a pencil eraser.

When the flowers appear, the blush is over. The red bud scales drop away. If there's still snow, the fallen scales scattered over it look like flakes of cayenne. The new twig growth hardens and turns color, and the hardwood uplands return once again to shades of brown, buff, and gray. But now they must turn green. And though it may be weeks before the first green appears on those same hills, the momentary flush of the maples is still a first flourish of spring, a sign that the elements are in place, if not yet quite ready — the toot of horns or ripple of strings that comes from behind the curtain and alerts the audience that the musicians, still invisible, have taken the stage.

MAY, THE FIFTH MONTH

The partial solar eclipse of May 21st is visible in the early morning hours across most of the Midwest and the West. Venus leaps higher in the predawn sky and reaches greatest brilliancy on the 6th, while Mars, fading rapidly in the western evening sky, passes through the north edge of the Beehive star cluster on the 12th (an event best seen by binoculars). Below still-bright Jupiter in the south these evenings is the little sail-shaped Corvus the Crow. Following kite-shaped Bootes with his bright star Arcturus in the northeast is the semicircle of Corona Borealis (the Northern Crown), plus Hercules and Arcturus's rival in brightness, Vega. The bright Moon hinders viewing of the Eta Aquarid meteors during the first week.

ASTRONOMICAL CALCULATIONS

○ Full Moon	5th day	22nd hour	35th min.
☾ Last Quarter	13th day	7th hour	20th min.
● New Moon	21st day	9th hour	8th min.
☽ First Quarter	28th day	13th hour	22nd min.

ADD 1 hour for Daylight Saving Time.

FOR POINTS OUTSIDE BOSTON SEE KEY LETTER CORRECTIONS — PAGES 198-202

Day of Year	Day of Month	Day of Week	☉ Rises h. m.	Key	☉ Sets h. m.	Key	Length of Days h. m.	Sun Fast m.	Full Sea Boston A.M.	Full Sea Boston P.M.	☽ Rises h. m.	Key	☽ Sets h. m.	Key	Declination of Sun ° '	☽ Place	☽ Age
121	1	Sa.	4 40	B	6 44	D	14 04	19	6¼	6¾	1 P.M. 40	D	1 A.M. 42	D	15N.13	SEX	10
122	2	C	4 39	B	6 45	D	14 06	19	7¼	7¾	2 54	D	2 12	C	15 31	LEO	11
123	3	M.	4 37	A	6 46	D	14 09	19	8¼	8¾	4 10	E	2 44	C	15 49	VIR	12
124	4	Tu.	4 36	A	6 47	D	14 11	19	9¼	9½	5 25	E	3 17	B	16 06	VIR	13
125	5	W.	4 35	A	6 48	D	14 13	19	10¼	10½	6 40	E	3 54	B	16 24	VIR	14
126	6	Th.	4 33	A	6 49	D	14 16	19	11	11¼	7 51	E	4 37	B	16 40	LIB	15
127	7	Fr.	4 32	A	6 50	D	14 18	19	—	12	8 55	E	5 25	B	16 57	SCO	16
128	8	Sa.	4 31	A	6 51	D	14 20	20	12	12¾	9 51	E	6 20	A	17 13	OPH	17
129	9	C	4 30	A	6 52	D	14 22	20	1	1½	10 39	E	7 20	B	17 29	SAG	18
130	10	M.	4 29	A	6 53	D	14 24	20	1¾	2½	11 18	E	8 23	B	17 45	SAG	19
131	11	Tu.	4 27	A	6 54	D	14 27	20	2½	3¼	11 P.M. 52	E	9 26	B	18 00	SAG	20
132	12	W.	4 26	A	6 55	D	14 29	20	3½	4¼	— —	–	10 28	C	18 15	CAP	21
133	13	Th.	4 25	A	6 57	D	14 32	20	4½	5	12 A.M. 20	D	11 A.M. 29	C	18 30	CAP	22
134	14	Fr.	4 24	A	6 58	E	14 34	20	5½	6	12 46	D	12 P.M. 28	C	18 44	AQU	23
135	15	Sa.	4 23	A	6 59	E	14 36	20	6¼	7	1 10	D	1 26	D	18 58	PSC	24
136	16	C	4 22	A	7 00	E	14 38	20	7¼	7¾	1 34	C	2 25	D	19 12	PSC	25
137	17	M.	4 21	A	7 01	E	14 40	20	8¼	8½	1 58	C	3 24	E	19 26	PSC	26
138	18	Tu.	4 20	A	7 02	E	14 42	20	9	9¼	2 26	B	4 24	E	19 39	PSC	27
139	19	W.	4 19	A	7 03	E	14 44	20	9¾	9¾	2 55	B	5 26	E	19 52	ARI	28
140	20	Th.	4 18	A	7 04	E	14 46	20	10½	10½	3 29	B	6 27	E	20 04	ARI	29
141	21	Fr.	4 17	A	7 05	E	14 48	19	11	11¼	4 09	B	7 27	E	20 17	TAU	0
142	22	Sa.	4 17	A	7 06	E	14 49	19	11¾	11¾	4 57	B	8 23	E	20 28	TAU	1
143	23	C	4 16	A	7 07	E	14 51	19	—	12½	5 51	B	9 14	E	20 40	TAU	2
144	24	M.	4 15	A	7 07	E	14 52	19	12½	1¼	6 52	B	9 59	E	20 51	GEM	3
145	25	Tu.	4 14	A	7 08	E	14 54	19	1¼	2	7 58	B	10 38	E	21 02	GEM	4
146	26	W.	4 14	A	7 09	E	14 55	19	2	2¾	9 08	C	11 13	D	21 12	CAN	5
147	27	Th.	4 13	A	7 10	E	14 57	19	3	3½	10 18	C	11 P.M. 45	D	21 23	CAN	6
148	28	Fr.	4 12	A	7 11	E	14 59	19	3¾	4½	11 A.M. 29	D	— —	–	21 32	LEO	7
149	29	Sa.	4 12	A	7 12	E	15 00	19	4¾	5½	12 P.M. 41	D	12 A.M. 14	D	21 41	LEO	8
150	30	C	4 11	A	7 13	E	15 02	19	6	6½	1 53	E	12 44	C	21 50	VIR	9
151	31	M.	4 11	A	7 14	E	15 03	18	7	7½	3 P.M. 06	E	1 A.M. 16	C	21N.58	VIR	10

MAY hath 31 days. 1993

May is a green as no other,
May is much sun through small leaves,
May is soft earth, /And apple-blossoms,
And windows open to a South wind.
— *Amy Lowell*

D. M.	D. W.	Dates, Feasts, Fasts, Aspects, Tide Heights	*Weather* ↓
1	Sa.	**Sts. Philip & James** • Rain means a fertile year. • Tides {10.1 10.1 •	*Up*
2	C	**3rd S. af. E.** • ☾ on Eq. • Hudson Bay Company chartered, 1670 •	*the*
3	M.	Invention of the Cross • ☌♃☾ • ☾ at perig. • Tides {10.4 11.3	*creek;*
4	Tu.	Union forces defeated at Chancellorsville, Va., 1863 • {10.6 11.8	*spring's*
5	W.	Full Flower ○ • James Beard born, 1903 • Tides {10.8 12.0	*sprung*
6	Th.	♀ Greatest Brilliancy • *Painting the pump won't clear the well.* • {10.8 12.1 •	*a leak.*
7	Fr.	☾ at ☊ • –15° F, White Mt., California, 1964 • Johannes Brahms born, 1833	*The*
8	Sa.	☾ runs low • Apple blossoms, Massachusetts, 1824 • Tides {11.9 10.3 •	*muck*
9	C	**4th S. af. E.** • Sale of birth-control pills approved, 1960 {11.5 10.0	*stops*
10	M.	☌♆☾ • ☌♅☾ • Water in May is bread all the year. •	*here,*
11	Tu.	**Three** • Skunks are born now. • Irving Berlin born, 1888 • {10.4 9.2 •	*tempor-*
12	W.	**Chilly** • 20-ton meteor fell near Blackston, Va., 1922 • Tides {9.9 9.0 •	*arily;*
13	Th.	**Saints** • *Three can keep a secret, as long as two are dead.* • Tides {9.4 8.9 •	*all*
14	Fr.	☌♄☾ • ♇ at ☍ • Lewis and Clark Expedition left St. Louis for West, 1804 •	*sing*
15	Sa.	☾ on Eq. • ☾ at perig. • ☿ at sup. ☌ • {8.8 9.0 •	*merrily!*
16	C	**Rogation S.** • Congress authorized new coin, soon called the nickel, 1866	*Keep*
17	M.	☌♀☾ • *If you can't bite, don't show your teeth.* • Tides {8.8 9.5 •	*a*
18	Tu.	Gamaliel Wayte planted his garden, Milne St., Boston, 1642 • Tornadoes, Ohio, 1825	*sandbag*
19	W.	**St. Dunstan** • Dark Day in New England, 1780 • {9.0 10.1 •	*in*
20	Th.	**Ascension** • 18 percent of tornadoes occur this month. • Peggy Lee born, 1920	*your*
21	Fr.	New ● • Eclipse ☉ • Tides {9.2 10.5 •	*handbag:*
22	Sa.	Last run of Orient Express across Europe, 1977 • Mary Cassatt born, 1844 {9.3 10.6	*You're*
23	C	**1st S. af. Asc.** • ☾ rides high • 6" snow Iowa, 1882	*dammed*
24	M.	**Victoria Day, Canada** • Anti-Saloon League founded, Oberlin, Ohio, 1893 • {10.7 9.5 •	*if*
25	Tu.	**St. Bede** • *The largest room in the world is the room for improvement.* • {10.7 9.5	*you*
26	W.	**Shavuot** • **St. Augustine of Canterbury** •	*do,*
27	Th.	☌♂☾ • Peter Stuyvesant inaugurated governor of New Amsterdam, 1647 {10.5 9.8	*and*
28	Fr.	Cast not a clout Till May be out. • Dionne quintuplets born, 1934 •	*damp*
29	Sa.	☾ on Eq. • Bob Hope born, 1903 • Wisconsin statehood, 1848 • {10.1 10.3 •	*if*
30	C	**Whit S.** • **Pentecost** • ☌♃☾ • Tides {10.0 10.6	*you*
31	M.	**Visit. of Mary** • **Memorial Day** • ☾ at perig. •	*don't!*

Farmer's Calendar

Contemplating the turning wheels of the carts that passed along the road, the ancient Chinese sage reflected that *The spoke need not strive; it need only wait.* As the wheel turns, each spoke returns to its original position — why? Because that is the way the universe happens to be set up. Therefore we ought to ask, if we would see a task completed, whether our best course isn't to do nothing, to wait like the spoke — or so it is in the Realm of the Wheel, and that's a mighty big realm, a realm beloved by the old philosophers of the East, by shiftless peasants in all times and places, and by me.

I have discovered that every tiresome seasonal chore belongs to the Realm of the Wheel. Whatever needs to be covered, put away, closed down, shut up, or in any other way set to rights is a fit subject for meditation along the lines suggested above. Lesser minds, blinkered Western minds, will call you lazy. Ignore them. All this past winter I have looked out my window at the hammock slung between two trees by the driveway. I have seen it crusted in ice and snow and snapping like a flag in the arctic gales. Some have mocked me. Some have suggested I ought to have put that hammock away six months ago. At first I thought so, too; at Christmastime, the hammock un-put-away, I felt remorse. But I did nothing, and presently I came to consider the wheel, endlessly turning, the spoke, forever coming around. Soon now I will go out to the hammock and gratefully lay me down, not without a pitying thought for vain strivers who must take their hammocks out of the shed and wearily hang them up, ignorant as they are of the *tao* of the hammock.

JUNE, THE SIXTH MONTH

Hawaii sees all of, and the western contiguous states see much of, the total lunar eclipse (1 hour 36 minutes of totality) before dawn and moonset on the 4th, although volcanic haze from Mount Pinatubo's eruption two years ago may render it a dark or deeply colored eclipse. On the 10th, Venus is at greatest elongation before sunrise; on the 17th, Mercury reaches greatest elongation after sunset. Saturn rises in the late evening, and telescopes show its rings less tilted than they have been for a decade. High in the west after nightfall, similarly bright Mars and Regulus form a striking pair for several days around the 22nd; Jupiter is prominent in the southwest evening sky in Virgo. Summer solstice arrives at 4 A.M., EST, on the 21st.

ASTRONOMICAL CALCULATIONS

O	Full Moon	4th day	8th hour	3rd min.
☾	Last Quarter	12th day	0 hour	37th min.
●	New Moon	19th day	20th hour	54th min.
☽	First Quarter	26th day	17th hour	45th min.

ADD 1 hour for Daylight Saving Time.

FOR POINTS OUTSIDE BOSTON SEE KEY LETTER CORRECTIONS — PAGES 198-202

Day of Year	Day of Month	Day of Week	☉ Rises h. m.	Key	☉ Sets h. m.	Key	Length of Days h. m.	Sun Fast m.	Full Sea Boston A.M.	Full Sea Boston P.M.	☽ Rises h. m.	Key	☽ Sets h. m.	Key	Declination of Sun ° '	☽ Place	☽ Age
152	1	Tu.	4 10	A	7 14	E	15 04	18	8	8¼	4 ᴘ ᴍ 20	E	1 ᴀ ᴍ 49	B	22N.07	VIR	11
153	2	W.	4 10	A	7 15	E	15 05	18	9	9¼	5 31	E	2 29	B	22 14	LIB	12
154	3	Th.	4 09	A	7 16	E	15 07	18	10	10	6 38	E	3 13	B	22 21	LIB	13
155	4	Fr.	4 09	A	7 17	E	15 08	18	10¾	11	7 38	E	4 05	B	22 28	OPH	14
156	5	Sa.	4 08	A	7 17	E	15 09	18	11½	11¾	8 30	E	5 03	B	22 35	OPH	15
157	6	C	4 08	A	7 18	E	15 10	17	—	12½	9 13	E	6 06	B	22 42	SAG	16
158	7	M.	4 08	A	7 18	E	15 10	17	12½	1¼	9 49	D	7 09	B	22 48	SAG	17
159	8	Tu.	4 08	A	7 19	E	15 11	17	1¼	2	10 20	D	8 13	C	22 53	CAP	18
160	9	W.	4 08	A	7 20	E	15 12	17	2¼	2¾	10 48	D	9 15	C	22 58	AQU	19
161	10	Th.	4 07	A	7 20	E	15 13	17	3	3½	11 12	D	10 16	C	23 02	AQU	20
162	11	Fr.	4 07	A	7 21	E	15 14	16	3¾	4½	11 ᴍ 36	C	11 ᴀ ᴍ 15	D	23 06	AQU	21
163	12	Sa.	4 07	A	7 21	E	15 14	16	4¾	5¼	— —	—	12 ᴘ ᴍ 13	D	23 10	PSC	22
164	13	C	4 07	A	7 22	E	15 15	16	5½	6	12 ᴀ ᴍ 01	B	1 12	D	23 14	PSC	23
165	14	M.	4 07	A	7 22	E	15 15	16	6½	7	12 26	B	2 12	E	23 17	PSC	24
166	15	Tu.	4 07	A	7 23	E	15 16	16	7½	7¾	12 55	B	3 13	E	23 19	PSC	25
167	16	W.	4 07	A	7 23	E	15 16	15	8¼	8½	1 27	B	4 14	E	23 21	ARI	26
168	17	Th.	4 07	A	7 23	E	15 16	15	9	9¼	2 04	B	5 15	E	23 23	ARI	27
169	18	Fr.	4 07	A	7 24	E	15 17	15	9¾	10	2 48	B	6 13	E	23 24	TAU	28
170	19	Sa.	4 07	A	7 24	E	15 17	15	10½	10¾	3 41	B	7 07	E	23 25	TAU	0
171	20	C	4 07	A	7 24	E	15 17	14	11¼	11½	4 40	B	7 55	E	23 26	GEM	1
172	21	M.	4 07	A	7 24	E	15 17	14	—	12	5 46	B	8 38	E	23 26	GEM	2
173	22	Tu.	4 08	A	7 25	E	15 17	14	12¼	12¾	6 57	B	9 15	D	23 26	CAN	3
174	23	W.	4 08	A	7 25	E	15 17	14	1	1½	8 08	C	9 48	D	23 25	CAN	4
175	24	Th.	4 08	A	7 25	E	15 17	14	1¾	2½	9 20	D	10 18	D	23 24	LEO	5
176	25	Fr.	4 08	A	7 25	E	15 17	13	2¾	3¼	10 32	D	10 48	C	23 22	SEX	6
177	26	Sa.	4 09	A	7 25	E	15 16	13	3½	4¼	11 ᴀ ᴍ 44	D	11 18	C	23 20	LEO	7
178	27	C	4 09	A	7 25	E	15 16	13	4½	5	12 ᴘ ᴍ 56	E	11 ᴍ 51	C	23 17	VIR	8
179	28	M.	4 10	A	7 25	E	15 15	13	5½	6	2 07	E	— —	—	23 14	VIR	9
180	29	Tu.	4 10	A	7 25	E	15 15	13	6¾	7	3 18	E	12 ᴀ ᴍ 27	C	23 11	VIR	10
181	30	W.	4 10	A	7 25	E	15 15	12	7¾	8	4 ᴘ ᴍ 25	E	1 ᴀ ᴍ 09	B	23N.08	LIB	11

JUNE hath 30 days. 1993

All the sun long it was running, it was lovely, the hay-
Fields high as the house, the tunes from the chimneys, it was air
And playing, lovely and watery
And fire green as grass.

— *Dylan Thomas*

D. M.	D. W.	Dates, Feasts, Fasts, Aspects, Tide Heights	*Weather* ↓
1	Tu.	♃ stat. • Tennessee statehood, 1796 • Nelson Riddle born, 1921 • {9.9 11.3	*Did*
2	W.	Ember Day • *Keep a thing for seven years and you will find a use for it.* • Tides {10.0 11.5	*we*
3	Th.	Japanese navy suffered major losses, Battle of Midway, 1942 • {10.0 11.7	*mention*
4	Fr.	Ember Day • ☾ at ☊ • Full Strawberry ○ • Eclipse ☾ {10.1 11.6	*a*
5	Sa.	**St. Boniface** • Ember Day • ☾ runs low • {10.0 11.5	*drenchin'?*
6	**C**	**Trinity** • First Pulitzer prizes awarded, 1917 •	*Schoolbooks*
7	M.	☌♆☾ • ☌♅☾ • *Old foxes want no tutors.* Tides {11.2 9.7	*close,*
8	Tu.	Ice cream first advertised, New York *Gazette,* 1786 • {10.8 9.5 •	*and kids*
9	W.	I.R.S. began tax withholding, called Pay As You Go Act, 1943 • {10.3 9.4 •	*are*
10	Th.	**Corpus Christi** • ♀ Gr. Elong. (46° West) • ☌♄☾ • ♄ stat. • {9.8 9.2	
11	Fr.	**St. Barnabas** • ☾ on Eq. • Vince Lombardi born, 1913	*liberated;*
12	Sa.	☾ at apo. • Baseball Hall of Fame dedicated, 1939 • Tides {9.0 9.1	*only*
13	**C**	**2nd S. af. P.** • 2° F, Tamarack, California, 1907 •	*to feel*
14	M.	**St. Basil** • Harriet Beecher Stowe born, 1811 • {8.5 9.3 •	*refrigerated.*
15	Tu.	127° F, Fort Mojave, Ariz., 1896 • C. Goodyear patented vulcanized rubber, 1844 •	*Showers*
16	W.	☌♀☾ • *Praise does a wise man good, but a fool harm.* • {8.5 9.8	*schoon*
17	Th.	☿ Gr. Elong. (25° East) • Battle of Bunker Hill fought on Breed's Hill, Charlestown, 1775 •	*over*
18	Fr.	☾ at ☋ • Appendicitis identified, 1886 • Tides {8.9 10.4 •	*meadows*
19	Sa.	☾ rides high • New ● • Lou Gehrig born, 1903 • {9.1 10.7 •	*flower-*
20	**C**	**3rd S. af. P.** • West Virginia statehood, 1863 {9.4 11.0 •	*strewn.*
21	M.	Summer Solstice • ☌☿☾ • *Marriage is a covered dish.* • Tides {— 9.7 •	*Is*
22	Tu.	**St. Alban** • John Dillinger and Carl Hubbell born, 1903 • Tides {11.1 9.9	*this*
23	W.	122° F, Overton, Nevada, 1954 • Rain tomorrow means a wet harvest. • {11.2 10.2	*Saska-*
24	Th.	**Nativ. John the Baptist** • ☌♂☾ • Midsummer Day	*toon?*
25	Fr.	☾ on Eq. • ☾ at perig. • *Many a good cow has a bad calf.* •	*Let*
26	Sa.	☌♃☾ • Financial panic began, 1893 • Tides {10.5 10.6	*summer*
27	**C**	**4th S. af. P.** • 100° F, Fort Yukon, Alaska, 1915	*commence*
28	M.	Cholera epidemic began in New York City, 1852 • Tides {9.7 10.8 •	*with*
29	Tu.	**Sts. Peter & Paul** • 109° F, Monticello, Fla., 1931 •	*Pomp &*
30	W.	☿ stat. • Meteorites struck Siberia, 1908 {9.4 11.0	*Circumstance!*

Sing a song of seasons, / Something bright in all,
Flowers in the summer, / Fires in the fall.

Farmer's Calendar

Surrounding my fenceless little garden are eight old posts indicating the line the fence took when the garden was bigger than it is today. Rusty nails and scraps of hex netting adorn these posts. They are gray, rough, cracked. None of them stands up straight, but they all lean this way and that, giving the property a look of ramshackle decay, as though the posts were ancient villagers, idle, disreputable, who sit all day in front of the store cackling at the follies of the industrious.

The garden posts are of different sizes. The top of the tallest must be nine feet off the ground, the shortest is the height of my shoulder. They're round, mostly six or seven inches thick. The fattest has a knothole where chickadees sometimes nest. The posts are made of black locust trunks, and unless I cut them up and burn them, they're here to stay. They held the remains of the garden fence when we came here 20 years ago, and they're visible in photos of the place taken 20 years before that. There used to be nine posts. I uprooted one of them and moved it into the cellar of the house to brace a broken floor joist. When I dug that post up, I found its buried third, at least 35 years in the earth, as sound as the section that was exposed. Locust posts set in the ground by the first colonists at Jamestown, Virginia, in 1607, were as good as new 100 years later.

Nothing that endures as long as these posts can be entirely good-natured. Try driving a fence staple into one of them. You might as well hammer a piece of cooked spaghetti into a steel girder. Best leave the posts to their retirement; let the beans climb up them, let the flycatcher in the long summer evening find atop the tallest its lofty perch.

1993 JULY, THE SEVENTH MONTH

On the 12th, the planets Uranus and Neptune come to opposition on the same day for the first time in 172 years (but binoculars and detailed star charts are needed to identify these dim, distant worlds in Sagittarius). Venus, still blazing in the pre-dawn sky, grazes by two naked-eye stars in Taurus on the 13th and 28th (on the latter date, a good telescope shows it also near the famous Crab Nebula). High in the east look for the Summer Triangle of brilliant stars Vega, Altair, and Deneb. In the south, Antares gleams in Scorpius the Scorpion. Fading Jupiter sets in the evening in Virgo, brightening Saturn rises in the evening in Aquarius. Delta Aquarid meteors can be seen late in the month after late-night moonsets. Earth is at aphelion on the 4th.

ASTRONOMICAL CALCULATIONS

○	Full Moon	3rd day	18th hour	46th min.
☾	Last Quarter	11th day	17th hour	50th min.
●	New Moon	19th day	6th hour	25th min.
☽	First Quarter	25th day	22nd hour	26th min.

ADD 1 hour for Daylight Saving Time.

FOR POINTS OUTSIDE BOSTON SEE KEY LETTER CORRECTIONS — PAGES 198-202

Day of Year	Day of Month	Day of Week	☉ Rises h. m.	Key	☉ Sets h. m.	Key	Length of Days h. m.	Sun Fast m.	Full Sea Boston A.M.	Full Sea Boston P.M.	☽ Rises h. m.	Key	☽ Sets h. m.	Key	Declination of Sun ° '	☽ Place	☽ Age
182	1	Th.	4 11	A	7 25	E	15 14	12	8¾	9	5 P.M. 27	E	1 A.M. 57	B	23N.03	SCO	12
183	2	Fr.	4 12	A	7 25	E	15 13	12	9¾	9¾	6 21	E	2 51	B	22 59	OPH	13
184	3	Sa.	4 12	A	7 24	E	15 12	12	10½	10¾	7 07	E	3 51	B	22 55	SAG	14
185	4	**C**	4 13	A	7 24	E	15 11	12	11¼	11½	7 46	E	4 54	B	22 49	SAG	15
186	5	M.	4 13	A	7 24	E	15 11	11	—	12	8 20	D	5 58	B	22 44	SAG	16
187	6	Tu.	4 14	A	7 24	E	15 10	11	12¼	12¾	8 49	D	7 01	C	22 38	AQU	17
188	7	W.	4 14	A	7 23	E	15 09	11	1	1½	9 15	D	8 03	C	22 31	AQU	18
189	8	Th.	4 15	A	7 23	E	15 08	11	1¾	2¼	9 39	D	9 03	D	22 25	AQU	19
190	9	Fr.	4 16	A	7 23	E	15 07	11	2½	3	10 04	C	10 02	D	22 18	PSC	20
191	10	Sa.	4 16	A	7 22	E	15 06	11	3¼	3¾	10 28	B	11 00	D	22 10	PSC	21
192	11	**C**	4 17	A	7 22	E	15 05	11	4	4½	10 55	B	11 A.M. 59	D	22 02	PSC	22
193	12	M.	4 18	A	7 21	E	15 03	10	4¾	5¼	11 P.M. 25	B	12 P.M. 59	E	21 53	PSC	23
194	13	Tu.	4 19	A	7 21	E	15 02	10	5¾	6	— —	–	1 59	E	21 45	ARI	24
195	14	W.	4 20	A	7 20	E	15 00	10	6¾	7	12 A.M. 01	B	3 00	E	21 35	ARI	25
196	15	Th.	4 20	A	7 19	E	14 59	10	7½	7¾	12 40	B	3 59	E	21 26	TAU	26
197	16	Fr.	4 21	A	7 19	E	14 58	10	8½	8½	1 28	B	4 55	E	21 16	TAU	27
198	17	Sa.	4 22	A	7 18	E	14 56	10	9¼	9½	2 25	B	5 47	E	21 06	TAU	28
199	18	**C**	4 23	A	7 17	E	14 54	10	10	10¼	3 29	B	6 33	E	20 56	GEM	29
200	19	M.	4 24	A	7 17	E	14 53	10	10¾	11	4 38	B	7 15	E	20 45	GEM	0
201	20	Tu.	4 25	A	7 16	E	14 51	10	11¾	11¾	5 51	C	7 48	D	20 34	CAN	1
202	21	W.	4 26	A	7 15	E	14 49	10	—	12½	7 05	D	8 21	D	20 22	LEO	2
203	22	Th.	4 27	A	7 14	E	14 47	10	12¾	1¼	8 19	D	8 51	C	20 10	SEX	3
204	23	Fr.	4 28	A	7 13	E	14 45	10	1½	2	9 33	D	9 22	C	19 58	LEO	4
205	24	Sa.	4 28	A	7 12	E	14 44	10	2½	3	10 46	E	9 54	C	19 45	VIR	5
206	25	**C**	4 29	A	7 11	D	14 42	10	3¼	3¾	11 A.M. 58	E	10 29	B	19 32	VIR	6
207	26	M.	4 30	A	7 10	D	14 40	10	4¼	4¾	1 P.M. 09	E	11 09	B	19 19	VIR	7
208	27	Tu.	4 31	A	7 09	D	14 38	10	5¼	5¾	2 16	E	11 P.M. 54	B	19 05	LIB	8
209	28	W.	4 32	A	7 08	D	14 36	10	6½	6¾	3 19	E	— —	–	18 52	SCO	9
210	29	Th.	4 33	A	7 07	D	14 34	10	7½	7¾	4 15	E	12 A.M. 45	B	18 38	OPH	10
211	30	Fr.	4 34	A	7 06	D	14 32	10	8½	8¾	5 04	E	1 42	B	18 23	SAG	11
212	31	Sa.	4 35	A	7 05	D	14 30	10	9½	9¾	5 P.M. 45	E	2 A.M. 43	B	18N.08	SAG	12

JULY hath 31 days. 1993

Beyond me in the fields the sun
Soaks in the grass and hath his will;
I count the marguerites one by one;
Even the buttercups are still.
— *Archibald Lampman*

D. M.	D. W.	Dates, Feasts, Fasts, Aspects, Tide Heights	*Weather* ↓
1	Th.	**Canada Day** • ☾ at ☊ • Tides {9.4 / 11.1 •	*Happy*
2	Fr.	☾ runs low • *Scatter with one hand, gather with two.* •	*Birthday,*
3	Sa.	Full Buck ○ • Dog Days begin. • Franz Kafka born, 1883 {9.5 / 11.1	*Uncle Sam!*
4	**C**	**Independence Day** • **5th S. af. P.** • ⊕ at aphelion ☌♆☾	
5	M.	Arthur Ashe won at Wimbledon, 1975 • Settlers adopt constitution, Oregon Territory, 1843	*Nature*
6	Tu.	Pirate Capt. Kidd captured, Boston, 1699 • Tides {10.8 / 9.6 •	*shoots*
7	W.	☌♄☾ • 127° F, Parker, Arizona, 1905 • Satchel Paige born, 1906 •	*off*
8	Th.	*Contentment to the mind is as light to the eye.* • {10.2 / 9.5	*Roman*
9	Fr.	☾ on Eq. • W. J. Bryan gave "Cross of Gold" speech, 1896 • Tides {9.8 / 9.4	*candles;*
10	Sa.	☾ at apo. • 134° F, Death Valley, Cal., 1913 • Tides {9.3 / 9.3 •	*fine*
11	**C**	**6th S. af. P.** • 118° F, Bennett, Colo., 1888 •	*for*
12	M.	♅♆ at ☍ • Andrew Wyeth born, 1917 • Tides {8.6 / 9.3	*shorts*
13	Tu.	114° F, Wisconsin Dells, Wis., 1936 • Northwest Ordinance passed, 1787 •	*and*
14	W.	☿ at inf. ☌ • Bastille Day • *Deeds are fruits, words but leaves.* {8.2 / 9.5	*sandals.*
15	Th.	**St. Swithin** • ☾ at ☋ • ☌♀☾ • Tides {8.3 / 9.7	*Golfers*
16	Fr.	*Whatever July and August do not boil, September cannot fry.* •	*vamoose*
17	Sa.	☾ rides high • U.S. got possession of Florida from Spain, 1821 • Tides {8.8 / 10.5	*from*
18	**C**	**7th S. af. P.** • Sikorsky helicopter stayed aloft 15 minutes, 1940	*Dr.*
19	M.	New ● • Rain ceases, wind increases. • Tides {9.7 / 11.3	*Zeus.*
20	Tu.	**St. Margaret** • *Full cups must be held steady.* • {10.2 / 11.5	*Your*
21	W.	110° F, Millsboro, Delaware, 1930 • 10° F, Painter, Wyoming, 1911 {— / 10.6 •	*garden*
22	Th.	**St. Mary Magdalene** • ☾ on Eq. • ☾ at perig. • ☌♂☾ •	
23	Fr.	Thoreau arrested for not paying poll tax, 1846 • Tides {11.4 / 11.1	*looks like*
24	Sa.	☌♃☾ • Now the state of the crops is known. • 118° F, Minden, Neb., 1936	*Eden*
25	**C**	**8th S. af. P.** • **St. James** • ☿ stat. • {10.5 / 11.0 •	*if*
26	M.	**St. Anne** • *He who tells his wife all is but newly married.* •	*you*
27	Tu.	Leo Durocher born, 1906 • Korean War Armistice, 1953 • Tides {9.5 / 10.7	*keep*
28	W.	☾ at ☊ • *Some rain, some rest; Fine weather isn't always best.* •	*up*
29	Th.	☾ runs low • U.S.-Japan trade agreement signed, 1858 • {9.0 / 10.5 •	*with*
30	Fr.	Medicare established, 1965 • Henry Ford born, 1863 •	*your*
31	Sa.	☌♆☾ • ☌♅☾ • Cornscateous air. Tides {9.2 / 10.6	*weedin'.*

Farmer's Calendar

Secret agents, undercover cops, and young women in nightgowns aren't the only ones who can have Hollywood adventures, action-movie escapes. The humblest rodent can tell of catastrophes.

Late one night, investigating a faint sound that came from the kitchen closet, I found a mouse trapped in a glass bottle up on a high shelf. It was a deer mouse, an outdoor creature, usually, and a great gatherer of seeds and nuts. The bottle was a clean, empty quart that had once held fancy vinegar. The mouse had evidently discovered our supply of birdseed and had hit on the plan of dropping sunflower seeds into the bottle for safekeeping. An elegant scheme, but at last the mouse perceived what others have learned in dealings with institutions of safekeeping: putting in is easy; taking out, not always so easy. With the bottle a quarter full of seeds, the mouse must have decided to visit his assets. Once in there, he couldn't get out.

I took the bottle down from the shelf. I wouldn't have hurt the mouse, but as I held him in his bottle, he looked up at me the way Fay Wray, atop the Empire State Building, looked at that big gorilla. I laid the bottle on its side in the closet and left it, so the mouse could walk out. Half an hour later he was still there. He couldn't or wouldn't leave. I could think of only one solution — a crash. I took the bottle outside, tilted it so seeds and mouse slid toward the neck, and gave its base a smart rap with a hammer. Nothing. Again. An explosion of glass, seeds, and escaping mouse. Sweeping up, I wondered what in the world he would tell his friends, what tale of Jules Verne out of Ian Fleming. Where would he begin?

1993 — AUGUST, THE EIGHTH MONTH

This could be a stupendous year for the Perseid meteor shower between the 11th and 13th, especially if its parent comet has recently passed. The best time may be after midnight on the 12th (but look on several nights). At peak, at least 40 to 60 Perseids per hour — possibly several hundred per hour! — may be seen flying from the northeast. On the 19th, golden Saturn is at opposition, brightest and closest for the year, in Aquarius. Bright Jupiter follows dimmed Mars down to the west horizon; Venus remains prominent before dawn. For a number of days around the 4th, Mercury puts in a fine morning appearance, though lower in the east than Venus and not as bright. On the 28th, the Galileo space probe encounters the asteroid Ida on its way to Jupiter.

ASTRONOMICAL CALCULATIONS

O	Full Moon	2nd day	7th hour	11th min.
☾	Last Quarter	10th day	10th hour	20th min.
●	New Moon	17th day	14th hour	29th min.
☽	First Quarter	24th day	4th hour	59th min.
O	Full Moon	31st day	21st hour	34th min.

ADD 1 hour for Daylight Saving Time.

FOR POINTS OUTSIDE BOSTON SEE KEY LETTER CORRECTIONS — PAGES 198-202

Day of Year	Day of Month	Day of Week	☼ Rises h. m.	Key	☼ Sets h. m.	Key	Length of Days h. m.	Sun Fast m.	Full Sea Boston A.M.	Full Sea Boston P.M.	☽ Rises h. m.	Key	☽ Sets h. m.	Key	Declination of Sun ° '	☽ Place	☽ Age
213	1	**C**	4 36	A	7 04	D	14 28	10	10¼	10½	6ᴹ20	E	3ᴬ46	B	17N.53	SAG	13
214	2	M.	4 37	A	7 03	D	14 26	10	11	11¼	6 51	D	4 49	C	17 37	CAP	14
215	3	Tu.	4 38	A	7 02	D	14 24	10	11¾	11¾	7 18	D	5 51	C	17 22	CAP	15
216	4	W.	4 39	A	7 00	D	14 21	10	—	12¼	7 43	D	6 51	D	17 06	AQU	16
217	5	Th.	4 40	A	6 59	D	14 19	10	12½	1	8 07	C	7 51	D	16 49	PSC	17
218	6	Fr.	4 42	A	6 58	D	14 16	10	1¼	1¾	8 32	C	8 50	D	16 33	PSC	18
219	7	Sa.	4 43	A	6 57	D	14 14	10	2	2¼	8 57	B	9 48	D	16 16	PSC	19
220	8	**C**	4 44	A	6 55	D	14 11	10	2½	3	9 26	B	10 48	E	15 59	PSC	20
221	9	M.	4 45	A	6 54	D	14 09	11	3½	3¾	9 58	B	11ᴬ47	E	15 42	ARI	21
222	10	Tu.	4 46	A	6 53	D	14 07	11	4¼	4½	10 35	B	12ᴾ46	E	15 24	ARI	22
223	11	W.	4 47	A	6 51	D	14 04	11	5	5½	11ᴹ19	B	1 45	E	15 07	TAU	23
224	12	Th.	4 48	A	6 50	D	14 02	11	6	6¼	—		2 41	E	14 49	TAU	24
225	13	Fr.	4 49	A	6 49	D	14 00	11	7	7¼	12ᴬ10	B	3 34	E	14 31	TAU	25
226	14	Sa.	4 50	B	6 47	D	13 57	11	8	8	1 09	B	4 22	E	14 12	GEM	26
227	15	**C**	4 51	B	6 46	D	13 55	12	8¾	9	2 16	B	5 05	E	13 53	GEM	27
228	16	M.	4 52	B	6 44	D	13 52	12	9½	9¾	3 27	C	5 43	D	13 34	CAN	28
229	17	Tu.	4 53	B	6 43	D	13 50	12	10½	10¾	4 42	C	6 17	D	13 15	CAN	0
230	18	W.	4 54	B	6 41	D	13 47	12	11¼	11½	5 57	D	6 50	D	12 55	LEO	1
231	19	Th.	4 55	B	6 40	D	13 45	12	—	12	7 13	D	7 23	C	12 36	LEO	2
232	20	Fr.	4 56	B	6 38	D	13 42	13	12¼	12¾	8 29	D	7 55	C	12 16	VIR	3
233	21	Sa.	4 57	B	6 37	D	13 40	13	1¼	1½	9 44	E	8 30	B	11 56	VIR	4
234	22	**C**	4 58	B	6 35	D	13 37	13	2	2½	10ᴹ54	E	9 09	B	11 36	VIR	5
235	23	M.	4 59	B	6 33	D	13 34	13	3	3½	12ᴾ08	M	9 54	B	11 16	LIB	6
236	24	Tu.	5 01	B	6 32	D	13 31	14	4	4½	1 13	E	10 43	B	10 55	SCO	7
237	25	W.	5 02	B	6 30	D	13 28	14	5	5½	2 11	E	11ᴹ39	B	10 35	OPH	8
238	26	Th.	5 03	B	6 29	D	13 26	14	6¼	6½	3 02	E	— —		10 14	SAG	9
239	27	Fr.	5 04	B	6 27	D	13 23	15	7¼	7½	3 45	E	12ᴬ37	B	9 53	SAG	10
240	28	Sa.	5 05	B	6 25	D	13 20	15	8¼	8½	4 22	E	1 39	B	9 32	SAG	11
241	29	**C**	5 06	B	6 24	D	13 18	15	9¼	9½	4 53	D	2 41	B	9 10	CAP	12
242	30	M.	5 07	B	6 22	D	13 15	15	10	10¼	5 21	D	3 42	C	8 49	AQU	13
243	31	Tu.	5 08	B	6 20	D	13 12	16	10¾	10¾	5ᴹ47	D	4ᴹ43	C	8N.27	AQU	14

AUGUST hath 31 days. 1993

The big doors of the country barn stand open and ready,
  The dried grass of the harvest-time loads the slow-drawn wagon,
The clear light plays on the brown gray and green intertinged,
  The armfuls are pack'd to the sagging mow.

— *Walt Whitman*

D. M.	D. W.	Dates, Feasts, Fasts, Aspects, Tide Heights	Weather ↓
1	C	**9th S. af. P. • Lammas Day** • Tides {9.3 / 10.6} •	*Glory*
2	M.	Full Green Corn ○ • First Lincoln penny issued, 1909 • {9.5 / 10.6}	*days*
3	Tu.	☿ Gr. Elong. (19° West) • ☌♄☾ • Columbus left Spain, headed west, 1492 •	*and*
4	W.	All U.S. telephones silenced for one minute on day of Alexander Graham Bell's funeral, 1922 •	*rain*
5	Th.	☾ on Eq. • *The devil can cite Scripture for his purpose.* Tides {10.3 / 9.7}	*delays.*
6	Fr.	**Transfiguration** • ♇ stat. • ☾ at apo. • Clara Bow born, 1905 •	*Sit*
7	Sa.	**Name of Jesus** • Washington established Purple Heart, 1782 • {9.7 / 9.6}	*on*
8	C	**10th S. af. P. • St. Dominic** • D.A.R. organized, 1890	*the*
9	M.	113° F, Perryville, Tenn., 1930 • Tides {8.9 / 9.4}	*seat o'your*
10	Tu.	**St. Laurence** • A fine day predicts a pleasant autumn. • {8.5 / 9.3}	*pants*
11	W.	**St. Clare** • Dog Days end. • Watts riots began, 1965 • {8.2 / 9.3} •	*and*
12	Th.	☾ at ☋ • 127° F, Death Valley, Cal., 1933 • Katherine Lee Bates born, 1859	*watch*
13	Fr.	☾ runs high • Soviets began building Berlin Wall, 1961 • Tides {8.3 / 9.7}	*the*
14	Sa.	☌♀☾ • *What is bitter to endure may be sweet to remember.* {8.6 / 10.2}	*Perseid*
15	C	**11th S. af. P. • St. Mary** • Princess Anne born, 1950	*meteors*
16	M.	Battle of Bennington, Vermont, 1777 • Gold strike, Yukon, 1896 Tides {9.7 / 11.2}	*dance.*
17	Tu.	New ● • Much fog this month means a severe and snowy winter. • Cat Nights begin.	*Tie*
18	W.	Last day of Woodstock Festival, N.Y., 1969 • Rosalynn Carter born, 1927 {10.9 / 11.8}	*down*
19	Th.	☾ on Eq. • ☾ at peri. • ♄ at ☍ • War began in Europe; U.S. neutral, 1914	*what's*
20	Fr.	☌♂☾ • ☌♃☾ • Paul Tillich born, 1886 • {11.7 / 11.6}	*essential;*
21	Sa.	*Burdens become light when cheerfully borne.* • Tides {11.5 / 11.7}	*hurricane's*
22	C	**12th S. af. P.** • Schooner *America* won yacht race, 1851 {11.0 / 11.5}	*rains*
23	M.	Fair tomorrow means a prosperous autumn. • *Ranger I* lunar probe launched, 1961 •	*are*
24	Tu.	**St. Bartholomew** • ☾ at ☊ • {9.8 / 10.8} •	*torrential!*
25	W.	☾ runs low • 5° F, Bowen, Montana, 1910 • Tides {9.3 / 10.4}	*Load*
26	Th.	Drake's oil rig struck oil, Titusville, Penn., 1859 • Linotype patented, 1884 •	*up the*
27	Fr.	☌♆☾ • ☌♅☾ • L.B.J. born, 1908 • {8.9 / 10.1}	*Winnebago;*
28	Sa.	**St. Augustine of Hippo** • M. L. King: "I have a dream . . ." 1963 •	*where*
29	C	**13th S. af. P.** • John the Baptist beheaded • ☿ at sup. ☌ •	*did*
30	M.	*There is no one luckier than he who thinks himself so.* • Tides {9.4 / 10.2} •	*the*
31	Tu.	☌♄☾ • Full Sturgeon ○ • Ted Williams born, 1918 •	*day go?*

Farmer's Calendar

It is around the middle of this month that the orange monarch butterflies begin to appear in numbers over the gardens, meadows, and roadsides. A monarch drifts across the yard, alights on a flower, leaves it, floats back the way it came, finds another flower, changes its mind and returns to the first, rests, then wanders on. Other butterflies may dart quickly here and there or move ahead in a businesslike way; the monarch has an utterly languid, purposeless style of flight that never seems to take it much of anywhere. It lingers at every flower, turns in early every day, and travels only when the weather is fine. This butterfly has all the time in the world. Its summer flights are like the progress of a lady of leisure killing an afternoon at Bloomingdale's.

The loitering flight of this laziest of butterflies is in contrast to the prodigious journey it is embarked on. So far from being the idling Sunday sailor it appears, the monarch *(Danaus plexippus)* is the insect world's Magellan. Individuals born in Canada and the northern states migrate each year as far as Mexico, and monarchs have been found hundreds of miles out over the ocean. There are birds that travel farther, but no migrator — no bird, no insect, no animal — makes its trip with more nonchalance. It's a wonder the monarch gets as far as the next county, so lackadaisical is its motion, so readily does it break its voyage to stop at a flower. I can imagine the monarch finally arrives at its tropical destination with something like surprise, as though our shopper, having left Bloomingdale's, just decided to pop into Bergdorf's for half an hour, then moved on down Fifth Avenue to Saks, and so on until she found herself in Acapulco.

"Oh, dear," she'd say.

1993 SEPTEMBER, THE NINTH MONTH

Jupiter and Mars have a splendid conjunction after nightfall on the 6th, when much dimmer and ruddier Mars is less than one Moon-width north of Jupiter (brightest evening object). From the 24th to 27th, Mercury joins Jupiter and Spica for a close grouping, but the three are very low in the dusk. Another spectacular conjunction occurs on the morning of the 21st, when Venus passes the star Regulus. The only really visible conjunctions of Uranus and Neptune between 1821 (before Neptune's discovery) and 2165 occur on the 17th and 28th, but you'll need binoculars and finder charts for these planets. The Moon is near perigee (closest) on the 16th, so look for rather high tides. The autumnal equinox is at 7:22 P.M., EST, on the 22nd.

ASTRONOMICAL CALCULATIONS

☾	Last Quarter	9th day	1st hour	27th min.
●	New Moon	15th day	22nd hour	12th min.
☽	First Quarter	22nd day	14th hour	33rd min.
○	Full Moon	30th day	13th hour	54th min.

ADD 1 hour for Daylight Saving Time.

FOR POINTS OUTSIDE BOSTON SEE KEY LETTER CORRECTIONS — PAGES 198-202

Day of Year	Day of Month	Day of Week	☉ Rises h. m.	Key	☉ Sets h. m.	Key	Length of Days h. m.	Sun Fast m.	Full Sea Boston A.M.	Full Sea Boston P.M.	☽ Rises h. m.	Key	☽ Sets h. m.	Key	Declination of Sun ° '	☽ Place	☽ Age
244	1	W.	5 09	B	6 19	D	13 10	16	11¼	11½	6 P.M. 11	D	5 A.M. 42	D	8N.05	PSC	15
245	2	Th.	5 10	B	6 17	D	13 07	16	11¾	—	6 36	C	6 41	D	7 44	PSC	16
246	3	Fr.	5 11	B	6 15	D	13 04	17	12¼	12½	7 01	B	7 40	D	7 22	PSC	17
247	4	Sa.	5 12	B	6 14	D	13 02	17	12¾	1	7 29	B	8 39	E	6 59	PSC	18
248	5	**C**	5 13	B	6 12	D	12 59	17	1½	1¾	7 59	B	9 38	E	6 37	PSC	19
249	6	M.	5 14	B	6 10	D	12 56	18	2	2¼	8 34	B	10 36	E	6 15	ARI	20
250	7	Tu.	5 15	B	6 08	D	12 53	18	2¾	3	9 14	B	11 A.M. 34	E	5 52	ARI	21
251	8	W.	5 16	B	6 07	C	12 51	18	3½	3¾	10 02	B	12 P.M. 30	E	5 30	TAU	22
252	9	Th.	5 17	B	6 05	C	12 48	19	4½	4¾	10 56	B	1 23	E	5 07	TAU	23
253	10	Fr.	5 19	B	6 03	C	12 44	19	5½	5¾	11 P.M. 57	C	2 12	E	4 44	GEM	24
254	11	Sa.	5 20	B	6 01	C	12 41	19	6½	6¾	— —	–	2 56	E	4 21	GEM	25
255	12	**C**	5 21	B	6 00	C	12 39	20	7¼	7½	1 A.M. 04	C	3 36	E	3 58	GEM	26
256	13	M.	5 22	B	5 58	C	12 36	20	8¼	8½	2 15	C	4 12	D	3 35	CAN	27
257	14	Tu.	5 23	B	5 56	C	12 33	20	9	9½	3 30	D	4 45	D	3 12	LEO	28
258	15	W.	5 24	B	5 54	C	12 30	21	10	10¼	4 46	D	5 17	B	2 49	SEX	0
259	16	Th.	5 25	B	5 53	C	12 28	21	10¾	11¼	6 03	D	5 49	A	2 26	LEO	1
260	17	Fr.	5 26	B	5 51	C	12 25	22	11½	—	7 21	E	6 26	B	2 03	VIR	2
261	18	Sa.	5 27	B	5 49	C	12 22	22	12	12¼	8 37	E	7 05	B	1 40	VIR	3
262	19	**C**	5 28	C	5 47	C	12 19	22	1	1¼	9 51	E	7 49	B	1 17	VIR	4
263	20	M.	5 29	C	5 46	C	12 17	23	1¾	2	11 A.M. 01	E	8 39	B	0 53	LIB	5
264	21	Tu.	5 30	C	5 44	C	12 14	23	2¾	3	12 P.M. 03	E	9 33	B	0 30	OPH	6
265	22	W.	5 31	C	5 42	C	12 11	23	3¾	4	12 57	E	10 32	B	0N.06	OPH	7
266	23	Th.	5 32	C	5 40	C	12 08	24	4¾	5	1 43	E	11 P.M. 33	B	0S.16	SAG	8
267	24	Fr.	5 33	C	5 39	C	12 06	24	5¾	6¼	2 22	E	— —	–	0 39	SAG	9
268	25	Sa.	5 34	C	5 37	C	12 03	24	7	7¼	2 55	D	12 A.M. 35	B	1 03	CAP	10
269	26	**C**	5 36	C	5 35	C	11 59	25	8	8¼	3 24	D	1 36	C	1 26	AQU	11
270	27	M.	5 37	C	5 33	B	11 56	25	8¾	9	3 51	D	2 37	C	1 49	AQU	12
271	28	Tu.	5 38	C	5 31	B	11 53	25	9½	9¾	4 16	C	3 36	D	2 13	AQU	13
272	29	W.	5 39	C	5 30	B	11 51	26	10	10½	4 41	C	4 35	D	2 36	PSC	14
273	30	Th.	5 40	C	5 28	B	11 48	26	10¾	11	5 P.M. 06	B	5 A.M. 33	D	2S.59	PSC	15

SEPTEMBER hath 30 days. 1993

Where long the shadows of the wind had rolled,
Green wheat was yielding to the change assigned,
And as by some vast magic undivined
The world was turning slowly into gold.
— *Edwin Arlington Robinson*

D. M.	D. W.	Dates, Feasts, Fasts, Aspects, Tide Heights	*Weather* ↓
1	W.	**St. Giles** • ☾ on Eq. • Tides {9.8 / 10.1 •	*Farewell*
2	Th.	126° F, Mecca, Cal., 1950 • Mark Antony defeated at Actium, 31 B.C. •	*to*
3	Fr.	☾ at apo. • Ferdinand Porsche born, 1875 • Tides {10.0 / 9.9	*summer;*
4	Sa.	*Though honey is sweet, do not lick it off a bear.* • Tides {9.8 / 9.9 •	*it's*
5	**C**	**14th S. af. P.** • 112° F, Centerville, Ala., 1925 • Tides {9.5 / 9.8	*cooler*
6	M.	**Labor Day** • ☌♂♃ • Pres. McKinley assassinated, 1901 • {9.2 / 9.6	*and*
7	Tu.	Cranberry harvest begins, Cape Cod, Mass. • 109° F, Weldon, N.C., 1954 •	*glummer.*
8	W.	**Nativity of Mary** • ☾ at ☋ • St. Augustine, Fla., founded, 1565	*Don't*
9	Th.	☾ rides high • *Knowledge without sense is twofold folly.* • Tides {8.3 / 9.3	*let*
10	Fr.	"Gunsmoke" TV debut, 1955 • Women got voting rights, New Zealand, 1893	*bright*
11	Sa.	Lucky day for reapers. • Jenny Lind's American debut, Castle Garden, N.Y.C., 1850 {8.5 / 9.8	*days*
12	**C**	**15th S. af. P.** • Beatles cut first record, 1962 • {8.9 / 10.2	*deceive*
13	M.	☌♀☾ • Henry Hudson entered N.Y. harbor, claimed area for Holland, 1609	*you —*
14	Tu.	**Holy Cross** • *A vacant mind is open to all suggestions.* Tides {10.3 / 11.2	*here's*
15	W.	☾ on Eq. • New ● • This day is fine six years out of seven. • {11.0 / 11.6 •	*a*
16	Th.	**Rosh Hashanah** • ☾ at perig. • *Mayflower* left England, 1620 {11.6 / 11.7	*wintry*
17	Fr.	**St. Lambert** • ☌☿☾ • ☌♃☾ • {12.1 / —	*preview.*
18	Sa.	☌♂☾ • Jane Addams moved into Hull House, Chicago, 1889 Tides {11.6 / 12.2	*High*
19	**C**	**16th S. af. P.** • 300 German immigrants arrived in Boston, 1752 {11.3 / 12.1	*school*
20	M.	☾ at ☊ • N.Y. Stock Exchange closed to stop panic, 1873 •	*bands*
21	Tu.	**St. Matthew** • Louis Joliet born, 1645 • {10.2 / 11.1	*playing*
22	W.	☾ runs low • Autumnal Equinox • Ember Day • Tunney beat Dempsey, 1927 •	*and*
23	Th.	Time capsule buried at New York World's Fair, 1938 • {9.2 / 10.1 •	*old*
24	Fr.	☌♆☾ • ☌♅☾ • ☌☿♃ • Ember Day •	*single*
25	Sa.	**Yom Kippur** • Ember Day • Glenn Gould born, 1932 Tides {8.9 / 9.7	*wings:*
26	**C**	**17th S. af. P.** • *The riches in the heart cannot be stolen.* •	*these*
27	M.	☌♄☾ • ♅ stat. • "Tonight Show" debut, 1954 Tides {9.3 / 9.8	*are a few*
28	Tu.	**St. Wenceslas** • ☾ on Eq. • Ed Sullivan born, 1902 •	*of my*
29	W.	**St. Michael** • ♆ stat. • Harvest Home • {9.8 / 9.9	*favorite*
30	Th.	**St. Jerome** • **Succoth** • Full Harvest ○ • ☾ at apo. •	*things.*
		Take out a six-month loan in the fall, and the winter will fly by like nothing.	

Farmer's Calendar

All through the New England hinterlands you find places called Beartown. It is evidently a name given by the old inhabitants to remote, wild districts that resisted settlement. Beartown was the deepest boonies, the other side of the mountain, where the land was so steep and so broken that even the ruggedest farm couldn't hope to hang on. A place, in short, for bears and not for people.

I know of six Beartowns in my state. In many of them conditions have changed some in the years since they were named. Those vertiginous mountainsides that couldn't be made to grow corn or even hay now yield abundantly the crop Recreation. The bears get around on skis and den up for the winter slopeside, in condominiums that cost more than most bears make in a couple of years. Bears who can no longer hack Beartown prices are obliged to move on. Where do they go?

My own community is no Beartown; it's pretty tame. But in the past couple of years, bears have begun turning up over here. My neighbor on her early walk sees them: big bears and little ones, going here, going there. Now, I don't know whether these bears are taking our neighborhood up or down, but that they are changing it I have no doubt. I was raised in a big city, and I understand these things. Pretty soon Beartown will be right here. For my part, I don't mind the prospect at all, but not everybody will feel the same way. And I'm not sure the schools can take it. Bears have little bears. In ten years you'll have a bear on the board of selectmen, bears will own the gas station, and the town will have gone to — well, anyway, not to the dogs.

1993 OCTOBER, THE TENTH MONTH

The Summer Triangle of Vega, Altair, and Deneb lingers in the west after increasingly early nightfalls. Deneb and the rest of Cygnus the Swan form the "Northern Cross," which stands upright as it reaches the horizon in mid-evening. High in the north, Cassiopeia the Queen hangs upside down. To her right in the northeast leaps Perseus, hero whose star of variable brightness, Algol, marks the head of monster Medusa. Turn to the south to find the Great Square of Pegasus. All bright planets but Saturn are poorly placed for viewing this month. The new Moon and perigee are close together on the 14th-15th. Predawn skies are moonfree for the Orionid meteor shower on the 20th. Clocks should be set back one hour on the 31st.

ASTRONOMICAL CALCULATIONS

☾ Last Quarter	8th day	14th hour	37th min.
● New Moon	15th day	6th hour	37th min.
☽ First Quarter	22nd day	3rd hour	53rd min.
○ Full Moon	30th day	7th hour	38th min.

ADD 1 hour for Daylight Saving Time until 2 A.M., October 31st.

FOR POINTS OUTSIDE BOSTON SEE KEY LETTER CORRECTIONS — PAGES 198-202

Day of Year	Day of Month	Day of Week	☉ Rises h. m.	Key	☉ Sets h. m.	Key	Length of Days h. m.	Sun Fast m.	Full Sea Boston A.M.	Full Sea Boston P.M.	☽ Rises h. m.	Key	☽ Sets h. m.	Key	Declination of Sun ° '	☽ Place	☽ Age
274	1	Fr.	5 41	C	5 26	B	11 45	26	11¼	11¾	5 P.M. 33	B	6 A.M. 32	E	3s.22	PSC	16
275	2	Sa.	5 42	C	5 25	B	11 43	27	11¾	—	6 02	B	7 30	E	3 46	PSC	17
276	3	C	5 43	C	5 23	B	11 40	27	12¼	12½	6 36	B	8 29	E	4 09	ARI	18
277	4	M.	5 44	C	5 21	B	11 37	27	1	1	7 14	B	9 27	E	4 32	ARI	19
278	5	Tu.	5 45	C	5 19	B	11 34	28	1½	1¾	7 58	B	10 23	E	4 55	TAU	20
279	6	W.	5 47	C	5 18	B	11 31	28	2¼	2½	8 49	B	11 A.M. 17	E	5 18	TAU	21
280	7	Th.	5 48	C	5 16	B	11 28	28	3¼	3¼	9 46	B	12 P.M. 06	E	5 41	TAU	22
281	8	Fr.	5 49	C	5 14	B	11 25	28	4	4¼	10 49	B	12 50	E	6 04	GEM	23
282	9	Sa.	5 50	C	5 13	B	11 23	29	5	5¼	11 P.M. 56	B	1 30	E	6 27	GEM	24
283	10	C	5 51	C	5 11	B	11 20	29	6	6¼	— —	–	2 07	D	6 50	CAN	25
284	11	M.	5 52	C	5 09	B	11 17	29	6¾	7¼	1 A.M. 06	C	2 40	D	7 12	LEO	26
285	12	Tu.	5 53	C	5 08	B	11 15	30	7¾	8¼	2 19	D	3 12	D	7 38	SEX	27
286	13	W.	5 54	D	5 06	B	11 12	30	8½	9	3 34	D	3 45	C	7 58	LEO	28
287	14	Th.	5 56	D	5 04	B	11 08	30	9½	10	4 51	D	4 19	C	8 19	VIR	29
288	15	Fr.	5 57	D	5 03	B	11 06	30	10¼	10¾	6 08	E	4 57	B	8 42	VIR	0
289	16	Sa.	5 58	D	5 01	B	11 03	30	11	11¾	7 25	E	5 39	B	9 04	VIR	1
290	17	C	5 59	D	5 00	B	11 01	31	—	12	8 39	E	6 27	B	9 26	LIB	2
291	18	M.	6 00	D	4 58	B	10 58	31	12½	12¾	9 48	E	7 22	B	9 47	SCO	3
292	19	Tu.	6 01	D	4 56	B	10 55	31	1½	1¾	10 47	E	8 21	B	10 09	OPH	4
293	20	W.	6 03	D	4 55	B	10 52	31	2½	2¾	11 A.M. 38	E	9 23	B	10 30	SAG	5
294	21	Th.	6 04	D	4 53	B	10 49	31	3¼	3½	12 P.M. 21	E	10 26	B	10 52	SAG	6
295	22	Fr.	6 05	D	4 52	B	10 47	32	4½	4¾	12 56	E	11 P.M. 29	C	11 13	SAG	7
296	23	Sa.	6 06	D	4 50	B	10 44	32	5½	5¾	1 27	D	— —	–	11 34	CAP	8
297	24	C	6 07	D	4 49	B	10 42	32	6½	6¾	1 55	D	12 A.M. 30	C	11 55	CAP	9
298	25	M.	6 09	D	4 48	B	10 39	32	7¼	7¾	2 19	D	1 30	C	12 16	AQU	10
299	26	Tu.	6 10	D	4 46	B	10 36	32	8¼	8½	2 44	C	2 28	D	12 36	AQU	11
300	27	W.	6 11	D	4 45	B	10 34	32	9	9¼	3 09	C	3 26	D	12 57	PSC	12
301	28	Th.	6 12	D	4 43	B	10 31	32	9½	10	3 36	B	4 24	D	13 17	PSC	13
302	29	Fr.	6 14	D	4 42	B	10 28	32	10¼	10½	4 05	B	5 23	E	13 37	PSC	14
303	30	Sa.	6 15	D	4 41	B	10 26	32	10¾	11¼	4 38	B	6 22	E	13 56	ARI	15
304	31	C	6 16	D	4 39	B	10 23	32	11¼	—	5 P.M. 14	B	7 A.M. 21	E	14s.16	ARI	16

OCTOBER hath 31 days. 1993

The mug of cider simmered slow,
The apples sputtered in a row,
And, close at hand, the basket stood
With nuts from brown October's wood.
— John Greenleaf Whittier

D. M.	D. W.	Dates, Feasts, Fasts, Aspects, Tide Heights	*Weather* ↓
1	Fr.	St. Remigius • Post office began Rural Free Delivery, 1896 • Tides {10.1 9.7}	*At*
2	Sa.	*Many who are ahead of their time must wait for it in uncomfortable quarters.* •	*times*
3	C	18th S. af. P. • Chubby Checker born, 1941 {9.6 10.1}	*these*
4	M.	St. Francis of Assisi • Watch for line storms — "lash of St. Francis" •	*climes*
5	Tu.	☾ at ☋ • 116° F, Sentinel, Arizona, 1917 • Tides {9.1 9.8} •	*seem*
6	W.	St. Faith • ☾ rides high • ☌☿♂ • Tides {8.8 9.7}	*almost*
7	Th.	*The best way to know God is to love many things.* • Yo-Yo Ma born, 1955	*Caribbean.*
8	Fr.	Chicago fire began, 1871 • Acadians expelled from Nova Scotia, 1755 {8.5 9.5}	*Then*
9	Sa.	St. Denis • *A mile walked with a friend has only 100 steps.* • {8.6 9.6} •	*all*
10	C	19th S. af. P. • This month always has 19 fine days. • Tides {8.9 9.8}	*of*
11	M.	Columbus Day • Thanksgiving Day (Canada) • Tides {9.5 10.2} •	*a*
12	Tu.	Columbus reached Bahamas, 1492 • Luciano Pavarotti born, 1935 {10.2 10.7}	*sodden,*
13	W.	☾ on Eq. • ☌♀☾ • ☿ Gr. Elong. (25° E.) • Art Garfunkel born, 1942	*you've*
14	Th.	☾ at perig. • *Winnie-the-Pooh* published, 1926 • Tides {11.6 11.3}	*gotten*
15	Fr.	New ● • "I Love Lucy" television debut, 1951 {12.1 11.4}	*amphibian!*
16	Sa.	Dry today means a dry spring. • ☌♂☾ • Yale College founded, 1701 {12.4 11.3}	*Of*
17	C	20th S. af. P. • St. Ethelreda • ☌☿☾	*autumn's*
18	M.	St. Luke • ☾ at ☊ • ☌♃☉ • {11.0 12.1} •	*wine,*
19	Tu.	☾ runs low • Gen. Cornwallis surrendered Yorktown, Va., 1781 • {10.5 11.6}	• *now*
20	W.	*Grief will take care of itself; joy must be shared.* • Art Buchwald born, 1925 •	*drink*
21	Th.	☌♆☾ • ☌♅☾ • Lord Nelson won at Battle of Trafalgar, 1805 {9.5 10.4}	*your*
22	Fr.	Opening night at Metropolitan Opera House, N.Y.C., 1883 • N. C. Wyeth born, 1882	*fill;*
23	Sa.	*A proverb is a short sentence based on long experience.* • Tides {9.0 9.5} •	*the*
24	C	21st S. af. P. • ☌♄☾ • Chartres Cathedral consecrated, 1260	*frost's*
25	M.	St. Crispin • ☿ stat. • Minnie Pearl born, 1912 • Tides {9.2 9.3}	*on*
26	Tu.	☾ on Eq. • Erie Canal opened, linking Midwest to Atlantic Coast, 1825 •	*the*
27	W.	☾ at apo. • *Variety* noted popularity of jazz in Chicago, 1916 • {9.7 9.4}	*pumpkin,*
28	Th.	Sts. Simon and Jude • ☌☿♂ • ♄ stat. • {9.9 9.4}	*and*
29	Fr.	–33° F, Soda Butte, Wyoming, 1917 • Charleston dance introduced on Broadway, 1923	*snow's*
30	Sa.	Full Hunter's ○ • *Time and truth are friends.* • Tides {10.2 9.4}	*on the*
31	C	22nd S. af. P. • All Hallows Eve • D.S.T. ends. •	*hill.*

Farmer's Calendar

Pliny the Elder, the Roman scholar whose *Natural History*, in 37 volumes, forms an encyclopedia of the ancient world's knowledge of the natural sciences, education, art, and society, had some quaint ideas about medicine. He believed, for example, that kissing the nostrils of a mule cured hay fever. He believed that an owlet's brains, eaten, were good for a sore throat. Pliny didn't invent these cures; he was a reporter only. Therefore, presumably, thousands of afflicted Romans must have been seen every day making unwelcome advances to mules and chasing after owlets who ran for their lives. And so the question arises, if Pliny didn't think this stuff up, who did? How did anybody first get the idea, for a third instance, that epilepsy could be treated by feeding the sufferer the afterbirth of a donkey?

Some of Pliny's cures make even other folk remedies look perfectly plausible by comparison. In fact, much of the antique medical lore has a kind of magical logic, rigorous enough in its own way. If you believe the common wildflower Solomon's seal to have some mystic connection with the ancient king of Israel, then it makes a kind of sense to suppose that by grinding up the plant and eating it you will gain fame, wisdom, and the Queen of Sheba for a girlfriend. Beside Pliny's regimens, that sounds no more extreme than "Take two aspirin and call me in the morning." Where, in contrast, is the logic behind Pliny's idea that a colicky baby can usefully be served roast lark? We'll never know. One thing is clear, though. Pliny was killed in the eruption of Mount Vesuvius in A.D. 79, when he apparently got a little too close to the action — proving to the most skeptical that a nearby volcano is a sovereign cure for natural history.

1993 NOVEMBER, THE ELEVENTH MONTH

This is a month of close meetings near or at the Sun. A partial solar eclipse on November 13th is seen only in the far southern latitudes. The start of a rare transit of Mercury — the planet passing in front of the Sun — on the 5th is seen from Hawaii and the Aleutians but nowhere else in the nation. All the country gets a look at two conjunctions low in the east before dawn: the bright-planet pair Venus and Jupiter on the 8th; the inner-planet pair Venus and Mercury on the 14th. Mercury puts in a fine morning appearance before and after its greatest elongation on the 22nd. The Leonid meteors are unbothered by moonlight in the hours just before dawn on the 18th. The Moon's total eclipse on the 28th-29th will be visible everywhere.

ASTRONOMICAL CALCULATIONS

☾	Last Quarter	7th day	1st hour	37th min.
●	New Moon	13th day	16th hour	35th min.
☽	First Quarter	20th day	21st hour	4th min.
○	Full Moon	29th day	1st hour	32nd min.

FOR POINTS OUTSIDE BOSTON SEE KEY LETTER CORRECTIONS — PAGES 198-202

Day of Year	Day of Month	Day of Week	☉ Rises h. m.	Key	☉ Sets h. m.	Key	Length of Days h. m.	Sun Fast m.	Full Sea Boston A.M.	Full Sea Boston P.M.	☽ Rises h. m.	Key	☽ Sets h. m.	Key	Declination of Sun ° '	☽ Place	☽ Age
305	1	M.	6 17	D	4 38	B	10 21	32	12	12	5 P.M. 57	B	8 A.M. 18	E	14 s.35	TAU	17
306	2	Tu.	6 19	D	4 37	B	10 18	32	12½	12½	6 46	B	9 13	E	14 54	TAU	18
307	3	W.	6 20	D	4 35	B	10 15	32	1¼	1¼	7 41	B	10 03	E	15 12	TAU	19
308	4	Th.	6 21	D	4 34	B	10 13	32	2	2	8 41	B	10 49	E	15 31	GEM	20
309	5	Fr.	6 22	D	4 33	B	10 11	32	2¾	2¾	9 45	C	11 A.M. 29	E	15 49	GEM	21
310	6	Sa.	6 24	D	4 32	B	10 08	32	3½	3¾	10 P.M. 52	C	12 P.M. 06	D	16 07	CAN	22
311	7	**C**	6 25	D	4 31	A	10 06	32	4½	4¾	— —	–	12 39	D	16 25	CAN	23
312	8	M.	6 26	D	4 30	A	10 04	32	5½	5¾	12 A.M. 02	C	1 10	D	16 43	LEO	24
313	9	Tu.	6 27	D	4 28	A	10 01	32	6¼	6¾	1 13	D	1 41	C	17 00	SEX	25
314	10	W.	6 29	D	4 27	A	9 58	32	7¼	7¾	2 25	D	2 13	C	17 17	VIR	26
315	11	Th.	6 30	D	4 26	A	9 56	32	8¼	8¾	3 41	E	2 48	B	17 33	VIR	27
316	12	Fr.	6 31	D	4 25	A	9 54	32	9	9¾	4 56	E	3 27	B	17 49	VIR	28
317	13	Sa.	6 32	D	4 24	A	9 52	32	10	10½	6 12	E	4 13	B	18 05	LIB	0
318	14	**C**	6 34	D	4 23	A	9 49	32	10¾	11½	7 24	E	5 05	B	18 21	LIB	1
319	15	M.	6 35	D	4 23	A	9 48	31	11½	—	8 29	E	6 03	B	18 36	OPH	2
320	16	Tu.	6 36	D	4 22	A	9 46	31	12¼	12½	9 26	E	7 06	B	18 51	SAG	3
321	17	W.	6 37	D	4 21	A	9 44	31	1¼	1¼	10 14	E	8 11	B	19 05	SAG	4
322	18	Th.	6 38	D	4 20	A	9 42	31	2	2¼	10 53	E	9 15	C	19 20	SAG	5
323	19	Fr.	6 40	D	4 19	A	9 39	31	3	3¼	11 27	D	10 19	C	19 34	CAP	6
324	20	Sa.	6 41	D	4 19	A	9 38	30	3¾	4	11 A.M. 56	D	11 P.M. 20	C	19 48	AQU	7
325	21	**C**	6 42	D	4 18	A	9 36	30	4¾	5	12 P.M. 23	D	— —	–	20 01	AQU	8
326	22	M.	6 43	D	4 17	A	9 34	30	5¾	6	12 47	D	12 A.M. 19	D	20 14	PSC	9
327	23	Tu.	6 45	D	4 17	A	9 32	30	6¾	7	1 12	C	1 18	D	20 26	PSC	10
328	24	W.	6 46	D	4 16	A	9 30	29	7½	8	1 38	B	2 16	D	20 38	PSC	11
329	25	Th.	6 47	D	4 15	A	9 28	29	8¼	8¾	2 07	B	3 15	E	20 50	PSC	12
330	26	Fr.	6 48	E	4 15	A	9 27	29	9	9½	2 38	B	4 14	E	21 01	ARI	13
331	27	Sa.	6 49	E	4 14	A	9 25	28	9½	10¼	3 13	B	5 13	E	21 12	ARI	14
332	28	**C**	6 50	E	4 14	A	9 24	28	10¼	10¾	3 54	B	6 11	E	21 23	TAU	15
333	29	M.	6 51	E	4 14	A	9 23	28	11	11½	4 41	B	7 07	E	21 33	TAU	16
334	30	Tu.	6 52	E	4 13	A	9 21	27	11½	—	5 P.M. 35	B	7 A.M. 59	E	21 s.43	TAU	17

NOVEMBER hath 30 days. 1993

And the dead leaves lie huddled and still,
No longer blown hither and thither;
The last lone aster is gone;
The flowers of the witch-hazel wither. . .
— *Robert Frost*

D. M.	D. W.	Dates, Feasts, Fasts, Aspects, Tide Heights	*Weather* ↓
1	M.	**All Saints** • ☾ at ☋ • Earthquake, Lisbon, Portugal, 1755 •	*After*
2	Tu.	**All Souls** • 7" snow, New York City, 1810 • Tides {9.2 10.2 •	*a*
3	W.	☾ rides high • Great flood, Vermont, 1927 • Stephen Austin born, 1793 •	*mist,*
4	Th.	*Virtues, like essences, lose their fragrance when exposed.* • Tides {8.9 10.0	*it's*
5	Fr.	☿ at inf. ☌ • Transit of ☿ • Roy Rogers born, 1912 •	*clear and*
6	Sa.	**St. Leonard** • Edsel Ford born, 1893 • Tides {8.9 9.8	*warm.*
7	C	**23rd S. af. P.** • Bolshevik Revolution began, 1917	*Inconsist-*
8	M.	☌♀♃ • *The secret of being a bore is to tell everything.* • Tides {9.5 9.8	*ent;*
9	Tu.	☾ on Eq. • Auspicious day for travel. • Great Lakes gale, 1913 {10.0 10.0	*now a*
10	W.	Marine Corps created by Continental Congress, 1775 • Tides {10.7 10.3 •	*storm.*
11	Th.	**St. Martin** • **Veterans Day** • Indian summer begins. •	*Hunters*
12	Fr.	☾ at perig. • ☌♃☾ • ☌♀☾ Tides {11.8 10.8 •	*hale*
13	Sa.	New ● • Eclipse of ☉ • Sadie Hawkins Day • {12.2 10.8 •	*and*
14	C	**24th S. af. P.** • ☾ at ☊ • ☌☿♀ • ☿ stat. • {12.4 10.8 •	
15	M.	45" snow, Watertown, N.Y., 1900 • Tides {12.3 —	*heavy-booted*
16	Tu.	☾ runs low • –53° F, Lincoln 14NE, Montana, 1959 • Tides {10.6 11.9	*crush*
17	W.	**St. Hugh of Lincoln** • ☌♇☉ • ☌♆☾ • ☌♅☾ •	*the*
18	Th.	**St. Hilda** • Julia Ward Howe wrote lyrics to "Battle Hymn of the Republic," 1861	*leaves,*
19	Fr.	*Life must be lived forward, but can only be understood backward.* • Tides {9.5 10.2	*their*
20	Sa.	Indian summer ends. • ☌♄☾ • Prune grapevines now. • {9.2 9.6	*colors*
21	C	**25th S. af. P.** • Mayflower Compact signed, 1620 • {9.1 9.1	*muted.*
22	M.	**St. Cecilia** • ☾ on Eq. • ☿ Gr. Elong. (20° W.) • {9.1 8.9 •	*You'll*
23	Tu.	**St. Clement** • *Solitude is impracticable, and society fatal.* •	*have to*
24	W.	☾ at apo. • Joseph Glidden patented barbed wire, 1874 • Tides {9.4 8.7	*ask*
25	Th.	**Thanksgiving Day** • East Coast blizzard, 57" snow, W. Va., 1950 •	*the*
26	Fr.	*If ice in November will bear a duck, There'll be nothing thereafter but sleet and muck.* •	*Navy*
27	Sa.	Peace march on Washington, D.C., 1965 • James Agee born, 1909 • Tides {10.0 9.0	*to*
28	C	**1st S. in Advent** • ☾ at ☋ • Tides {10.2 9.1 •	*pass*
29	M.	Full Beaver ○ • Eclipse of ☾ • Louisa May Alcott born, 1832 {10.4 9.1	*the*
30	Tu.	**St. Andrew** • ☾ rides high • Thunder this month means a fertile year. •	*gravy!*

Arguments are to be avoided: they are always vulgar and often convincing. — Oscar Wilde

Farmer's Calendar

The multitudes of summer hate to see it end. They keep on coming back. Like an aging tenor or a superannuated generalissimo, a hundred creatures that thrived abundantly in June, then retired with the deep frosts, return on a warm, bright day and take up their careers all over again. But now, although the creatures themselves are real, everything else is different. This is no mere Indian summer, no simple matter of a mild day in autumn: A summer day in November is more like a mysterious moment in a play or movie — it's a flashback, a memory happening now, a dream.

The summer birds have been gone for eight weeks, the garden closed down for six. The trees are bare. A week or two of winter cold has turned the meadows brown and the earth gray. Often there is a thin cover of snow in the morning. The sun is pale and far off. Then two days of flashback supervene, and forgotten life emerges. Little brown snakes curl on the flagstones by the defunct flower garden. Chipmunks are seen poking about. The paper wasps wake up in their cold cracks and buzz around the eaves. Hibernating butterflies, including my favorites, the big tortoiseshells, bask in the sun on the porch floorboards and fly slowly over the clipped dead flower stalks. Little brown and gray moths suddenly appear in the woods and come to lights at night, just as they did in July. For a couple of days you're in a kind of dream of summer, but as in a real dream, everything that is so convincingly the same is also profoundly changed. It's as though dreams are lit differently from waking life, and so it is here; summer is back, but it's summer without the colors, summer without green.

The Geminid meteor shower peaks around new Moon this year. In clear country skies, observers should see up to 60 per hour late in the evening of the 13th and early after midnight on the 14th. Earlier, Gemini and its two brightest stars, Castor and Pollux, are still low in the northeast. The eastern sky above and to the right of them is decorated with the dipper-shaped Pleiades star cluster and arrowhead-shaped Hyades star cluster in Taurus, and the pentagon-shaped constellation Auriga with its bright star Capella. Rising due east is glorious Orion, with blue Rigel, red Betelgeuse, three-star belt, and nebula-spotted sword. An hour after Orion rises, the brightest star, Sirius, comes up to dominate the sky. Winter begins at 3:26 P.M., EST, on the 21st.

ASTRONOMICAL CALCULATIONS

☾ Last Quarter	6th day	10th hour	50th min.
● New Moon	13th day	4th hour	28th min.
☽ First Quarter	20th day	17th hour	26th min.
○ Full Moon	28th day	18th hour	7th min.

FOR POINTS OUTSIDE BOSTON SEE KEY LETTER CORRECTIONS — PAGES 198-202

Day of Year	Day of Month	Day of Week	☉ Rises h. m.	Key	☉ Sets h. m.	Key	Length of Days h. m.	Sun Fast m.	Full Sea Boston A.M.	Full Sea Boston P.M.	☽ Rises h. m.	Key	☽ Sets h. m.	Key	Declination of Sun ° '	Place	☽ Age
335	1	W.	6 54	E	4 13	A	9 19	27	12¼	12¼	6 ᴘᴍ 35	B	8 ᴀᴍ 47	E	21s.52	ORI	18
336	2	Th.	6 55	E	4 13	A	9 18	27	1	1	7 38	B	9 30	E	22 01	GEM	19
337	3	Fr.	6 56	E	4 13	A	9 16	26	1½	1¾	8 44	C	10 07	E	22 09	CAN	20
338	4	Sa.	6 57	E	4 12	A	9 15	26	2¼	2½	9 52	C	10 41	D	22 17	CAN	21
339	5	**☾**	6 58	E	4 12	A	9 14	25	3¼	3½	11 ᴘᴍ 01	D	11 13	D	22 25	LEO	22
340	6	M.	6 59	E	4 12	A	9 13	25	4	4¼	— —	–	11 ᴀᴍ 43	D	22 32	SEX	23
341	7	Tu.	7 00	E	4 12	A	9 12	24	5	5¼	12 ᴀᴍ 11	D	12 ᴘᴍ 13	C	22 39	LEO	24
342	8	W.	7 01	E	4 12	A	9 11	24	6	6½	1 23	D	12 46	B	22 46	VIR	25
343	9	Th.	7 01	E	4 12	A	9 11	24	6¾	7½	2 35	E	1 21	B	22 51	VIR	26
344	10	Fr.	7 02	E	4 12	A	9 10	23	7¾	8½	3 49	E	2 02	B	22 57	VIR	27
345	11	Sa.	7 03	E	4 12	A	9 09	23	8¾	9½	5 01	E	2 50	B	23 02	LIB	28
346	12	**☾**	7 04	E	4 12	A	9 08	22	9½	10¼	6 09	E	3 44	B	23 06	SCO	29
347	13	M.	7 05	E	4 12	A	9 07	22	10½	11¼	7 09	E	4 45	B	23 12	OPH	0
348	14	Tu.	7 06	E	4 12	A	9 06	21	11¼	—	8 03	E	5 50	B	23 14	SAG	1
349	15	W.	7 06	E	4 12	A	9 06	21	12	12¼	8 47	E	6 56	B	23 17	SAG	2
350	16	Th.	7 07	E	4 13	A	9 06	20	12¾	1	9 24	E	8 01	C	23 20	SAG	3
351	17	Fr.	7 08	E	4 13	A	9 05	20	1¾	1¾	9 56	D	9 05	C	23 22	AQU	4
352	18	Sa.	7 08	E	4 13	A	9 05	19	2½	2½	10 24	D	10 06	D	23 23	AQU	5
353	19	**☾**	7 09	E	4 14	A	9 05	19	3¼	3½	10 50	C	11 ᴀᴍ 06	D	23 25	AQU	6
354	20	M.	7 09	E	4 14	A	9 05	18	4	4¼	11 15	C	— —	–	23 26	PSC	7
355	21	Tu.	7 10	E	4 15	A	9 05	18	5	5¼	11 ᴀᴍ 40	C	12 ᴀᴍ 05	D	23 26	PSC	8
356	22	W.	7 10	E	4 15	A	9 05	17	5¾	6¼	12 ᴘᴍ 08	B	1 03	D	23 26	PSC	9
357	23	Th.	7 11	E	4 16	A	9 05	17	6¾	7¼	12 37	B	2 02	E	23 25	PSC	10
358	24	Fr.	7 11	E	4 16	A	9 05	16	7½	8	1 11	B	3 01	E	23 24	ARI	11
359	25	Sa.	7 12	E	4 17	A	9 05	16	8¼	9	1 49	B	4 00	E	23 22	ARI	12
360	26	**☾**	7 12	E	4 18	A	9 06	15	9	9¾	2 34	B	4 57	E	23 20	TAU	13
361	27	M.	7 12	E	4 18	A	9 06	15	9¾	10½	3 25	B	5 52	E	23 17	TAU	14
362	28	Tu.	7 13	E	4 19	A	9 06	14	10½	11	4 24	B	6 42	E	23 14	ORI	15
363	29	W.	7 13	E	4 20	A	9 07	14	11¼	11¾	5 27	B	7 27	E	23 11	GEM	16
364	30	Th.	7 13	E	4 20	A	9 07	13	11¾	—	6 34	B	8 08	E	23 08	GEM	17
365	31	Fr.	7 13	E	4 21	A	9 08	13	12½	12½	7 ᴘᴍ 43	C	8 ᴀᴍ 44	D	23s.03	CAN	18

DECEMBER hath 31 days. 1993

O World, thou choosest not the better part!
It is not wisdom to be only wise,
And on the inward vision close the eyes,
But it is wisdom to believe the heart.
— *George Santayana*

D. M.	D. W.	Dates, Feasts, Fasts, Aspects, Tide Heights	Weather ↓
1	W.	Marines rescued 1,200 U.S. soldiers, Chosin, Korea, 1950 • Tides {9.2 10.5 •	*It's*
2	Th.	*The finger of God never leaves identical fingerprints.* • John Brown hanged, 1859 •	*sleety,*
3	Fr.	Beware the Pogonip. • Illinois joined Union, 1818 • Tides {9.3 10.4 •	*sweetie.*
4	Sa.	The Grange (Patrons of Husbandry) founded, 1867 • Tides {9.4 10.2 •	*On*
5	**C**	**2nd S. in Adv.** • Walt Disney born, 1901 • {9.5 10.0	*northern*
6	M.	**St. Nicholas** • ☾ on Eq. • Ira Gershwin born, 1896 •	*peaks*
7	Tu.	*Soup and fish explain half the emotions of life.* • Tides {10.0 9.7	*the*
8	W.	**Conception of Virgin Mary** • 100° F, LaMesa, Calif., 1938	*snow*
9	Th.	**Chanukah** • Tanganyika independence, 1961 • {10.8 9.8 •	*is*
10	Fr.	☌♃☾ • ☾ at perig. • 70° F, New York City, 1946 {11.2 9.9	*heaping;*
11	Sa.	☾ at ☊ • First U.S. helicopters and crew arrived in Saigon, Vietnam, 1961 •	*pile*
12	**C**	**3rd S. in Adv.** • Blizzard, New England, 1960 • Tides {11.8 10.2	*on*
13	M.	**St. Lucy** • ☾ runs low • New ● • Tides {11.9 10.2	*blankets*
14	Tu.	*Great riches have sold more men than they have bought.* • Washington died, 1799 •	*for*
15	W.	☌♆☾ • ☌♅☾ • Ember Day • J. Paul Getty born, 1892 • {10.1 11.5	*good*
16	Th.	Great earthquake rocked Miss. River valley near New Madrid, Mo., 1811 •	*sleeping.*
17	Fr.	Ember Day • *Reason is God's gift, but so are the passions.* • Tides {9.8 10.6 •	*Shop*
18	Sa.	☌♄☾ • Ember Day • Battle of Verdun ended with 750,000 casualties, 1916 •	*and*
19	**C**	**4th S. in Advent** • ☾ on Eq. • Tides {9.3 9.4	*shiver —*
20	M.	Halcyon days. • Missouri imposed $1 per year tax on bachelors, 1820 •	*blessed's*
21	Tu.	**St. Thomas** • Winter Solstice • Benj. Disraeli born, 1804 • Tides {9.1 8.5	*the*
22	W.	☾ at apo. • Continental Congress established navy, 1775 • *Snow White* opened, 1937 •	*giver.*
23	Th.	Baseball arbitrator established "free agent" status, 1973 • {9.2 8.2	*Gather nigh*
24	Fr.	Green Christmas, White Easter. • Fire burned ⅔ of Library of Congress collection, 1851 •	*the*
25	Sa.	**Christmas Day** • Wind today brings a fruitful year. {9.6 8.4	*festive*
26	**C**	**1st S. af. Ch.** • **St. Stephen** • ☾ at ☋ • ☌♂☉	*tree,*
27	M.	**St. John** • ☾ rides high • Radio City Music Hall opened, N.Y.C., 1932 •	*and*
28	Tu.	**Holy Innocents** • Full Cold ○ • Tides {10.4 9.1 •	*wave*
29	W.	Battle of Wounded Knee, S.D., 1890 • Pablo Casals born, 1876 • {10.6 9.4	*good-bye*
30	Th.	*Be at war with your vices, at peace with your neighbors, and let every new year find you a better man.* (B. Franklin)	*to*
31	Fr.	**St. Sylvester** • *Begin the new year square with every man.* (R. B. Thomas) {9.6 10.8	*'93!*

Farmer's Calendar

Now, as the season of storms approaches, a bewildering multiplicity of snow shovels has gone on display in practically every store in town. With winter coming, you can buy a snow shovel in a grocery store, a drugstore, a sporting-goods store. Snow shovels are hawked with special fervor at those curious hybrid establishments known as "home centers." (In more plain-spoken times they were called "hardware stores" and "lumberyards.") And what snow shovels they are! There are snow shovels that look like shovels, there are others that look like really large dental tools, there are even snow shovels that look like Eskimo perambulators. There are snow shovels with straight handles, snow shovels with bent handles; with fat blades, with thin blades; with D grips, with T grips. Some snow shovels are plastic and cost a couple of bucks; others are so expensive that it seems wrong to expose them to a substance, like snow, that comes for free. What to do?

It took me a number of winters to discover that very often the best snow shovel is not a shovel at all. Get yourself a simple broom, one with long, stiff straw. A broom will take care of better than half the snow you'll get in a winter, and it won't break your back, burst your heart, or dig up your grass by mistake. For cleaning snow off the car, the broom is far superior to the shovel because it can't scratch your paint job. And if you are equipped with a broom and you should, at last, get a fall of snow too deep for your broom to overcome, you can simply hop on it and fly south until you get to a latitude where snow is unknown and the home centers sell only those shovels that come with pails for use at the beach.

The Seven Sisters

To the naked eye, they're the loveliest of all star clusters. And now that there's a danger we may lose sight of them, they've become even more precious.

by Fred Schaaf

They are among the few starry sights mentioned in the Bible. Their rising at dusk determined when the Druids would hold the holiday that has become our Halloween. Today you can see a stylized version of them on a popular make of car (Subaru, Japanese for Pleiades), more than 4,000 years after they were first mentioned in Chinese annals.

They are the Pleiades, or the Seven Sisters, the loveliest of all star clusters to the naked eye. If you're lucky enough to be stargazing far from city lights, you can see them in their full splendor in the east on autumn evenings or south on winter evenings. They look like nothing else the naked eye can see: a pocketful of stellar gems, a minute but perfect formation of stars sparkling not quite together and therefore all the more beautifully. Although only the seven brightest stars in the cluster can be distinguished unaided, binoculars will reveal many more, and the world's largest telescopes have confirmed more than 500 stars in the cluster.

Much farther back in time than humanity's earliest legends about the Pleiades was their birth as stars in space. This may have occurred about 50 million years ago — a stupendously long time by human standards, though little more than one percent of the way back to Earth's beginning. The hot blue stars burst into view from their nebula after the last dinosaur died — and maybe about the time that the first flowers opened.

The Pleiades are young enough for careful telescope users and experienced astrophotographers to detect glowing traces of the original gases and dust of the nebula. Some people have even claimed to see these wisps with the naked eye, bringing to mind Tennyson's famous lines from "Locksley Hall":

Many a night I saw the Pleiads,
*   rising thro' the mellow shade,*
Glitter like a swarm of fire-flies
*   tangled in a silver braid.*

Great legends and literature as old as three thousand years mention the Pleiades. In the Book of Job in the Bible, there is the famous line in God's speech from out of the whirlwind: "Canst thou bind the sweet influences of the Pleiades, or loose the bands of Orion?" Both Homer and Hesiod have beautiful passages involving the star cluster, and Euripides called them time-keepers of the night. It was the ancient Greeks who called these stars the Seven Sisters, the daughters of Pleione and the giant Atlas, and told stories of their flight from the lascivious Orion. The daughters, also called the Seven Virgins, escaped to the heavens, but Orion continued to pursue them.

An American Indian legend portrays the Pleiades as maidens who were chased by a vast, evil bear. To escape, they climbed a mountain whose sides the bear scratched. Finally they were lifted to the heavens far beyond his reach. That mountain is known today as Devils Tower in Wyoming, complete with odd striations on its side (and made famous in Steven Spielberg's movie, *Close Encounters of the Third Kind*).

A Polynesian legend tells of the Pleiades' once being a single great star, bright as a half-moon, which was vain about its beauty and so got broken into pieces — pieces that still gaze longingly at their reflection in still waters.

An equally haunting story is mysteriously found in one version or another in cultures all over the world: the tale of the Lost Pleiad. In the stories of ancient Greece, Japan, Australia, Africa, and other lands, we are told that one of the original Pleiades is now missing. The poet Alfred Austin wrote: "The Sister Stars that once were seven/ Mourn for their missing mate in Heaven." A Mongolian legend says the lost sister is one who was carried off to the north, where she can now be glimpsed as Alcor, the little companion to the star at the bend in the Big Dipper's handle. Astronomers have noticed that one of the stars, Pleione (actually the mother of the Pleiades in Greek myth), has varied somewhat in brightness during the 20th century — perhaps it dimmed too much to be seen with the naked eye at some point in history? More likely is that only sharp-eyed people can see the seventh star,

leading to a discrepancy in the reported number.

A beautiful thing becomes all the more precious when it is in danger of being lost. Unfortunately, that is the case with the Pleiades today. It is not really the cluster, hundreds of light years away, that is being threatened, of course. It is our view of these stars — and all stars.

The problem is "light pollution" — society's excessive outdoor lighting. A scientific study in 1988 estimated that poorly shielded and misdirected outdoor lighting in the United States was sending at least $1.6 billion worth of energy uselessly out into space every year. An organization called the International Dark-Sky Association (IDA) offers information about light pollution and how we can reduce it. They also offer a chart and questionnaire about how many Pleiades stars you can see from where you live or visit; to participate, send a self-addressed, stamped long envelope and a request for the Pleiades form to: IDA, 3545 N. Stewart, Tucson, AZ 85716.

Perhaps the Seven Sisters can help us save our view of themselves and of all the starry heavens for the generations to come. Our children can then be like the great stargazer, Leslie Peltier, who in old age recalled from his own childhood his first and possibly dearest sight: "... seven little stars that sparkle in a long-gone autumn sky." □□

Pleiades star-finder chart, with magnitudes. All stars brighter than 7.0 in this field are shown.

• 6.9 • 6.6
PLEIONE
ATLAS • 5.1 • 7.0
• 6.7 • 3.6
• 6.2 • 6.8
• 6.8 ASTEROPE
ALCYONE • 2.9 • 5.6
• 6.3 6.4 •• 5.8
MAIA • 3.9
TAYGETA • 4.3
• 7.0 CELAENO
• 5.4 MEROPE • 4.2 • 5.5
ELECTRA • 3.7

RECYCLE BRUSH PILES INTO *FREE* WOOD CHIPS, MULCH, AND COMPOST!

Why put up with unsightly brush piles that ruin the good looks of your place? Turn *all* your organic "throw-aways" into useful wood chip, mulch and compost material...and beautify your home, instead!

Have the kind of place you've always dreamed of – more easily than you ever thought possible – with the quick and efficient SUPER TOMAHAWK® Chipper/Shredder! Send for FREE INFORMATION!

Send for your FREE CATALOG!
Learn how the TROY-BILT® Chipper/Shredder can help you reduce and recycle yard waste – from leaves and lawn clippings to giant limbs up to 4"-thick! See the built-in durability that gives it the industry's best warranty! Send for your FREE Catalog TODAY!

Small Property 3HP Junior Model   *Mid-Sized 5HP Model*   *Big Power 8 HP Models*

A Modest Collection of
PIGORABILIA

Pig tipping, filthy pigs, pigs-in-a-poke,
and other beastly lore about our most
productive barnyard animal . . .

BY MARTHA WHITE

– illustrated by Andrea Barrett

For centuries, pigs have suffered a bad rap. If you're piggish, you're considered filthy or greedy; if you're pigheaded, you're too stubborn. Someone who is a hog is selfish — as in road hog or gas hog — and to live (or eat) high off the hog is to take more than your share. We laugh at a clumsy friend, saying he's "like a pig on ice." Even going hog wild is taboo; it's not just excitement, it's intemperate enthusiasm. "But what can be expected of a sow but a grumph?" asks an old English homily.

THE EVOLUTION OF THE PIG

Of the genus *Sus* and family Suidae, swine are cloven-hoofed mammals known domestically as pigs or hogs. An ancestor, the European wild boar or *Sus scrofa*, still has wild-roaming descendants in Tennessee, North Carolina, and elsewhere. Some believe the word *hog* comes from the Hebrew *choog*, for "to surround," while others attribute it to an Arabic source meaning "with narrow eyes." Pigs are also related to the warthog of the southern African plains. With their small eyes they cannot see well, but their sense of smell serves as keen compensation.

Pigs are excellent swimmers and have been found on remote islands. Borneo has bearded pigs. The largest wild pigs live in the forests of Africa: they measure about six feet long and weigh in at 600 pounds. The smallest are the pygmy pigs of India, at about two feet long.

In addition to 44 teeth, male pigs generally grow two, sometimes four, tusks for fighting and rooting. The babirusa boar from the Celebes has useless (except for sexual display) curved tusks that grow toward its eyes. The modern hog has more flesh on the sides and quarters than its wild ancestor and a longer intestine for more efficient feeding. Pigs have a single

We laugh at a clumsy friend, saying he's "like a pig on ice..."

stomach, unlike cows, sheep, or goats. In fact, their digestive tracts resemble man's. The wild boar had a straight, droopy tail, unlike the tight, curly ones evident today. And finally, wild boars of China and Europe were nocturnal, but our modern equivalent has become a night-sleeper.

The ace of diamonds is a pig's eye for its beady shape...

PIG-IN-A-POKE
(or when a pig is not a pig)

Numerous colorful terms slung throughout our language derive from pigs. A *pigboat*, for instance, is slang for a submarine, just as a locomotive might be called a *hog* or *pig* and the engineer known as a *hogger, hoghead, hog jockey, hog mauler,* or *grunt.* Tennessee has sometimes been known as the *Hog and Hominy State* for that favorite combination of fatback and cornmeal.

Pig iron derives from the use of a *sow* or channel into which melted iron runs. The lateral branches of the sow are known as *pigs* and the cooled iron is, thus, *pig iron.* A *pig-in-a-poke* is a bad bargain, where a pig is bought unseen and might turn out to be a cat. When the *poke,* or large pocket, is opened, the cat is let out of the bag and the buyer knows he hasn't gotten his suckling pig.

The ace of diamonds is a *pig's eye* for its beady shape. *Piggin* is a small wooden milk pail in which the handle is formed by a stave reaching above the rim. Similarly, a *pig* might be a crock, mug, jar, or potter's clay, and a *pig-wife* is a female crockery dealer. In England names like *Pig and Whistle* abound for

pubs and inns, *pig* referring to the mug and *whistle* to the wassail.

FILTHY PIG?

Are the slanderous tales true? Most are pure hogwash. Sure, a hearty enthusiasm for food has contributed most heinously to the pig's poor reputation. But consider, it was the farmer who penned the pig and agreed to deliver its swill. Provided with a sturdy, untippable trough that they can't walk into, pigs' manners are vastly improved.

Filthy pig is a misnomer and reflects poorly on the farmer's methods of husbandry. Pigs prefer to be clean, as it turns out, and enjoy a shower bath with the hose second only to a good meal. Their muddy wallows are attempts to keep cool and eliminate parasites. Give them a foot-deep concrete pool of clean water and they'll use that instead. Since they have no sweat glands, sun and heat pose a life-threatening problem. With sufficient shade, clean straw in their houses, and a regularly alternated field to root in, pigs keep a cleaner yard and profile than cows or sheep. They'll deposit their manure in one corner, away from their sleeping quarters, and they won't pick up sticks or other "toys" that have been dirtied by it.

OUR AMERICAN "MORTGAGE LIFTERS"

Their reputation for greediness comes from their appetites, but ponder this: Since the 1800s hogs have become known as the American "mortgage lifters" because of their reliability as efficient meat producers. They retain over 35 percent of the weight of their feed — compared with about 11 percent for cows or sheep. What's more, the slaughtered hog yields 70 to 80 percent in edible material, as against 48 percent for sheep or 60 percent for cows. Hogs also give a higher-density meat and lard than other animals. There's a reason we put our pennies in piggy banks; these thrifty creatures give a solid return!

On the small farm or homestead, pigs earn their keep by "bare-fallowing" the land, harvesting the last of the potatoes, rooting up unwanted weeds like twitch and spear grass, and turning the soil. There is no quicker way to compost than by running the kitchen scraps through a pig, and their manure is easily spread simply by rotating the field in which they are penned or tethered.

EVERYTHING IS USABLE EXCEPT THE SQUEAL

As a matter of fact, even the squeal was once marketed. The Porco-Forte, invented in the 1800s, divided pigs into compartments by musical notes. The instrument was played by squeezing the pigs' tails, and the squeals produced, well ... something akin to music.

More common

SOME INTERESTING PIG STATISTICS

☞ In 1790 six million pounds of pork and lard were exported from the U.S.

☞ In 1890 there were an estimated 48,130,000 hogs on U.S. farms. In 1990 there were an estimated 53,852,000 hogs on U.S. farms.

☞ In 1930 farmers received $8.84 per hundred pounds for their hogs. In 1987 that figure was up to $51.20 per hundred pounds.

☞ More than half the corn grown in the U.S. is used to feed pigs. (The Corn Belt of the Midwest is the largest hog-raising region in the U.S.)

☞ Over one-third of the world's red-meat supply is pork.

head cheese leaves no part wasted.

Because pigs are so like humans, especially in their hearts and teeth, they have frequently been used for medical research. Human heart valve transplants utilize pig valves, and modern pharmaceutical uses include insulin and skin for burn victims.

SUPER PIG STUD SERVICES

Swinish in their sensuality? Lucky for the farmer! One sow might give 20 to 30 piglets a year, if well kept. An average litter is about a dozen piglets, one to a nipple, but the official world's record litter was 34 piglets, born in 1961 to a sow in Denmark. Boar walkers take their boars around to stud, and what studs! In a single shot a good boar will release an average of 45,000,000,000 sperm, more than three times that of the fertile jackass (14,500,000,000), well over six times that of a bull or ram, and 90 times that of humans (500,000,000). Even the prolific

uses today include everything from ham, bacon, and lard to pigskin footballs and gloves, pig bristle brushes, and ball bearings. Laurence Sterne (1713-1768), in *Tristram Shandy,* claimed the impossibility of making "a velvet cap out of a sow's ear," but hog's

A pig might be a crock, mug, jar, or potter's clay...

rabbit tallies in at a mere 64,000,000 sperm per ejaculation.

A PIG'S IQ

Some aficionados say pigs are highly intelligent and easier to train than dogs. Their keen sense of smell led to their use not only as truffle hounds and clammers, but as highly trained pointers for hunters. In France they were harnessed for driving and used to clear forests. Legend has it that Louis XI (1423-1483), the superstitious (and some say manic) king of France, ordered pigs to dance in his bedroom, bedecked in pantaloons and ribbons and accompanied by bagpipes. Many tales describe trained pigs in street fairs and circuses playing card tricks or ringing bells to a tune.

There are farmers who argue that pigs communicate quite well, shrieking in terror and raising their bristles like a dog, barking an alarm, grunting with pleasure, or roaring in hunger. Most farmers agree that the maternal pig grunts contentedly to her litter. Piglets choose one of the sow's 12 nipples and nurse only from that nipple (about every two hours initially) until they are weaned. A pig may sidle up to an owner to be scratched or nudge the breakfast-pail toter with a wet kiss. They like to play with each other and with toys, such as a bucket or feed sack or a strip of cloth tied to the

Louis XI ordered pigs to dance in his bedroom bedecked in pantaloons and ribbons...

fence. Pigs are tryers and will climb, dig, or jump to escape a fence.

PIG WEATHER PROGNOSTICATORS

Perhaps another sign of their intelligence is their renown as storm indicators. The Roman poet, Virgil, described pigs "tossing their snouts" at the approach of a storm. Many farmers agree that, like other farm animals, pigs get agitated by foul weather. An English weather rhyme states:

Grumphie smells the weather,
An' Grumphie sees the wun';
He kens when clouds will gather,
And smoor the blinkin' sun.

Another ditty reads:

When pigs carry sticks,
The clouds will play tricks.
When they lie in the mud,
No fears of a flood.

SOME HANDY PIG HOW-TO'S

The pigheaded pig is definitely obstinate when it comes to doing what it doesn't want to do, like being shipped to slaughter. Here are some hints that might be useful:

☞ Avoid prick-eared pigs like the Large White — they tend to wander and escape. The floppy-eared varieties have ears that hang down over

For the truth is precious and divine,

Too rich a pearl for carnal swine.

– <u>Samuel Butler</u> (1612-1680)

TOURIST: "What do you do for fun out here in the sticks?"

COUNTRY BOY: "Oh, we like to go 'round at night and tip over the pigs when they're sleeping."

A PIG BY ANY OTHER NAME . . .

To understand pigs, you first have to understand the language (and no, it's not pig Latin). A farmyard guide would include these terms:

BARROW: castrated young boar

BOAR: male pig

CHUFFY: a hog raised for lard

FARROWING: to have a litter of piglets

FEEDER PIG: a swine of 25 to 220 pounds, being fattened for market

GILT: young female pig

HOG: the domestic swine, male or female, over 120 pounds

MASTING: running swine through the woods in autumn to forage

PIG: young male or female swine, under 120 pounds

PIGLET: baby pig

RUNT: littlest pig, especially if there are more than 12 in a litter

SHOAT: a weaner pig, 25 to 40 pounds

SOW: female, mother pig with 12 nipples

STAG: an old boar, castrated prior to butchering

STY: pigpen or piggery

SWINE: the domestic hog or pig, male or female

WALLOW: water pool or mudhole for cooling and parasite control

WEANERS: straight off the sow at eight to ten weeks old

their eyes, and they're more likely to stay penned.

☞ If a pig does escape, don't panic. Try food as a lure, shaking a bucket of pellets and backing toward the pen. Pigs follow a leader, so concentrate on capturing just one.

☞ "When the Lord made pigs, He put the head on the wrong end." To get a pig up a ramp into a truck, put a bushel basket over its head and guide it by the tail, backing it up the ramp.

☞ A rope around a back leg will also work, helping you to back a pig into its pen. Commercial pig snares over the snout are more dubious; electric prods are not recommended because they can cause stress-related deaths.

☞ To weigh a pig if you can't get him onto the scales, try measuring him. An approximate formula is to take the heart-girth measurement (just behind the front legs), multiply it by itself, then multiply that times the length of your pig. Divide by 400, and you'll have a weight accurate to within about three percent.

To weigh a pig if you can't get him onto the scales, try measuring him...

☞ And, oh, by the way, pigs travel better at night.

PIG HOPEFULS AND PIG RECORD BREAKERS

In 1968 "Pigasus the Pig" was entered as a presidential candidate. Among television audiences, the Muppets' famous Miss Piggy stole the hearts of millions when she said, "Never eat more than you can lift."

In 1973 a champion Duroc pig from Missouri sold to Soga-No-Yo Swine Farms in Japan for a record price of $38,000. That figure was topped in 1983 when a Texan crossbred boar named "Bud" sold for $56,000. Years earlier, we had the famous Big Bill, a Tennessee Poland-China hog, that weighed a stunning 2,552 pounds and measured nine feet long. His belly dragged on the ground, but this little piggy didn't go to market. When he was chloroformed in 1933, he was mounted and displayed.

As James Boswell put it in *The Life of Samuel Johnson*, "the pigs are a race unjustly calumniated. Pig has, it seems, not been wanting to man, but man to pig."

□□

Now We Must All Thank the

LOWLY LEECH

Believe it or not, these slimy, icky, revolting little devils are actually useful — and becoming more so every day.

BY RICHARD CONNIFF

A lot of us live under the happy misconception that we are unlikely to run into leeches unless we are foolish enough to slog through a steamy equatorial swamp, as Humphrey Bogart did in *The African Queen*. The uncomfortable truth is that these slimy, wormlike creatures thrive almost everywhere, from mountains to desert oases. Even worse, we may have reason to be thankful for it.

North America and Europe are prime leech territory, particularly farther north where the glaciers of the last Ice Age scooped out an excess of watery habitat. In Minnesota, for instance, leeches can be so abundant that trappers, who sell them for fishing bait, sometimes get violent over the rights to prized ponds. In a year they harvest 70 tons of leeches for sale to walleye fishermen at the prime sirloin price of $10 to $12 a pound. Fluttering on the end of a hook, the bait leech has a tantalizing effect on fish. Iowans sometimes use another species, a semiterrestrial leech measuring up to a foot in length, to catch catfish (something squeamish sorts might describe as a case of the inedible in pursuit of the abominable, or vice versa).

Though they may be everywhere, there is nonetheless good news about leeches:

Contrary to a second popular misconception, most leeches do not feed on humans. Many of the 650 species do not suck blood at all. A typical freshwater pond in North America or Central Europe might contain ten different leech species that coexist by partitioning the food supply. Minnesota's bait leech, for example, feeds mostly on algae and microscopic invertebrates. Other species gobble up whole midges, worms, or even other leeches. Some insert a straw-like proboscis and suck up the soft tissue from snails and mosquito larvae.

But probably the most serious misconception about leeches is that — except perhaps as bait — they are useless and even contemptible, or as Bogart put it, "If there's anything in the world I hate, it's leeches — the filthy little devils!" Indeed, leeches are almost a case study in how humans, busy with the self-appointed task of subduing the Earth, can misjudge an animal's importance.

Until recently, the scientific world and almost everybody else dismissed leeches as one of the more revolting instruments of primitive medical superstition. Therapeutic uses of the leech date back at least to the second century B.C., when a Greek author prescribed leeches as a treatment for venomous bites. But modern disdain for the leech was largely a reaction to the leechmania of the 19th century, when doctors often applied leeches 50 at a time to cure patients of everything from nosebleeds to gross obesity. It was the last gasp of the medieval belief that disease was caused by an excess of corrupt blood or by an imbalance in bodily humors. Thus in 1852 Russian novelist Nicolai Gogol, on his deathbed, was doused in cold water while six leeches fed at his nostrils. Crying, "Take the leeches off, take the leeches off my mouth," the patient had to be physically restrained. A witness commented, "All this probably helped him die much faster."

And yet leeches have made a comeback. Over the past two decades, research labs around the world have come to regard them as an important source of biological insights. Leeches have also turned up lately as a valuable tool in the most sophisticated microsurgical operating rooms.

In the laboratory, leeches are now a standard model for figuring out how nervous systems work. Scientists are using the leech, for instance, to learn why some nerve pathways can regenerate themselves after traumatic injury. Medicinal leeches, the species applied to Gogol, have large and unusually accessible nerve cells, making them an ideal animal for studying how the parts of the nervous system connect and communicate. The leech's nerve cells are also relatively easy to map, because there are only about 10,000 of them, versus the estimated ten billion in the human nervous system. Yet leeches do many of the complicated things that other animals do, including rhythmic activities like swimming. It is, of course, a huge leap from an understanding of these processes in leeches to an application of that knowledge in humans, but it is a start.

Leeches have also shown more immediate promise: Biochemicals evolved by the leech for the nasty business of getting and digesting blood have produced startling results in cardiovascular research. At the Mayo Clinic and New York's Mount Sinai Medical Center, for example, researchers are working with a genetically engineered version of hirudin, a blood-thinning substance in the saliva of medicinal leeches. Experiments in pigs indicate that it may be ten times more effective than the widely used drug, heparin, at preventing deadly blood clots. In another experiment, they found that hirudin in combination with a highly touted new drug dissolved clots faster and far more reliably than when the drug was used by itself. Some

Leeches are already helping surgeons save reattached ears, lips, fingertips, and other surgical grafts.

A 1639 handbook on the medicinal use of animals showed how to apply a leech to an afflicted area.

Some leeches can penetrate the skin of a hippopotamus; others can feed only through soft mucous membranes such as the throats and nasal passages of ducks.

A 1671 treatise on blood-letting instruments included these wiggly, hungry leeches.

researchers suggest that substances in the leech's saliva may also inhibit the spread of tumors.

Leeches are already helping surgeons save reattached ears, lips, fingertips, and other surgical grafts. In February of 1992 in Akron, Ohio, for instance, a 45-year-old factory worker caught his hand in a bread-slicing machine. A microsurgeon named Brian Davies spent 13 hours reconnecting both the hand, which was held on by only a few tendons, and three fingers, which were completely severed. After a day, one of the fingers became congested and discolored, a common problem in such cases. While it is relatively easy to reestablish arterial flow into a graft, it often takes time for capillaries to grow together and get the blood back out again. Meanwhile, the reconnected limb or tissue can die. Led by the Europeans, plastic surgeons discovered in the 1980s that the gentlest way to prevent this was with leeches.

On the factory worker's hand, the first leech soon attached itself to the pinky and arched its neck, which began to pulse subtly — a sign that bloodsucking had begun. During a half-hour feeding, the leech would extract seven to nine times its starting weight in blood; because of biochemicals like hirudin, the engorged finger would also bleed for hours afterward. With the application of a new leech every four hours, healthy color returned to the pinky, and the patient ultimately regained use of his entire hand.

The feeding mechanism of bloodsucking leeches is a remarkably delicate business. (The method also varies considerably among species. Some leeches can penetrate the skin of a hippopotamus or an elephant; others can feed only through soft mucous membranes, such as the gums of a Nile crocodile or the throats and nasal passages of ducks.) Humans ordinarily become a meal in the wild when hungry leeches detect the ripples as we move through the water. Leeches are wonderful swimmers, flattening out their bodies and fluttering through the water with the rhythmic up-and-down undulation of sea monsters. Among other skills, they can tread water next to a person's leg while their front end probes delicately for a suitable place to fasten on.

The medicinal leech secretes a mucus to help it cling to the skin with its sucker and also for lubrication. Within the sucker it has three toothed cutting plates like saw blades. These plates reciprocate their way into the flesh, opening the wound in three directions at

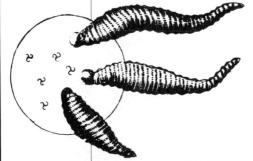

once. (Admirers say that the radial arrangement of these plates produces a scar resembling the hood ornament of a Mercedes-Benz.) One chemical in the leech's saliva dilates the victim's (or the patient's) blood veins; another breaks down cell membranes and disperses the salivary secretions. The pharyngeal muscles begin to pump, and within the leech's gut the anticoagulant hirudin keeps the meal liquid during digestion, which may take as much as six months. Rather than using its own enzymes to digest the blood meal, the leech depends on a kind of intestinal bacterium that puts out an antibiotic to kill other bacteria that might cause putrefaction. Leeches apparently pass this commensal bacterium from generation to generation, like a treasured heirloom, at the time of egg laying.

During the leechmania of the 19th century, demand was so great that the Russian government was forced to establish a closed season on leechgathering. The modern leech business is far smaller in scale. The largest supplier, a company called Biopharm, operated by leech biologist Roy Sawyer in Swansea, Wales, ships an annual total of 100,000 medicinal leeches worldwide (compare this with a single consignment of five million leeches sent from Germany to England in 1824). It also sells an array of leech-derived biochemicals. Instead of relying on wild-caught medicinal leeches, which remain threatened in Europe, Biopharm raises its own in darkened, temperature-controlled rooms. The company keeps about 80,000 leeches, which cling to the sides of buckets and fiberglass tanks in knotty, glistening clumps.

Sawyer, author of the definitive three-volume *Leech Biology and Behaviour,* is a soft-spoken, slightly distracted man, with hanks of sandy hair combed across his balding scalp. He has the ability to turn any conversation toward leeches, and his green eyes pop just perceptibly when he hits pay dirt. (His wife reports that during their courtship, he took her out one night in party clothes and rubber boots to search a Florida swamp for a species that hadn't been seen since the 1930s. They failed, but in the morning she heard an ecstatic whoop: The leech had turned up inside one of her boots. She married him anyway.) Sawyer, who is working on another leech anticoagulant called hementin, has predicted that secretions from bloodsucking animals will one day do for cardiovascular medicine what penicillin did for treatment of infectious disease. The tired old image of leeches as "filthy little devils" might thus be laid to rest. But then Sawyer adds that the source of hementin is an 18-inch-long giant Amazonian leech known to penetrate the skin and suck up mammalian blood with a threadlike proboscis. So the nasty image may just stick. ☐☐

In a book published in Paris in 1598, author Denis Heracleot was depicted attempting to lose weight by attaching quantities of leeches to his person.

In Search of the Orphan

In 1854 the first of hundreds of trainloads of orphans from eastern cities headed west in search of new homes for the lonely, bewildered children. By the time the program ended 75 years later, more than 150,000 children, of whom nearly 600 are still alive today, had been "placed out." Each child's story was different and yet the same...

From the age of five, little Alice Bullis, nicknamed "Toots," took care of her younger siblings born one after the next: Pearl, who became sick with whooping cough and scarlet fever; the identical twins, Lesley and Wesley, who called her "Too-Too"; and Elmer, the baby. The way Toots saw it, her mother hatched them for her to raise. The family was her father's third, and he didn't come home much to the tent where they lived for a summer in the woods of upstate New York. Toots fetched stagnant water and picked strawberries to eat.

One day in 1929 agents arrived from the city. They took Toots and her siblings back with them and placed the boys in one institution, Pearl in another, and Toots in the Goodhue Home for Girls on Staten Island. The staff at Goodhue taught Toots how to "act like a lady" — how to set a table, how to dress, eat, and speak properly. They fattened her up and sanded rough words such as "bull" out of her vocabulary. When she was well enough, they planned to put her on a train (as they did with all the girls) and send her west to live with a new family.

This practice of sending children west was initiated in 1854 by the Reverend Charles Loring Brace, one of the founders of the Children's Aid Society in New York. The city had too many people, too little housing,

– courtesy Alice Bullis Ayler

Train Riders

by Christine Schultz

too few jobs. The conditions bred poverty, disease, and disillusionment; in desperation many were forced to leave babies on doorsteps and let the young ones loose to find their way. A population of "street arabs" grew up earning pennies as newsboys or shoeshiners, as beggars or thieves. The Reverend Brace wanted to move children like Toots away from the influence of the "dangerous classes" in the city into the "better homes" of the farm families out west. But what Toots wanted, more than a new family, was to care again for her old one.

One day an agent from Goodhue took Toots into the city to meet her baby brother

Alice "Toots" Bullis (left, *at 3 years old) was sent west in 1930. She was preceded by thousands of other orphaned children from the East, including the group below, circa 1900.*

and the twins. Others always mixed the twins up, but Toots recognized the three-year-olds instantly — Wesley the shy one and Lesley whose eyes jumped with life. She wanted to hold them for a long time, but the meeting was brief. The train would leave soon, taking the boys with it. Since no family would want a sickly girl, only Toots would stay behind. The twins held tightly to her dress. "Too-Too, please don't go away," they cried. "Please don't go away."

She had been through a lot in her nine years, but nothing so sad as that separation. The months passed, and all the other girls left on the orphan trains. She was one of the last three orphans to go.

When at last she boarded the Pullman in October 1930, she had no idea what to expect. The train ride thrilled her. She ate

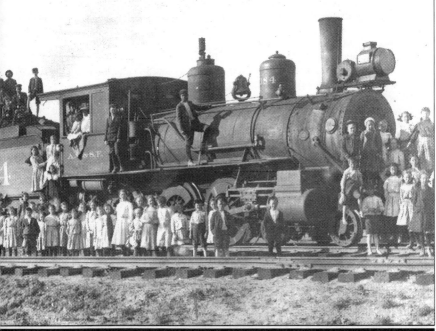

fancy meals served in the diner as the landscape flew past and lay at night in a berth that rocked her to sleep over the rumble of rails. Three days later, all the world was new. This place they called Kansas rolled on and on with fields and cows and (dare she say it?) . . . bulls! She was Dorothy set down in the fascinating land of Oz, but still far from any place she could call home.

It is estimated that well over a million Americans are descendants of orphan train riders.

She stayed for a while in each of the houses where her brothers lived. And though it warmed her heart to be near them again, she could not tolerate the father's treatment of her in either place. She got permission from the agent, Georgia Greenleaf, to be moved to a new family. But in the next house she found conditions equally trying. At night she pressed her ear to the radio listening through her loneliness to the familiar voice of President Roosevelt reading his Fireside Chat.

The woman who cared for Toots ridiculed her background. She told the orphan girl she was dumb and wouldn't amount to anything. But Toots proved her wrong; she became a psychologist, married an optometrist, Donald Ayler, gave birth to a boy, and adopted a girl. She made a home for her family that was better than those she had known herself as a girl. When Toots was in her late twenties, her brother Elmer tracked her down for a heartfelt reunion. She met her three brothers in St. Louis, and they had a ball together. "They thought they were something, having their big sister back with them," Toots says. She's 72 now, is called Alice, and lives in Oklahoma City. "They just love me. There was something special in that early bonding."

Many of the 150,000 or so children who were sent west over the 75 years of the "placing-out program" later criticized the

system for breaking those early bonds. When other institutions, such as the New York Foundling Hospital and the New England Home for Little Wanderers, later undertook a similar program, they altered the process by selecting families for the children before sending them west.

The Reverend Brace had found it difficult to match individual children to a family's specifications. He had more luck placing thousands of children by sending them in groups. In his book, *Dangerous Classes of New York,* Brace explains the process: "We formed little companies of emigrants, and after thoroughly cleaning and clothing them, put them under a competent agent, and first selecting a village where there was a call or opening for such a party, we dispatched them to the place."

Farm families often learned of the orphans through an advertisement in the local newspaper or a sign posted in town: "WANTED: Homes for Children; of various ages and of both sexes, well disciplined." The orphan train pulled into town with its unusual cargo. Children piled out and lined up at the front of a church or town hall for townspeople to inspect. The Children's Aid Society asked that the children be taken care of in sickness and in health; that they be fed, clothed, and given religious training and education to age 16. Boys over 17 were to be paid for their work. The Reverend Brace describes what generally happened after the agent told the history of the orphans to the gathering of townspeople: "The sight of [the children's] worn faces was a most pathetic enforcement of [the agent's] arguments. People who were childless came forward to adopt children; others, who had not intended to take any into their families, were induced to apply for them; and many who really wanted the children's labor pressed forward to obtain it." Those who saw it as an opportunity to gain healthy farmhands often squeezed the young ones' limbs to check their strength.

But no one poked at six-year-old Robert Gayer in 1923. He sat with a group of orphan boys on the stage of the City Hall in Blair, Nebraska. He was too young then to be much help on a farm. In fact, he hadn't ever seen a farm. He'd been living in New York City under the care of his 14-year-old brother, Archie. After their mother died and their father deserted the two boys in a New York City park, Archie sold newspapers and delivered telegrams to feed his brother. They stayed in a boardinghouse for newsboys until an agent arrived one day and took Bob to the Children's Aid Society orphanage. Archie was left behind to fend for himself. Now, sitting before this crowd of unfamiliar faces in a place called Nebraska, Bob desperately missed his brother. He was just an average kid, more curious than most, one who needed and deserved to be loved. One by one the couples chose a boy from the stage, completed the paperwork, and left for home. When the crowd cleared that Saturday, Bob was one of five boys left behind.

He went with the agent to a hotel and waited as she asked around town about other families who might care for a child. On Monday morning she took the boys in a taxi to visit Pearl and Jens Petersen's farm. Bob stared through the window at the immense trees lining the long lane. He looked with amazement at the big red barn and the strange creatures in the fields. Except for the large white dog, he had never seen anything like them.

A woman came out of the farmhouse, and the agent explained the situation. Pearl Petersen said she and her husband were too old to raise a child, but would take one boy for the afternoon. Her husband, Jens, came in from the field, and they chose the boy Bob with the brown hair, blue eyes, and ears that stuck out just a little. Bob remembers that day well. "From the minute I saw the farm and saw the Petersens," he

later wrote, "I wanted to stay with them forever, but I was willing to accept the idea of at least spending the afternoon at this beautiful place."

The rest of that afternoon unfolded like a fairy tale: Bob helped Mrs. Petersen shell

The Children's Aid Society sent this group of children west for "placing out" in 1890.

peas for lunch; he ate heartily, wandered the fields with Mr. Petersen, and studied the workings of the harness and plow. He learned the names of the animals — cows and hogs and horses. Later that afternoon while visiting a neighbor with Mrs. Petersen, he couldn't help asking, "Could I stay with you forever?" "No," Mrs. Petersen replied; she had promised to return him that evening to the hotel in town where the agent waited.

Before sunset, Bob said good-bye to the beautiful 40-acre farm and climbed into the car with the Petersens. He sat anxiously in the hotel lobby while the Petersens talked in private with the agent. After a long time, he looked up to see the couple coming down the stairs. He stood up to say good-bye. "Bob," Mr. Petersen said to him, "how would you like to come live with us?" Bob's heart overflowed with joy.

"From the time we left the hotel that night," he remembers, "there was never any doubt in my mind or the minds of my folks, that I was their boy. We never even talked about just trying it out; it was assumed that I was going to be with them from then on. They were Mother and Dad and I was their son, and nobody would ever tell us otherwise."

To this day he considers himself one of the luckiest orphan train riders. "It was just pure chance that I ended up in a good home," he says. "Believe me, a lot of the others didn't." Many children never outgrew the feeling of being outsiders in the families that raised them. Yet most believe their lives would have been worse had they been left alone in the streets of New York City. The Children's Aid Society documented a success rate of 87 percent in 1910, based on a survey of the number of children who stayed out west and didn't run away or get arrested. Many later achieved successful careers as governors, congressmen, sheriffs, district attorneys, artists, railroad officials, journalists, and farmers.

In 1987 Mary Ellen Johnson founded the Orphan Train Heritage Society of America, Inc., in Springdale, Arkansas, to preserve the history and act as a clearinghouse of information. Seven hundred people joined. She now edits a quarterly newsletter called *Crossroads* for and about orphan train riders. As executive director of the organization, she oversaw the recent construction of the Orphan Train Riders Research Center. Records on more than 3,000 riders are kept there. "As long as word gets out," Johnson says, "this history won't be forgotten — it touches a lot of people's lives." She estimates that well over a million Americans are descendants of orphan train riders.

Every month more relatives track each other down through the directory, through the help of Helen Steinman at the Children's Aid Society in New York City, or through word of mouth. Sometimes, as in Bob Petersen's case, a lot depends on hope and fate.

One day in 1938, while waiting for a haircut in an Iowa barbershop, Bob happened to flip through a copy of *Look* magazine. He noticed a story about the New York World's Fair. One photo of a carnival man caught his eye. Under the photo was the man's name: Archie Gayer. On the off

chance that this was his Archie, Bob wrote a letter and sent it to the World's Fair. Much later he received a reply. It was signed by his long-lost brother.

In the years that followed, the two men talked of many things, as brothers do, but the one thing they never really spoke of were those early years when Archie cared for his little brother on the streets of New York. Since Archie's death a dozen years ago, there's been no way for Bob to flesh out his story. "I'm sorry we didn't talk about it more," says Bob, now a lawyer in

Alice Bullis Ayler (center) and her twin brothers Wesley (left; now Thomas Bankston) and Lesley (now Alan Bankston), and their wives, at a reunion.

Omaha. "I have no memory of those first six years. That's always bothered me." He tried some years ago to have a hypnotist unbury the memories, but had no luck. Most likely, the hypnotist told him, something so traumatic had happened that Bob had completely blocked it out.

These half-remembered stories of Bob and others like him create a bond among the orphan train riders. "Everyone had a different kind of life," Alice (Bullis) Ayler says, "but everyone had the same loss." Each year most of the nearly 600 survivors travel to join in the reunions around the country. They share their stories and pass their histories on to the thousands of interested descendants. "On the whole," Alice Ayler says of orphan train riders, "we're the sort of people who don't cry much. But at those reunions everyone cries. It's such a relief to talk to others who understand. We're all a big old family — not by blood, by something greater." □ □

For more information: Orphan Train Heritage Society of America, Inc., 4912 Trout Farm Road, Springdale, AR 72764; 501-756-2780 (evenings and weekends only).

The House with the Most Cats Under One Roof in North America

You'll never believe how many.

BY ADAM CORELLI

In the beautiful and historic Canadian city of Kingston (population 61,000), located at the eastern spout of Lake Ontario, live Jack and Donna Wright and their 640 cats. The Wrights have more cats living with them than any other home-owner in North America. The Wrights' penchant for all things feline has made them famous. They have appeared on television shows the world over. They have been in dozens of magazines and newspapers. Visitors, from veterinarians to the cat-curious, stream into their two-story home.

The cats seem content. They stand around, blinking, purring, and pouncing, doing the regular sorts of things that cats do. A small, furry mountain shimmers by the front door. Dozens of eyes blink and tails wave. The cats are curious and friendly. This living rug of cats at the entrance is not trying to escape the house. They simply want to crawl all over whoever dares enter.

Within moments of coming in the door, I find nearly a dozen cats hanging from me. Claws gripping gently, they hang from my arms and legs, and a couple more, stretched thin, dangle down my back. One more has wrapped itself around my neck like a fur scarf. For a brief eternity, a catatonic moment, I find myself wearing a live cat-hair coat. I remember that I am dogged by feline allergies.

Cats are everywhere in the Wrights' house. They occupy all the chairs and tables. They sit in partly opened drawers. They lie in the sink, on the toilet seat, on the washing machine, and on the stove. They even manage to somehow obscure the giant television screen in the living room. "When a film crew comes in, you can't get rid of them," laughs Jack. "They crawl all over the crew and the equipment. They get into boxes, go for the lights, and can't wait to have their photos taken. They just love people."

This multicultural crowd of cats assumes a cosmopolitan disdain: the Himalayan lives peacefully with the Burmese, Siamese, Persian, and Angora. The purebred coon cat seems more stylishly disheveled than the Heinz-57s it hangs out with. The cats enjoy each other immensely. They lie together in piles. They leap at each other. Indeed, after all their years of cat collecting, the Wrights can recollect only one fight, a cataclysmic brawl involving about 40 cats.

The house is surprisingly clean. The Wrights got rid of their rugs years ago to make cleanups easier. While there is an odor of ammonia and something else (cat breath, perhaps?), it is not disgusting. Hired help, as well as several friends, help to keep things in order.

Every cat has a name, although there are several duplicates (three Boots, three Taras). Amazingly, Jack can call out a name, and from the crowd of fur at one end of the room the sole cat beckoned will emerge. "You

Donna and Jack Wright relax in their kitchen with several cats, including Arnold (top left) and Boots II (top right).

know how people call a cat by saying, 'Kitty kitty,'" Jack says. "I've got one named Kitty Kitty. When I call her, she's the only one who will come forward."

The Wrights have a lot of mouths to feed. Chow time runs 24 hours a day. Each day the cats eat 180 14-ounce cans of cat food plus about 50 pounds of dry food and nine quarts of milk. Holiday meals involve a dozen 20-pound turkeys, a few pot roasts, and dozens of cans of pink salmon and tuna. In return, the cats use up seven 20-pound bags of kitty litter each day, enough to fill nearly nine large garbage bags with waste.

The feeding frenzy takes place throughout the eight first-floor rooms in the Wrights' 15-room house. It all begins each

morning at 5:30, when 52-year-old Jack spends the first 20 minutes of his day at an electric can opener. He leaves food in giant bowls and on trays in each room before heading out to work (he and Donna, who is 47, run a painting and decorating business). All but one of the cats eats just enough and no more. The exception has an eating disorder that has made it obese. "The cats are not greedy," Jack says. "They will take only enough to make them happy."

The Wrights' extended family started more than 20 years ago, not too long after they were married, when they acquired Midnight. By 1981, when the cat family numbered 45, the Wrights moved to a bigger house. As the number kept increasing, so did

To this day, they always leave cat food on their front stoop for strays. The sign above the stoop reads Cat Crossing.

their reputation within the community. Kingston has a large student population, thanks to Queen's University. The collection kept growing as students and other locals, unable to continue caring for their cats, brought them to the Wrights.

By the beginning of 1987, the collection hit 145 cats. A family friend noticed that the tabloid *National Inquirer* was holding a contest to find out who had the most cats under one roof in North America. The Wrights entered, and not surprisingly, they won. Suddenly the press attention, as well as the cat population at 94 Elm Street, soared. "It just snowballed," Jack says. "People started coming from all over with their cats. We got them from Toronto, from Ottawa, from Cardinal [Ontario]. We've got some from Pennsylvania. There are cats from all over North America in this house."

It wasn't a conscious decision to attain feline fame. The Wrights could simply never turn away a pet in need. To this day, they always leave cat food on their front stoop for strays. The sign above the stoop reads Cat Crossing. Jack says the animals are peaceful; they bring him contentment, a purpose in life.

"The cats weren't put on this earth to be put to sleep," he says pleadingly. "The problem is that people who have them can't look after them. It's nice to have a pet, but if you are not prepared to look after a pet like you would a human being, then don't bother having one. They are quite a comfort. I've seen people sick in the hospital without much happiness, and you take their pet to them and they perk right up."

As the Wrights' cat collection has grown in recent months, reaction within the community has been mixed. The local city council recently passed a law limiting to six the number of cats allowed in one house, although the Wrights got a grandfather clause and can keep their cats. The Wrights' next-door neighbor is also upset, complaining that her 640 furry neighbors are triggering her allergies.

Yet the local humane society is one of the Wrights' biggest fans. Ron McMillan, the director of the Kingston Humane Society, has visited the house to inspect the pets' living conditions. "I'm impressed," McMillan says. "We have a full-time job looking after the 60 cats we have, and we have seven staff. I think he is doing a good job. If he wasn't there, we would have to euthanize them."

While Jack dreams of establishing a foundation to care for cats, Donna says they are unlikely to take in too many more because of the complaints and the cost. They spend $306 a day on their pets in food and veterinary bills (a vet visits every week or when needed). "We go around to the different stores for the specials," Donna says. Even so, the expense of caring for the pets nearly cost the Wrights their house earlier this year. They fell about $8,000 behind in their mortgage payments. But a story in the local newspaper about their plight brought in donations of nearly $15,000 from cat lovers around the world.

Both Jack and Donna say they have no regrets about the amount of time, money, and emotional support they've devoted to their feline family. They simply provide too much enjoyment. "You never want to get rid of them, but sometimes you wonder what you are doing with them all," Jack concedes. He says getting out of bed at night is a risk because the cats will take the warm, cozy spot in the bed. He has spent more than one night sleeping elsewhere in the house, forced from his own bed by napping cats. "One will get on your lap, and one will get on top of him, and they will just pile right up until they are past your chin. It can make it difficult to watch television or just sit around.

"But I just love them." □□

OUT IN THE MIDDLE OF NOWHERE

☞ **Loving County has more registered voters than residents.**

☞ **Kalawao County's only residents are 88 leper patients and staff.**

☞ **Kenedy County has the greatest maldistribution of wealth in the nation.**

☞ **The world's only church constructed of baled straw still stands in Arthur County.**

According to the 1990 census, there are 26 counties in America with populations below two people per square mile. This author recently visited ten of them in order to report what life is really like there . . .

BY DAYTON DUNCAN

☐ ONE CENTURY AFTER HISTORIAN FREDerick Jackson Turner proclaimed the closing of the frontier, a part of America still exists miles from nowhere. In a nation where 78 percent of us now live an urban existence, these anachronistic places instead have "towns" that sometimes consist of only a combined gas station/store/post office/house. These quirky, individualistic communities can be a day's drive away from the closest fast-food franchise.

The census of 1990 revealed 27 counties with populations of 999 or less, three more than in 1980. All but one have population densities below two people per square mile, the criterion once used by the Census Bureau to delineate the frontier line between settled and unsettled spaces. Together, the 27 "three-digit" counties cover 25,063 square miles — about three times the size of Massachusetts. Yet their total population in 1990 was 18,272, or 0.7 resident per square mile.

Here are the ten counties with the tiniest populations — and a tiny bit about each one:

LOVING COUNTY, TEXAS

population 107

Nestled between the Pecos River and the state border with New Mexico, Loving County has the double distinction of being both the nation's least populated county and the one with the lowest population density (0.2 person per square

– illustrated by Randy Chewning

mile). It's named for Oliver Loving, who, with partner Charles Goodnight, established a famous cattle trail that cut right through the county in the 19th century. In many respects, Loving County is defined more by what it doesn't have than by what it does: no school (students are bused to another county), no church (except a historic building used occasionally for special services), no grocery store, no medical services, and no place that accepts credit cards. There's no potable water supply, so the county trucks water in and sells it for 15¢ a barrel. Although a handful of individual graves are scattered within its borders — the most recent one holds the remains of Shady Davis, a cowboy dragged to death by his horse in 1912 — Loving County is also probably the only county in America without a cemetery. Mentone, the county seat and sole town, has a gas station, a café, a courthouse, a post office, and 17 residents.

What Loving County does have in abundance are oil and gas wells. Without them — and especially the tax revenues they generate — the county would have to be dissolved. Being the principal source of employment, county government is the focus of fiercely fought elections, many of them decided by small margins and write-in campaigns. A glitch in local election laws has given rise to yet another distinction: Loving County is the only one in the nation with more registered voters (110) than residents.

KALAWAO COUNTY, HAWAII

population 130

In the 1860s King Kamehameha V of Hawaii created a leper colony on the island of Molokai's Kalaupapa Peninsula, a flat piece of land surrounded on three sides by the Pacific Ocean and on the fourth by steep cliffs rising 2,000 feet. Hawaiians suffering from leprosy were unloaded there and left to fend for themselves. "They were strangers to each other, collected by common calamity, disfigured, mortally sick, banished without sin from home and friends," wrote Robert Louis Stevenson after a visit. "In the chronicle of man there is perhaps no more melancholy landing than this."

In 1873 the Belgian priest Father Damien arrived to provide more humane treatment, and the peninsula became famous worldwide, particularly after Father Damien, currently under consideration for canonization, died from the disease. When Hawaii became a territory (and then a state), the peninsula was designated as a separate county. Until 1969 Hawaiians with leprosy were dispatched there.

Today the only residents are the 88 remaining patients and the staff of the state-run facility. Although it has no governmental functions, Kalawao is still considered a county. With the exception of an automated Coast Guard light-

☞ Hinsdale County's colorful past includes a hungry prospector named Alferd.

☞ Petroleum County has plenty of oil wells but only one gas station.

☞ In McPherson County cattle outnumber people 70 to 1.

☞ Teddy Roosevelt set aside thousands of Blaine County acres as a forest preserve, even though there weren't any forests.

house, all 14 square miles of the county are owned by the state. When the last of the patients dies (the youngest is age 50, the oldest 98) and the facility is closed, the empty settlement is scheduled to become a national historic park.

KING COUNTY, TEXAS

population 354

Located near the base of the Texas panhandle, King County is the home of the 6666 Ranch, whose 208,000 acres cover more than a third of the county. In Guthrie, the county seat, most of the houses are owned either by the ranch or the school district, both of which provide housing for their employees as an inducement. The main ranch house, on a hill dominating the town, is larger than the courthouse, which in 1982 received national attention for finally getting indoor plumbing.

KENEDY COUNTY, TEXAS

population 460

Five huge cattle ranches (with lucrative oil leases) comprise most of this county on the lower Gulf Coast. Other than U.S. Highway 77 and seven miles of county roads, all the roads in its 1,389 square miles (bigger than Rhode Island but smaller than Delaware) are privately owned and maintained. Kenedy

County has been cited as having the greatest maldistribution of wealth in the nation: Although oil royalties to a minority of the households rank the county near the top in per capita income, 35 percent of its residents live below the poverty line, one of the country's higher percentages.

ARTHUR COUNTY, NEBRASKA

population 462

Of the 27 "three-digit" counties, eight are in northwestern Nebraska's eerie Sand Hills, the largest sand-dune area in the Western Hemisphere. A treeless area half the size of Ohio, the Sand Hills are filled with huge dunes, some 400 feet high and 20 miles long and stabilized by a loose grass cover, yet also pocked with lush lowland marshes watered by the Ogallala aquifer. They have been called "God's Cow Country." The world's only church constructed of baled straw, erected in 1927, still stands in Arthur County. Residents' telephone numbers are listed on a sheet of typing paper; there being no local doctor or nurse, the names of people who have first-aid training are marked with an asterisk for quick reference in a medical emergency.

HINSDALE COUNTY, COLORADO

population 467

In 1874 Alferd Packer and five fellow prospectors wandered into the snow-covered San Juan Mountains to search for gold. The next spring only Packer, looking uncommonly well fed, emerged. Suspicions were aroused, and Packer eventually confessed to eating his compatriots over the winter. One account of the ensuing trial claims the judge shouted at Packer: "Stand up, y' man-eating son iv' a bitch, STAND UP! They was sivin Dimmycrats in Hinsdale County and ye et five iv thim, God damn ye!"

Lake City, the county seat, a former mining boom town filled with well-pre-

served Victorian houses and buildings, is Colorado's largest historical district. It is quiet in the winter, but in the summer bustles with tourists, many of whom buy sweatshirts decorated with a picture of Alferd the cannibal and carrying slogans like, "Have a Friend for Dinner" or "Dedicated to Serving His Fellow Man." The county remains a Republican stronghold.

PETROLEUM COUNTY, MONTANA

population 519

The dry plains and the rough, broken coulees at the confluence of the Musselshell and Missouri rivers in eastern Montana were among the last places in the nation to be homesteaded. Most of the settlement took place in the 1910s, a good 20 years after the frontier supposedly "closed." Petroleum County was organized in 1924, after a brief oil boom that gave the county its name. The wells are still producing, but because of the county's sparse population (0.3 person per square mile), there is only one retail gas station in Petroleum County.

McPHERSON COUNTY, NEBRASKA

population 546

This is another Sand Hills county, where cattle outnumber people 70 to 1. To keep busy and supplement his salary, the sheriff cleans septic tanks, runs the only motel ($12 for a single), has a leather shop, and sells cassettes of "Don Nicholson, the Singing Sheriff" for two bucks each. Tryon, the county seat, is said to be named either for a Colonial governor from the East or for "Let's keep tryin' to have a town."

MINERAL COUNTY, COLORADO

population 558

Like Hinsdale County and San Juan County (population 745), Mineral County sits in the midst of the imposing San Juan Mountains of southwestern Colorado, where the Continental Divide makes a sharp U-turn. Long on scenery, longer on winters, and short on roads and year-round residents, these counties witnessed their peak populations during the silver and gold rushes more than a century ago. Their economies now rely on the summer rush of tourists.

Creede, Mineral County's seat, was known as a wild mining town and the place where Robert Ford, the man who shot Jesse James, ran a profitable saloon until he, too, was shot down in 1892. Creede's current claim to fame is a respected summer repertory theater and an active artists' community.

BLAINE COUNTY, NEBRASKA

population 675

The lack of trees in the Sand Hills vexed promoters of farming and homesteading near the turn of the century: No trees meant no wood for homes, fences, and fuel. In 1902 President Teddy Roosevelt was persuaded to set aside thousands of Sand Hills acres as a forest preserve, even though there weren't any forests to preserve. The U.S. Forest Service's first tree nursery was soon started on the border of Blaine and Thomas (population 851) counties. Today, the Nebraska National Forest is the largest man-made forest in the Western Hemisphere.

But the trees matured too late to spur any sustained settlement boom. After doubling between 1900 and 1920, the population started a steady descent as most of the homesteaders gave up and moved out. In 1990 the Sand Hills region had about the same number of residents as it did in 1890. Thanks to the forest, however, the porcupine population has increased dramatically. □□

Dayton Duncan is the author of *Miles from Nowhere* (Viking Penguin, 1993), about life in the most sparsely populated parts of America.

HOW LONG WILL YOU LIVE?

 The average life expectancy for men and women in the United States is at best a very general statistic. Individual life spans vary greatly; the reasons are sometimes genetic, but some are under a person's control. To get a more precise idea of how long you may expect to live — and what you can do about it — find the average life expectancy for someone your age in the accompanying chart, then answer the life-style questions below.

Average Life Expectancy

YOUR AGE NOW	AVERAGE LIFE EXPECTANCY FOR MEN	AVERAGE LIFE EXPECTANCY FOR WOMEN
25	73	79
35	74	80
45	75	80
55	76	81
65	80	84

1 For every 5 years that your father lived past 70, add 1 year to your average life expectancy. Add 1 year for every 5 years your mother lived past 78. _____

2 If you are single, deduct 1 year for each decade you are un-married after age 25. _____

3 If you are married, add 5 years. If there is an unusual amount of family strife, subtract 2 years. _____

4 If you live in a city, subtract 2 years. If you live in a small town or on a farm, add 2 years. _____

5 If you have been either poor or wealthy most of your life, sub-tract 3 years. _____

6 If you're over 40, subtract a year for every 5 pounds above your best weight. Men only: Deduct 2 years per inch that your waist measurement exceeds your chest measurement. _____

7 If you exercise moderately but regularly, add 3 years. If you regularly do vigorous exercise, add 5 years. _____

8 If you think you have a hard-driving, competitive personality or are often tense, deduct 5 years. Add 5 years if you're usually cheerful and easygoing. _____

9 If you drink heavily, subtract 5 years; very heavily, 10 years. If you take recreational drugs, subtract 5 years. _____

10 If you smoke ½ to 1 pack of cigarettes daily, subtract 3 years. If you smoke 1 to 1½ packs, subtract 5 years; 2 packs, 10 years. _____

11 If you have regular medical and dental checkups, add 3 years. If you're often ill, subtract 2 years. _____

12 If your diet is high in fats, salt, and sweets, deduct 4 years. If you eat a balanced diet with plenty of fruit, vegetables, and low-fat proteins, add 4 years. _____

YOUR LIFE EXPECTANCY _____

THE WORST DISASTER

*In only ten months it killed more Americans than those who
died in all the wars of this century combined . . .* **BY DEBRA SANDERSON**

Only in retrospect did people realize that the first appearance of the Spanish influenza was actually in the United States in March of 1918. Although more than a thousand workers at Detroit's Ford Motor Company were sent home with the flu in March, the disease was considered mostly a nuisance rather than a dangerous health threat. Influenza, or the grippe as it was called, was not considered a reportable disease, so very few records were kept.

As the first wave of the flu was dying out in the United States in April, it was just beginning an incredible sweep across Europe, war or no war, striking soldier and civilian alike. The flu picked up its name as it swept across Spain, infecting some eight million Spaniards. Although it killed many during that summer — estimated tens of thousands — the mortality rate was relatively low. Most folks, including health-care professionals and those in charge, considered it to be yet another go-around with the traditional flus of the day.

Spanish influenza rounded the globe in four months. As the virus passed from host to host and country to country, it proved to be extremely mutable, changing its outer surface to make itself less vulnerable to specific human antibodies. It also became much more virulent. By August 1918 it stood poised for its real attack on humanity. And humanity was totally unprepared.

On August 27, 500 of the 600 workers at the Sierra Leone Coaling Company failed to report for work due to illness. The flu ripped through the native population and was carried onto transport ships with other cargo. Local officials in Sierra Leone estimated that three percent of the total indigenous population died as a result of Spanish influenza by the end of September. In Brest, France, where the rate of infection was similar, the impact was even greater: Brest was the chief port of disembarkation for the American Expeditionary Force.

Boston's Commonwealth Pier was "grossly overcrowded" by the Navy's own admission when the flu arrived. The epidemic blossomed from two or three sick sailors on the first day, August 27, to 106 on the fifth day. Within the first two weeks of its arrival at the Pier, 2,000 officers and sailors of the First Naval District were stricken.

Not only was the flu spread from one person to another with incredible rapidity, but the course of the disease within the individual was amazingly swift as well. Once infected, a

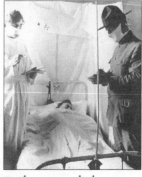

*Lucky to get a bed, a
soldier was admitted to a
makeshift hospital.*

– photos: Culver Pictures

IN RECORDED HISTORY

The American Red Cross was called out day and night to help transport the sick to hospitals, the dead to morgues.

the flu. In 1918 viruses were unknown and antibiotics were still many years of medical research away. The best that could be done for flu patients was to provide fresh air, bed rest, and good nursing care, which was in very short supply during the height of the pandemic.

person would pass from apparent good health to near prostration in only one or two hours. For most of them the worst would be over in several days, followed by a longer recovery period. But for five to ten percent, a severe and massive pneumonia followed. For some, the rapid course from health to illness to death lasted only a few days. The lungs of those who died quickly were completely unlike those seen in autopsies on "traditional" pneumonia victims. Instead of the gross, nodular, almost liverlike lung tissue normally seen as a result of pneumonia, the doctors found severely abnormal, waterlogged lungs filled with vast quantities of bloody fluid. The medical authorities were at a complete loss to explain how something as "innocuous" as the flu could wreak such devastation.

They were also helpless in combating

While it was clear to the surgeon general of the United States Public Health Service that a strict military and civilian quarantine was necessary, it was not legally or politically possible to impose one. As Colonel S. M. Kennedy, chief surgeon of the New York port of embarkation said, "We can't stop this war on account of Spanish or any other kind of influenza." So the troop transports continued sailing for Europe that fall, and although troops bound for overseas were examined for flu symptoms at the training camps, at the embarkation camps, and again before boarding their ships, many soldiers died before ever reaching a battlefield.

The story of Private Robert James Wal-

In the second week of October, 2,600 Philadelphians died and in the third week 4,500.

lace on board the *Briton* was probably representative of many. When Private Wallace awoke one morning with the flu, he reported to the medical officer and was told to gather up his blanket and gear and make himself a pallet on deck, since all available hospital space was taken. With a fever of 103° F, they did not want him below decks infecting the others. While the open air would do him good, the gale-force winds and soaking waves would not. His mess kit, cap, and puttees were swept overboard one miserable night, but he was really too sick to care, as he drifted in and out of his feverish delirium. After many days, he was picked up and moved to a carpeted floor in a salon, where he was at least warm and dry, and he was fed several times a day. There he finally received some nursing care. When a kindly nurse offered to wash his feet, she discovered this sick soldier had not removed his shoes for 12 days.

Private Wallace was among the lucky ones who survived the voyage, though his ordeal was not over. But those who were not so lucky presented yet another problem for their fellow travelers. The transport ships were not equipped to embalm and store the mounting number of corpses. By October 12, the directive requiring the return of bodies to America could no longer be obeyed. Many of America's fighting men were buried in the unmarked graves of the sea, never having been in combat. The Navy Department's annual report would show that almost twice as many American sailors died as the result of Spanish influenza in 1918 than as the result of enemy action.

Meanwhile, back at home the pandemic was sweeping the country. War bond parades and rallies brought thousands of people together to sing patriotic songs and breathe each others' germs. In Philadelphia, one of the hardest hit of all major U.S. cities, a Liberty Loan Parade on September 28 attracted 200,000 to watch the parade, which stretched 23 city blocks. On October 1, 635 new cases of flu were reported. Many other cases went unreported.

The shortage of doctors and especially nurses and hospital beds was acute. As more and more people succumbed, essential services began to collapse. The telephone company in Philadelphia was forced to restrict calls to those relating to the epidemic or to the war effort. Police, firefighters, garbage collectors, and all city agencies suffered from high absentee rates. In Philadelphia the essential services of morticians and undertakers came closest to total collapse. In the second week of October, 2,600 died, and in the third week 4,500 died of flu and pneumonia. The city's only morgue had a normal capacity of 36 bodies.

Police in Seattle, December 1918, wore masks made by the local Red Cross.

— Culver Pictures

The city's only morgue had a capacity of 36 bodies.

In all large cities, visiting public health nurses witnessed grisly scenes reminiscent of 14th-century plague years. One nurse on a home visit discovered a sick woman with newly born twins lying in the same room with her dead husband. In the 24 hours since the death and births, the mother had eaten only an apple that was lying within reach. In Boston a social worker went to the home of a hospitalized 14-year-old to check on his family. She found devastation. A baby and an older child had died of the flu, and the father and two more children were ill. The father was too sick to work so there was no money. The baby had remained on the kitchen table for three days after it died before anyone was able to contact the Board of Health.

For most U.S. cities, the worst of the Spanish influenza hit during the fall of 1918. Philadelphia experienced only the fall wave, which peaked in mid-October. San Francisco's fall wave peaked in late October and seemed to be largely over by the third week in November, but late December saw a resurgence that caused about half as many deaths as in the fall. For most communities, the mortality rates had stabilized by the summer of 1919.

In his book *America's Forgotten Pandemic, the Influenza of 1918*, Alfred W.

Crosby states that the combined battle deaths of the United States Armed Forces in World War I, World War II, and the Korean and Vietnam conflicts totaled 423,000, a figure far below what the country lost to Spanish influenza in ten months in 1918. The world mortality figure generally cited is 21 million, but Crosby considers this a gross underestimation, since reputable estimates put the mortality rate in India alone at about 20 million.

Stepping back in history to look at the Spanish influenza pandemic of 1918 leaves us with more questions than answers. Perhaps the most important of these is: Could it happen again? Would the world in 1993 be as ill-prepared as the world of 1918?

Dr. Louisa Chapman, a medical epidemiologist at the Centers for Disease Control in Atlanta, says it's not impossible that an extremely virulent strain of virus such as that experienced in 1918 could recur, but that we are much better equipped to cope with it if it does.

"One of the most interesting and frustrating things about flu virus is the way it manages to change," Dr. Chapman commented. "But we now have an elaborate international tracking system, so within a matter of days we would know about a significant new virus, even if it starts in a remote corner of the Earth." Although she admitted there would be a time delay between identifying a new virus and having large quantities of vaccine ready to inoculate the public, Dr. Chapman stressed that other treatments are currently available besides vaccination. In addition to oxygen therapy and antibiotics (for secondary infections), the drug amantadine hydrochloride has also proven effective in combating influenza type A. Vaccination itself greatly decreases the risk of contracting the flu among healthy young adults (the group most affected by the 1918 Spanish flu) and lowers the chances of hospitalization and death for all age groups.

Modern medical communication systems, new treatment options, and the ability to formulate effective vaccines are major differences between 1918 and now. But one very important similarity remains.

"People just don't take flu seriously," Dr. Chapman said. "It's hard to convince them that it could be a real hazard." □□

The Startling Saga of the

Not the hockey championship finals. Rather, we're referring to the actual silver cup awarded to the winning team each year. Its first 100 years have been unusual . . .

by Jim Matheson

The Stanley Cup turns 100 this year, and it has the weathered look that comes with time. It has fallen on its head, been tossed into a river, and been held for ransom. It has been bruised and battered, but it's still alive and well with many stories to tell.

The Stanley Cup, awarded every spring, is the most prized trophy in hockey, perhaps the most revered of all sports awards. It goes to the winner of the National Hockey League playoffs, in which the victorious team has to take four consecutive best-of-seven series. It's the oldest trophy awarded for professional sports in North America. When grown men lift the Cup over their heads, they become kids again.

The saga of the Cup began in England in March of 1892. Frederick Arthur, Baron Stanley of Preston, the governor general of Canada, sent his aide-de-camp, Captain Colville, out to purchase a presentation cup, perhaps a bowl on a wooden base. Baron Stanley's sons played for an Ottawa hockey team called the Rideau Hall Rebels, and the baron decided to award a prize to the best amateur hockey team in Canada in honor of his sons' love for the game. Captain Colville spent 10 guineas (about $50) for the 7½-inch, gold-lined, silver bowl set on an ebony base. Lord Stanley donated the Cup in 1893; it has been presented to the top professional team since 1910.

The Stanley Cup literally has history written all over it: More than 1,600 names have been engraved on the Cup, going back to the championship of 1894, when 5,000 people showed up to watch the Montreal AAA team beat the Ottawa Generals 3-1. The earliest champions' names were engraved around the neck and shoulders of the Cup, which has necessarily been enlarged and modified over

The original cup presented by Baron Stanley of Preston (opposite) now reposes in the Hockey Hall of Fame and Museum in Toronto.

Stanley Cup

the years to accommodate all the winners. In 1926 the newly formed National Hockey League inherited the trophy and began enlarging it to its present height of 35½ inches and heft of 32 pounds.

The names of Cup winners are stamped into specially fitted bands that encircle the structure. The Cup experienced a major overhaul in 1947, when a Montreal silversmith named Carl Peterson renovated the trophy in stages until each part was copied. He made five new bands and had the names stamped (exactly ⅟₃₂ inch deep) rather than engraved. He placed the names closer together to make more room for future winners and reworked the framework hull in hollow aluminum to streamline it. The bowl itself had to be copied because it had been dented so much. The original, made of nickel silver and alloys, is in the Hockey Hall of Fame and Museum in Toronto. The sterling silver replica, with the names of all winners painstakingly matched by Peterson, also spends most of the year in the Hall of Fame — except when Stanley Cup time rolls around.

In Canada, where fathers get out hoses in the late fall and pour water into flower gardens and backyards to make ice rinks, kids grow up dreaming of the Stanley Cup. It's hockey's Holy Grail, and the stories about where the Cup has been are the stuff of legend:

☞ "I remember Stanley was there with us the day my wife and I got married," said Edmonton Oiler masseur Stew Poirier. "Stanley wasn't the best man, but he was the main attraction."

☞ The Cup was booted into the Rideau Canal in Ottawa by a tipsy group of Silver Seven players in the early 1900s. Fortunately, the water was frozen, and the Cup was still there in the snow the next morn-

ing, a little bruised but still in one piece.

☞ A few years later, at an Ottawa Senators' victory party, the Cup was tossed over a wall into a graveyard, contributing further to its general dented appearance.

☞ When the New York Islanders won their first Cup in 1980, Clark Gillies brought his German shepherd, Hombre, to the party and let him drink from the Cup. A passerby was shocked that Gillies would let Hombre slurp from the trophy. "Why not? He's a good dog," said Gillies.

☞ When the Calgary Flames won their only Cup in 1989, assistant trainer Al Murray let his horse eat oats from the bowl.

☞ In 1987 Edmonton players took the Stanley Cup to a strip show at a hotel across the street from the rink. NHL executives saw red and ordered the Oilers to keep the Cup in more genteel surroundings.

☞ The Cup was abandoned in 1924 when a group of Montreal Canadiens en route

> In 1987 Edmonton players took the Stanley Cup to a strip show ... NHL executives saw red and ordered the Oilers to keep the Cup in more genteel surroundings.

to a party had a flat tire. They put the Cup on the sidewalk and drove off without it. After a few hours, when they returned in panic to retrieve the orphaned trophy, it was still there, right where they'd left it.

☞ The collar of Lord Stanley's original cup was stolen from the Hockey Hall of Fame in 1970 and wasn't recovered until 1979, when an anonymous tip sent Toronto police to the back room of a dry cleaner. There the collar was, all wrapped up like a Christmas present.

☞ In 1962 a Montreal fan named Ken Kilander walked into Chicago Stadium to watch a playoff game with the Canadiens and saw the Cup on display in a glass case in the lobby. He opened the case. Unbelievably, no sirens went off. He and the Cup were half a dozen steps from freedom when a cop glanced at him. "Hey, where are you going with that?" the police officer demanded. "I want to take it back where it belongs ... back to Montreal," said Kilander, still angry that the Blackhawks had beaten his team in the finals the year before.

☞ Stealing the Cup doesn't make much sense — it's far too well known to take to the local pawnshop. But, if you've actually won the Cup, you can ask nicely and be allowed to take it wherever you want. Former Edmonton goalie Andy Moog's daughter took it to school one day for one of the best show-and-tells of all time.

Today the Cup literally runneth over with names. After 100 years of champions, the NHL will likely retire the top band of winners to the Hall of Fame in 1993, leaving four engraved bands and a blank new one for future winners. Lord Stanley never dreamed his $50 trophy would become a jewel, but it's insured for $75,000 today. To players and would-be winners, it's a priceless treasure. □□

BEAUFORT'S SCALE OF WIND SPEEDS

"Used Mostly at Sea but of Help to all who are interested in the Weather"

A scale of wind velocity was devised by Admiral Sir Francis Beaufort of the British Navy in 1806. The numbers 0 to 12 were arranged by Beaufort to indicate the strength of the wind from a calm, force 0, to a hurricane, force 12. This adaptation of Beaufort's scale is used by the U.S. National Weather Service.

FORCE	DESCRIPTION	STATUTE MILES PER HOUR
0	Calm	less than 1
1	Light air	1 to 3
2	Light breeze	4 to 7
3	Gentle breeze	8 to 12
4	Moderate breeze	13 to 18
5	Fresh breeze	19 to 24
6	Strong breeze	25 to 31
7	Moderate gale	32 to 38
8	Fresh gale	39 to 46
9	Strong gale	47 to 54
10	Whole gale	55 to 63
11	Storm	64 to 75
12	Hurricane	more than 75

GET IN ON THE PROFITS OF
SMALL ENGINE SERVICE AND REPAIR
START YOUR OWN MONEY MAKING BUSINESS & BEAT INFLATION!

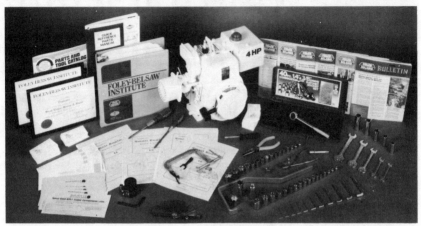

**You get all this Professional equipment with your course,
PLUS 4 H.P. Engine... ALL YOURS TO KEEP... All at NO EXTRA COST.**

Work part time, full time right at home. In just a short time, you can be ready to join one of the fastest growing industries in America... an industry where qualified men are making from **$25.00 to $30.00 per hour.** Because the small engine industry has grown so quickly, an acute shortage of qualified Small Engine Professionals exists throughout the country. When you see how many small engines are in use today, it's easy to understand why qualified men command such high prices — as much as $49.95 for a simple tune-up that takes less than an hour.

65-million small engines are in service today!

That's right — there are over sixty-five million 2-cycle and 4-cycle small engines in service across the U.S.A.! With fully accredited and approved Foley-Belsaw training, you can soon have the skill and knowledge to make top money servicing these engines. Homeowners and businessmen will seek you out and pay you well to service and repair their lawn mowers, tillers, edgers, pow-

er rakes, garden tractors, chain saws, mini-bikes, go-carts, snowmobiles... the list is almost endless.

No experience necessary.

We guide you every step of the way, including tested and proven instructions on how to get business, what to charge, how to get free advertising, where to get supplies wholesale... all the 'tricks of the trade'... all the inside facts you need to assure success right from the start.

Send today for FREE facts!

You risk nothing by accepting this offer to find out how Foley-Belsaw training can give you the skills you need to increase your income in a high-profit, recession-proof business of your own.

Just fill in and mail coupon below (or send postcard) to receive full information and details by return mail. DO IT TODAY!

FOLEY-BELSAW INSTITUTE
6301 Equitable Rd., Dept. 52122
Kansas City, Mo. 64120

NO OBLIGATION... NO SALESMAN WILL CALL
RUSH COUPON TODAY FOR THIS FACT-FILLED
FREE BOOKLET!

Tells how you quickly train to be your own boss in a profitable Spare time or Full time business of your own PLUS complete details on our 30 DAY NO RISK Trial Offer!

FOLEY-BELSAW INSTITUTE
6301 EQUITABLE RD., DEPT. 52122
KANSAS CITY, MO. 64120

☐ YES, please send me the FREE booklet that gives full details about starting my own business in Small Engine Repair. I understand there is no obligation and that no salesman will call.

NAME _____

ADDRESS _____

CITY _____

STATE _____ ZIP _____

H O W   T O   B E C O M E   A
WORLD RECORD
HOLDER

Most people think Ashrita Furman is nuts. In fact, this guy just might be one of the nuttiest people on earth. Still, he does have his very own category in the *Guinness Book of World Records.* There he is in the 1990 edition on page 311, under "Versatility" — pogo-sticking, juggling, jumping rope, rowing, milk-bottle-balancing — grinning triumphantly, looking famous. All told, since he began 13 years ago, he's set 32 official records; nine of them stand in the 1992 edition (see 126). Nutty or not, Ashrita Furman apparently knows a thing or two about this business of achievement.

The question is, How does he do it? What does it take? Let's face it. We've all spent our share of time contemplating the possibility of becoming famous for *something.* But by now you may have given up your dream of dodging deftly past the defense for the winning touchdown. You've abandoned the possibility of warbling your way to success as a country music star. And you never really looked that good in a tutu. What else is there?

Ashrita Furman, record holder among record holders, just might have the answer: It may be that you simply haven't found the right outlet for your talents — or, more accurately, maybe you haven't found the right talents. Take the *Guinness Book,* for example. This collection of world records and unusual human feats is one route to fame — or a few lines of it, at least. It's second only to the Bible in number of copies sold, it's updated every year, and unlike the Bible, anyone can get in. Even you.

Ashrita, a 5'10", 165-pound health-food-store manager from Queens, New York, insists there's nothing special about him. "Anybody has the capability," he says. In fact, he loves it when people break his records. "It just inspires me to do better." Well, there it is: an invitation to break the records of the world-record-holding champion himself. He even offers some tips for success based on his past experience. Study them carefully. He knows what he's talking about.

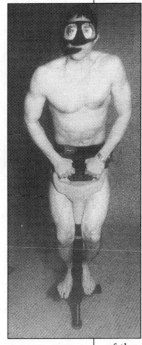

Ashrita tried for the underwater pogo-stick jumping record in 1986. He made 3,303 jumps in a pool in 3 hours and 20 minutes.

BY SUKI CASANAVE

Motivation

First of all, you need the right initiation experience. For Ashrita, a self-described former wimp once destined for life as a lawyer, it all started with a bike race. For 24 hours Ashrita rode, along with thousands of others, around and around Central Park. Unlike most of the others, he pedaled 405 miles, coming in third overall, a remarkable feat, especially given the fact that he'd hardly trained at all. "I wasn't in great shape physically," says Ashrita, "so obviously it had to be something much deeper."

Ashrita credits his success to a combination of meditation and sheer determination. As part of his study of Eastern philosophy with teacher Sri Chinmoy, Ashrita, whose given name is Keith, received his new name, which means "protected by God" — not a bad appellation given the grueling, and occasionally life-threatening, stunts he has undertaken. While he admits that some of his feats draw more laughter than awe, each one, he says, is a challenge. Each physical obstacle is a means to transcendence of self. The bike race was only the beginning.

Find the Right Activity

One time early in his career of record-breaking, Ashrita managed to juggle 100,000 times in a row, drawing an admiring crowd as he stood in Grand Central Station. Pleased with his creativity, he submitted his record to the *Guinness Book,* only to find that they wouldn't accept it because the category didn't exist. Since then, he's managed to set some unusually creative records (page 126), but he advises new record breakers to stick to the established categories.

Know the Rules

The second time Ashrita tried to get into the book, he went after the pogo-sticking record for the most continuous number of jumps. He completed 100,000 jumps in a record 13 hours, and then, as if that weren't enough, he continued. He actually jumped for 24 hours, only to find that the occasional rests he took after each hour were longer than the legal time allowed. The record was void. Not an encouraging start.

Choose Things You Love

Ashrita's all-time favorite record is one he set in Japan, where he pogo-sticked up and down the foothills of Mount Fuji for 11½ miles. "It was exhilarating, and the Japanese people loved it," says Ashrita. "Of course, someone eventually broke my record on flat land — they did 12 miles. But I broke it right back again and did 13." The record for continuous clapping, on the other hand, just wasn't worth defending. "I did it for 50 hours — 140 claps a minute audible at 100 yards. Eventually somebody broke my record," says Ashrita, "but it was just too boring to do again."

Don't Forget Media Coverage

This is an important part of the verification process. (You must also have official witnesses who are not friends.) "They can't send fact checkers all over the world," says Ashrita, "so they expect you to provide some proof." But it can be hard to attract press attention. The key is to surprise them. If you're going for the deep-knee-bend record, for example, don't just do it in a gym. "It's kind of hard to get anybody to come watch a guy stand and squat for hours on end," says Ashrita, who figured what he needed was a piano. He rented a baby grand, got a friend to play, and he stood on top and huffed his way to another record.

You may not, of course, always want media coverage. During the somersaulting record, for example, when *People* magazine was there to cover the story, along with lots of local newspaper and TV crews, Ashrita was so nauseated after the first two miles, he thought he'd have to quit. Another tip: don't eat four slices of pizza before attempting to somersault for 12 miles.

Moral Support

Just because you can't have friends as official witnesses doesn't mean they can't come along and cheer you on. Sometimes they may even be able to save your life. When Ashrita decided to somersault his way along the entire 12.5-mile route of Paul Revere's midnight ride between Charlestown (in Boston) and Lexington (that's 8,341 somersaults), friends walked alongside to keep him from getting run over by traffic.

Occasionally a police escort may be more appropriate — if you decide, for example, to row along the New Jersey Turnpike from New York City to Philadelphia. Ashrita's rowing feat began on the Staten Island Bridge as a policeman sang, "Row, row, row your boat," over the loudspeaker on his car. Seven hours later, sailing along on his rowing machine with wheels, he arrived in the city of Philadelphia, having been escorted by the police force in every town along the way.

Choose Appropriate Workout Conditions

Although Ashrita's not on any sort of rigid training schedule, there are times when he must put aside all pride in pursuit of his goal — well, almost all pride. "People already think I'm crazy," he points out. "What do you think they'd say if they saw me out there somersaulting around a track?" The master tumbler trains for his somersaulting records in the dark of night on a 200-meter dirt track at his old high school. He wears a helmet and a strip of foam to protect his backbone, but comes home covered with mud and grit.

Ashrita set a world record (since surpassed) in 1982 when he completed 33,000 jumping jacks in 7 hours, 32 minutes, and 28 seconds.

When Ashrita decided to try to pogostick to the top of the Canadian National

The record for continuous clapping just wasn't worth defending. "I did it for 50 hours — 140 claps a minute audible at 100 yards. Eventually somebody broke my record, but it was just too boring to do again."

– courtesy AP/Worldwide Photos

GETTING BALD?
You May Not Have To!
Try This – Results Guaranteed!

HOUSTON, Texas – While chances of growing hair on a bald head are very slim, you can now at least save and thicken the hair you still have without the risk and cost of dangerous drugs, **or, it costs you nothing.**

A way has been found to reduce and control excessive hair loss caused by the acid-laden sebum discharged by the sebaceous glands in the scalp. This maintains the hair loss to where it is minimal, helps stop or at least slow down the thinning, balding process, thickens the hair, and helps promote natural, normal hair growth.

A survey of this system was completed by 45 dermatologists across the country; and, a study was completed by two medical schools which showed that 95% of the subjects reduced and maintained their hair loss to where it was minimal in just 60 days or less.

If you have one or more of the following symptoms, sebum could be the cause of your excessive hair loss: **oily, greasy forehead; dandruff, dry or oily; itchy scalp; excessively dry or oily hair, and hair that pulls out easily on top of your head.**

Experts believe that the majority of cases of excessive hair fall and baldness are the beginning and more fully developed stages of male pattern baldness and cannot be helped.

However, if your excessive hair loss is caused or affected by the discharge of acid-laden sebum, you certainly can be helped by this technology developed by Loesch Laboratory Consultants, Inc., who have been distributing quality hair, scalp and skin products since 1951.

This scientific hair care system has proven so successful, the firm invites you to try it for 30 days, at their risk, and see for yourself. So, if you have sebum symptoms and want to stop excessive hair loss and thicken your hair... now is the time to do something about it, before it's too late.

For more information write to Loesch Laboratory Consultants, Inc., Dept. 9, **or call toll free 1-800-231-7157, 24 hours.**

If you want to save time and get started saving your hair, send in the 30 day trial coupon with a 100% unconditional money back guarantee, or, order toll free and use a credit card (Visa or MasterCard). No C.O.D.'s please. Adv. ©

Railways (CN) tower in Toronto, the logical place to train was the five flights of stairs in his father's office building. "People would pass me as I sweated and hopped my way up those stairs. Usually they were too afraid to say anything," says Ashrita. Occasionally they'd attempt a polite question: "Ah, is that good exercise?"

Be Creative (Eventually)

At some point, you may want to get more daring and creative. You could try something like the Pogo-Sticking-Among-Piranhas-in-the-Amazon-River stunt, which Ashrita dreamed up a few years ago. "I know it sounds totally kooky," he says, "but I just wanted to do something different." Of course, he practiced first, in a pool and then in San Francisco Bay, where he nearly drowned. But there was no stopping him. Before long he was off to Peru in search of water that was relatively piranha free. He traveled through the jungle, by plane, speedboat, and dugout canoe, got plenty of advice from the locals, did some serious meditation to overcome his fear, and then pogo-sticked his way to another record: three hours and 40 minutes jumping up and down in eight feet of water.

Don't Quit Your Day Job

One thing to remember about fame: it doesn't always bring fortune. Ashrita makes no money for his fantastic feats, relying instead on his job as a store manager to support himself. He also has a job as the organizer of worldwide trips for his meditation group. This position, although it doesn't draw a salary, has an important benefit: The organizer flies for free. That means plenty of exotic spots in which to set new world records.

Always Have Another Goal

"The great thing about this," says Ashrita of his record-breaking career, "is that it's one adventure after another. There's no limit to what we can do. I found another record I'm really excited about — running a marathon wearing a 40-pound pack on my back and combat boots." Sound like fun? Perhaps something with a bit of cultural flair would appeal more: Six years after his grueling 12-mile somersaulting stunt, Ashrita says he's ready for the Great Wall of China. He's also considering deep knee bends in quicksand.

See, there are plenty of things to choose from. All you need are a few records that get you really excited, revved up, and ready to roll — or run or juggle or row or jump — and off you go. Grab your pogo stick and start practicing. □ □

The 1992 edition of the *Guinness Book of World Records* lists nine records held by Ashrita Furman (eight of them are athletic):

1 Most completed games of hopscotch in 24 hours: 307 *(Zurich, Switzerland; April 5-6, 1991)*

2 Greatest distance walked with full pint of milk on head: 43.7 miles *(New York, New York, park; August 12, 1990)*

3 Greatest distance for pogo-stick jumping: 13.06 miles *(New York, New York; in 5 hours 23 minutes; September 15, 1989)*

4 Most continuous forward somersaults: 8,341 *(12 miles 390 yards; Lexington to Charlestown, Massachusetts; in 10 hours 30 minutes; April 30, 1986)*

5 Most squats in one hour: 2,550 *(Philadelphia, Pennsylvania; November 3, 1989)*

6 Most burpees in one hour: 1,551 *(New York, New York; March 13, 1990)*

7 Fastest time for a marathon (26 miles 385 yards) while juggling three objects: 3 hours, 22 minutes, 32.5 seconds *(1988)*

8 Longest distance while juggling three objects: 50 miles *(in 8 hours, 52 minutes, 7 seconds; 1989)*

9 Most expensive wreath: $3,500 *(New York, New York; 10,000 flowers; 1983)*

GENERAL WEATHER FORECAST
1992 - 1993

(For details see regional forecasts beginning on page 130.)

NOVEMBER THROUGH MARCH is expected to be quite variable over the country, with temperatures averaging slightly above normal in New England and from the middle Great Plains across to the Southwest and much of California; well above normal from the Middle Atlantic states westward to the lower Great Lakes and all across the Southeast and West; and below normal from Minnesota west to the Northwest and northern California. Precipitation may be quite variable with below-normal amounts all down the Atlantic seaboard, in the central and southern Great Plains, and across the southwest; above-normal west of the Appalachian mountains through the Mississippi and Ohio River valleys, and from the western Great Lakes and upper Great Plains across to the Northwest. Snowfall may be below normal across southern regions, from the mountains of southern California across the lower Great Plains through the Ohio River valley and the Middle Atlantic states; near normal from the southern Sierra Nevada mountains across the southern Rockies through the central Great Plains, northern New York, and New England. Possibly well above normal amounts may fall on the northern Sierra Nevada, Rockies, and Cascades and across the northern Great Plains and northern Great Lakes.

APRIL THROUGH OCTOBER: Spring will be warmer than normal east of the Mississippi River except for northern New England, the extreme northern region of the Pacific coast, and along the Gulf. The region west of the Mississippi River will be cooler than normal and considerably colder in the Great Basin and Southwest. Most of the country will experience above-normal precipitation except for the Pacific Coast, the Middle Atlantic region, and the lower Great Plains to the southern Ohio Valley. Heavy precipitation in the central and upper Great Plains and in the South will cause flooding, while the combination of above-normal snowfall and heavy springtime precipitation in the southern Great Basin may well result in further increases in the level of the Great Salt Lake.

Summer will be warmer than normal over most of the region east and north of the Mississippi and Ohio rivers, along the Gulf coast, the southern Great Basin, and the Northwest, with the rest of the country being cooler than normal. Above-normal precipitation is expected in the Middle and Southern Atlantic states, the western Great Plains, and in eastern New England; the rest of the country will receive below-normal amounts. Portions of the Northeast may experience drought conditions until late August, when relief is expected.

Early fall should be cooler than normal east of the Rockies and warmer west, with central regions quite close to normal and even slightly above in some sections. Only northern New England, the Middle and Southern Atlantic states, the southern Great Plains, and southern Texas will have above-normal precipitation, while the rest of the country will be drier than normal, particularly in the eastern Great Plains, the lower Ohio Valley, and the Pacific Northwest.

U.S. WEATHER REGIONS

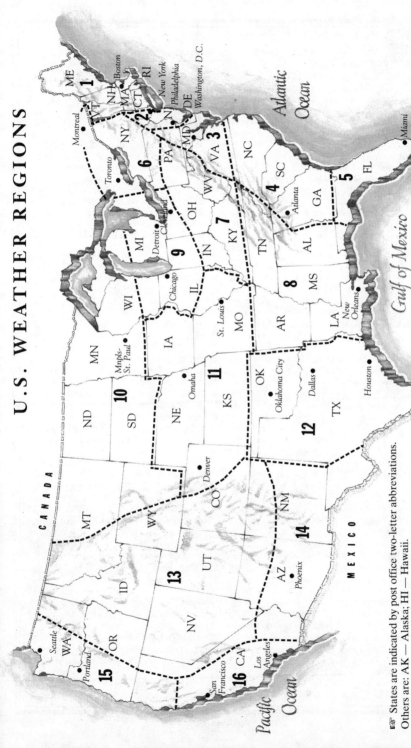

☞ States are indicated by post office two-letter abbreviations. Others are: AK — Alaska; HI — Hawaii.

☞ Weather predictions for each of the numbered regions shown begin on page 130.

NEW ENGLAND

For regional boundaries, see map page 129.

SUMMARY: *November through March is expected to have variable temperatures, averaging close to normal in the south but slightly above normal in the north. December through February will be warmer than normal over the whole region. Precipitation should be below normal in the south and east, but near normal north. Snowfall may be 20 percent below normal. Following a cold wave early in the second week, November will be mild until shortly before Thanksgiving, when cold with frequent precipitation should prevail through mid-December. Except for a snowstorm at the beginning of December and another before mid-January, precipitation will be frequent but light, and cold and mild spells will alternate until mid-February. Wintry conditions with frequent and heavy snows should begin after mid-February and continue until the spring equinox.*

April and May will see cool periods partially offset by warm spells, while precipitation will be frequent but light, except for a storm near mid-April. Sunny, bright days are expected from late May through June. East-central sections may be fairly dry. Summer temperatures will be close to normal; rainfall will be light except for storms early in July and August and from a possible offshore hurricane at the end of August. September will be cool. October will be generally sunny and warm, with near-drought conditions except for rainfall at the middle and end of the month.

NOV. 1992: Temp. 44° (1° below avg.); Precip. 3" (1" below avg.; avg. north). 1-2 Sunny & mild. 3-6 Rain; clearing. 7-10 Rain, snow north; cold. 11-15 Clearing, mild; showers west. 16-18 Seasonable; rain. 19-22 Sprinkles. 23-25 Cold, snowstorm north. 26-28 Flurries. 29-30 Freezing rain.

DEC. 1992: Temp. 36° (3° above avg.; 6° above north); Precip. 2.5" (1.5" below avg.). 1-3 Snow, then rain. 4-6 Cloudy, cold. 7-10 Light snow. 11-13 Severe cold. 14-16 Mild & rainy. 17-20 Cold. 21-26 Sunny, very mild. 27-28 Cold wave, snow. 29-31 Mild, rain.

JAN. 1993: Temp. 34° (5° above avg., 8° above north); Precip. 3" (0.5" below avg.; 1" above north). 1-4 Rain ending; clear, cold. 5-9 Thaw, light rain. 10-13 Snow, then clear & cold. 14-16 Light snow, seasonable. 17-21 Rain, snow north; mild. 22-24 Cold, snow. 25-29 Freezing rain, snow north. 30-31 Sunny, mild.

FEB. 1993: Temp. 30° (1° below avg.; 2° above north); Precip. 4.5" (0.5" above avg.). 1-2 Clear, mild. 3-5 Snowstorm. 6-9 Cloudy, light snow. 10-12 Cold snap, clear. 13-15 Rain, snow north; milder. 16-17 Cloudy, seasonable. 18-20 Heavy snowstorm. 21-23 Snowy, seasonable. 24-25 Severe cold. 26-28 Snowstorm.

MAR. 1993: Temp. 33° (6° below avg.); Precip. 3" (1" below avg.; 1" above north). 1-2 Cloudy, frigid. 3-5 Snow, seasonable. 6-8 Cold snap, cloudy. 9-11 Sunny, mild. 12-14 Snow, heavy north. 15-18 Cloudy & cold; snow. 19-22 Cold, snowy. 23-25 Clear, milder. 26-28 Storm, snow mountains. 29-31 Sunny, normal.

APR. 1993: Temp. 47° (1.5° below avg.); Precip. 2.5" (1" below avg.). 1-3 Rain, snow inland; cold. 4-5 Sunny, mild. 6-9 Rain, warm. 10-15 Cold; showers. 16-18 Rain, snow inland. 19-22 Sunny, warm. 23-25 Heavy rain, seasonable. 26-28 Cold, light rain. 29-30 Rain, light north.

MAY 1993: Temp. 56.5° (2° below avg.; avg. north); Precip. 1" (2" below avg.). 1-4 Rain, turning cold. 5-8 Sprinkles, some sun. 9-10 Sunny, warm. 11-14 Rain; cold. 15-17 Sunny, warm; sprinkles north. 18-20 Cloudy & cool. 21-23 Cold, heavy rain. 24-26 Clear & warm. 27-31 Rainy; clearing north.

JUNE 1993: Temp. 70° (2° above avg.); Precip. 1.5" (1.5" below avg.; 0.5" above west). 1-4 Heavy rain, cool. 5-8 Sunny & warm; rain. 9-13 Sunny, very warm. 14-16 Cold, rain. 17-20 Showers, some sun; seasonable. 21-24 Cold, sprinkles. 25-27 Clear, warm; showers north. 28-30 Drizzle; sunny & warm north.

JULY 1993: Temp. 73° (0.5° below avg.; 1° above north). Precip. 1.5" (1.5" below avg.). 1-3 Rain; seasonable. 4-5 Sun & showers. 6-9 Thunderstorms. 10-13 Clear, hot. 14-17 Showers; cooler. 18-20 Cloudy, mild. 21-22 Warm, showers. 23-26 Cool, showers, then warming. 27-31 Sprinkles.

AUG. 1993: Temp. 71° (1° below avg.); Precip. 3" (Avg.). 1-2 Sunny, warm. 3-5 Rain; cool. 6-10 Cloudy, showers. 11-14 Sunny, warm. 15-17 Cloudy, sprinkles; mild. 18-20 Clear, warm; showers west. 21-24 Heavy rain from offshore hurricane, cool. 25-27 Clearing, warming. 28-31 Warm, showers.

SEPT. 1993: Temp. 61.5° (3° below avg.); Precip. 1" (2" below avg.; 1" above inland). 1-5 Rain; cool. 6-9 Showers. 10-12 Sunny, warm. 13-17 Showers, heavy west; cold. 18-20 Sunny & seasonable; showers west. 21-23 Sunny, few showers; cool. 24-30 Cold; showers.

OCT. 1993: Temp. 54.5° (Avg.; 1.5° above inland); Precip. 2" (1" below avg.). 1-2 Cloudy, mild. 3-7 Sunny, warm. 8-9 Cool, showers. 10-13 Clearing, warming. 14-17 Heavy rain, cold. 18-24 Sunny, warm days. 25-28 Cold wave, rain. 29-31 Clear, cold; light snow north.

1993   OLD FARMER'S ALMANAC   131

For regional boundaries, see map page 129.

SUMMARY: *November through March is expected to be milder and drier than normal with below-normal snowfall. November will be mild and dry except for a cold wave during the second week; a colder and wetter period late in the month will last until mid-December. Frequent mild spells interspersed with brief cold waves will persist through January and early February. Precipitation will be frequent but lighter than normal. Wintry conditions will then set in and persist through March, bringing well above normal precipitation and snowfall.*

April through June should be colder and drier than normal. Below-normal temperatures in April and early May will be partially offset by brief warm spells in April, after which more springlike weather should prevail. Precipitation will be frequent but generally light.

July through September should be cooler and wetter than normal. Brief hot spells early in July and August will be more than offset by cool and rainy periods through to late September, with the possibility of an offshore tropical storm in mid-September.

Warm spells in early and late October will result in a warmer than normal month; significant rainfall is expected only at the middle and end of the month.

NOV. 1992: Temp. 47.5° (0.5° above avg.); Precip. 1.5" (2" below avg.). 1-4 Rain, turning heavy; mild. 5-7 Rain, colder; then clearing. 8-10 Sprinkles, cold. 11-15 Clear & pleasant. 16-18 Rain. 19-21 Sunny, pleasant. 22-24 Cold wave, light rain. 25-28 Sunny; warm with cold snap. 29-30 Rain, snow north; cold.

DEC. 1992: Temp. 38.5° (2.5° above avg.); Precip. 2.5" (0.8" below avg.). 1-2 Cold, snow. 3-5 Some sun, seasonable. 6-8 Cold wave, snow. 9-10 Clearing, warming. 11-14 Cold wave, flurries. 15-17 Rain, mild. 18-21 Cloudy & cold. 22-25 Mild, rain, then clearing. 26-27 Mild, rain. 28-29 Cold snap. 30-31 Rain, mild.

JAN. 1993: Temp. 39° (8° above avg.); Precip. 2" (1" below avg.). 1 Rain ending. 2-5 Sunny, cold. 6-9 Light rain, then clearing; mild. 10-13 Rain turning to snow, cold. 14-15 Mild, rain. 16-17 Freezing rain. 18-20 Mild, sprinkles. 21-22 Freezing rain. 23-25 Cloudy & cold. 26-27 Sunny, milder. 28-31 Rain, warm.

FEB. 1993: Temp. 35° (2° above avg.); Precip. 5" (2" above avg.). 1-6 Rain, heavy snow north. 7-9 Sunny, cold. 10-12 Freezing rain, then clear & cold. 13-16 Milder, rain, then clearing. 17-20 Heavy rain, snowstorm north. 21-23 Clearing, seasonable. 24-27 Cold; snow north, rain south. 28 Clear, seasonable.

MAR. 1993: Temp. 35° (6° below avg.); Precip. 3" (1" below avg.). 1-4 Clear, cold. 5-6 Rain & snow. 7-8 Clear, cold. 9-11 Sunny & mild. 12-15 Rain, then clear & cold. 16-18 Rain, seasonable. 19-21 Clear & cold. 22-25 Cold, rain & snow. 26-28 Rain. 29-31 Rainy, seasonable.

APR. 1993: Temp. 49° (3° below avg.); Precip. 1.5" (2.5" below avg.). 1-2 Rain, mild. 3-4 Clear, cold. 5-9 Light rain, warming. 10-14 Sunny, cold; sprinkles. 15-17 Rain, seasonable. 18-20 Cold. 21-23 Clear & warm. 24-26 Cool, rain; then clearing. 27-30 Cold & rainy.

MAY 1993: Temp. 59° (3° below avg.); Precip. 2.5" (1" below avg.). 1-2 Rain, cool. 3-6 Cold, rain. 7-8 Sunny & pleasant. 9-11 Light rain, then clear & warm. 12-18 Mild, few showers. 19-21 Rain, cool. 22-24 Cold; rain. 25-26 Clear & warm. 27-31 Cool, rain; then clearing.

JUNE 1993: Temp. 69.5° (1.5° below avg.); Precip. 3" (0.5" below avg.). 1-5 Intermittent rain, cool. 6-7 Sunny, warm. 8-9 Heavy rain. 10-14 Clear, hot. 15-19 Cool, showers. 20-21 Clearing, seasonable. 22-25 Rain, cool. 26-27 Clear. 28-30 Sprinkles, turning hot.

JULY 1993: Temp. 74° (2° below avg.); Precip. 5" (1" above avg.). 1-2 Clear & hot. 3-6 Sprinkles, seasonable. 7-10 Rain. 11-13 Sunny, warm. 14-15 Rain, cool. 16-17 Seasonable. 18-20 Showers, cool. 21-23 Sunny, warm. 24-27 Rain, then clear. 28-31 Showers.

AUG. 1993: Temp. 73.5° (2° below avg.); Precip. 3" (0.5" below avg.). 1-2 Showers, warm. 3-4 Clear & hot. 5-11 Cool; showers. 12-13 Sunny, warm. 14-16 Light rain, seasonable. 17-22 Clear, warm. 23-24 Heavy rain, cooler. 25-27 Sunny, showers. 28-31 Clear.

SEPT. 1993: Temp. 65.5° (2.5° below avg.); Precip. 4" (0.5" above avg.). 1-5 Rain, warm. 6-9 Clearing, mild; showers. 10-13 Clear & pleasant. 14-17 Possible offshore tropical storm. 18-22 Clearing, mild. 23-26 Scattered light showers. 27-30 Cold wave, sunny.

OCT. 1993: Temp. 58° (1° above avg.); Precip. 2" (1" below avg.). 1-3 Cool & sunny. 4-7 Clear, warm. 8-11 Showers, cool. 12-14 Rain, warming. 15-17 Rain, cool. 18-20 Cloudy & cool. 21-26 Clear & warm. 27-29 Showers, cool. 30-31 Clear & cold.

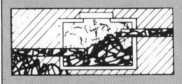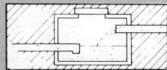

3 MIDDLE ATLANTIC COAST

For regional boundaries, see map page 129.

SUMMARY: *November through March is expected to be warmer and drier than normal, but with great variability from month to month and well below normal snowfall. November will be near normal, with cold spells offset by a warm period at midmonth, while heavy rains the first week will bring normal amounts of precipitation. Frequent warm spells from mid-December to early February, with light precipitation, will be partially offset by frequent cold waves through January. After early February, temperatures may be close to normal; then cold, wet wintry weather, with snow in the north and mountains, will persist through March.*

April through June may be colder and wetter than normal in central and southern sections, but drier than normal in the north. Most of April and early May will be colder than normal, offset by brief mild spells, with frequent but light precipitation. Above-normal rainfall is expected in May and June, and warm spells will relieve the frequent cold waves.

July through September will be cooler and wetter than normal, with cool spells and heavy rains in mid-July, early August, and late September, along with warm rains in early September.

October will average close to normal in temperature and precipitation, with sunny, warm periods early and late in the month and cold, wet periods near midmonth and at the end.

NOV. 1992: Temp. 49° (Avg.); Precip. 3" (Avg.). 1-5 Heavy rain, turning warm. 6-7 Sunny & cold. 8-10 Sprinkles, cold wave. 11-15 Clear & warm. 16-17 Rain, seasonable. 18-20 Clear, mild. 21-23 Cold wave, sprinkles. 24-26 Clear, mild; then cold snap. 27-30 Sunny, then rain & cold.

DEC. 1992: Temp. 41° (2° above avg.); Precip. 2" (1" above avg.). 1-3 Rain, milder. 4-8 Cold; few sprinkles, snow north. 9-11 Sunny, warming; rain. 12-14 Cold wave, snow. 15-17 Milder, rain. 18-21 Cloudy, cold. 22-24 Mild, light rain. 25-27 Unseasonably mild; showers. 28-29 Cold snap. 30-31 Rain, mild.

JAN. 1993: Temp. 44° (9° above avg.); Precip. 1.5" (1" below avg.). 1-2 Clear, mild. 3-5 Cold wave. 6-7 Rain, seasonable. 8-10 Clear. 11-13 Cold, rain & snow. 14-15 Clear, warm. 16-20 Cold, flurries, then sunny & mild. 21-24 Rain, snow north; cold. 25-27 Clear, warm; showers north. 28-30 Showers, warm. 31 Cold.

FEB. 1993: Temp. 40.5° (3° above avg.); Precip. 3" (0.5" above avg.). 1-6 Sleet & snow. 7-9 Clear, cold. 10-12 Rain, snow north, then clearing & cold. 13-14 Rain, milder. 15-16 Sunny, cold nights. 17-19 Rain, snow north. 20-23 Seasonable, sprinkles & flurries. 24-28 Cold, then milder; rain, snow north.

MAR. 1993: Temp. 41° (5° below avg.); Precip. 3.5" (0.5" above avg.). 1-3 Cold, flurries. 4-5 Seasonable, showers. 6-10 Clear; cold, then mild. 11-13 Rain, heavy north. 14-15 Cold. 16-19 Rain, snow north. 20-23 Cold & rainy, then clearing. 24-27 Heavy rain, snowstorm north & west. 28-31 Warming; rain north.

APR. 1993: Temp. 53° (3.5° below avg.); Precip. 1.5" (1" below avg.). 1-2 Rain. 3-5 Cold, sunny. 6-9 Rain, warm. 10-14 Cold; sprinkles. 15-17 Rain, snow mountains; turning colder. 18-19

Clear & cold. 20-23 Warm, showers. 24-26 Showers, cool. 27-30 Rain, warming.

MAY 1993: Temp. 65° (1° below avg.); Precip. 5" (1.5" above avg.). 1-3 Showers; sunny south. 4-7 Rain, heavy south; cool. 8-11 Few showers, hot. 12-13 Sunny, cool. 14-18 Sunny & warm, showers south. 19-21 Heavy showers. 22-24 Rain, cold. 25-26 Sunny, warm. 27-31 Showers; warm.

JUNE 1993: Temp. 73° (1° below avg.); Precip. 4" (0.5" above avg.). 1-3 Rain, cool; then clear & warm. 4-10 Rain, then clearing & warm. 11-13 Clear & hot. 14-15 Rain, mild. 16-20 Clear & cool, then showers. 21-22 Sunny, seasonable. 23-25 Rain, cool. 26-30 Clear, hot.

JULY 1993: Temp. 77° (2° below avg.); Precip. 5.5" (1.5" above avg.). 1-2 Clear & hot. 3-6 Showers, then clear & warm. 7-9 Rain, mild. 10-12 Clear & pleasant. 13-15 Rain, cool. 16-17 Sprinkles. 18-21 Rain, cool. 22-23 Sunny & warm. 24-25 Rain. 26-31 Showers, cool.

AUG. 1993: Temp. 75.5° (2.5° below avg.); Precip. 6.5" (3" above avg.). 1-5 Showers, then sunny & hot. 6-7 Heavy rain, cool. 8-13 Sprinkles, then clear. 14-16 Light rain, warm. 17-22 Sunny, warm. 23-24 Heavy rain. 25-27 Sunny, cooler; then rain, heavy south. 28-31 Clear & warm.

SEPT. 1993: Temp. 69.5° (2° below avg.); Precip. 5" (2" above avg.). 1-5 Rain, warm. 6-7 Showers, cooler. 8-11 Clearing, cold. 12-16 Heavy rain, seasonable. 17-19 Cloudy, cool; rain north. 20-23 Sunny, cool; few showers. 24-26 Rain. 27-30 Cold.

OCT. 1993: Temp. 60° (0.5° above avg.); Precip. 3" (Avg.). 1-3 Clear & cold. 4-7 Sunny, warm. 8-11 Cloudy, cool, then showers. 12-16 Rain, mild. 17-19 Cloudy & cool; clear & warm south. 20-23 Clear & pleasant. 24-27 Heavy rain, seasonable. 28-31 Showers, cool.

PIEDMONT & SOUTHEAST COAST

For regional boundaries, see map page 129.

SUMMARY: *November through March is expected to be considerably warmer and drier than normal, with well below normal snowfall. Cool and warm spells will alternate in November and December, with infrequent rainfall from the second week of November until late December. Temperatures will swing between normal and well above normal from late December through January, and much of February; precipitation will be below normal. March, however, will be colder than normal, with near-normal precipitation and above-normal snowfall.*

April through June should be close to normal in temperature but with below-normal precipitation. April will be highly variable with frequent cold waves and relatively dry, particularly in southern sections. May will be warm and wet in coastal and southern sections, but drier west. June, near normal in temperature and rainfall, will close with a hot, dry spell.

July through September should be cooler than normal due to cool periods in July and August and a cool, wet spell in early September from a possible hurricane. July will have frequent heavy rains; August will be fairly dry; September will be near normal in precipitation.

October will be dominated by fair weather, but watch for a possible hurricane from Florida toward the end of the month.

NOV. 1992: Temp. 49° (2° below avg.); Precip. 4" (1" above avg.). 1-5 Heavy rain, warming. 6-8 Clearing, cool. 9-11 Clear; cold nights, frost. 12-16 Sunny, few sprinkles; warm. 17-19 Light rain, seasonable. 20-23 Cold wave. 24-25 Clear & mild. 26-28 Cold snap. 29-30 Rain, locally heavy; cold.

DEC. 1992: Temp. 45.5° (2° above avg.); Precip. 2" (1.5" below avg.). 1-2 Clear, warming. 3-4 Rain, warm. 5-10 Sunny, few sprinkles; cold nights. 11-14 Rain, then cloudy & cold. 15-17 Rain, warm. 18-21 Cold wave; heavy rain, then clearing. 22-27 Light rain, mild. 28-29 Cold. 30-31 Rain, mild.

JAN. 1993: Temp. 49° (10° above avg.); Precip. 2" (1.5" below avg.). 1-5 Clear; turning cold. 6-7 Warming, showers north. 8-11 Showers, warm. 12-13 Cold snap. 14-19 Intermittent rain, mild. 20-23 Heavy rain. 24-26 Sunny, seasonable. 27-30 Clear & warm. 31 Rain.

FEB. 1993: Temp. 47° (5° above avg.); Precip. 1" (2.5" below avg.). 1-4 Cold wave, rain. 5-7 Sunny & warm. 8-10 Clear, cold. 11-14 Rain, heavy south. 15-16 Cloudy, seasonable. 17-19 Mild & rainy. 20-25 Sunny, seasonable days, cold nights. 26-28 Rain, heavy south.

MAR. 1993: Temp. 48.5° (2° below avg.); Precip. 3.5" (1" below avg.). 1-3 Sunny days, cold nights. 4-5 Heavy rain. 6-8 Cold wave. 9-12 Heavy rain; mild days, cold nights. 13-15 Clear & mild. 16-19 Rain, then clearing. 20-23 Showers, seasonable. 24-26 Cold; rain, heavy north. 27-31 Sunny, few showers; hot.

APR. 1993: Temp. 57° (3° below avg.); Precip. 2" (1" below avg.). 1-2 Rain, cold. 3-5 Cold wave, sunny. 6-9 Showers, locally heavy; seasonable. 10-12 Cold snap. 13-15 Sunny & pleasant. 16-20 Cold wave, few showers. 21-

23 Sunny, warm. 24-26 Cool, showers. 27-28 Clear & warm. 29-30 Rain, heavy south.

MAY 1993: Temp. 70.5° (3° above avg.); Precip. 2" (1.5" below avg.). 1-3 Clearing & warming. 4-7 Heavy rain, seasonable. 8-10 Clear, hot. 11-13 Sunny, showers north; seasonable. 14-16 Hot, showers. 17-19 Heavy rain, milder. 20-23 Sunny, showers; warm. 24-26 Rain south; cool. 27-31 Sunny, hot; showers north.

JUNE 1993: Temp. 76° (1° above avg.); Precip. 3" (0.3" below avg.). 1-3 Showers; warm. 4-8 Heavy showers; sun. 9-11 Clear, cooler. 12-15 Rain, seasonable. 16-17 Clear & warm. 18-20 Showers. 21-23 Sunny, warm. 24-26 Few showers. 27-30 Clear & hot.

JULY 1993: Temp. 77.5° (1° below avg.); Precip. 7" (3" above avg.). 1-2 Sunny, hot. 3-5 Rain north, sun south; seasonable. 6-10 Showers & sun. 11-14 Rain; milder. 15-20 Rain, seasonable. 21-24 Sunny & hot; few showers. 25-26 Rain, milder. 27-31 Sunny, then rain.

AUG. 1993: Temp. 75.5° (2° below avg.); Precip. 2" (1.5" below avg.). 1-2 Rain. 3-6 Sunny & hot; showers. 7-14 Clear, mild. 15-19 Few showers. 20-23 Showers; hot. 24-27 Showers north, sunny south. 28-31 Showers south.

SEPT. 1993: Temp. 71° (1° below avg.); Precip. 3.5" (Avg.). 1-5 Rain, seasonable. 6-8 Clear & hot. 9-13 Possible hurricane with heavy rain; much cooler. 14-18 Few showers; sunny & hot. 19-22 Seasonable, few showers. 23-25 Clear & hot. 26-27 Heavy rain. 28-30 Cooler, clear.

OCT. 1993: Temp. 62.5° (2° above avg.); Precip. 3" (Avg.). 1-4 Cloudy & mild, showers south. 5-7 Sunny & pleasant. 8-11 Mild, showers. 12-14 Light rain. 15-22 Clear & pleasant. 23-25 Possible hurricane. 26-28 Light rain, seasonable. 29-31 Clear, warm.

"DO YOU KNOW THESE LITTLE-KNOWN NATURAL HEALING FOODS? WHAT YOUR DOCTOR NEVER TELLS YOU. PLUS, FIVE FOODS YOU SHOULD NEVER BUY."

NEW NATURAL HEALING SECRETS REVEALED!
420 WAYS TO PERFECT HEALTH.

(By Frank K. Wood)

"How many of these little-known health secrets do you know? Could one of them save your health?"

FC&A, a Peachtree City, Georgia, publisher, announced today the release of a new book for the general public, *"Natural Health Secrets Encyclopedia."* In their book, the authors claim many health benefits with full explanations.

▶ Deadly Alzheimer's senility — could a common painkiller prevent this tragedy?

▶ Shed fat without breaking a sweat — drink this all-natural, nutrient-loaded beverage from your supermarket three times a day!

▶ Going deaf? Eating this may help.

▶ When a low-salt diet for high blood pressure can backfire!

▶ How timing breast cancer surgery to the menstrual cycle can mean life or death!

▶ Heart attacks and strokes! How to develop your body's own natural, clot-busting protection.

▶ Joint agony from arthritis? You might break out of your painful prison with this new treatment!

▶ Stop snoring this easy way.

▶ Kill the pain of shingles with this new application of an old remedy!

▶ Mysterious cough? Eat this and halt your hacking!

▶ Weak bladder? How to strengthen it!

▶ This nutrient puts a ceiling on your high blood pressure!

▶ How to read your nails for an instant picture of your health!

▶ Add years to your life? Why fresh make-up and clean clothes make a big difference!

▶ "Skin tags": How to read this early-warning sign of future cancer in time to beat it.

▶ Memory loss? It could be the way you sleep!

▶ Stomach pains? Scared it's ulcers? Painless, new, doctor-approved, at-home treatment for ulcers cures nine out of 10!

▶ Hope for alcoholics — is this amazing mix of nutrients the key to long-term recovery?

▶ "Crucify" your breast cancer risk with this powerful food with the cross-shaped flowers!

▶ How some blood pressure drugs trigger diabetes.

▶ Pump up your weak bones to greater strength this all-natural way!

▶ Trying to kick the smoking habit? Don't be sabotaged by this common part of your daily diet!

▶ Psoriasis getting worse? Stop drinking this!

▶ Check your feet for these diabetes early-warning signs!

▶ Boost your immune system with this quick "killer-cell diet"!

▶ Lung power! This nutrient shields your lungs from cigarette smoke!

▶ Is your vitamin supplement working? A quick test you can make in your kitchen!

Learn all these natural healing secrets. Book includes 420 ways to perfect health. To order a copy, just return this notice with your name and address and a check for $5.99 plus $2.00 shipping and handling to our address: **FC&A, Dept. MOF-93,** 103 Clover Green, Peachtree City, GA 30269. Make checks payable to FC&A. We will send you a copy of *"Natural Health Secrets Encyclopedia"* right away.

Save! Return this notice with $11.98 plus $2.00 for two books. (No extra shipping and handling charges.)

You get a no-time-limit guarantee of satisfaction or your money back.

You must cut out and return this notice with your order. Copies will not be accepted!

IMPORTANT — FREE GIFT OFFER EXPIRES WITHIN 30 DAYS

All orders mailed within 30 days will receive a free gift, <u>guaranteed</u>. Order right away!

FLORIDA

For regional boundaries, see map page 129.

SUMMARY: *November through March is expected to be warmer and drier than normal overall. November will see cold waves early and late in the month with precipitation close to normal. A pleasant first half of December may be followed by cold waves with heavy rains. Most of January and February will be sunny and warm with a few light showers. A cold wave late February may bring a freeze to the north. Variable temperatures and frequent rains will follow in March.*

April through June is expected to average close to normal in temperature but below normal in rainfall overall. April will see several cold waves and storms. A warm, dry first half of May will be followed by a variable, wet second half. The first half of June may be close to normal in temperature before closing with a hot spell; showers will be frequent but light.

July through September may be cooler than normal, with above-normal rainfall. July is expected to be cool and wet except for south-central sections, which will be drier than normal. August will be dry except for a possible tropical storm at the end and continuing into the first days of September. After a second possible onshore hurricane the second week, September should be near normal.

Temperatures will be above normal in October, as will rainfall, although a possible mid-month hurricane could bring an extra 10" of rain to central and northern sections.

NOV. 1992: Temp. 65.5° (3° below avg.); Precip. 1.5" (0.5" below avg.). 1-2 Rain; warming. 3-5 Heavy rain north, light south; warm. 6-11 Clear & pleasant. 12-14 Rain, seasonable. 15-16 Sunny. 17-19 Rain. 20-23 Cold, sunny. 24-28 Clear, variable. 29-30 Cold, rainy.

DEC. 1992: Temp. 64° (1.5° above avg.); Precip. 4" (2" above avg.). 1-3 Clearing, warmer. 4-5 Showers, warm. 6-10 Sunny; warm days, cold nights. 11-13 Showers, seasonable. 14-18 Clear, warm. 19-21 Cold wave, rain. 22-24 Sunny & warm; showers south. 25-28 Cold, showers. 29-31 Rain, warming.

JAN. 1993: Temp. 67° (7° above avg.); Precip. 0.5" (2" below avg.). 1-3 Heavy rain south, light north. 4-6 Partial clearing. 7-11 Light showers, warm. 12-14 Seasonable, clearing. 15-19 Sunny, very warm. 20-23 Few showers, continued warm. 24-26 Sprinkles, seasonable. 27-31 Clear, warm; showers south.

FEB. 1993: Temp. 65° (3.5° above avg.); Precip. 0.5" (2.5" below avg.). 1-7 Clear, warm; sprinkles south. 8-11 Showers. 12-14 Sunny & warm. 15-19 Showers, warm. 20-25 Cold, light frost north. 26-28 Rain, seasonable.

MAR. 1993: Temp. 66° (1° below avg.); Precip. 3" (0.5" below avg.). 1-5 Sunny, variable. 6-8 Cold snap, showers north. 9-12 Heavy rain, warming. 13-14 Cold snap. 15-17 Clear, warm. 18-20 Rain, cool. 21-22 Sunny, cool. 23-26 Rain, warm then cooling. 27-31 Clear, warm.

APR. 1993: Temp. 68° (4° below avg.); Precip. 4" (2.5" above avg.). 1-2 Warm rain. 3-5 Cold snap, possible frost. 6-7 Clear, warming. 8-10 Rain, heavy south; turning cold. 11-12 Cold. 13-17 Clear, warm. 18-21 Cold wave. 22-24 Light rain, warm. 25-27 Clear & cold. 28-30 Rain, seasonable.

MAY 1993: Temp. 78.5° (1.5° above avg.); Precip. 4" (0.5" above avg.). 1-2 Rain, warm. 3-5 Clear, warm; rain north. 6-10 Clear & hot. 11-13 Showers, warm. 14-17 Clear, cool nights. 18-21 Rain, warm. 22-24 Clear & hot. 25-28 Rain, milder. 29-31 Clear & hot.

JUNE 1993: Temp. 83.5° (2.5° above avg.); Precip. 4" (3.5" below avg.). 1-5 Showers, heavy south; scattered north. 6-11 Showers, heavy south; hot. 12-15 Showers, seasonable. 16-21 Mostly clear & seasonable. 22-27 Showers, hot. 28-30 Very hot, few showers.

JULY 1993: Temp. 81.5° (1° below avg.); Precip. 10" (3" above avg.). 1-2 Showers; clear & hot north. 3-6 Showers, hot. 7-11 Rain. 12-15 Showers, milder. 16-18 Few showers, hot. 19-21 Rain, heavy south. 22-24 Sunny, hot. 25-29 Showers, hot. 30-31 Clear & hot.

AUG. 1993: Temp. 82.5° (Avg.); Precip. 2.5" (3.5" below avg.). 1-5 Showers north; sunny & hot south. 6-8 Scattered showers, heavy south. 9-11 Sunny, milder. 12-17 Showers, heavy south; hot. 18-24 Mostly sunny & hot; light rain. 25-29 Rain, heavy central & east. 30-31 Showers, heavy south; milder.

SEPT. 1993: Temp. 81° (0.5° below avg.); Precip. 8" (2.5" above avg.). 1-4 Rain, possible hurricane. 5-6 Showers, hot. 7-11 Possible onshore hurricane, cooler. 12-16 Clear, warm. 17-20 Showers, heavy south; hot. 21-24 Showers, milder. 25-28 Clear; hot. 29-30 Showers.

OCT. 1993: Temp. 77.5° (2° above avg.); Precip. 2" (Avg.). 1-4 Rain, heavy north; mild. 5-7 Showers, seasonable. 8-11 Sunny, showers south. 12-13 Rain. 14-17 Clear, warm. 18-22 Heavy rain central & north from possible hurricane. 23-25 Clear & pleasant; rain north. 26-31 Sunny & mild; showers south.

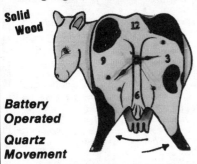

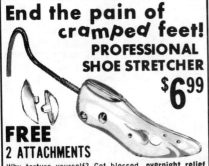

UPSTATE N.Y.-TORONTO AND MONTREAL

For regional boundaries, see map page 129.

SUMMARY: *November through April is expected to be milder than normal with below-normal precipitation in the east but above-normal in the west and north. Snowfall will be close to normal, with the major amounts expected in February and March. Except for a cold spell the latter half of November through the first half of December, temperatures may vary from normal to well above normal, with a few instances of subnormal temperatures in early November and from mid-December through February. Look for a possible heavy snowstorm in the west before Thanksgiving with otherwise below-normal snowfall in November and December. January may have little snow despite above-normal precipitation. February through March will be quite wintry, with well below normal temperatures and above-normal snowfall.*

April through June will be cooler and drier than normal with cold spells in April and above-normal snowfall in the east. May will see some mild days, with rains throughout the month, while June will be wet in the mountains, but drier in the north and west.

July through September will be cooler than normal with above-normal precipitation, but with below-normal in the west and north. Mostly normal temperatures are expected until a cold period arrives in late September. Below-normal rainfall may prevail through July and August, but heavy rains are anticipated in September. October may be warmer and slightly drier than normal, with several warm and sunny spells.

NOV. 1992: Temp. 37° (2° below avg.); Precip. 1" (1" below avg.; 2" above west). 1-2 Clear, warm. 3-5 Rain, seasonable. 6-7 Clear; rain west. 8-10 Cold wave, snow. 11-14 Clear, mild. 15-18 Rain. 19-21 Snowstorm, heavy west & north; seasonable. 22-25 Cold, snow. 26-27 Cold snap. 28-30 Snow, heavy north.

DEC. 1992: Temp. 30° (4° above avg.); Precip. 2" (0.5" below avg.). 1-3 Cold wave, snow. 4-5 Sunny, seasonable. 6-11 Light snow, some sun. 12-14 Cold wave, flurries. 15-17 Snow changing to rain; mild. 18-21 Cold, flurries. 22-24 Rain & snow; milder. 25-26 Rain, mild. 27-29 Cold wave, snow west. 30-31 Rain, mild.

JAN. 1993: Temp. 30° (9° above avg.); Precip. 3" (0.5" above avg.; 2" above west). 1-6 Cold, flurries. 7-9 Mild; rain. 10-11 Snowstorm, seasonable. 12-13 Cold snap, flurries. 14-16 Rain, snow mountains; mild then cold. 17-20 Rain, snow north; mild. 21-24 Cold, snow. 25-29 Snow turning to rain. 30-31 Clear, mild.

FEB. 1993: Temp. 25° (2° above avg.); Precip. 4.5" (2" above avg.). 1-4 Cold, then mild & rain. 5-9 Seasonable; sunny west. 10-13 Snow, then clear & cold. 14-16 Sleet; mild. 17-20 Snowstorm, seasonable. 21-23 Light snow. 24-28 Cold wave, then heavy snow & seasonable.

MAR. 1993: Temp. 28° (6° below avg.). Precip. 2" (0.5" below avg.). 1-3 Very cold, flurries. 4-5 Seasonable, snow. 6-8 Severe cold. 9-11 Sunny, cold nights. 12-14 Heavy snowstorm, cold. 15-19 Snow, heavy west & north. 20-23 Cold, intermittent snow. 24-28 Seasonable, sleet & snow. 29-31 Sunny, then heavy rain.

APR. 1993: Temp. 43° (3° below avg.) Precip. 1.7" (1" below avg.). 1-2 Rain, very mild. 3-6 Sunny, cold. 7-9 Warm, rain. 10-11 Cold. 12-13 Light snow & rain, cold. 14-15 Clearing, seasonable.

16-18 Snowstorm. 19-23 Clear, warm. 24-26 Cold, rain. 27-30 Some sun, some rain; milder.

MAY 1993: Temp. 58° (Avg.); Precip. 2.8" (1" below avg.). 1-5 Some sun, then cold & rainy. 6-10 Warming, showers; sunny west. 11-12 Clear, cold nights. 13-14 Rain, seasonable. 15-17 Sunny, cool. 18-24 Showers, turning cool. 25-27 Sunny. 28-31 Warming, showers.

JUNE 1993: Temp. 67° (1° above avg.); Precip. 2.5" (1" below avg.). 1-2 Cold, rain east. 3-7 Heavy rain, seasonable. 8-10 Clearing, cool. 11-13 Clear, warm. 14-16 Showers, cool. 17-20 Warming, light showers. 21-23 Heavy rain, then clear & cold. 24-25 Seasonable, showers. 26-27 Clear, warm. 28-30 Showers.

JULY 1993: Temp. 70° (1.5° below avg.); Precip. 2.7" (1" below avg.). 1-5 Showers, cool west. 6-10 Rain, seasonable east. 11-13 Clear, warm. 14-17 Rain. 18-20 Clear & mild. 21-24 Rain, heavy west; seasonable. 25-27 Sunny. 28-29 Rain, heavy west. 30-31 Sunny, warm.

AUG. 1993: Temp. 68.5° (0.5° below avg.); Precip. 3.0" (0.5" below avg.). 1-5 Rain, seasonable. 6-8 Rain, cooler. 9-14 Sunny & warm, showers. 15-17 Mild, sprinkles. 18-21 Clear. 22-24 Rain, cool. 25-27 Clear, warm. 28-31 Cloudy, warm.

SEPT. 1993: Temp. 58° (3° below avg.); Precip. 6" (3" above avg.; 1" above west). 1-5 Heavy rain, mild. 6-9 Showers, cooler. 10-13 Sunny, warm. 14-16 Rain, heavy east; cool. 17-20 Rain, colder. 21-22 Cold snap. 23-25 Showers, milder. 26-28 Cold, rain. 29-30 Clear & warmer.

OCT. 1993: Temp. 52° (2° above avg.); Precip. 2" (1" below avg.). 1-6 Sunny, warm. 7-9 Cold wave, showers. 10-13 Clear & warm, showers. 14-17 Heavy rain, turning cold. 18-23 Clear, warming. 24-26 Sunny, seasonable. 27-29 Cold; light rain, snow mountains. 30-31 Clear, cold.

12 Great Reasons to Own America's Favorite Small Tiller

1. **Weighs just 20 pounds.** Mantis is a joy to use. It starts easily, turns on a dime, lifts nimbly over plants and fences.
2. **Tills like nothing else.** Mantis bites down a full 8" deep, churns tough soil into crumbly loam, prepares seedbeds in no time.
3. **Has unique "serpentine" tines.** Our 36 tine teeth spin at up to 240 RPM — twice as fast as others. Cuts through tough soil and vegetation like a chain saw cuts through wood!
4. **Weeds faster than hand tools.** Reverse its tines and Mantis is a precision power weeder. Weeds an average garden in 20 minutes.
5. **Digs planting furrows.** With the Planter/Furrower, Mantis digs deep or shallow furrows for planting. Builds raised beds, too!
6. **Cuts neat borders.** Use the Border Edger to cut crisp edges for flower beds, walkways, around shrubs and trees.
7. **Dethatches your lawn.** Thatch in your lawn prevents water and nutrients from reaching the roots. The Dethatcher quickly removes thatch.
8. **Aerates your lawn, too.** For a lush, healthy carpet, the Aerator slices thousands of tiny slits in your lawn's surface.
9. **Trims bushes and hedges!** Only Mantis has an 16" or 30" Trimmer Bar to prune and trim your shrubbery and small trees.
10. **No Risk FULL YEAR Trial.** The Mantis Promise — Try any product that you buy from Mantis with NO RISK! If you're not completely satisfied, send it back to us within one year for a complete, no hassle refund.
11. **Lifetime tine warranty.** Our tines are so strong that we guarantee them for life against breakage.
12. **Just $20 a month.** With our Easy Payment Plan, if you qualify, you can own a Mantis for as little as $20 a month...with no money down!

Learn more about Mantis today! For **FREE** details,

call TOLL FREE,
1-800-366-6268
Or mail coupon.

GREATER OHIO VALLEY

For regional boundaries, see map page 129.

SUMMARY: *November through March is expected to be much milder and wetter than normal, but with considerable variability. Snowfall will be below normal except for extreme northeastern sections, which should receive close to normal amounts. A mild and dry first half of November should be followed by cold and rain, persisting through mid-December in the east. The rest of December and all of January should have frequent mild, wet spells, interrupted by cold spells. February should approach normal conditions until a cold wave at the end of the month ushers in a quite cold March, with frequent and occasionally heavy snows in the north and east.*

April through June should have below-normal temperatures, with below-normal precipitation in the west but above in the east. April may experience several quite cold periods with above-normal snowfall, while May and June should see some cold and rainy periods offset by warm and drier spells, except for heavy rains expected in the east.

July through September may be considerably cooler in the west and slightly so in the east, with above-average precipitation. July may have consistently cool temperatures, while August through September should see alternating warm and cool waves, possibly continuing through mid-October, when an Indian summer-like spell should take over.

NOV. 1992: Temp. 46.5° (1° above avg.); Precip. 2" (1" below avg.; avg. east). 1-2 Sunny & mild. 3-5 Cloudy, cold; rain east, then clearing. 6-10 Very cold, rain & snow east. 11-16 Sunny, warm. 17-18 Rain, cooler. 19-22 Cold, then rain, snow east. 23-24 Clearing. 25-30 Cold, rain & snow.
DEC. 1992: Temp. 37.5° (3° above avg.); Precip. 5" (2" above avg.). 1-5 Clearing, milder; rain east. 6-8 Light rain, mild; snow, cold east. 9-10 Sunny, mild. 11-13 Cold, snow. 14-17 Rain, warm. 18-20 Sunny, very cold. 21-23 Rain, sleet; milder. 24-26 Rain, mild. 27-29 Cold, snow east. 30-31 Rain & snow.
JAN. 1993: Temp. 37° (8° above avg.); Precip. 5" (3" above avg.; 1" above east). 1-4 Sunny, mild. 5-8 Rain, very warm. 9-12 Cold; snow. 13-16 Rain, mild; turning cold. 17-19 Rain, warm. 20-22 Sunny. 23-25 Cold snap, flurries. 26-28 Rain; warmer. 29-31 Mild, then cold; rain.
FEB. 1993: Temp. 34.5° (2° above avg.; 4° above east); Precip. 2" (Avg.; 2" above east). 1-2 Mild, rain. 3-6 Cold; snow. 7-9 Sunny, turning mild. 10-12 Light freezing rain. 13-15 Rain & snow then clearing, mild. 16-19 Snowstorm. 20-24 Cold nights; flurries, snow east. 25-28 Snow, turning very cold.
MAR. 1993: Temp. 38.5° (5° below avg.); Precip. 3" (1" below avg.; 0.5" above east). 1-2 Cold, flurries. 3-7 Seasonable, then cold; snow. 8-11 Sunny, warm west. 12-14 Cold, light snow; clearing. 15-18 Seasonable, then cold; snow. 19-20 Clear, cold. 21-23 Sunny, seasonable. 24-26 Snowstorm, cold. 27-29 Snow. 30-31 Warm, rain.
APR. 1993: Temp. 50.5° (5° below avg.); Precip. 3" (0.5" below avg.). 1-3 Light snow, cold. 4-5 Clear, seasonable. 6-9 Rain & snow, cold. 10-12 Sunny, then cloudy & cold. 13-16 Light rain, mild, then cold. 17-19 Clear, very cold. 20-22 Sunny & mild. 23-25 Cold & rainy. 26-27 Sunny,

seasonable. 28-30 Rain, warming.
MAY 1993: Temp. 65° (1° above avg.); Precip. 2" (2" below avg.; 1" above east). 1-2 Clear, cold west. 3-5 Rain, cold. 6-8 Showers, warming. 9-10 Thundershowers. 11-13 Clear. 14-15 Showers, cold. 16-18 Sunny. 19-26 Showers, warm. 27-29 Clear, very warm. 30-31 Showers, cool.
JUNE 1993: Temp. 71° (1° below avg.; avg. east); Precip. 4.5" (1" above avg.). 1-6 Showers, seasonable. 7-8 Heavy rain, cool. 9-13 Clear, seasonable, warm east. 14-15 Heavy showers, cool. 16-20 Rain, seasonable. 21-24 Cold, showers. 25-27 Warm. 28-30 Showers, warming.
JULY 1993: Temp. 71° (5° below avg.; 2° below east); Precip. 5" (1" above avg.; avg. east). 1-5 Light showers, cool. 6-9 Showers, mild. 10-16 Sunny & warm west; showers, mild east. 17-18 Showers, cool. 19-20 Clear & pleasant. 21-24 Rain, seasonable. 25-26 Clear, mild. 27-29 Heavy showers, 30-31 Clearing, warm.
AUG. 1993: Temp. 72° (3° below avg.; avg. east); Precip. 3" (1" below avg.). 1-3 Clear & warm, showers east. 4-6 Showers, cooling. 7-11 Sunny, few showers. 12-15 Rain, seasonable. 16-18 Clear & mild. 19-21 Warmer, showers. 22-24 Showers, cool. 25-30 Sunny & warm. 31 Showers.
SEPT. 1993: Temp. 66.5° (2° below avg.; 1° above east); Precip. 2.5" (Avg.; 1" above east). 1-7 Rain, milder. 8-11 Clear & cool. 12-14 Showers, sunny east; seasonable. 15-19 Heavy rain east, showers west; cool. 20-22 Sunny, warming. 23-26 Rain, seasonable. 27-30 Cold, sunny.
OCT. 1993: Temp. 59° (3° above avg.); Precip. 1.5" (1" below avg.). 1-6 Sunny & warm, few showers west. 7-8 Cold wave, light rain. 9-10 Clear, seasonable. 11-14 Heavy rain, cool. 15-18 Sunny, warm; cold & rainy east. 19-24 Clear, very warm. 25-27 Scattered showers, cooling. 28-31 Sunny & seasonable, then rain.

Amazing New Product Gives Crisp, Clear TV Reception WITHOUT Cable!

Until recently, the only convenient way to guarantee great TV reception was to get cable installed. But who wants to pay those irritating monthly cable fees just to clear reception? Now, thanks to years of micro-electronic research, a new device has been developed that's so advanced it actually makes other antennas a thing of the past. It's called the SWEDA™ Power Antenna and is without a doubt "the single most important thing you should own if you have a TV!"

A PICTURE OF ADVANCED TECHNOLOGY!

Just imagine watching TV and seeing a picture so brilliantly clear that you'd almost swear you were there live! Just plug this tiny 2" x 4" Power Antenna into any ordinary AC outlet, connect your TV and get ready for the best reception you've ever had without cable. You'll watch in amazement as YOUR TV set suddenly displays a sharp, focused picture. You literally "won't believe your eyes!" Even older TV sets suddenly come to life. The Power Antenna is so easy to install, so convenient to use, and so incredibly effective that you'll wonder how you ever got by without it!

A THOUSAND FOOT ANTENNA?

Power Antenna is a highly sophisticated electronic product (like a transistor radio) with a simple function. It takes the electrical wiring in your house or apartment (hundreds or thousands of feet) and turns it into a giant TV reception station! It's almost like having an antenna the size of your entire house! Imagine how effective that would be. But there's more, because Power Antenna takes that signal and electronically boosts it before it gets to your TV set. The results are amazing! You can finally enjoy your favorite prime time shows or sports events the way they were meant to be watched.

LIMITED TIME OFFER!

Electronic antennas like this one normally sell for $50 or more! But now, for a limited time (if you respond before December 31, 1993), you can have the amazing SWEDA™ Power Antenna for just $19.95. Experience the best reception you've ever had or simply return it within 30 days for a prompt and courteous refund. You absolutely must see it to believe it! ORDER TODAY.

P.S. Works just as good for radio reception too! Limit 3 per order.

© *U.S. Buyers Network 1992, (2697).*
Allow up to 60 days for shipment.

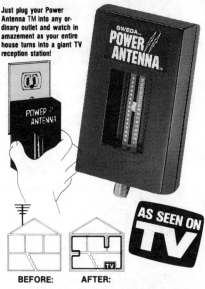

Just plug your Power Antenna ™ into any ordinary outlet and watch in amazement as your entire house turns into a giant TV reception station!

BEFORE: **AFTER:**

RESPOND BEFORE DECEMBER 31ST FOR THIS SPECIAL OFFER!

YES! Please rush me the following SWEDA™ Power Antenna(s)!

☐ One Power Antenna for just **$19.95** plus $4 P&H.

☐ **SAVE $5!** Two for just **$34.95** plus $5 P&H.

☐ **SAVE $10!** Three for just **$49.95** plus $6 P&H.

__Qty. **Extra length 6 foot connection cable** just $2 ea. (a $5.00 value).

Enclosed $_____. VA residents add sales tax.

Payment method: (Check one)
☐ Check ☐ Money Order ☐ VISA ☐ Mastercard
☐ Amex ☐ Diners ☐ Discover ☐ Carte Blanch

Card # _____

Exp. Date _____/_____

Name _____

Address _____

Apt. _____ City _____

State _____

Zip _____

U.S. Buyers Network, Dept. AT4836
One American Way, Roanoke, VA 24016

1993   OLD FARMER'S ALMANAC   143

DEEP SOUTH

For regional boundaries, see map page 129.

SUMMARY: *November through March should be much colder than normal, with above-normal precipitation, but below-normal snowfall. After a cold, wet beginning, November through early December will be milder and drier than normal. A warm spell in mid-December, with rain in the northwest, will usher in variable weather with frequent, heavy rains bringing flooding in January and February. Cold waves will alternate with mild spells from before Christmas through March.*

April through June is expected to have slightly below normal temperatures with well below normal precipitation. April may be much cooler and drier except for very brief seasonable spells early and late in the month. May and June will be warmer and drier than normal except for cool and rainy periods early in both months and at mid-May.

July through September will be cooler than normal with slightly above normal precipitation. Near-normal temperatures will prevail in the south, except for a brief cold wave in early September. Expect prolonged subnormal temperatures in the north, broken by seasonable spells in late August and in September. July should be fairly wet, but a drought may develop by September in the extreme south. Watch for possible tropical storms in early September.

October will be slightly warm due to a pleasant period after midmonth, while rainfall will be below normal in the south, but slightly above normal north.

NOV. 1992: Temp. 54.5° (1.5° below avg.); Precip. 2" (3" below avg.). 1-2 Sunny. 3-5 Cold, heavy rain. 6-8 Sunny, showers northeast. 9-11 Clear & cool, frost. 12-15 Clear, very warm. 16-17 Rain, cooling. 18-22 Clear, seasonable, then cold, frost. 23-24 Clear, warm. 25-27 Cold. 28-30 Seasonable.

DEC. 1992: Temp. 52° (3.5° above avg.); Precip. 3.5" (2" below avg.; 1.5" above north). 1-3 Cloudy, showers east; warm. 4-6 Clear, frost north. 7-9 Showers, seasonable. 10-13 Rain, turning cold. 14-16 Rain, warm. 17-20 Cold, hard frost. 21-26 Rain, milder. 27-29 Cold, hard frost. 30-31 Rain, mild.

JAN. 1993: Temp. 54° (10° above avg.); Precip. 7" (2" above avg.; 5" above north). 1-4 Sunny, warm; showers east. 5-8 Rain, warm. 9-11 Cold; rain, snow north. 12-13 Clearing, milder. 14-18 Rain, warm. 19-22 Sunny, warm. 23-26 Cold; rain, snow north; clearing. 27-29 Sunny, warm. 30-31 Rain, colder.

FEB. 1993: Temp. 55° (7° above avg.); Precip. 8" (3.5" above avg.; 6" above north). 1-2 Showers, warming. 3-6 Cold wave; heavy rain, very heavy north. 7-9 Clearing, seasonable. 10-14 Rain, mild. 15-18 Very heavy rain. 19-21 Cold snap, sunny. 22-24 Scattered showers, seasonable. 25-28 Moderate rain, clearing.

MAR. 1993: Temp. 56.5° (Avg.; 1° below north); Precip. 6" (0.5" below avg.; 1" above north). 1-3 Sunny, cool. 4-5 Rain, mild. 6-10 Cold then warming, warm. 11-14 Cold, showers north. 15-17 Heavy rain, warm then cooling. 18-23 Cool, intermittent rain. 24-27 Showers, cold nights. 28-31 Very warm; rain.

APR. 1993: Temp. 61° (4° below avg.); Precip. 3" (3" below avg.). 1-4 Cold wave, sunny. 5-8 Rain, then clearing south; warming. 9-11 Cold snap. 12-14 Sunny & warm. 15-16 Rain, cool. 17-20 Cold wave, clear. 21-23 Rain, cool. 24-27

Sunny, turning warm. 28-30 Rain, cooler.

MAY 1993: Temp. 75° (3° above avg.); Precip. 5" (Avg.). 1-2 Showers, warm. 3-7 Rain, cool. 8-9 Clear, warm. 10-12 Heavy rain, cool north; showers, warm south. 13-14 Clear, warm. 15-19 Rain, cool. 20-22 Clear, very warm. 23-25 Rain, cool. 26-31 Very warm, few showers.

JUNE 1993: Temp. 79° (Avg.); Precip. 3.5" (0.5" above avg.; 0.5" below north). 1-4 Showers, seasonable. 5-9 Rain, heavy north, then clearing; cool. 10-12 Sunny & warm, showers south. 13-15 Moderate rain, seasonable. 16-23 Clear, unseasonably hot. 24-26 Rain, warm. 27-30 Clear & hot.

JULY 1993: Temp. 80° (2° below avg.); Precip. 5.5" (1.5" above avg.). 1-3 Scattered showers, mild. 4-6 Sunny & warm. 7-10 Rain, cooler. 11-14 Clear, warm. 15-17 Showers, locally heavy; mild. 18-21 Heavy rain, cool then warming. 22-27 Showers; seasonable, cool north. 28-31 Showers, heavy north.

AUG. 1993: Temp. 80° (1.5° above avg.; 3° below north); Precip. 3.5" (0.5" below avg.). 1-3 Heavy rain, light northeast; cool. 4-5 Sunny & warm. 6-9 Rain, cool. 10-13 Clear, then showers. 14-18 Sunny, warm. 19-22 Showers, warm. 23-26 Clear. 27-29 Heavy rain north, sunny & warm south. 30-31 Showers.

SEPT. 1993: Temp. 75° (1.5° below avg.); Precip. 3.5" (Avg.; 0.5" above north). 1-6 Possible tropical storm, heavy rain; mild. 7-10 Sunny. 11-13 Rain, possible hurricane east; quite cool. 14-16 Clear, warm. 17-20 Rain, cool. 21-23 Clear, hot. 24-26 Showers, cooling. 27-30 Sunny, very cool.

OCT. 1993: Temp. 67° (2° above avg.); Precip. 2.5" (1" below avg.; 0.5" above north). 1-2 Showers, mild. 3-7 Sunny, warm. 8-12 Showers, cool, then warming. 13-16 Clear, pleasant. 17-20 Clear, very hot. 21-23 Rain, cloudy north. 24-27 Heavy rain, warm. 28-31 Sunny.

CHICAGO & SOUTHERN GREAT LAKES

For regional boundaries, see map page 129.

SUMMARY: *November through March should be warmer than normal with above-normal precipitation, slightly below normal snowfall in the south and slightly above in the north. The first half of November will be fairly dry and cold, followed by a mild spell, after which generally cold weather with frequent snow continues through mid-December. Warm spells, interspersed with brief cold snaps, and moderately heavy precipitation may prevail through January. More wintry weather should set in in early February and persist through March except for mild spells mid-February and mid-March. Precipitation and snowfall should be above normal, particularly in the east.*

April through June is anticipated to be colder than normal, with above-normal precipitation and snowfall in the northeast, near normal northwest, and below normal south. March's wintry weather will continue through April and early May with several warm spells bringing some relief. A warm spell the second week of May will usher in more normal temperatures in June, with only some heavy rains in the east in June bringing above-normal precipitation.

July through September will average colder than normal due to frequent cool spells, while less than normal shower activity will prevail except during late July.

A cold, wet mid-October should be offset by a warm spell early in the month and Indian summer-like weather toward the end.

NOV. 1992: Temp. 41° (0.5° above avg.); Precip. 2" (1" below avg.). 1-2 Sunny & warm. 3-5 Cold snap, clear. 6-9 Sleet, cold. 10-15 Clear & mild. 16-18 Rain, seasonable. 19-22 Cold, snow, heavy east. 23-25 Seasonable, then cold, rain & snow. 26-27 Clear & cold. 28-30 Snow, cold.

DEC. 1992: Temp. 29° (3° above avg.); Precip. 5" (2.5" above avg.). 1-4 Milder; flurries, sprinkles south. 5-6 Cold snap, snowstorm. 7-9 Some sun, seasonable. 10-13 Cold wave, light snow. 14-16 Heavy rain, very mild. 17-20 Very cold, clear. 21-23 Mild, freezing rain. 24-26 Heavy rain, mild. 27-31 Cold wave, then snowstorm.

JAN. 1993: Temp. 29° (8° above avg.); Precip. 4.5" (3" above avg.). 1-3 Sunny & mild. 4-8 Snow, then heavy rain, warming. 9-12 Seasonable, snow, then clearing. 13-14 Turning mild, rain. 15-21 Seasonable to mild, heavy rain. 22-24 Cold, snow. 25-26 Sunny, milder. 27-30 Heavy rain, very mild. 31 Cold snap.

FEB. 1993: Temp. 27° (2° above avg.); Precip. 2" (0.5" above avg.; 2" above east). 1-2 Sunny, sprinkles east; milder. 3-5 Flurries, seasonable. 6-9 Clear, warming. 10-13 Freezing rain & snow. 14-16 Clearing, milder. 17-19 Snow. 20-24 Seasonable, light snow. 25-28 Colder; snow.

MAR. 1993: Temp. 33° (4° below avg.); Precip. 1.5" (1" below avg.; 0.5" above east). 1-3 Very cold, light snow east. 4-6 Snowstorm, turning very cold. 7-11 Sunny, warming. 12-14 Cold, light snow. 15-17 Cold; snow. 18-22 Sunny, cold, then snow. 23-28 Seasonable, some freezing rain. 29-31 Heavy rain, milder.

APR. 1993: Temp. 43° (5° below avg.); Precip. 4.5" (1" above avg.). 1-3 Cold wave, flurries. 4-8 Heavy rain, snow north; seasonable. 9-12 Cold, snow, then clearing. 13-15 Snow turning to rain. 16-19 Very cold, light snow. 20-22 Warm, light rain. 23-25 Cool, showers. 26-30 Heavy rain, seasonable then cooling.

MAY 1993: Temp. 60° (1° above avg.; 0.5° below east); Precip. 1" (2.5" below avg.; 0.5" below east). 1-5 Very cold & rainy. 6-10 Sunny, very warm, sprinkles. 11-13 Cold, rain. 14-17 Sunny, warming. 18-21 Showers, seasonable. 22-25 Cool, then milder, showers. 26-29 Heavy rain, very warm. 30-31 Cold snap.

JUNE 1993: Temp. 69° (1° above avg.); Precip. 4.5" (1" below avg.; 0.5" above east). 1-5 Sunny & warm, few showers. 6-7 Rain, cool. 8-12 Clear, warming. 13-15 Rain, then clearing. 16-20 Rain, seasonable. 21-24 Cold; rain. 25-27 Warming, showers. 28-30 Heavy rain, then clearing, very warm.

JULY 1993: Temp. 69° (2° below avg.); Precip. 5.5" (2" above avg.; avg. east). 1-5 Showers, cool. 6-8 Rain. 9-15 Sunny, warm, hot west. 16-18 Cooler; rain, then clearing. 19-24 Intermittent rain, warm, then cool. 25-26 Clear. 27-29 Heavy rain, seasonable. 30-31 Sunny, seasonable.

AUG. 1993: Temp. 68° (2° below avg.; avg. east); Precip. 2.5" (1.5" below avg.). 1-3 Clear, hot. 4-6 Showers; cool. 7-10 Sunny. 11-12 Clear, cool. 13-15 Rain, seasonable. 16-18 Clear, mild. 19-21 Sunny, hot, showers north. 22-24 Mild, showers. 25-29 Clear, hot; showers north. 30-31 Rain.

SEPT. 1993: Temp. 63.5° (1° below avg.); Precip. 3" (0.5" below avg.). 1-2 Rain, hot. 3-6 Mild; rain. 7-10 Clear & warm. 11-13 Sunny, much warmer. 14-18 Heavy rain, cooling. 19-21 Clear & pleasant. 22-26 Intermittent rain, seasonable. 27-29 Cold. 30 Clear, warm.

OCT. 1993: Temp. 55° (3° above avg.); Precip. 1.5" (1" below avg.; 1" above east). 1-3 Light rain, warm. 4-5 Clear, very warm. 6-7 Cold wave, rain. 8-10 Clear, gradual warming. 11-12 Heavy rain, cool. 13-18 Rain east, showers west; cool. 19-25 Clear & warm. 26-29 Light showers, cold. 30-31 Rain, warming.

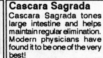

SUMMARY: *November through March is expected to be colder than normal, particularly in the west, with below-normal precipitation in central sections, but above in the east and west. Snowfall should be above normal except for some southeastern sections, which may be slightly below. November and early December should be warm and fairly dry, although heavy snows may occur in the east during late November. More wintry conditions will then persist through March, with severe cold waves, heavy snow, and near-blizzard conditions, especially in central and western sections. Brief mild spells will offer some respite in January, mid-February, and mid-March.*

April through June will be very cold and dry, with above-normal snowfall, conditions that may persist through mid-April. Relief arrives from warm spells late in the month, with cold returning for the first half of May. Thereafter, frequent warm and dry spells will offset the few cool periods.

July through September will be much cooler than average with below-normal rainfall in the east, but near normal or above central and west. July may be quite cool, with heavy shower activity. Warm spells will partially offset cool ones in August and dominate the first half of September before closing cool and wet.

Following a cold and wet beginning, October will be quite mild and pleasant until the arrival of a cold wave at the close of the month.

NOV. 1992: Temp. 36°(3° above avg.; 5° above west); Precip. 1" (0.5" below avg.). 1-2 Sunny, warm. 3-6 Variable; cold, showers; sunny & mild. 7-14 Sunny, warm; sprinkles north. 15-18 Seasonable; rain & snow. 19-22 Cold; cloudy, snow east. 23-24 Milder; snow, sunny west. 25-30 Cold, turning milder west; flurries.

DEC. 1992: Temp. 19° (0.5° above avg.); Precip. 1" (Avg.). 1-5 Mild; sunny central, sleet west & east. 6-9 Cloudy, turning cold. 10-12 Cold, light snow. 13-16 Snowstorm, near blizzard. 17-19 Cold wave, flurries east. 20-23 Milder; sunny, flurries. 24-27 Very cold, light snow. 28-29 Sunny, milder. 30-31 Seasonable, snow.

JAN. 1993: Temp. 11° (1° below avg.; 5° below west); Precip. 1.5" (0.5" above avg.). 1-3 Sunny, seasonable. 4-7 Snow, turning cold. 8-9 Clearing, very cold. 10-12 Mild east, seasonable west. 13-18 Variable, some snow. 19-23 Cold, flurries. 24-29 Turning seasonable, heavy snow. 30-31 Cold snap, heavy snow east.

FEB. 1993: Temp. 15.5° (2° below avg.); Precip. 1" (Avg.; 0.5" above west). 1-4 Very cold, light snow. 5-9 Clear, seasonable. 10-14 Mild; sunny central, snow east & west. 15-18 Turning cold, heavy snow. 19-22 Seasonable, cold west; flurries. 23-26 Some snow, colder. 27-28 Cold, snow.

MAR. 1993: Temp. 25° (5° below avg.); Precip. 2.5" (0.5" above avg.). 1-2 Very cold, snow west. 3-5 Seasonable, sunny. 6-8 Cold, snow east. 9-10 Sunny, mild. 11-14 Snow, cold. 15-18 Clear, very cold. 19-21 Sunny, milder; snow. 22-24 Clear, cold. 25-29 Seasonable, cold west; snow. 30-31 Snow.

APR. 1993: Temp. 41.5° (5° below avg.); Precip. 2.5" (Avg.; 1" below west). 1-2 Storm ending, turning cold. 3-4 Sunny, seasonable. 5-7 Snow, cold. 8-11 Clear, cold nights. 12-15 Snow. 16-18 Clear, cold. 19-21 Sunny, turning mild. 22-24 Cold wave, snow. 25-27 Clear, mild. 28-30 Cold; snow.

MAY 1993: Temp. 55° (4° below avg.); Precip. 3.5" (Avg.). 1-4 Cold; cloudy, snow south. 5-6 Clearing, milder. 7-10 Snow west, heavy rain east. 11-13 Cold, rain & snow. 14-18 Sunny & warm. 19-21 Seasonable, cold east; showers. 22-25 Rain. 26-28 Rain, warm. 29-31 Clear & cold.

JUNE 1993: Temp. 69° (1° above avg.); Precip. 2" (2" below avg.). 1-2 Sunny, seasonable; showers west. 3-7 Rain, then cooler. 8-10 Sunny & hot. 11-14 Seasonable, showers west & east, cloudy central. 15-19 Hot, showers. 20-22 Cold & wet. 23-25 Warming, showers. 26-29 Showers, hot. 30 Cooler, heavy rain east.

JULY 1993: Temp. 70° (4° below avg.); Precip. 3.5" (Avg.; 0.5" above west). 1-5 Mild, showers. 6-10 Cooler; sunny, showers west. 11-15 Showers, seasonable. 16-25 Rain, much cooler. 26-29 Scattered showers, mild. 30-31 Clear, seasonable.

AUG. 1993: Temp. 68° (2.5° below avg.); Precip. 1.5" (2" below avg.; 0.5" below west). 1-2 Sunny, hot. 3-5 Heavy showers, cooling. 6-10 Seasonable, showers west. 11-13 Sunny, warm; showers, rain west. 14-17 Cooler, rain. 18-21 Clear & hot. 22-26 Widely scattered showers, cool. 27-29 Showers, seasonable. 30-31 Mild.

SEPT. 1993: Temp. 61.5° (1° above avg.); Precip. 2" (1" below avg.; 0.5" above west). 1-2 Cool, rain. 3-6 Clear & warm, hot west. 7-11 Sunny. 12-14 Clear & warm east, rain west. 15-17 Cooling; rain. 18-19 Sunny, warm. 20-22 Showers. 23-25 Showers, cool. 26-30 Clear, warm.

OCT. 1993: Temp. 50° (1° above avg.); Precip. 2" (Avg.). 1-2 Showers, seasonable. 3-6 Heavy rain, then cold. 7-9 Clear, warming. 10-12 Showers, cool. 13-16 Sunny, seasonable. 17-19 Scattered showers, pleasantly warm. 20-24 Sunny, quite warm. 25-27 Cold wave, light rain. 28-31 Gradual warming, showers east.

SUMMARY: *November through March is expected to be much warmer than normal in central and southern sections and slightly warmer in northern ones, with below-normal precipitation except the southeast, which may be quite wet. Snowfall will be well below normal, but slightly above in the northeast. Very warm and dry conditions will dominate the weather until mid-December, when cold waves partially offset warm spells through January, with above-normal precipitation in the east and southeast. February will be cold with heavy snows in the north, but mild south, and wet southeast. March will be generally cold and dry except for heavy snow in the northeast.*

April through June will be quite cold, with below-normal precipitation except in the northeast. April through early May should see cold and wet periods alternating with mild and dry spells, but with below-normal precipitation except in the southeast. Closer to normal conditions will then prevail except for subnormal precipitation in the southwest.

July through September will be quite cool. Precipitation will vary, from dry in the east and northwest to heavy showers in central and southwestern sections during July and August. Warm and dry spells will partially balance cold waves during September. Following a cold wave in early October, Indian summer-like weather is expected until a late-month cold wave.

NOV. 1992: Temp. 41° (2° above avg.; 4° above west); Precip. 0.5" (1" below avg.). 1-2 Clear, warm. 3-4 Cold, showers south. 5-9 Seasonable, showers southeast. 10-15 Clear, very warm. 16-18 Rain, cooling. 19-22 Sunny, seasonable; showers northeast. 23-25 Clear & warm. 26-28 Rain, mild. 29-30 Clear, warm.

DEC. 1992: Temp. 27.5° (2.5° above avg.); Precip. 1" (0.5" below avg.; 2" above southeast). 1-4 Clear & mild. 5-11 Cloudy, cooler. 12-15 Cold; storm, near blizzard north. 16-17 Clearing, warm. 18-20 Severe cold wave. 21-23 Sunny, mild. 24-26 Snowstorm, cold. 27-29 Clear, cold nights. 30-31 Seasonable, heavy rain southeast.

JAN. 1993: Temp. 23° (4° above avg.; 1° above west); Precip. 1" (Avg.; 5" above southeast). 1-2 Sunny, mild. 3-5 Freezing rain. 6-8 Rain turning to snow; cold. 9-12 Clearing, mild; snow southeast. 13-16 Cloudy, mild; rain south. 17-21 Mild, cold nights; flurries. 22-24 Cold. 25-28 Sunny, warm. 29-31 Snow, cold.

FEB. 1993: Temp. 22° (2° below avg.; 2° above south); Precip. 1.5" (0.5" above avg.; 2" below northwest). 1-2 Mild, cold nights. 3-4 Very cold, snow. 5-10 Clearing, mild. 11-14 Snow, then clearing. 15-18 Snowstorm, cold. 19-24 Seasonable. 25-28 Rain southeast, snow north.

MAR. 1993: Temp. 33° (3° below avg.; 1.5° below west); Precip. 1" (1" below avg.; avg. west). 1-2 Very cold. 3-4 Rain, snow northeast; milder. 5-6 Cold. 7-10 Clear, very mild. 11-12 Cold wave; snow, blizzard northwest. 13-17 Very cold; snow. 18-21 Seasonable, rain south. 22-25 Cold, snow. 26-29 Clear warm. 30-31 Cold, storm east.

APR. 1993: Temp. 47° (4° below avg.); Precip. 2" (1" below avg.; 2" below west; avg. southeast). 1-3 Cold. 4-5 Warming. 6-8 Rain, snow north. 9-12 Cold, then seasonable. 13-15 Showers, cooler. 16-18 Cold. 19-21 Rain, seasonable. 22-

25 Showers, cold. 26-28 Rain, warm. 29-30 Cold.

MAY 1993: Temp. 59.5° (3° above avg.; 1° below south); Precip. 5.5" (2" above avg.; 2" below southwest). 1-4 Rain, snow north; cold. 5-7 Sunny, warming. 8-9 Rain. 10-11 Sunny, seasonable. 12-14 Rain, cool. 15-21 Intermittent sun, showers; warm. 22-25 Rain, cool. 26-28 Clear, very warm. 29-31 Cold wave, heavy rain.

JUNE 1993: Temp. 70.5° (1° below avg.); Precip. 4.5" (0.5" above avg.; 0.5" below south). 1-2 Rain ending, warming. 3-4 Sunny, seasonable. 5-7 Rain, cold. 8-12 Sunny, warm. 13-15 Rain, cool. 16-20 Thundershowers, very warm. 21-24 Cold; rain. 25-29 Showers, warm. 30 Cooling.

JULY 1993: Temp. 72° (5° below avg.); Precip. 3" (0.5" below avg.; 4" above west). 1-5 Sunny & mild, showers west. 6-8 Rain, seasonable. 9-11 Clear. 12-16 Showers, cool. 17-19 Clear, warm. 20-24 Thunderstorms, cool. 25-29 Showers, cool. 30-31 Clear, warm.

AUG. 1993: Temp. 70° (4° below avg.); Precip. 2.5" (2" below avg.; 3" above central). 1-2 Sunny & warm, showers west. 3-11 Showers, milder. 12-15 Seasonable, scattered showers. 16-19 Rain, mild then seasonable. 20-24 Very cool, showers. 25-28 Clear, warm. 29-31 Heavy rain, cool.

SEPT. 1993: Temp. 62° (3° below avg.); Precip. 1.5" (2" below avg.; avg. southeast). 1-2 Rain, cool. 3-6 Sunny, warm; rain southeast. 7-10 Clear, cooler. 11-13 Warm days, cold nights; rain southeast. 14-16 Cold, rain. 17-20 Clear east, rain west. 21-22 Clear, warm. 23-25 Rain, cooling. 26-27 Clear. 28-30 Cold.

OCT. 1993: Temp. 57° (3.5° above avg.); Precip. 1.5" (1" below avg.). 1-4 Showers, then clearing & warming. 5-7 Cold; rain, very heavy north. 8-9 Clear, warm. 10-12 Rain, cool. 13-25 Indian summer-like weather. 26-28 Cold; cloudy, heavy rain southeast. 29-31 Sunny and mild.

TEXAS-OKLAHOMA

For regional boundaries, see map page 129.

SUMMARY: *November through March is expected to be warmer than normal, but close to normal in the panhandle. Precipitation will be below normal, but above normal in central and southeastern sections. Snowfall will be well below normal. After a cool and slightly wet beginning, November through early December should be quite warm and dry, followed by variable weather. Cold spells during the middle and end of December and January, in early February, and after mid-March will bring snow to central and northern sections, but will be offset by mild periods before Christmas and intermittently through March.*

April through June should be slightly cooler than normal, but slightly warmer in the southern Gulf, with below-normal precipitation in the north and west but well above normal in central and southern sections. April may be quite warm and dry the first half but cool and wet after midmonth, while May through mid-June should see frequent cool, wet spells alternating with warm, dry ones.

July through September may be cooler and wetter than normal except in the southern Gulf, which may be warmer and drier. July through early August should be fairly mild with frequent, heavy showers. Warm periods will alternate with mild, wet ones at the middle and end of August and the last half of September.

Following a mild and wet first half, October should be sunny and warm until a cool and wet spell arrives near the end of the month.

NOV. 1992: Temp. 58° (2° above avg.; 1° below south); Precip. 1" (1.5" below avg.). 1-2 Clear, seasonable. 3-5 Cold, showers. 6-11 Clear; mild days, cold nights. 12-14 Sunny, very warm. 15-17 Rain, cool. 18-21 Clear. 22-24 Sunny, very warm. 25-27 Cold. 28-30 Clear, very warm.

DEC. 1992: Temp. 51° (2.5° above avg.); Precip. 2" (0.5" below avg.; 1" above south). 1-4 Sunny, warm then milder. 5-8 Showers, seasonable. 9-11 Sunny, warm. 12-14 Rain, cool. 15-16 Showers, warm. 17-20 Cold, rain south. 21-23 Sunny, warm, showers. 24-26 Showers, turning cold. 27-29 Clear, cold. 30-31 Showers.

JAN. 1993: Temp. 50° (5.5° above avg.); Precip. 2.5" (0.5" above avg.; 1" below south). 1-2 Clear, mild. 3-5 Rain. 6-10 Rain, changing to snow; cold. 11-13 Clear, warming. 14-17 Rain, mild. 18-23 Showers, warm. 24-26 Cold. 27-29 Clear, very warm. 30-31 Cold, snow north.

FEB. 1993: Temp. 50° (1.5° above avg.; 5° above south); Precip. 2" (0.5" below avg.; 3" above east). 1-2 Clear, warm. 3-6 Snow, very cold. 7-9 Warming, rain south. 10-14 Clear & warm, then showers. 15-17 Rain, mild. 18-19 Cold. 20-23 Clear & warm, then seasonable. 24-26 Showers, cooler. 27-28 Clear, warm.

MAR. 1993: Temp. 58.5° (1.5° above avg.; 1° below north); Precip. 2.5" (0.5" below avg.; 1" above south). 1-4 Clear, warm. 5-8 Cold, rain & snow. 9-11 Clear, pleasant. 12-14 Cold. 15-17 Rain, dry west. 18-22 Sunny, warm. 23-25 Cold, showers. 26-31 Clear, very warm; sprinkles east.

APR. 1993: Temp. 64° (2.5° below avg.; 1° above south & west); Precip. 3.5" (Avg.; 2" below northeast). 1-4 Clear, cold nights. 5-7 Showers, very warm. 8-11 Sunny, cold. 12-15 Clear, warming. 16-21 Rain, very cool. 22-24 Warmer, scattered showers. 25-28 Sunny, warm; few showers. 29-30 Clear, cool, then warming.

MAY 1993: Temp. 75° (1° above avg.; 0.5° below north); Precip. 7.5" (3" above avg.; 1" below southwest). 1-3 Rain, dry west; warm. 4-6 Rain central & east, cool. 7-10 Sunny, warm, then showers. 11-14 Clear, warm; rain north. 15-18 Rain, mild. 19-22 Sunny, hot. 23-25 Rain. 26-28 Clear, warm. 29-31 Rain, cool.

JUNE 1993: Temp. 80° (1.5° below avg.; 1° above west); Precip. 4" (1" above avg.; 3" above south). 1-4 Sunny west, rain east; warm. 5-10 Heavy rain, very cool. 11-13 Sunny, seasonable. 14-16 Showers, quite warm. 17-23 Clear, hot. 24-26 Showers, heavy north & southeast; cooler. 27-30 Sunny & hot.

JULY 1993: Temp. 82° (4° below avg.; avg. south); Precip. 5" (3" above avg.; 1" below south). 1-3 Showers, cooler. 4-7 Cloudy, mild. 8-13 Showers, cool. 14-19 Rain central & north, sprinkles elsewhere. 20-22 Showers, cool. 23-26 Rain north, sunny south. 27-31 Showers, cool.

AUG. 1993: Temp. 82.5° (3° below avg.; avg. south); Precip. 3" (1" above avg.; 1" below south). 1-3 Showers, rain north, mild. 4-10 Scattered showers, warming. 11-16 Hot, sprinkles. 17-19 Sunny, hot; showers west. 20-24 Rain, then clear & cool. 25-27 Showers. 28-30 Clear, warm. 31 Heavy rain.

SEPT. 1993: Temp. 74° (4° below avg.; 2° above south); Precip. 3.5" (Avg.; 2" below north). 1-3 Showers, cooler. 4-6 Cloudy, very cool. 7-9 Heavy rain, cool. 10-13 Sunny, warming. 14-16 Showers, mild. 17-20 Rain, cool. 21-24 Seasonable; showers. 25-28 Sunny & pleasant. 29-30 Showers, cool.

OCT. 1993: Temp. 70° (2.5° above avg.); Precip. 2" (2" below avg.; avg. south). 1-4 Clear, pleasant. 5-7 Showers, cool. 8-10 Sunny, warm. 11-13 Sprinkles, cool. 14-21 Clear, warm. 22-24 Seasonable, rain central. 25-27 Partly cloudy, cool. 28-31 Sunny, warm.

ROCKY MOUNTAINS

For regional boundaries, see map page 129.

SUMMARY: *November through March is expected to be colder than normal in the north with above-normal precipitation and snowfall, but slightly warmer central and south, with below-normal precipitation and near-normal snowfall. November through mid-December will be warm and dry, followed by cold through early February, except for mild spells in early and late January. Expect milder weather through mid-March, then a wintry latter half of March.*

April through June should be much cooler than normal in central and northern sections and slightly so in the west and south. Precipitation may be well below normal, but only slightly below in the west, and above normal in the north. Snowfall, however, will be well above normal for this period. Watch for an extended cold wave in early May and brief cold snaps in mid- and late June. Most of the precipitation is expected in early April and May and during mid-June.

July through September may be cooler than normal central and south, but slightly warmer in the north and west. Late July and early August may have cool spells, while late August and early September may see some heat waves. Precipitation should be below normal, but slightly above normal in the west.

Following a cold beginning, October should be warmer than normal until the end of the month, with most of the shower activity occurring in the north.

NOV. 1992: Temp. 43° (3° above avg.; 5° above south); Precip. 1" (0.5" below avg.; avg. north). 1-2 Sunny, mild; showers north. 3-11 Clear, warm. 12-15 Cold; rain, snow mountains. 16-18 Clear, warming; showers north. 19-24 Sunny, mild. 25-28 Cold north, rain & snow; sunny, mild south. 29-30 Sunny, mild.

DEC. 1992: Temp. 30.5° (0.5° above avg.; 0.5° below south); Precip. 1.5" (Avg.; 0.5" below south). 1-4 Sunny, mild south; showers, cool north. 5-12 Seasonable; sunny south, showers north. 13-15 Snow. 16-18 Clearing, very cold. 19-22 Snow, seasonable. 23-25 Cold, snow south. 26-30 Snow, seasonable. 31 Clearing.

JAN. 1993: Temp. 28° (Avg.; 1° below west); Precip. 1.5" (0.5" above avg.; 1" below south). 1-4 Clear, mild. 5-8 Rain & snow, very cold. 9-11 Clear, very cold then warming. 12-15 Snow north, sunny south. 16-20 Snow, turning cold. 21-27 Sunny, mild; snow then rain north. 28-31 Cold, snow.

FEB. 1993: Temp. 33° (1° below avg.; 4° below north, 2° above south); Precip. 1.5" (Avg.; 0.5" below south). 1-3 Very cold north; snow, milder south. 4-8 Very cold, flurries. 9-11 Seasonable, sleet north; mild south. 12-17 Cold, rain & snow. 18-20 Sunny, warming; sprinkles. 21-24 Clear, warm south. 25-28 Sunny, warm south; rain.

MAR. 1993: Temp. 43° (1° above avg.; 1° below west & north); Precip. 1" (1" below avg. 0.5" above north). 1-2 Sprinkles north; sunny, mild south. 3-6 Sunny, showers south. 7-9 Sunny, warm; showers north. 10-14 Seasonable; rain north. 15-18 Cold, snow. 19-27 Rain north, snow mountains; warm south. 28-31 Snow, cold.

APR. 1993: Temp. 50.5° (0.5° above avg.; 2° below north); Precip. 1" (1" below avg.; avg. north & west). 1-3 Clear, warming. 4-7 Clear, rain north. 8-10 Sunny, mild. 11-13 Cold; rain, snow north. 14-16 Clear, seasonable. 17-19 Cold, light rain & snow. 20-26 Clear, warm. 27-30 Sunny south; showers north.

MAY 1993: Temp. 56° (3° below avg.); Precip. 2" (1" above avg.; avg. north & south). 1-4 Rain, then clearing; cooler. 5-12 Rain, snow; cold. 13-20 Clearing, warm; sprinkles. 21-23 Showers, snow mountains; cold. 24-26 Clear, warm. 27-31 Sunny, cool; warming; snow east.

JUNE 1993: Temp. 66° (3° below avg.); Precip. 0.4" (0.5" below avg.; 2" above north). 1-5 Clear, pleasant. 6-9 Sunny, seasonable; cool, sprinkles central. 10-12 Cold; rain, snow north; sunny south. 13-14 Clear, seasonable. 15-19 Cold, rain north. 20-26 Sunny, warm; showers. 27-30 Cold; rain north, dry south.

JULY 1993: Temp. 76.5° (1° below avg.; 0.5° above north & west); Precip. 0.8" (Avg.; 0.5" above south). 1-5 Clear, warm. 6-9 Sunny, rain south. 10-15 Cooling; heavy rain, light north. 16-19 Sunny, warm; few sprinkles. 20-23 Sunny, mild; thundershowers south. 24-31 Clear, hot north; rain, cool south.

AUG. 1993: Temp. 73° (2° below avg.; avg. north & west); Precip. 0.4" (0.5" below avg.). 1-3 Light rain, cool. 4-7 Clearing, seasonable. 8-10 Cool, rain; dry west. 11-20 Seasonable, showers, heavy south. 21-25 Clear & hot; light rain south. 26-28 Rain; cool, clear central. 29-31 Clear, warm.

SEPT. 1993: Temp. 65.5° (0.5° above avg.; 2° above north & west); Precip. 1.2" (Avg.; 0.5" above west). 1-9 Clear, hot. 10-14 Rain, cool, sprinkles north. 15-20 Sunny, mild; showers central & east. 21-23 Rain, cool south; showers, seasonable north. 24-27 Clear, warm. 28-30 Rain, clear south; cooler.

OCT. 1993: Temp. 55° (2° above avg.; 5° above south); Precip. 1" (0.5" below avg.; 0.5" above north & west). 1-5 Cold, showers central. 6-9 Sunny, seasonable; rain north. 10-14 Clear, showers north. 15-17 Sunny, warm. 18-22 Rain, seasonable. 23-27 Clear, mild. 28-31 Rain; cloudy, cool.

SOUTHWEST DESERT
For regional boundaries, see map page 129.

SUMMARY: *November through March is expected to be warmer than normal, particularly in the east, with below-normal precipitation in the west and slightly below in the east. November through mid-December will be quite warm and dry except for a cool spell in mid-November. Cold spells with hard frosts during the last half of December, the second week of January, and the beginning of February will be offset by warm spells in early and late January and before the middle and end of February and March. The main precipitation is expected at mid-December and mid-February, with lesser amounts in early January and early March.*

April through June is anticipated to be slightly warmer than normal in the west with close to normal precipitation, but slightly cooler and drier in the east. April should be quite warm with little precipitation, while May will be close to normal except for a cool period near midmonth. Expect cool nights in mid-June in the west while the east is enjoying above-normal temperatures.

July through September should be cooler than normal, with below-normal precipitation in the west, but above in the east. July begins with a heat wave, followed by a mild, wet week. Look for milder periods with thundershowers during the latter part of July, the beginning of August and during September, and hot, dry spells at the end of August and beginning of September.

Following some shower activity in early October, the rest of the month should be quite dry with well above normal temperatures.

NOV. 1992: Temp. 64° (2.5° above avg.); Precip. 0.3" (0.4" below avg.). 1-3 Clear, warm. 4-5 Cold snap. 6-11 Clear, warm. 12-15 Increasing clouds, turning cold; rain west. 16-20 Clearing, warming. 21-24 Clear, warm. 25-26 Cloudy, cool east. 27-30 Sunny, warm.

DEC. 1992: Temp. 53° (1° below avg.; 1° above east); Precip. 1" (Avg.). 1-3 Clear, warm. 4-6 Cooling, showers. 7-12 Sunny, turning seasonable. 13-15 Cold, rain. 16-18 Clear, cold; frost. 19-23 Showers, seasonable. 24-26 Cold, rain. 27-31 Clearing, warm days, cold nights.

JAN. 1993: Temp. 51° (1° below avg.; 3° above east); Precip. 0.2" (0.5" below avg.). 1-4 Clear, pleasant, rain east. 5-7 Increasing clouds, showers; milder. 8-10 Clear, cold, hard frost. 11-14 Seasonable, sprinkles. 15-17 Rain, cooler. 18-21 Clearing, warming. 22-28 Clear, very warm. 29-31 Cold, showers.

FEB. 1993: Temp. 58.5° (1° above avg.; 4° above east); Precip. 1" (0.3" above avg.). 1-3 Clear, cold nights; light frost, then rain. 4-7 Sunny, seasonable. 8-13 Clear, warm. 14-16 Cold, rain. 17-19 Clear, warming. 20-23 Clear, very warm. 24-25 Showers. 26-28 Clear; warm.

MAR. 1993: Temp. 63° (1° above avg.; 2° above east); Precip. 1" (Avg.; 0.2" below east). 1-3 Clear, very warm, then heavy rain. 4-6 Seasonable, showers. 7-10 Sunny, warm. 11-15 Sunny, seasonable, then warming. 16-19 Clear, cool. 20-28 Clear, warm. 29-31 Cold, rain.

APR. 1993: Temp. 72.5° (3° above avg.); Precip. 0" (0.2" below avg.). 1-2 Clearing, warm; cold nights. 3-7 Sunny, warm, sprinkles. 8-11 Very warm, increasing clouds. 12-14 Cold, showers. 15-20 Clearing, seasonable; rain east. 21-25 Clear, hot. 26-27 Sprinkles, cooler. 28-30 Seasonable.

MAY 1993: Temp. 77° (1.5° below avg.; avg. east); Precip. 0" (0.1" below avg.). 1-6 Clear, warm. 7-9 Cold, rain. 10-13 Warm days, cool nights. 14-16 Clear, warm; rain east. 17-20 Clear, turning hot. 21-24 Seasonable, cool nights; scattered showers. 25-27 Sunny, hot. 28-31 Seasonable, showers then clearing.

JUNE 1993: Temp. 86.5° (1.5° below avg.; 1° above east); Precip. 0.1" (Avg.; 1" above south). 1-3 Clear & hot. 4-6 Light rain, seasonable. 7-9 Clear, hot. 10-12 Light rain, mild. 13-24 Clear; seasonable, cool nights; sprinkles east. 25-27 Rain, mild. 28-30 Clear, seasonable.

JULY 1993: Temp. 92° (1° below avg.; 2° below east); Precip. 0.7" (0.1" below avg.; 1" above south & east). 1-4 Clear, very hot. 5-8 Showers, very hot. 9-13 Thundershowers, cooler. 14-16 Clearing, hot; showers east. 17-19 Clear, very hot. 20-23 Rain, milder. 24-26 Showers, cooler. 27-31 Rain, then clearing; seasonable.

AUG. 1993: Temp. 90° (1° below avg.); Precip. 0.5" (0.4" below avg.). 1-4 Thundershowers, cooler. 5-7 Clear, hot. 8-9 Showers, milder. 10-13 Clear, turning very hot. 14-16 Rain, seasonable. 17-19 Clear, turning very hot; rain east. 20-24 Clear & hot. 25-29 Scattered showers, milder. 30-31 Clear & hot.

SEPT. 1993: Temp. 84° (1.5° below avg.; avg. east); Precip. 0.5" (0.3" below avg.). 1-5 Clear, very hot. 6-8 Seasonable, rain east. 9-12 Rain, seasonable, cool nights. 13-20 Clear, cool nights, slightly mild. 21-23 Thundershowers, slightly mild. 24-26 Cold, rain. 27-30 Clearing, turning hot; rain east.

OCT. 1993: Temp. 79° (5° above avg.); Precip. 0" (0.7" below avg.). 1-3 Clear & hot. 4-6 Clear; seasonable, cool nights. 7-9 Sunny, hot; showers south & east. 10-17 Clear; hot nights. 18-25 Sunny, hot, few showers. 26-31 Clear, warm.

PACIFIC NORTHWEST

For regional boundaries, see map page 129.

SUMMARY: *November through March will be colder and wetter than normal, with well above normal snowfall, but with considerable variability from month to month. November may be warm with below-normal snowfall, but with rain at midmonth and after Thanksgiving. Beginning in December, progressively colder, wetter, and snowier weather is anticipated through early February, with mild temperatures between Christmas and New Year and in late January. By mid-February, seasonable temperatures are expected, continuing through early March before becoming subnormal again. Precipitation will be well above normal, with snow at higher elevations.*

April through June is anticipated to be slightly warmer and drier than normal in the north, but slightly cooler and wetter in the south. Cold, wet periods, with snow at high elevations, will alternate with brief warm spells through April and the first half of May, but then sunny and warm periods should dominate until early June. The rest of June should be cold and wet.

July through September should be warmer than normal with near-normal precipitation. Sunny and warm periods in early and late July and the end of August will be partially balanced by brief cool, wet periods, while September will be close to normal, with little rainfall until a storm at the end of the month.

October is expected to turn quite cold and wet after a clear beginning.

NOV. 1992: Temp. 50° (4° above avg.); Precip. 5.5" (Avg.). 1-2 Heavy rain, seasonable. 3-10 Clear, very mild. 11-15 Heavy rain, seasonable. 16-18 Heavy rain north, light south. 19-22 Sunny south, showers north; mild. 23-25 Clear, cold nights; cloudy north. 26-30 Heavy rain, quite mild.

DEC. 1992: Temp. 41.5° (1° above avg.); Precip. 5" (1" below avg.). 1-2 Rain, cooler. 3-6 Rain, snow mountains; seasonable. 7-13 Rain, snow mountains. 14-16 Cold wave, snow. 17-22 Seasonable, cold, freezing rain & snow. 23-25 Cold wave, flurries. 26-31 Rain, snow mountains.

JAN. 1993: Temp. 33.5° (6° below avg.); Precip. 9" (4" above avg.). 1-2 Rain, mild. 3-5 Turning cold, snow. 6-9 Cold wave, light snow. 10-14 Rain & snow, seasonable. 15-17 Snow, colder. 18-22 Cold wave; light snow. 23-26 Heavy snow changing to rain; milder. 27-31 Cold, snow.

FEB. 1993: Temp. 40.5° (3° below avg.); Precip. 5" (1" above avg.). 1-7 Cold; clear north, snow south then clearing. 8-10 Snow, warming to normal. 11-16 Freezing rain, snow mountains; seasonable. 17-20 Heavy rain, slightly mild. 21-25 Showers, seasonable. 26-28 Heavy rain, heavy snow mountains.

MAR. 1993: Temp. 46° (1° below avg.; 1° above north); Precip. 5" (1.5" above avg.; 4" above north). 1-2 Rain, snow mountains; milder. 3-5 Sunny. 6-10 Heavy rain, snow mountains; slightly mild. 11-17 Cold; light rain & snow. 18-24 Sprinkles, then rain, snow mountains; seasonable. 25-31 Rain & snow, cold.

APR. 1993: Temp. 49° (2° below avg.; avg. north); Precip. 2.5" (Avg.). 1-7 Cloudy, then rain, snow mountains; seasonable. 8-9 Sunny & mild. 10-12 Rain & snow south, intermittent north; seasonable. 13-15 Showers. 16-21 Heavy rain, then slackening; colder. 22-25 Sunny & mild. 26-30 Light showers, turning cold.

MAY 1993: Temp. 55° (2° below avg.); Precip. 1" (1" below avg.). 1 Cold & rainy. 2-4 Sunny & mild. 5-10 Rain, snow mountains; quite cold. 11-13 Clear; seasonable, cool south. 14-20 Sunny & warm, then seasonable. 21-23 Cold wave, rain. 24-25 Clear, mild. 26-28 Cool, showers. 29-31 Clear, very warm.

JUNE 1993: Temp. 62° (1° above avg.; 1° below north). 1-3 Cool, showers. 4-7 Clear, very warm. 8-10 Cold wave, then cloudy. 11-13 Rain, cool. 14-15 Clear & warm, rain south. 16-18 Cold, light rain. 19-24 Showers then clearing, warm. 25-28 Rain, cool. 29-30 Clearing, warm.

JULY 1993: Temp. 68° (Avg.); Precip. 0.5" (Avg.). 1-10 Clear, warm. 11-14 Showers, cool. 15-17 Sunny & warm. 18-20 Cloudy & cool. 21-23 Rain, seasonable. 24-29 Sunny, pleasantly warm. 30-31 Scattered showers, turning very cool.

AUG. 1993: Temp. 69° (1° above avg.); Precip. 1" (Avg.). 1-2 Rain, very cool. 3-6 Clearing & warming. 7-11 Sunny, quite cool; showers. 12-17 Sunny, warm. 18-20 Heavy rain, cool north; showers & warm south. 21-25 Clear, very warm. 26-28 Rain, cool. 29-31 Clearing & warm.

SEPT. 1993: Temp. 64° (1° above avg.); Precip. 1" (0.5" below avg.). 1-3 Sunny, seasonable. 4-6 Clear, quite warm. 7-9 Scattered showers, cooler. 10-12 Sunny, mild. 13-16 Variable; cool, then warm. 17-19 Cool, few showers. 20-21 Sunny, mild. 22-24 Cool. 25-27 Clear, warm. 28-30 Rain, seasonable.

OCT. 1993: Temp. 53° (1.5° below avg.); Precip. 5" (2.5" above avg.). 1-2 Showers, cool. 3-6 Clear, cold nights. 7-9 Heavy rain, very cool. 10-11 Clearing & warming. 12-14 Heavy rain, cool. 15-20 Showers, quite cool. 21-24 Heavy rain, seasonable. 25-27 Partial clearing, cool. 28-31 Rain, seasonable.

CALIFORNIA
For regional boundaries, see map page 129.

SUMMARY: *November through March is expected to be slightly colder than normal in the far north, but warmer in central and southern sections with below-normal precipitation, particularly in the south. Snowfall in the mountains should be well above normal in the north and slightly above east of the San Joaquin valley, but below normal in the mountains of southern California. November through early December may be quite warm and dry except for a storm in mid-November. Frequent cold, wet spells are expected through mid-February, interspersed with warm, dry spells in early and late January. Most of March will be fairly warm and dry until a cold wave and heavy rain end the month.*

April through June is anticipated to be quite variable while averaging warmer than normal in the north and south. Precipitation will be generally below normal. Cool, wet periods before mid-April and in early May will be offset by warm, dry spells in early and late April and the latter half of May. A hot early June will be followed by a fairly prolonged period of milder weather.

July through September should be warmer than normal with the usual lack of precipitation. Hot spells in early July, late August, and early September should be partially offset by mild periods in the latter part of July, the first half of August, and the middle of September.

October may start with a cool spell, then be generally clear and warm until a heavy rainstorm in central and northern sections closes out the month.

NOV.1992: Temp. 59° (5° above avg.); Precip. 1.5" (1" below avg.; 0.5" above south). 1-8 Clear & hot. 9-11 Rain, cooling. 12-14 Heavy rain, very cool. 15-19 Clearing; warming, hot south. 20-22 Clear, very warm. 23-26 Slight cooling, fog inland. 27-30 Clear, warm.

DEC.1992: Temp. 49° (0.5° above avg.; 0.5° below south); Precip. 3" (Avg.; 1" above south). 1-3 Sunny, warm; cloudy, cool south. 4-8 Cooling; cloudy, showers inland. 9-12 Rain. 13-17 Clear; cold, frost inland. 18-20 Rain, seasonable. 21-23 Rain. 24-28 Sunny, cold nights. 29-31 Warm days, cold nights.

JAN.1993: Temp. 46° (2° below avg.); Precip. 6" (2" above avg.; 1" below south.). 1-4 Mild, cold nights, frost inland. 5-7 Rain, snow mountains, cold. 8-11 Clear. 12-18 Rain, heavy snow mountains; cold. 19-22 Clearing, then rain, warming. 23-24 Sunny, warm. 25-28 Mild, rain. 29-31 Cold; rain, snow mountains.

FEB.1993: Temp. 50.5° (1° below avg.); Precip. 2.5" (1" below avg.). 1-2 Rain, snow mountains; cold. 3-7 Clear, cold, frost inland. 8-10 Heavy rain, seasonable. 11-13 Sunny, cold nights. 14-16 Rain. 17-23 Clear, mild. 24-28 Clear, sprinkles south.

MAR.1993: Temp. 52° (0.5° below avg.); Precip. 1.5" (1.5" below avg.). 1-4 Sunny, mild; few showers. 5-8 Partly cloudy, seasonable. 9-13 Cooling, showers. 14-19 Clear, cold nights. 20-26 Rain, seasonable. 27-31 Heavy rain, heavy snow mountains; cold.

APR.1993: Temp. 57° (2° above avg.; 4° above south); Precip. 1" (0.5" below avg.). 1-6 Clear, warm. 7-9 Cloudy, milder. 10-13 Heavy rain, cold. 14-16 Clear, pleasant. 17-19 Showers, cool. 20-24 Clear, very warm. 25-27 Cloudy, seasonable. 28-30 Sunny.

MAY1993: Temp. 57° (1.5° below avg.); Precip. 0.2" (0.1" above avg.). 1-4 Clear & warm. 5-7 Cold wave; rain, snow mountains. 8-11 Clearing; colder than normal, seasonable south. 12-16 Clear, turning hot. 17-21 Sunny, warm, scattered showers. 22-25 Clear, very hot. 26-28 Mild spell. 29-31 Clear, very hot.

JUNE1993: Temp. 60° (2° below avg.); Precip. 0.1" (Avg.). 1-3 Clear, hot. 4-6 Sunny, warm; sprinkles south. 7-9 Clear, warm. 10-13 Showers, very cool, then clearing. 14-21 Showers; cool, seasonable south. 22-26 Clear, hot. 27-30 Clear & mild, sprinkles south.

JULY1993: Temp. 62° (2° below avg.; 2° above inland); Precip. 0" (Avg.). 1-5 Clear, very hot. 6-9 Increasing clouds, cooling. 10-14 Scattered showers, mild. 15-18 Clear, turning hot. 19-22 Clear, cooling. 23-29 Sunny, warm; few showers. 30-31 Cloudy, cooler.

AUG.1993: Temp. 62° (2° below avg.; 1° above inland); Precip. 0" (Avg.). 1-4 Clearing; warming, cooler south. 5-9 Showers, cooler north; clear & warm south. 10-15 Clear, mild; hot south. 16-18 Sunny, seasonable. 19-24 Clear, very hot. 25-27 Clear, warm. 28-31 Sunny, warming.

SEPT.1993: Temp. 64.5° (Avg.); Precip. 0.1" (0.1" below avg.). 1-4 Clear & warm, cool north coast. 5-9 Clear, very warm. 10-16 Showers, quite cool. 17-20 Partly cloudy, cool. 21-23 Showers, very cool. 24-28 Clear, pleasantly warm. 29-30 Cloudy, seasonable.

OCT.1993: Temp. 62° (1° above avg.; 3° above south & inland); Precip. 1.5" (0.5" above avg.; 0.5" below south). 1-2 Clear, warm. 3-6 Clear, cold. 7-9 Sunny; warm south, showers north. 10-13 Clear, warm. 14-17 Clear, very warm. 18-21 Cooler; cloudier, showers north. 22-26 Clear, pleasant. 27-31 Rain, cooler.

Be Your Own Boss and Make

$18.00 to $30.00 AN HOUR!

Find out how by sending now for your Free Lifetime Security Fact Kit!

Your FREE Lifetime Security Fact Kit tells you how to make $18.00 to $30.00 an hour in your own Foley-Belsaw Full-Service Saw and Tool Sharpening Business. Your FREE Fact Kit explains how you can:

— **be your own BOSS!**
— **work full time or part time, right at home.**
— **do work you enjoy and take pride in.**
— **operate a CASH business where 90¢ of every dollar you take in is clear cash profit.**

And it is so easy to learn. Foley-Belsaw gives you all the facts and instructions. No previous experience or special training necessary. All you need is the desire and ambition to be your own boss. Foley-Belsaw tells you everything you need to know to be successful. There's plenty of business where you live to keep you busy. It doesn't matter whether you live in a big city, small town or a small farm community.

Earn While You Learn

You'll quickly be able to develop the skills necessary to earn a steady income. You'll be able to sharpen all types of saws, garden and shop tools for home, farm and industry. Profits from your Foley-Belsaw Full-Service Sharpening Business can provide...

... **CASH for future security or supplemental income**
... **CASH for travel, vacations, fishing trips**
... **CASH for things you've always wanted!**

And you'll be able to set your own hours and not have to worry about layoffs and strikes. There are no franchise fees. Best of all — age or physical condition is no barrier — any age person can succeed.

You can be like Steve Taylor of Brookville, Ohio, who told us:
"... the first year I grossed $21,000.00."

Or James B. Jones, of Albuquerque, NM who reported:
"This past summer my sales and service amounted to almost $6,000.00 a month."

But you've got to get the FACTS before you can get started. So WRITE NOW for your FREE Lifetime Security Fact Kit. It's yours to keep with NO OBLIGATION!

FOLEY BELSAW

Foley-Belsaw Co.
6301 Equitable Rd.
Dept. 21093
Kansas City, Mo. 64120

FREE Lifetime Security
FACT KIT

Foley-Belsaw Co.
6301 Equitable Rd., Dept. 21093
Kansas City, Mo. 64120

☐ **YES,** I want to know more! Please rush my FREE Lifetime Security Fact Kit. No obligation and no salesman will call.

Name

Address

City   State   Zip

(   )
Area Code Phone

Catching Fireflies for Fun

There's a bounty on lightning bugs. A St. Louis chemical company will pay you one cent each for fireflies, dead or alive. Alive is preferred, said Sue Hardwick of the Sigma Firefly Scientists Club; the fresher the firefly, the higher the quality of the luciferin and luciferase in the tail. The company's clients want the light-producing luciferin and the catalyzing enzyme luciferase, which causes luciferin to light up, for various research projects.

Although fireflies can be successfully hatched in a lab, they cannot be reared easily because of exacting nutritional requirements and a two-year gestation period. So Sigma relies on catchers, 600 of them in a good year. Some catchers may turn in a total of only 100, but others supply many more.

A catcher gets a $5 bonus for 5,000 ($50) and up to a $600 bonus for 200,000 ($2,000), so families often submit under one name, Hardwick said. One supplier in Chambersburg, Pennsylvania, turned in 32,000 one summer. An Apple Creek, Ohio, catcher provided 44,000; a Fredericksburg, Ohio, catcher submitted 41,000.

An average respectable harvest rate might top 9,000 in a good year. Hardwick said she did have one Pennsylvania family that turned in 30,000 in a week, although she nets only about 150 a night herself on her farm. In trying to achieve that kind of goal, some people have tried creative approaches. One farmer erected a net on his pickup truck and drove around. But he then had to pick the fireflies out of the other bugs he caught. He gave that up. Then there was the woman who drove around in her car with a large net hanging out the side window. She caught a baby fox. "Fortunately, she didn't try to mail it to us," Hardwick recalled.

When suppliers come up with more than 5,000 a week, Hardwick calls them and advises them to ship the fireflies overnight in an ice-cooled container. However you ship them, Sigma refunds postage. They even provide canisters containing a drying agent for shipment of the fireflies through the regular mail.

The Firefly Club also has "live catchers" to supplement their supply. In 1991 there was one in Illinois and one in Iowa. "These two people have children catching for them, and they ship them to us overnight delivery on ice. We'll get those alive," Hardwick said. Hardwick recalled one live catcher from Allison, Iowa, who got involved in a project to build a community swimming pool. Fireflies paid for a portion of that pool, which has since been built.

You can store your fireflies in the refrigerator in a jar or in the shipping canister to accumulate them before mailing. But don't wait beyond five days. The chemicals are no good to Sigma after that. In any event, don't freeze them — it will ruin the chemical reaction.

There's no minimum shipment. One Sigma employee's son came up with two shipments hand-carried in by Mom, and he got his money like everyone else — 6¢ for the first bunch, 14¢ for the second.

Sigma's fireflies come mostly from the Midwest, said Hardwick, with some from the East, and virtually none from west of Colorado. Warm humid conditions are required. Summarized by Hardwick: "Can't be too hot, can't be too cold, can't

The money you can make in a year won't buy you a car, but with the right weather conditions, it's easy enough money to come by ...

and Profit

have too much rain, can't have too little. They're kind of fragile."

Sigma's catchers harvest two basic varieties of firefly. One is the common firefly beetle, *Photinus pyralis.* The other is *Photuris pennsylvanica.* With the cannibalistic female of the latter species, the firefly's flash is not a courting signal. It's a dinner bell. And the unwary male answering the signal is dinner. Fortunately for the continuation of the species, sometime prior to becoming the entrée, the male manages to copulate. (This type of behavior by the larger, stronger females is very common in insects. The female firefly beetle subdues and consumes her mate in order to nourish her egg mass and provide the protein for yolk production.)

"Can't be too hot, can't be too cold, can't have too much rain, can't have too little. They're kind of fragile."

During their two-year gestation, the firefly larvae feed on snails and slugs. Those larvae that have the firefly's glow are referred to as "glowworms." So are the flightless females of some species.

There are 1,900 species of this beetle worldwide. They are distinguished by two pairs of "wings," the outer pair of which have evolved to form a hard, protective pair of wing covers that fold out of the way when the insect uses the inner pair for flight. In Jamaica they're known to gather by the thousands in trees, transforming them into "fire trees." Similar "fire trees" in the Far East are also filled with fireflies, but they flash in a synchro-

by Nick Howes

– illustrated by Robert Lawson / represented by Creative Freelancers

nized pattern (the significance of which is unknown). The glowing larvae of New Zealand fireflies light up rooms in caverns, creating tourist attractions. Fireflies in Japan are traditionally regarded as ghosts of heroic warriors slain in battle. Around the Mediterranean, fireflies are spirits marking graves.

Last summer I caught about 1,200 fireflies over a couple of weeks' time. I started just before dusk when you can still see them, especially with the momentary flash as a guide. I enjoyed my-self immensely. It took only two years to work up the nerve to leap around the yard with a firefly net while the neighbors watched.

For a member's handbook describing how to make a net, store and ship fireflies, send to:

Sigma Firefly Scientists Club
Division of Sigma Chemical
  Company
3500 DeKalb Street
St. Louis, MO 63118 ☐☐

Other Bugs That Make Money:
SOME TIPS FOR ENTREPRENEURS

As always in any business venture, check state and local licensing requirements and zoning limitations.

☞ **FISHING WORMS** can be sold wholesale to local bait shops at about half the retail price or from your garage with a hand-lettered sign by the road. Retail prices run $1 per dozen in some places. Red worms are best for breeding because they breed in shallow soil and can be reared in old-fashioned wash tubs or in homemade wooden beds. Sell the enriched "nightsoil" they create to gardeners or people with houseplants.

☞ **CRICKETS** or **MEALY WORMS** can be raised for pet shops. One bait dealer said both do require temperature control, but crickets are very popular with pet shops, bringing 50¢ to 75¢ per dozen, wholesale. Cricket and mealy worm gourmets include birds, lizards, and tarantulas.

☞ **CRICKETS** can be sold as pets. (Cricket cages are

available from bait shops.) Cricket pets are an old tradition in Hong Kong and elsewhere in the East. Entomologist David Shetler told CBS News he thought cockroaches would make good pets. They eat anything, they're not smelly like mice or hamsters, but he admitted, "Most moms and dads, I think, would be absolutely horrified." He suggests crickets as an alternative.

☞ Do what I did ... write about insects.

WHAT DO RESEARCHERS DO WITH ALL THOSE FIREFLIES?

☞ In North Carolina, Dr. Joseph Bonaventura found that firefly extract paralyzed Atlantic sharp-nosed sharks and ultimately killed them.

☞ NASA once rocketed firefly extract into space. On-board instruments could detect the flash produced by the exposure of firefly luciferin and luciferase to even one-quadrillionth of a gram of adenosine triphosphate (ATP), the energy source for the firefly's light.

☞ California researchers transferred the luciferase-producing gene into tobacco plants. This aids research into the plant's genetic functions and may be adaptable to other plants.

☞ Sigma sends live fireflies to a Boston hospital for on-going neurological research.

☞ Firefly extract can help biochemists distinguish cancerous cells from healthy ones because cancerous cells produce more ATP than background normal cells. Firefly extract also detects bacterial contamination in water and milk and is part of a diagnostic test used with heart-attack victims.

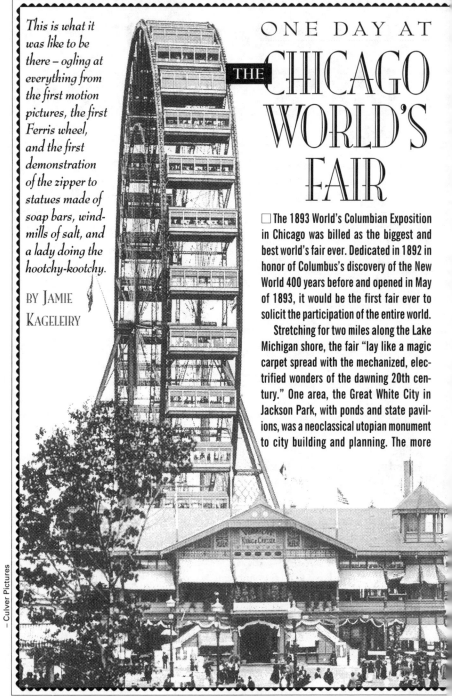

This is what it was like to be there – ogling at everything from the first motion pictures, the first Ferris wheel, and the first demonstration of the zipper to statues made of soap bars, windmills of salt, and a lady doing the hootchy-kootchy.

BY JAMIE KAGELEIRY

ONE DAY AT

THE CHICAGO WORLD'S FAIR

☐ The 1893 World's Columbian Exposition in Chicago was billed as the biggest and best world's fair ever. Dedicated in 1892 in honor of Columbus's discovery of the New World 400 years before and opened in May of 1893, it would be the first fair ever to solicit the participation of the entire world.

Stretching for two miles along the Lake Michigan shore, the fair "lay like a magic carpet spread with the mechanized, electrified wonders of the dawning 20th century." One area, the Great White City in Jackson Park, with ponds and state pavilions, was a neoclassical utopian monument to city building and planning. The more

– Culver Pictures

honky-tonk Midway Plaisance, which was run officially under the auspices of a Department of Ethnology, catered to the more recreational diversions. The Ferris wheel – the world's first – turned out to be one of the most thrilling wonders of the fair and ended up being a giant centerpiece. Queen of the Midway, it was called.

It was a late summer day. Engineer George Washington Gale Ferris stood looking up at the wheel he had built for the exposition. It stood four stories higher than the world's tallest building. Two perfect pinion wheels, 250 feet across, hung on an axle 45 feet long, weighing 70 tons — the largest steel shaft ever forged. Between the wheels were suspended 36 cars the size of trolleys that could hold 60 people each. It was the first of its kind, the largest ever in America.

THE FERRIS WHEEL

- ☞ Eight foundation towers, each 20 feet square and 35 feet high, were made of solid concrete.

- ☞ The giant axle that turned the wheels was the largest steel shaft ever forged. It weighed 70 tons, as much as an ordinary locomotive.

- ☞ 2,200 tons of pig iron went into the making of the wheels.

- ☞ A single 1,000-horsepower engine drove the wheel (with another engine in reserve).

- ☞ Ninety-two percent of all the people who attended the fair rode the Ferris wheel at 50¢ a ride (ten times the cost of the merry-go-round).

The great wheel was America's answer to the Eiffel Tower, the showpiece of the awesome Paris Exposition of 1889. Eager to prove to the world that America was indeed the vigorous new land of invention and bold ideas, it had taken George Ferris only 20 minutes to sketch his vision and the engineering specifications necessary to build it. Words of warning echoed in Ferris's head: "It can't be done!" said fellow engineers. The gales of Lake Michigan, "strong enough to strip the fur off a buffalo," would collapse the wheel, or worse, would send it rolling into the lake. Ferris had such confidence in the idea, such dash, that he didn't even feel compelled to test his invention before sending it, in parts, to be assembled on the Midway. And there it was, untouched by the 110-mile-an-hour winds of a ferocious storm the month before, lilting toward heaven in the golden afternoon light. On the ground, George Ferris turned to the Midway to enjoy the rest of the fair.

"I am dazzled, captivated, and bewildered, and return to my room, tired in mind, eyes, ears, and body. So much to think about, so much to entice you on from place to place."

– Horace Benson, Denver attorney

At the very top of the 250-foot Ferris wheel sat a Ceylonese monk, Dharmapala, orange-robed, smiling. He'd come to attend the world's first Parliament of Religion. From his perspective, the monk could see all of the World's Columbian Exposition spread before him; beyond lay all of Chicago and a long stretch of Lake Michigan shoreline. Suspended thus, the monk exclaimed to his companion, "All the joys of heaven are in Chicago!" Dr. Alfred Momerie, a Christian from the English Anglican church, gazed at the bustle below and replied, "I wish I were sure that all the joys of Chicago are to be in heaven!"

Chicago was a microcosm of the whole world that summer of 1893, of a world big enough to surprise each person with its gifts, and small enough still to be represented in all its color at a single event. The fair was a crossroads, not just of the East and West of the monk and the reverend or the collision of the spiritual and the technological, but of old and new, past and future. All roads led to the Chicago fair, converging like the spokes of the great wheel.

At the base of the wheel, a young girl from Kansas pulls away from her mother's hand and spins past Ferris down the Midway. So much to see! Here an ostrich farm, and right next door a Lapland village and a muscle-flexing strongman. And the sounds! Annie Oakley practicing sure-shots with Buffalo Bill's Wild West Show across the street, and other sounds she's never heard before and doesn't have a name for: African drumming, scratchy phonograph records, the screech of steel, and the clang of gears. On the Street of Cairo a peddler yells, "Nicey, freshy, bum-bum candy. Hot, hot, paneycakey, good!"

"It [the fancy beaux-arts architecture of the Great White City] has penetrated deep into the constitution of the American mind, effecting there lesions significant of dementia."

— Chicago "modern school" architect Louis Sullivan

A Wisconsin farm boy turns to stare. It's hard concentrating, with everything here in one place. The Liberty Bell, a cannon captured at Yorktown, the first and last guns fired in the Civil War, even the anchor from Columbus's ship. And more — statues made of soap bars, windmills of salt, and a hut of gilded coconuts. He remembers a poem he'd heard earlier that summer: "Come, boys, let's away to the Midway Plaisance. There are visions of loveliness there to behold..." Four lions roar, and the hootchy-kootchy hawkers pull the boy forward, his eyes wide. Inside the tent, Little Egypt would be doing her "danse du ventre," better known as the belly dance or hootchy-kootchy. He ponders. His father strolls up, and with a long look around the tent flap himself, snatches the lad by the collar and heads with him toward the exclamations emanating from a building ahead.

Picture this: An audience sits in

Above: Neoclassical pavilions in the Great White City. Right: Little Egypt warming up the Midway Plaisance.

photos Culver Pictures

THE NUMBERS

☞ During construction in 1891-1892, including an "icy hell of a winter," 7,000 men worked on the fair. Eighteen were killed and 700 were injured in accidents.

☞ On Dedication Day, October 23, 1892: 5,000 singers celebrated the opening; 100,000 people attended; 70,000 people ate the lunch provided.

☞ By the end of the fair, one in every ten Americans had attended.

☞ On "Chicago Day," 716,881 local citizens were admitted at a reduced price.

☞ To spend just ten minutes at each of the fair's exhibits would have taken 21 years.

☞ Fast food: 17,000 people could sit and eat at one time at the various dining establishments. Fifty cattle were killed each morning to feed the crowds.

☞ Over the course of the fair, 6,000 experts in 200 fields of human endeavor came to deliver their views on major issues like the role of modern women and the future of labor.

FIRSTS

☞ First side-buttoned lady's boot

☞ First Sousa band performance

☞ First carnival midway

☞ Introduction of motion pictures

☞ First muscle-flexing strongman

☞ First use of saccharin

☞ Introduction of Cracker Jack candied popcorn

☞ First large-scale demonstration of electricity; also the founding of Underwriters Laboratories after a "number of fires" in electrical devices

☞ First ham baked electrically

☞ First use of concrete paving

☞ First large-scale debuts of the telephone, the phonograph, the incandescent lamp, the Linotype machine, and the "sliding clasp locker and unlocker for shoes," later known as the zipper!

walls. A man in white tie and tails walks out to center stage, quiet, barely noticed in his cork-bottomed shoes. The man, Nicola Tesla, the inventor of alternating current, stops, stretches his arms out. In one hand is a glass bulb. Now all eyes are on him, and all is silent. The boy holds his breath. Several hundred thousand volts of electricity from a nearby Tesla coil course over the man's body, and the light bulb in his hand — unconnected to any wire or source of power — blooms with light. The audience gasps. To heighten the effect, Tesla strikes a Statue of Liberty pose. His invention would make Edison's electrical lights and other gadgets safe and cheap for the whole world. The light glints from the boy's amazed face.

The girl from Kansas, meanwhile, is whirling from world to world. She enters a logger's camp, then an Indian school, and alights at the heliographic exhibit. There are Algerian beggars, Arabian carpenter shops, Moorish barbers, Egyptian shoe stores, the Duke of Veragua, and the Marquis of Barboles. A light stops her. She stares up at the newest creation of Louis Tiffany, the one that would catapult him to international fame. The window is splendid, unbelievable, like nothing she's ever seen — five parakeets of many colors, perched in the branches of a blossom-laden tree. And a fish bowl with goldfish, hanging from a bough. All in glass that looks like jewels. The amber light that bathes her face also catches the woman next to her.

"You could see every muscle in her body at the same time!"

– Chicago policeman after witnessing Little Egypt's hootchy-kootchy

Ida Wells was, one historian would say, "a black woman who spent her life traveling in search of riots or lynchings so she could write editorials about them." She was one of the founders of the NAACP. It had been a long trip from the South by train. The conductor had tried to force her to ride in the smoking car,

an exhibition hall. People clear their throats and appraise their neighbors. Gaslights throw tentative shadows on the

> *"I ain't afraid anymore of the world bustin' up. People that made the machinery that I've seen have too much sense."*
>

and Ida (70 years before Rosa Parks!) refused. (She later sued the railroad.) Ida Wells had come to protest the segregated "Negro Day" at the exposition. She may have wondered at the irony of a "Parliament of Religion," supposedly emblematic of tolerance, sitting side by side with exhibitions intended to keep black people out.

Ida Wells lifts her head to go. Puzzled, she passes a woman dressed as her grandmother would have been. Aunt Jemima made her debut, too, at the Chicago World's Fair.

The girl's mother finds her and leads her off to the "fair proper" to sip tea and eat quail on toast at the rooftop garden of the Woman's Building, headed by Mrs. Potter Palmer as president of the Board of Lady Managers. Sophia Hayden, the first female graduate of MIT's architecture school, designed the building, called a "focal point for the vanguard of the women's movement." (It was said that the 21-year-old Sophia suffered a nervous breakdown from the stress of such an important project. Though she lived to be 87, Sophia Hayden never designed another building.) Inside on this day a woman doctor, dressed in bloomers, tells her audience, most of whom are squeezed into whalebone corsets, that the tight lacing is responsible for more than 30 percent of female health disorders.

Standing outside is Daniel H. Burnham, the chairman of the fair, who'd stood on this then-swampy spot 2½ years earlier on a hellish January day. "Make no small plans," he'd said then, envisioning what could rise. Chicago was chosen as the site for the fair only after a volley of intercity boasting (especially with New York) so gaseous that journalist Charles Dana called the winner "That Windy City."

Burnham, a leading architect in town, had decreed that all buildings in his envisioned city be made of dazzling white artificial marble (called staff, it was a mixture of plaster of Paris and hemp) and that all cornice heights be exactly the same. He expressed the hope that "the classic forms" of the beaux-arts style would be employed in the design. And all white the Great White City was, sparkling there in front of him, gossamer-like, reflecting in the pools puddling the acres of greenery that Frederick Law Olmsted had designed. All white, that is, except Louis Sullivan's bright Transportation Building. Sullivan was one of the fathers of the skyscraper and the Chicago School of Modern Architecture, so while Burnham stood this day with hands clasped and a smile on his face, Sullivan shook his head. Half a century, he guessed; architecture would be set back half a century. "The whole imperial beaux-arts layout is an unspeakable disaster. It has penetrated deep into the constitution of the American mind, effecting there lesions significant of dementia," Sullivan stated.

After a few years, these buildings would disappear: They were built of temporary materials. Only the Palace of Fine Arts survived — stripped down to its steel frame, it was rebuilt in stone and reincarnated as the Museum of Science

"Make no small plans; they have no magic to stir men's blood."

– Daniel Burnham

GHOSTS OF THE FAIR

So many things that inhabit our everyday lives first showed up at the fair. But other, quieter reminders are so much a part of our landscape that we overlook them. Some dwell quietly in dusty cellars, some are disguised, and some appear out of nowhere. Like ghosts.

THE COLUMBIAN EXPOSITION HALF-DOLLAR

☞ Congress authorized the minting of $2½ million in special half-dollars, with the stipulation that the gates to the Midway Plaisance be locked tight on Sundays.

Fair promoters found a loophole in the agreement, and the gates were thrown open. When Congress tried to compromise by closing the hootchy-kootchy exhibits on Sundays, the crowds stayed away in droves. Eventually the good times won out. If a Columbian Exposition half-dollar crosses your palm these days, hang on to it. Or sell it — it's worth almost $100.

MUNICIPAL ARCHITECTURE

☞ Look around your town — is the post office or city hall rendered in a neoclassical style? Perhaps the buildings are the offspring of the Great White City, created by town fathers who'd

swooned at the fair that summer of 1893.

THE EL

☞ You hear it coming and look up. With a whoosh and a roar, it's gone. The El, Chicago's rapid transit, built to link the exposition grounds to the city, still embodies for most Chicagoans the old glory of the city.

CHRISTOPHER COLUMBUS'S ANCHOR

☞ "In a storage room at the Chicago Historical Society, among crates of relics, is a corroded iron anchor thought to belong to the Santa Maria," reported the Chicago Tribune in 1989. Over 100 years ago, Doctor Alejandro Llenas was walking

in the jungles of the Dominican Republic when he practically tripped over it. There were four other anchors contending for the title, but after much research, the Dominican government concluded that Llenas's anchor was most probably from Columbus's ship. Llenas brought the anchor to the fair for display. In 1932 the Dominicans asked for the anchor back, saying that Llenas had only loaned it to the fair. But officials at the Field Museum, where the anchor was taken after the fair, said it had been donated. The nine-foot anchor still lurks in the depths of the Chicago Historical Society.

and Industry. The rest of the Great White City and Olmsted's parklike grounds would have an impact beyond their brief existence, for they would inspire Americans to beautify and design the urban landscape.

So while Burnham and Sullivan ponder in their separate orbits, the girl and her mother dash past for a last ride on Ferris's wheel before the sunlight fades. In line behind them are the boy from Wisconsin and his father. And disembarking, reluctantly, are Dharmapala and Dr. Momerie. Horace Benson, an attorney visiting from Denver, rests on a bench and writes a letter home: "I am dazzled, captivated, and bewildered and return to my room each night, tired in mind, eyes, ears, and body. So much to think about...." George Ferris looks up, proud. It has been a long day, an amazing summer.

Historian Henry Steele Commager would call the World's Columbian Expo-

sition the "primary representative event of an era that was the watershed of American history." Think about it, historian Henry Adams invited: "Men who had never put their hands on a lever, had never touched an electric battery or talked through a phone" were shaken into wonder. Men who had arrived by horse and wagon, read by candlelight, and plowed their fields by hand had witnessed Algerian barbers, America's first belly dance, all-electric homes, and the world's first moving pictures. The world after the World's Columbian Exposition would never be the same — a fitting celebration for Christopher Columbus's "discovery" of the New World. □□

"Hello and good-bye, hail and farewell"

— Henry Adams on what the Chicago fair represented about the 20th and 19th centuries

The OLD FARMER'S ALMANAC

1993

OLD AND NEW

MATHEMATICAL PUZZLES

Blanton C. Wiggin, Puzzle Editor

For 1993, here are 15 classical, original, or timely puzzles from our readers. There should be something to interest everyone, and we hope they are challenging. Everyday common sense and a little agility are all you'll need; you won't need calculus, computers, alertness to tricks, or specialized knowledge, though sometimes they may be helpful. Some puzzles may require information obtainable from your local library.

The answers to puzzles 12 through 15 are omitted. We will award one prize of $50 for the best set of solutions to these four received before February 1, 1993.

We use a point system to judge the prize set. A basic, unadorned, correct answer is 20 points. For a thorough analysis, an elegant or novel answer, up to 5 points extra. Numerical errors lose only 2 or 3 points, if it is clear that the method is understood.

Please use a separate sheet for each puzzle or answer. Be sure to put your name and address on each sheet.

Explanations and prize-set answers will be sent after June 15, 1993 to anyone sending $1 and a self-addressed stamped envelope to "Puzzle Answers," *The Old Farmer's Almanac,* Dublin, NH 03444. Copies of prize-set puzzles and answers for previous years (1973 to the present) may be obtained from *The Old Farmer's Almanac* for $1 and a one-ounce stamp for each year requested; a self-addressed envelope should be included.

We will also pay $15 for any original puzzles we use in *The Old Farmer's Almanac* for 1994. Closing date for submissions is February 1, 1993. Entries become the property of Yankee Publishing Incorporated and cannot be acknowledged or returned.

In 1992, there were excellent entries in the prize-set contest. Winner by a point was last year's co-winner, Robert Henderson of Belleville, Michigan, with 95.5. A keen mind! Hervey Vigour, Charlottesville, Virginia, was the close second; followed by George Hall, Tucson, Arizona; Robert Griffin, Montclair, New Jersey; and Leon Kreidler, Sheboygan, Wisconsin. All scored over 92! Congratulations!

Have fun with these 1993 puzzles and send your answers early. Answers to puzzles 1-11 appear on page 174.

1. WET MATCHES

Difficulty: 1

☞ Noah's harbor agent phoned Noah that he was sending out a herd of 5 male and 6 female zebras. Soon the 11 animals randomly swam up to the ark. What is the largest number that Noah might have to fish out to be sure he embarked one of each gender?

Old Classic

2. Third Dimension

Difficulty: 1

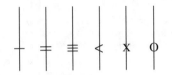

a) Here are six different types of sticks of equal length. Using these sticks as edges, construct cubes in which no two sticks of the same type touch each other, using:

1) Three each of types I, II, III, and V
2) Two each of all six types.

b) What is the maximum number of trees you can plant so that each one is equidistant from every other tree?

Harry Van Tassel
Three Rivers, Michigan

3. Like Lightning

Difficulty: 2

☞ An auto traveled one mile at 30 miles an hour. How fast would it have to travel another mile in order to average 60 miles an hour for the two miles?

Rob Connors
Brookline, Massachusetts

4. Coins and Stamps

Difficulty: 2

a) What combination of 9 U.S. or Canadian coins of values less than one dollar can be used to make all payments from 1 to 99 cents, inclusive?

b) A frequent mailer was left with many 25-cent stamps when rates changed recently. He then bought a lot of 29s.

Using only 25- and 29-cent stamps, what is the largest amount of postage he cannot affix exactly?

Kevin Wall
Union City, New Jersey
Sidney Kravitz
Dover, New Jersey

5. Make Your Own

Difficulty: 2

a) Choose any number between two and 28, divisible by three. Multiply by 37. Add 241,000. Add the six digits together, forming a two-digit sum. From this sum, subtract your original choice. What is your answer?

b) Choose any number at all. If even, divide it by two; if odd, multiply it by three and add one. Do the same to the result and keep repeating. What is the last number before the series repeats?

Dan Lytle
Clayton, Oklahoma

6. Simple Moves

Difficulty: 3

a) Holding one conventional machine screw steady, head toward you, slide an identical screw, head away, clockwise around it, threads engaged. Do not rotate; the screwdriver slots should always point in the same direction. Do the heads approach or recede?

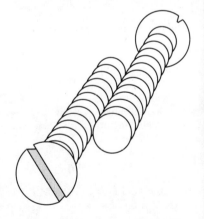

b) What is the next number in this sequence?

2; 6; 30; 210; 2310

Tina Virzi
Plattsburgh, New York

7. DIVIDING PRIME NUMBERS

Difficulty: 3

☞ Before bulk pickup, how did dairy farmer Brown divide 7 full, 7 half-full, and 7 empty milk cans among 3 milk haulers so that each hauler carried away equal amounts of milk in the same quantities in each of the same number of cans?

Doreen Morin
Toronto, Ontario

8. WHAT DAY IS TODAY?

Difficulty: 3

a) Why is the same full Moon shown on, say, the 14th on some calendars and the 15th on others?

b) Is it ever just one day all over the planet?

c) Are there ever 3 different days observed simultaneously on our planet?

d) When is it exactly 500 years since Columbus landed in the New World?

Raymond Cloutier
Bellevue, Nebraska

9. NEW MATH FOR 1993

Difficulty: 4

a) If $A = (1+9+9-3)^{1993}$
and $B = (-1-9-9+3)^{1993}$
what is $(1+9+9+3)^{A+B}$

b) Using all 9 digits, 1-9, but no zeros, create the precise fraction 1/9. Then make 1/8, 1/7, etc., right up to 1/2.

Jerry Curtright
Carpentersville, Illinois

10. AGE-OLD PROBLEMS

Difficulty: 4

☞ This is about the ages of Ann, Bea, Cam, Dot, and Eve. Four of the five are teenagers. "Age" is the commonly used integer value.

The product of Ann's and Cam's ages equals the product of Bea's and Dot's ages, plus one.

When Dot is three times Cam's present age, Eve will be twice Dot's present age, plus one year, and Cam will be four times Eve's present age, plus one year. How old is Ann?

Hervey Vigour
Charlottesville, Virginia

11. ARRAYS AND SQUARES

Difficulty: 4

☞ Arrange the five different girls' initials from puzzle 10 in a 5x5 Latin Square array, so that

a) no initial is repeated in any row, column or diagonal and, done that way

b) the cyclic order of the initials is uniform in all the rows, and separately in all the columns as well.

Dan W. M. Burns
Chicago, Illinois

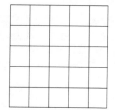

12. CENTERS OF TRIANGLES

Difficulty: 5

☞ Here's a chance to doodle, develop, and describe. Take any triangle and locate all its centers and related centers.

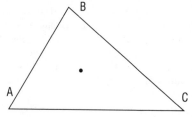

Margaret Arnold Nash
Mount Pleasant, Michigan

13. GOLDBACH REVERSED

Difficulty: 5

☞ What is the longest sequence N, of consecutive integers that can be rearranged into N/2 pairs, where the sum of each pair is a prime number and no prime appears more than once among the N/2 sums? Both members of each pair should be within the sequence. Both positive and negative primes may be used and need not be consecutive or uninterrupted.

Robert L. Henderson
Belleville, Michigan

14. POLYOMINO PACKS

Difficulty: 5

☞ These little pieces are glued-together assemblies of four to seven small cubes. None is hidden. Can you fit, by rotating and/or flipping:

a) the 12 shapes of set A into a 9x7x1 flat; into a 3x7x3 solid, and

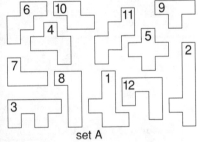

set A

b) the six shapes of set B into a cube.

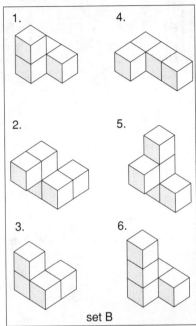

set B

Please label your drawings with the piece numbers. For the solid and the cube, please show each layer *and* at least three surfaces of each overall assembly with each piece number marked. Judging is virtually impossible without identifying pieces.

C. J. Bouwkamp
Amsterdam, Holland

15. PLANETARY WEEK

Difficulty: 5

☞ Last year's 200th anniversary edition of *The Old Farmer's Almanac* showed how the five obvious planets were associated with classical Western deities. The days of the week and the hours of the day were similarly ruled, including the Sun and the Moon, as the seven regularly repeating, bright sky objects. There is remarkable agreement today, millennia later, on this Western pantheon of the week (allowing for equivalents, translations, and a few local exceptions): Sun, Moon, Mars, Mercury, Jupiter, Venus, and Saturn.

Is there a mathematical system to the *order* of the concepts behind the Western names of the days of the week?

Ruth Clark
Hollis, New Hampshire

Answers to

OLD AND NEW MATHEMATICAL PUZZLES

on pages 170-173

1. 7

2. a)

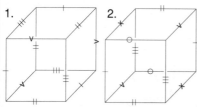

1. 2.

One type in each dimension   **Parallel edges on opposite sides**

b) 3 on a plane, or 4, if one tree can be elevated to be the vertex of a regular tetrahedron (triangular pyramid).

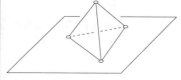

3. Infinitely fast; impossible to do.

4. a) 1 half dollar; 1 quarter; 1 dime; 2 nickels; 4 pennies.
  b) $6.71

5. a) Always 7
  b) Always 1

6. a) Neither. They hold steady.
  b) 30030

7. By any of at least four methods:
  a) Empty 2H into 2H = 9F, 3H, 9E
  b) Divide 1F into 1E = 6F, 9H, 6E
  c) Divide 4F into 4E = 3F, 15H, 3E
  d) Divide 7F into 7E = 0F, 21H, 0E

8. a) The Moon's phases are usually computed in Universal (Greenwich) Time. It may be after midnight in England and before midnight in America.

The Old Farmer's Almanac always shows Eastern Standard Time, if unlabelled.
b) Theoretically, yes, for an instant daily. Actually, no, owing to squiggles in the International Date Line.
c) Yes, for up to 1 hour, 45 minutes daily. Tuesday begins in Tonga and the Chatham Islands *before* Sunday is over in Kwajalein and Eniwetok.
d) October 21, 1992. October 12, 1492 is the old Julian-style calendar date.

9. a) 1. $(A + B = 0)$

b) $\dfrac{1}{9} = \dfrac{6381}{57429}$ $\qquad \dfrac{1}{5} = \dfrac{2769}{13845}$

$\dfrac{1}{8} = \dfrac{3187}{25496}$ $\qquad \dfrac{1}{4} = \dfrac{4392}{17568}$

$\dfrac{1}{7} = \dfrac{2394}{16758}$ $\qquad \dfrac{1}{3} = \dfrac{5832}{17496}$

$\dfrac{1}{6} = \dfrac{2943}{17658}$ $\qquad \dfrac{1}{2} = \dfrac{6729}{13458}$

10. 17

11. Two unique possibilities, of many:

B	E	A	C	D
A	D	E	B	C
D	B	C	A	E
C	A	D	E	B
E	C	B	D	A

B	D	A	C	E
C	E	B	D	A
D	A	C	E	B
E	B	D	A	C
A	C	E	B	D

a.) Varying Cycles   **b.) Uniform Cycles**

12-15.   PRIZE SET.
SEE INSTRUCTIONS PAGE 170.

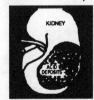

Insights into
Traditional Amish Cooking

Seemingly sort of grim, austere folks, the Amish of Lancaster County, Pennsylvania, have two areas in which they exercise color: in their quilts and in their food!

by Phyllis Pellman Good

The bountiful food served at Amish and Mennonite tables has always nourished both bodies and souls. Sprung from productive gardens and kitchens, these dishes have also grown out of a healthy community. The well-tended earth, as well as a cultivated and deliberate life as a people, has kept a distinctive food tradition thriving among the Old Order Mennonites and Amish.

Here we will focus on the Old Order Amish of Lancaster County, Pennsylvania, the oldest continuing settlement of Amish in the world and a group that still maintains a distinguishable identity.

Because they are highly disciplined, the Amish are often perceived as being grim, austere folks who live as ascetics. They do live ordered lives and, in general, are restrained in their outward expression. But in two areas they have exercised color — in their quilts and in their food!

By the mid-1850s and during the next several decades, a food tradition evolved that included a collection of dishes from a variety of sources. The Amish brought their own cultural taste preferences from Switzerland and Germany (a love of pork, noodles, and dumplings, for example). Those preferences affected what they copied and adapted from the diets of their English and Native American neighbors (pies and sweetened preserves came from the British; cornmeal dishes from the local tribes). The geography and climate in the parts of the New World where they made their homes also shaped their eating (beef and apples entered their diets in much greater proportion than before). In these ways, however, they were little different from the other German folk who settled in William Penn's colony.

How, then, did the Amish develop and retain a distinctive food tradition? With their sustained rural base, the Amish have continued to cultivate productive gardens and fields. In addition, they have

illustrated by Sara Mintz Zwicker

large families and stay closely connected to their extended families. Consequently, adults are able to convey the love of traditional dishes to their children and show them how to make those specialties, many of which are better learned by "feel" than by reading a cookbook. Finally, the Amish enjoy a vital community life that supports food traditions — at gatherings favorite dishes appear, undergirding the event, whether it be a school picnic, a funeral, or sisters' day.

Several principles prevail among these people with as much strength now as they did when the first Amish built their homesteads in Pennsylvania: To waste is to destroy God's gift. To be slack, workwise, is to be disrespectful of time and resources. To go hungry is to ignore the bounty of the earth (furthermore, there is no reason that eating shouldn't be a pleasure!).

Many myths exist about the Amish and their food. Separated as they are from the larger world in their dress and transportation choices, they are not immune to the many food options in the grocery stores of their communities. They shop, and so they pick up packaged cereal, boxes of fruit-flavored gelatin, and cans of concentrated soup. Although tuna noodle casserole and chili con carne turn up on the tables of Amish homes, and chocolate chip cookies and lunch meat are packed into the lunch boxes of Amish schoolchildren, cornmeal mush and chicken pot pie are still favorites.

The Amish are hard workers whose efforts on the land have been rewarded with fruitful fields and gardens. And so they have eaten well. In fact, their land has been so productive that Amish cooks have undertaken massive "pickling" operations, preserving the excess from their gardens in sweet-and-sour syrups. It is likely that one amazed guest who sat at the table of an Amish cook or who witnessed her well-stocked canning shelves began the apocryphal tale of "seven sweets and seven sours" served at meals.

Desserts are eaten daily in most Amish homes. But multiple desserts at one meal are usually eaten when there is company. Thus the story of manifold pastries available at every meal has only a shade of truth in it.

What do the Amish of Lancaster County, Pennsylvania, eat today that is part of their historical food tradition?

Chicken pot pie, the staple that may have first been prepared as a one-pot open-hearth stew, is still a favorite meal on Amish homesteads. Its basic ingredients are at hand — chicken, potatoes, and the wherewithal to make the pot pie noodles. The dish requires little tending. Several extra potatoes or a few more handfuls of noodles can easily be added to accommodate additional mouths around the table.

Steamed crackers, once made with homemade wafers of wheat flour, still make a filling meal, despite the current reliance on store-bought soda crackers.

(The Amish taste for starch is as strong as ever.) As easily prepared for one or 21, steamed crackers make a hearty breakfast (topped with fried eggs) or a sturdy supper (dressed up with chunks of pink salmon or cooked chicken).

Cornmeal mush is one dish that has survived from Colonial days with little change or adaptation. Filling and satisfying, it is still eaten on winter mornings in many households.

Although most mush is made now from store-bought, roasted cornmeal, choice ears of field corn were traditionally roasted at home in large bakeovens in the fall. Mush is eaten in two forms. The first is when it is puddinglike, immediately after it has been boiled to the proper thickness. Family tradition and personal preference determine the time of day when it is eaten and what one mixes with it — sugar or molasses, ketchup or milk. After it cools for several hours, mush can be sliced and fried. Some families make a batch big enough to last for several days.

Apples, which grow abundantly in eastern Pennsylvania, are cooked for hours to make apple butter. In years past no sweetening was added, making the preserves almost medicinal in flavor. With the increased influence of the English, who had a tradition of sweetened preserves, and the greater availability of sugar, apple butter came to be sweetened, and consequently grew in favor.

Apples dried for an extended time become a chewy, sweet-tart snack food known as schnitz. It's a practical way to handle an abundant apple crop (drying prevents spoilage); it allows a fruit pie to be made in any season; and its preparation requires little equipment (trays of apple slices can be dried over a stove or on the roof of an outbuilding).

Chowchow, along with its many other cousins in the relish family, is a continuing feature in traditional Amish menus; it has been so from the time of their earliest settlements in the New World.

Sweet-and-sour pickled mixes balance the rich meats and starches that have been the foundation of this diet. Chow-chow also puts to productive use the gardens' extra bounty. Virtually a pickled vegetable soup, chowchow is often made as a group project. A woman and her daughters or sisters typically gather to do the monotonous chopping and cooking that chowchow requires — another occasion when food brings life to community.

CHICKEN POT PIE

3½- to 4-pound chicken
1 onion, diced
4 medium-sized potatoes, peeled and
   cut into chunks
3 carrots, sliced (optional)
salt and pepper to taste
pot pie squares

Cook the chicken in 2 quarts water until it is partly tender. Then add the onion, potatoes, and carrots and cook until they and the chicken are completely tender. Remove meat from bones and set aside; remove vegetables and reserve. Bring broth to a boil. Drop pot pie squares into boiling broth and cook 20 minutes or until tender. Return chicken and vegetables to the broth and serve steaming hot.

Pot Pie Dough:

2 eggs
2 cups flour
2 to 3 tablespoons milk or cream

Break the eggs into the flour. Work together, adding the milk or cream to make a soft dough. Roll out the dough as thin as possible and cut into 1x2-inch rectangles with a knife or pastry wheel. Drop into boiling broth.

CORNMEAL MUSH

2 quarts cold water
2 cups roasted yellow cornmeal
1 teaspoon salt

Put 1 quart cold water in a bowl. Combine the cornmeal and salt and stir into the cold water. In a heavy kettle, bring the other quart of water to a boil. Slowly add the cornmeal mixture to it, stirring constantly to prevent lumps. When the mixture is smooth, cover and cook over low heat for 1 to 3 hours, so the mush "glops" slowly. Stir frequently to keep from sticking to bottom of pan. Serve.

Pour balance into loaf pans to mold. Let set until cool. Place in refrigerator for several hours until it is fully congealed. Cut into ¼-inch-thick slices and fry in margarine, butter, or lard until brown. Turn and brown on the other side until crisp. Serve.

STEAMED CRACKERS

¼ to ½ pound (about 50 to 60) saltine crackers
2½ cups milk
2 tablespoons butter or margarine
¾ cup milk

Butter the bottom and sides of a 1½-quart casserole. Lay dry crackers in the casserole. Heat the 2½ cups milk to scalding. Pour over crackers. Cover casserole and let stand at least 5 minutes, checking once to make sure the crackers are covered with milk. Just before serving, heat the butter until browned. Add ¾ cup milk and heat mixture until warm. Then pour over the crackers and serve. Makes 4 to 5 servings.

Variations

1. Mix pieces of cooked pink salmon with the crackers as they are layered into the casserole. Proceed with recipe.

2. Mix small pieces of cooked chicken with the crackers as they are layered into the casserole. Proceed with recipe.

3. While crackers are standing, prepare 4 fried eggs in skillet. When crackers are finished, spoon onto 4 dinner plates. Top each with a fried egg.

CHOWCHOW

4 cups lima beans
4 cups green string beans
2 cups yellow wax beans
4 cups cabbage, chopped
4 cups cauliflower florets
4 cups carrots, sliced
4 cups celery, cut in chunks
4 cups red and green peppers, chopped
4 cups small white onions
4 cups cucumbers, cut in chunks
4 cups corn kernels
6 cups granulated sugar
4½ cups apple cider vinegar
2 cups water
1 tablespoon pickling spices

1 tablespoon mustard seed
1 tablespoon celery seed

Cook each vegetable separately until tender but not mushy. When each is finished, lift out of hot water with a slotted spoon, and rinse with cold water to stop its cooking and preserve its color. Drain, then layer into a large dishpan.

Combine the sugar, vinegar, water, and spices in a 15-quart stockpot (or do half a batch at a time in an 8-quart kettle) and bring to a boil. Make sure the sugar is fully dissolved, then spoon all the vegetables (or half of them depending upon the size of the kettle) into the syrup and boil for 5 minutes. Stir gently, only to mix the vegetables well. Spoon into hot sterilized jars and seal.

SCHNITZ PIE

3 cups dried apples
2¼ cups warm water
1 teaspoon lemon extract
⅔ cup brown sugar
pastry for 9-inch double-crust pie

Soak apples in the warm water, then cook over low heat until soft. Mash apples and add lemon extract and sugar. Pour into unbaked pie shell. Cover with top crust. Seal edges. Bake at 425° F for 15 minutes; then at 350° F for 30 minutes. Serve warm. Makes one 9-inch pie.

APPLE BUTTER IN THE OVEN

8 quarts thick applesauce
8 quarts fresh cider
4 cups brown sugar
1 teaspoon salt

Make applesauce. Place hot applesauce into the oven at 400° F. Pour cider into large kettle and boil until half has evaporated. Add cider to sauce in the oven. Allow oven door to stand slightly ajar so steam can escape. Stir occasionally. After about 2 hours add sugar and salt. Mix well. Allow about 2 more hours of cooking time until apple butter is the desired consistency, remembering to stir occasionally. Seal in hot sterilized jars.

□□

Phyllis Pellman Good is the book editor for Good Books in Intercourse, Pennsylvania. She is the author of Cooking and Memories *and* The Best of Amish Cooking; *she is co-author of* From Amish and Mennonite Kitchens *and* The Best of Mennonite Fellowship Meals, *all published by Good Books.*

HOW TO REALLY ENJOY CARP

Carp used to be a popular fish. And, says this writer, it still ought to be today – if you don't mind smelling it for three days after you've cooked it.

BY LEON MANDELL

When a trout fisherman catches a carp by accident, he often mutters obscenities, calls them roaches, and heaves them back. When a bass angler hooks one in a tournament, his reaction is even stronger. When an environmentalist sees a carp, he uses unflattering terms because he notices the waters are muddy and polluted. Perhaps the largest contingent of Americans who express loathing for our poor trash fish are consumers. They turn up their noses at what they consider a brackish, oily taste.

Apparently our tastes change as the centuries go by. At the turn of this century Americans ate carp the way we eat canned tuna today. Carp was so popular that canneries sprang up all over the country. Today, with carp vilified as a food, a sport fish, and a denizen of our lakes and rivers, most of the carp canneries are closed except for a few that make cat food.

My personal experiences and observations refute the perceptions many people have about the fish.

When the ancient Chinese discovered the carp's ability to grow protein-rich flesh quickly in fresh water, they offered the world an aquatic domestic animal to supplement land animals. To this day,

Chinese and other Asian cultures recognize the carp's importance as a food. Songs and poems extol the graceful beauty of carp swimming in garden pools.

About 2,000 years ago, the Romans discovered that carp can live with little or poor water and are easier to transport live than most fish — they are so hardy they can travel for two hours in just a wet sack. They carted them into their conquered territories to culture them for food. Soon every pond, lake, and river in Europe housed this prized fish. By the year 1500, carp was a staple food across the Continent. (It is still considered a prized catch in England and on the Continent.)

In the middle of the 19th century, entrepreneurs started importing carp from Europe to America and selling them as "the fish for millions." The fecundity of the species made this come true. A 20-pound female carp can lay two million eggs. The fish can grow to four pounds in just three years and can easily dominate any aquatic system, sometimes to the detriment of native plants and other aquatic life. Carp were sold all over the United States, Canada, and Central America by promoters.

In 1876 the U.S. Fish Commission began importing and cultivating carp to bolster the nation's food supply. Soon thousands of fingerlings were being shipped to the states in special railroad tank cars that held 20,000 fish. Sportsmen liked the strong fighting qualities of this fish, and newspapers praised the table qualities.

But everything has a saturation point, and soon

The author and his colleague recently netted a small carp.

– photo by Bill Byrne /courtesy Leon Mandell

there were more carp than pots to cook them in. With lessened demand, the commercial carp fisheries began to go downhill. People started looking at carp habitat — often waters unfit for swimming or for other fish to live in — and, instead of admiring the fish for surviving in waters polluted by humans, associated it with the foul conditions. It is a matter of record that the U.S. Fish Commission has spent millions of dollars trying to eliminate the very fish it so enthusiastically introduced.

My own experience in fishing for carp has been exhilarating. They are strong and wily and give a good account of themselves before coming to the net. I don't always catch and release as the British do because I have a route of friends — Russians, Turks, Germans, and Jews in our local elderly housing — who eat this fish with enthusiasm.

Here is a simple recipe a Russian elder gave me for carp. She fed ten people who ate without talking. She uses the entire fish except for the gills (which are bitter) and the gut and scales.

In a cast-iron pot large enough to receive the steaks and head of an 8-pound carp, pour enough olive oil to cover the bottom. Cut up 3 potatoes, a few carrots, a few beets, and several onions, and layer them in the pot alternating with carp steaks. Add one bay leaf, some sugar (no amount given!), salt, and pepper. Simmer on top of the stove for 1 hour and bake in the oven at 350° F for 1 hour. Add paprika for color.

The resulting odor is guaranteed to remain in your apartment for three days.

My prediction is that the carp will be the sport fish of the future. The fertility of the female and virility of the male plus their adaptability to low-oxygenated waters could make them one of the few survivors. They are a remarkable fish. Like mosquitoes and cockroaches, they are here to stay. □□

BEST FISHING DAYS, 1993

(and other fishing lore from the files of *The Old Farmer's Almanac*)

Probably the best fishing time is when the ocean tides are restless before their turn and in the first hour of ebbing. All fish in all waters — salt or fresh — feed most heavily at that time.

Best temperatures for fish species vary widely, of course, and are chiefly important if you are going to have your own fish pond. Best temperatures for brook trout are 45° to 65° F. Brown trout and rainbows are more tolerant of higher temperatures. Smallmouth black bass do best in cool water. Horned pout take what they find.

Most of us go fishing when we can get off, not because it is the best time. But there are best times:

• One hour before and one hour after high tide, and one hour before and one hour after low tide. (The times of high tides are given on pages 56-82 and corrected for your locality on pages 204-205. Inland, the times for high tides would correspond with the times the Moon is due south. Low tides are halfway between high tides.)

• "The morning rise" — after sunup for a spell — and "the evening rise" — just before sundown and the hour or so after.

• Still water or a ripple is better than a wind at both times.

• When there is a hatch of flies — caddis or mayflies, commonly. (The fisherman will have to match the hatching flies with *his* fly — or go fishless.)

• When the breeze is from a westerly quarter rather than north or east.

• When the barometer is steady or on the rise. (But, of course, even in a three-day driving northeaster the fish isn't going to give up feeding. His hunger clock keeps right on working, and the smart fisherman will find something he wants.)

• When the Moon is between new and full.

MOON BETWEEN NEW & FULL

Jan. 1-8	July 19-Aug. 2
Jan. 22-Feb. 6	Aug. 17-31
Feb. 21-Mar. 8	Sept. 15-30
Mar. 23-Apr. 6	Oct. 15-30
Apr. 21-May 5	Nov. 13-29
May 21-June 4	Dec. 13-28
June 19-July 3	

WINNING RECIPES
in the 1992 RECIPE CONTEST

HOMEMADE SOUPS

HUNGARIAN GARDEN VEGETABLE CHICKEN SOUP

3½- to 4½-pound chicken, left whole
6 (13¾-ounce) cans chicken broth
1 large onion, chopped
1 bunch scallions, sliced (white and light green parts only)
2 large carrots, thinly sliced
2 stalks celery, thinly sliced
1 bag (4 to 5) parsnips, thinly sliced
1 medium zucchini, thinly sliced
1½ cups chopped green cabbage
2 medium tomatoes, skinned, seeded, and finely diced
¼ cup minced fresh parsley (or 2 tablespoons dried)
1 tablespoon minced fresh dill (or 1 teaspoon dried)
1 teaspoon freshly ground pepper
1 tablespoon Hungarian paprika
1 cup fine, dry egg noodles

Place chicken in a large pot and pour chicken broth over, adding water if necessary, so chicken is completely covered. Bring to a boil in covered pot, then lower heat and simmer until chicken is tender (45 to 60 minutes). Remove chicken and refrigerate broth, preferably overnight. Skim off the top layer of fat and return broth to large pot. Remove meat from chicken bones, shred or dice, and add to broth. Add all the remaining ingredients except the egg noodles, bring to a boil, lower heat, partially cover, and simmer until vegetables are barely tender, about 30 minutes. Add noodles and simmer until tender, about 5 minutes. (Note: This soup freezes well.) Serves 15 to 20.

Julie DeMatteo, Clementon, New Jersey

SPICY VEGGIE NUT STEW

1 to 2 tablespoons oil (peanut, vegetable, etc.)
1 medium yellow onion, chopped
4 to 6 cloves garlic, minced
1 teaspoon chopped fresh ginger (½ teaspoon dried)
1 to 2 dried red chilis, seeded and chopped, or 1 teaspoon crushed red pepper flakes (or to taste)
1 tablespoon ground cumin seed
1½ teaspoons curry powder (or to taste)
1 (6-ounce) can tomato paste
3½ cups chicken broth (canned is fine)
1 (16-ounce) package frozen mixed vegetables
⅓ cup fresh cilantro leaves
¼ cup peanut butter, creamy or crunchy style
salt and black pepper to taste
1 tablespoon chopped green onions and/or peanuts, per bowl, as garnish

In a stockpot (at least 4 quarts) heat oil and quickly sauté onion, garlic, and ginger for 3 to 4 minutes. Add chilis, cumin, and curry powder; stir, and cook for another minute. Add tomato paste and chicken stock; stir well, and bring to a boil. Add frozen vegetables, bring to a boil again, then turn heat to low. Add cilantro leaves and simmer, uncovered, for 10 minutes. Add peanut butter, stir to dissolve, and heat 4 to 5 minutes more. Add salt and black pepper, as desired. Pour into bowls and garnish with green onions and/or peanuts. Serves 4 to 6.

Sara Perkins, Dallas, Texas

RUSSIAN SOUP WITH PICKLES

2 tablespoons medium barley
3 cups water
4 cups (three 10½-ounce cans)
  consommé
2 cups (one 13¾-ounce can) chicken
  broth
2 cups diced potatoes
3 tablespoons butter or margarine
1 large onion, minced
1 veal kidney (or 5 lamb kidneys),
  trimmed and sliced
1 tablespoon all-purpose flour
2 small dill pickles, thinly sliced
½ cup sour cream, at room
  temperature
2 tablespoons minced parsley
pepper to taste

Cook barley in the water for about 1 hour, drain, and reserve. In a large kettle combine consommé and chicken broth. Add potatoes and cook until half-tender. In a separate pan, heat butter and cook onion until soft but not browned. Add kidneys and cook, stirring constantly, about 3 minutes. Stir in flour and cook an additional 3 minutes. Add pickles, barley, onion, and kidneys to soup mixture, bring to a boil, then lower heat and simmer, covered, for 15 minutes. Skim fat if needed. Pour sour cream into a large soup tureen, add a few teaspoons of soup, and beat vigorously to prevent curdling. Pour remaining soup over mixture. Sprinkle with parsley and pepper. Serves 6 to 8.

Melanija Wozniak, Vernon, Connecticut

BROWN BUTTER POTATO SOUP

5 tablespoons butter
3 tablespoons flour
9 to 10 cups water
4 cups diced potatoes
1½ cups diced celery
½ cup chopped onion
1½ cups chopped fresh parsley
salt and pepper to taste
drop noodles

In a soup kettle brown butter and flour until a dark caramel color. Add remaining ingredients, bring to a boil, then simmer until potatoes are tender. Just before serving time, make and add the drop noodles. Serves 10 to 12.

Drop noodles:

3 eggs
¾ to 1 cup flour
½ teaspoon salt
  Mix together with spoon until mixture is thick but pourable. Pour by the spoonful into the boiling soup and cook until firm.

Marge Larson and Patty Johnson (mother and daughter), Mora, Minnesota

OYSTER SOUP WITH PARSLEY CUBES

1 quart oysters
2 tablespoons butter
2 tablespoons flour
4 cups milk
salt and pepper to taste
parsley cubes

Drain oysters, saving liquor, and wash well to remove shell fragments. Heat oyster liquor and strain through double cheesecloth. Make a cream sauce of butter, flour, milk, and seasonings, and add oyster liquor and oysters. Heat until oyster edges curl. Serve garnished with parsley cubes.

Parsley Cubes:

4 eggs
½ teaspoon salt
¼ teaspoon black pepper
¼ cup milk
4 teaspoons parsley, minced
  Beat eggs until thick and smooth. Add salt, pepper, milk, and parsley. Pour into 8x8-inch greased pan, and set pan in water. Bake in 325° F oven until firm, about 20 minutes. Cut into squares, and drop into soup in serving dishes. Serves 6.

Arlene Deline, Menomonie, Wisconsin

ITALIANO MEATBALL MINESTRONE

Meatballs:

1½ pounds ground beef
½ cup Italian seasoned bread crumbs
2 tablespoons finely chopped onion
2 teaspoons salt
¼ teaspoon EACH pepper and anise

seeds
1 package (10½-ounce) frozen chopped spinach, thawed and squeezed dry
1 large egg, beaten
1 to 2 tablespoons olive oil

Combine beef, bread crumbs, onion, spices, spinach, and egg. Shape into balls; brown in heated oil. Set aside.

Beef Stock:

8 cups beef stock, homemade or canned
7 cups water
1 (15-ounce) can kidney beans, undrained
1 (29-ounce) can tomatoes, coarsely mashed
½ teaspoon EACH oregano and basil
2 stalks celery, sliced
2 large carrots, peeled and sliced
1 cup green beans, cut in 1-inch pieces
1 to 2 cups mostaccioli pasta, uncooked
freshly grated Romano or Parmesan cheese
finely chopped cilantro (optional)

Bring beef stock, water, kidney beans, tomatoes, oregano, and basil to a slow boil; simmer 10 minutes. Add celery, carrots, and green beans; return to boil and simmer 10 minutes. Add pasta and meatballs; boil 10 minutes. Remove from heat, allowing pasta to absorb liquid (15 minutes). Serve with grated cheese; garnish with cilantro. Serves 6 to 8.

Marie Rizzio, Traverse City, Michigan

1993 RECIPE CONTEST

RECIPES USING CHOCOLATE

For 1993, prizes (first prize, $50; second, $25; third, $15) will be awarded for the best original recipes using chocolate. All entries become the property of Yankee Publishing Incorporated, which reserves all rights to the materials submitted. Winners will be announced in the 1994 edition of *The Old Farmer's Al-*

manac. Deadline is February 1, 1993. Address: Recipe Contest, *The Old Farmer's Almanac,* Dublin, NH 03444.

WINNING ESSAYS *in the* 1992 ESSAY CONTEST

MY FAVORITE CURE FOR THE COMMON COLD

FIRST PRIZE

Father and Brother ran trap lines during the winter months. Being a thrifty man by nature, Father used as much of anything that came to hand as he could.

Skunks were quite prevalent in those days, so naturally we had a good supply of skunk furs stretched on boards in the basement. Father boiled the carcasses to feed the chickens and, after scraping the pelts, rendered the fat.

This grease had several uses around the farm. It could be used to oil harnesses, boots, or a squeaking axle in a pinch. Another use I remember quite well. Whenever one of us caught a cold, Mother's remedy was to sprinkle sugar on onion pieces and feed us a spoonful at bedtime. Father's remedy was to slather skunk grease on our chests. All the time I was in grade school, I seldom had a cold. I might catch one — but after that, nobody came close enough the rest of the winter to give me another.

Lura O'Briant, Oxford, Iowa

At age 14, I came home from school with a nasty cold. Later that evening, with fever, watery eyes, and runny nose, and huddled in a blanket doing my homework, my elderly great-aunt Mary said she had an old remedy for my cold. I groaned at the thought of an "old remedy," perhaps in the form of cooked tree bark or worse. With homework done, I headed for bed. Aunt Mary stopped me with steaming cup in hand. "Drink this, and you will feel much better." Marveling at the excellent health of my tall, slender, 75-year-old great-aunt, I took and emptied the cup, asking "What did I drink?" With a warm smile and "never-you-mind look" she tucked me into bed.

Waking after a night's peaceful sleep, I asked her for the recipe. She said, "I cooked a chopped onion in water, discarded the onion, added milk and a pinch of black pepper."

This became my favorite cure for the common cold, and to this day, some 40 years later, I think of Great-aunt Mary when the sniffles and chills begin — and start chopping the onion.

Ann McGraw, Defiance, Ohio

The only way to cure a cold is to catch it before it gets you down. At the first hint of a cold or flu, sip the following tea. Mix a batch ahead, using 2 handfuls of mint and 1 handful of each of the other ingredients:

Mix the leaves of spearmint, red raspberry, catnip, mullein, and comfrey with red clover flowers and rose hips. Steep about 2 tablespoons of the mixture in hot water with a sprig of white pine bark (don't omit this key ingredient — the white inner bark is best) for about 10 minutes. Put the white pine bark sprig in your cup and pour in the tea. Sweeten with honey if desired. Drink about 3 cups a day, adding another sprig for each cup.

Get plenty of rest.

Kayo Fraser, Gold Creek, Montana

1993 ESSAY CONTEST

THE BEST DOG I EVER KNEW

For 1993, prizes (first prize, $50; second, $25; third, $15) will be awarded for the three best 200-word essays on this topic: "The Best Dog I Ever Knew." All entries become the property of Yankee Publishing Incorporated, which reserves all rights to the materials submitted. Winners will be announced in the 1994 edition of *The Old Farmer's Almanac.* Deadline: February 1, 1993. Address: Essay Contest, *The Old Farmer's Almanac,* Dublin, NH 03444.

Special Report to Readers

"Name the Earth and Moon" Contest

In the 1992 edition we invited readers to submit their choices of proper names for the Earth and Moon. We received over 700 answers! Especially gratifying were the submissions from several elementary, junior high, and high schools — from Colorado to New York — whose students chose the contest as a class project.

Wading through the answers proved challenging, but we finally established that about 50 percent of our respondents chose mythology as their inspiration. Gaea (Gaia), Greek goddess/ Mother Earth was the choice of the majority, and Luna, Roman goddess of the Moon, was a clear favorite, but just about all the Greco/Roman deities had their adherents — from Artemis to Zeus and Apollo to Vesta. Other writers turned to other pantheons: Egyptian gods and Sumerian gods, Norse, Teutonic, and Indian gods, and gods whose origins we could not identify. Some chose names from ancient texts — Hebrew, Mesopotamian, and Sanskrit.

Of the remaining 50 percent, two-thirds showed such variety and diversity that we were hard put to find any duplicate names, let alone favorites. By and large, this group fell into the following categories:

☞ THE PHYSICISTS — Biochromisphere, Terraquea

☞ THE ROMANTICS — Romeo and Juliet

☞ THE POETS — The Star of Mirrors

☞ THE LOVERS — "Call the Moon 'Sherry,' because moonbeams flow soft like Sherry's hair."

☞ THE SPACE ENTHUSIASTS (the Moon) — Neil, Armstrong, or ANAEBA (for Apollo [landing] of Neil Armstrong and Edwin "Buzz" Aldrin)

☞ THE CYNICS — "How about Lethargy and Apathy?"

☞ THE ENVIRONMENTALISTS — Polluto and Polluto Annexia

☞ THE PROSAIC — Betty and Bob, Aldo and Patrizia (the latter from Rome, Italy)

☞ One writer suggested "Mickey and Pluto, because the Earth and Moon orbits are like a person walking an untrained dog." He added that in 1994 we could have a "Rename the Planet Pluto" contest!

The final third came from the dissenters. Many were outraged at the idea of renaming the Earth, quoting Genesis to point out that God had already named the planet, and "What's good enough for God is good enough for me." Others just *like* Earth and Moon. We thought a sixth-grader from Wilmington, North Carolina, summed it up best: "People who are against it in all of the other countries in the world might get pretty mad, and it's not fair to them for not having a chance to vote for a name or choose a name they like."

So there it is, over 700 imaginative, humorous, original responses. The results have been sent to the International Astronomical Union, and if the Working Group for Planetary System Nomenclature ever seriously considers renaming Earth and Moon, we think they'll all have plenty of help.

Thanks to all for your interest! □□

AN · ACCOUNT · OF

The First

MANNED BALLOON FLIGHT IN AMERICA

Frenchman Jean Pierre Blanchard looked to the skies above Philadelphia early on the morning of January 9, 1793. He thought the day would be fine for flying.

So did President George Washington, four future presidents (Adams, Jefferson, Madison, and Monroe), and 40,000 city residents. They hoped to see the first manned balloon voyage in America.

If anyone could perform the feat, it would be Blanchard. The French had pioneered the science of ballooning, also called aerostation. And although it still was an art in its infancy — men had been going aloft in Europe for less than ten years — Blanchard was a veteran aeronaut. He already had made 44 ascents, including the first crossing of the English Channel.

A month earlier, Blanchard had arrived in Philadelphia, then the United States capital, aboard the brig *Ceres* out of Hamburg, Germany. Everything necessary for the American flight had been unloaded from the ship. The balloon, which had been used in five prior ascents, was constructed of heavily varnished yellow silk enveloped by strong netting. A spangled blue basket would hang below. Lift would be initiated by 4,200 pounds of sulfuric acid (also called oil of vitriol), enough for just one flight. Added to iron scraps, the acid would produce hydrogen, the lighter-than-air gas that would cause the balloon to inflate and rise.

The 39-year-old aeronaut found lodgings at 9 North Eighth Street in the city. Manned balloon flight was an expensive venture, and Blanchard immediately sought a way to defray his costs. He alerted journalists to his presence and his planned ascent. Their stories so aroused the public that some readers wanted to accompany Blanchard on his journey. However, the extra acid that would be needed for greater lift was not available in Philadelphia.

Others intended to chase Blanchard's balloon on horseback. He discouraged them. "If the day is calm . . . I shall ascend perpendicularly," he explained, "but if the wind blows, permit me, gentlemen, to advise you not to attempt following, for the swiftest horses will be unable to keep up with me, especially in a country so intersected with rivers and so covered with woods."

All of Philadelphia planned to see the flight. Letters were written to Blanchard in care of local newspapers, pleading with him to reveal launch details well in advance so those traveling from the country could be there.

Blanchard seized on all the excite-

It began
exactly 200
years ago in
Philadelphia
with a send-off
by George
Washington
and ended near
Woodbury,
New Jersey,
where a bottle
of wine came
in handy.

BY DANN
HOWELL

Blanchard's balloon,
sketched as it rose
over Philadelphia,
January 9, 1793.

– from THE EAGLE ALOFT by Tom D. Crouch, courtesy National Air and Space Museum Library

ment. He received permission from city fathers to use — free of charge — the Walnut Street Prison courtyard for the ascent. It was an ideal site, centrally located and one of the few large open areas in tree-rich Philadelphia. The courtyard also was enclosed by high walls. Blanchard could control access to the launch, sell tickets, and raise money. "Everything seemed to succeed to my wishes and to ensure my success," he remarked. Blanchard announced the balloon would lift off at 10 A.M. on January 9. Tickets, priced at $5 and $2, went on sale at Oeller's Hotel.

The morning of the great event dawned hazy and overcast. Temperatures were unseasonably mild, eventually warming to near 50° F. As cannons signaled the time until ascent, city residents converged on the prison neighborhood. President Washington and his

Blanchard also learned that his lodestone — a magnetic rock — would not lift as much weight as on the ground.

cabinet arrived; so did visitors from New York, Baltimore, and elsewhere. Philadelphia was teeming with people. Small towns in the area were nearly deserted. Hotels were filled.

Much to Blanchard's disappointment, however, most spectators did not purchase tickets to view the launch. Thousands perched upon roofs or hung from open windows outside the prison instead.

By 8 A.M. a brass band had begun playing, and the balloon was being inflated. Those in the courtyard watched from a safe distance. Hydrogen was dangerous. Fire and explosion were possible. A newspaper editorial had warned onlookers to "not crowd too near or interrupt Mr. Blanchard whilst employed in his preparations, as it might be attended with fatal effects should he be incommoded."

The rising sun burned away the clouds and haze. At 9:30 A.M., Blanchard readied his basket for the flight. He attached bladders in case he was forced to land on water. Then he loaded the basket with an anchor and nine 24-pound bags of sand for ballast, a large barometer to measure altitude, and instruments to conduct scientific experiments. His equipment also included a compass, spyglass, and thermometer. He added a silk flag acknowledging both the United States and France. Friends supplied provisions of biscuits and wine. Another gave the aeronaut a small black dog to keep him company.

Shortly after 10 A.M., Blanchard reported the weather as "clear, serene, and propitious." He secured the basket to his now fully inflated balloon. George Washington stepped forward and wished him a safe flight. The president gave Blanchard, who did not speak English, a document to present upon landing asking "all citizens of the United States" to "receive and aid him with that humanity and good will which may render honor to their country. . . ."

Cannons fired a final volley. The band was silent. So was the crowd. Blanchard, wearing a plain blue suit and cocked hat with white feathers, climbed into the basket. He tossed out a few bags of ballast. At 10:10 A.M. the balloon ascended slowly. Floating above the prison walls, Blanchard flourished his hat and, with the flag, saluted the spectators. They waved back. Shouts of "Oh! Oh! Good voyage!" erupted from the masses. Prominent Philadelphia physician Benjamin Rush called the launch "a truly sublime sight. Every faculty of the mind was seized, expanded, and captivated by it. Forty thousand people concentrating their eyes and thoughts at the same instant, upon the same object, and all deriving nearly the same degree of pleasure from it. . . ."

Blanchard was equally impressed with the crowd. "I, for a long time, followed their rapid motions," he enthused. "For a long time could I hear the cries of joy which rent the air. I thought myself carried on the vows of their hearts."

A sudden breeze arose, steering the balloon toward the southeast at around 20 miles per hour. Several men on horseback gave chase, but they could not keep up.

Blanchard abandoned his anchor and ascended more quickly. The Delaware River came into view. It appeared to Blanchard as "a ribbon of the breadth of about four inches."

Twenty-five minutes after lift-off, the balloon reached a maximum altitude of just over 5,800 feet. The dog seemed to

Blanchard, a veteran aeronaut, made a total of 59 ascents before his death in 1809.

– Culver Pictures, Inc.

grow ill and tried to escape from the basket, "but finding no landing place, he took the prudent part to remain quietly beside me," the aeronaut noted.

Blanchard performed his scientific experiments. He collected air samples and measured his pulse, which was slightly faster than before the ascent. Blanchard also learned that his lodestone — a magnetic rock—would not lift as much weight as on the ground.

Atmospheric conditions suggested the wind was increasing below. Blanchard prepared to land. He hurriedly ate some biscuits and drank a bit of wine. Then he found a bottle of ether, which friends had placed in the basket without his knowledge. After sniffing a few drops, he noted that he felt "refreshed."

Blanchard stowed everything that was breakable. The basket's bladders obstructed his vision, so he removed them. Venting hydrogen from the balloon, he descended. Thick woods covered the ground, and Blanchard aborted two attempted landings. Finally he spotted a clearing. He released more hydrogen and the balloon approached the treetops. Moments later, the basket touched down. Blanchard stepped out at 10:56 A.M. His 46-minute journey had taken him over 15 miles from Philadelphia, to a landing one mile east of Woodbury, New Jersey.

The aeronaut examined his equipment. All was intact except the barometer, which had broken. The dog ran to drink from a nearby puddle. Blanchard heard a noise among the trees, and a man came forth. He had seen the descent and was frightened by the balloon. Since Blanchard did not speak English, he tried to calm the witness another way by offering a bottle of wine, considering it "the happiest sign of friendship and concilia-

tion." The man accepted Blanchard's hospitality and began helping to fold the deflated balloon.

Others soon appeared. They asked questions Blanchard could not understand. He displayed the president's document. "How dear the name of Washington is to this people!" Blanchard observed. They eagerly packed his balloon into the basket, fed him, and arranged his transportation back to Philadelphia.

Blanchard lost money on the flight, but it was an aeronautical success. As Dr. Benjamin Rush saw it 200 years ago, the ascent was a mandate for the future of flight. "The first command to man to subdue the earth, like every other divine command, must be fulfilled," he declared. "The earth certainly includes water and air as well as dry land. The first and the last have long ago yielded to the dominion of man. It remains for him only to render the air subservient to his will." ☐ ☐

On January 9, 1993, in Philadelphia, the United States ballooning community, to celebrate the 200th anniversary of Blanchard's flight, will reenact the event with a replica of his balloon plus many more events. For information call 215-322-8764.

SECRETS OF THE ZODIAC

Famous Debowelled Man of the Signs

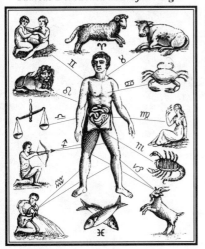

Ancient astrologers associated each of the signs with a part of the body over which they felt the sign held some influence. The first sign of the zodiac — Aries — was attributed to the head, with the rest of the signs moving down the body, ending with Pisces at the feet.

♈	Aries, head. ARI Mar. 21-Apr. 20
♉	Taurus, neck. TAU Apr. 21-May 20
♊	Gemini, arms. GEM May 21-June 20
♋	Cancer, breast. CAN June 21-July 22
♌	Leo, heart. LEO July 23-Aug. 22
♍	Virgo, belly. VIR Aug. 23-Sept. 22
♎	Libra, reins. LIB Sept. 23-Oct. 22
♏	Scorpio, secrets. SCO Oct. 23-Nov. 22
♐	Sagittarius, thighs. SAG Nov. 23-Dec. 21
♑	Capricorn, knees. CAP Dec. 22-Jan. 19
♒	Aquarius, legs. AQU Jan. 20-Feb. 19
♓	Pisces, feet. PSC Feb. 20-Mar. 20

ASTROLOGY AND ASTRONOMY

In ancient times, astrology and astronomy were the same science. "Wise men" looked into the heavens, noted the passage of planets through the vault of the sky, and summarily attached meaning to these events. They were able to find the Christ Child by the appearance of an extraordinary "star," and their counsel was sought by kings.

During the Middle Ages and beyond, the separation of church and state and the rise of science had a negative effect on astrology. Matters of the spirit were given over to religious institutions, and the business of everyday living was subjected to the scientific model. Astronomy became solely the study of the physical properties of the universe.

Yet astrology persists. This ancient art attempts to explain human behavior and even predict the future according to the astrological placement of the two luminaries (the Sun and the Moon) and the eight known planets (Mercury, Venus, Mars, Jupiter, Saturn, Uranus, Neptune, and Pluto) in the 12 signs of the zodiac. It is important to note that *the planetary placements through the signs of the zodiac are not the same astrologically as they are astronomically.* This is because astrologers figure according to a 24,000-year cycle they have identified as the Great Ages; astronomy takes into account precession of the equinoxes and the actual placement of the planets and constellations in the heavens.

Astrologers believe we have spent the past 2,000 years in the Age of Pisces, exploring the realm of compassion and religion. The dawning of the scientific model was due to the influence of Virgo, a dissecting, analyzing, data-oriented energy.

According to astrologers, we are now poised on the brink of the Age of Aquarius. This age will be one of intuition and self-knowledge. As Aquarius is concerned with all of humanity, global awareness and male-female equality will increase.

ASTROLOGY AS A TOOL

Astrology is the study of cycles. Just as the Moon waxes and wanes, everything in life is in a state of flux. An astrologer can provide an individual birth chart, including the astrological position of all of the planets, to describe a person's initial orientation in time and space. An individual's Sun sign (the astrological sign in which the Sun was located at birth) will describe the active, conscious personality (see pages 194-197); one's work should be compatible with the qualities of this sign. The Moon, on the other hand, shows the passive personality as well as the habits. One's emotional well-being is nourished by the qualities of the sign the Moon occupied at birth.

Many readers have asked us which signs are best suited for various activities. Astrologers use Moon signs for this determination; a month-by-month chart showing appropriate times for certain activities is provided on the next page. (To find the astrological place of the Moon in the zodiac, as well as detailed gardening information, see page 211. *Do not confuse this with the astronomical position of the Moon, as listed on the Left-Hand Calendar Pages [56-82]; because of precession and other factors the astrological and astronomical zodiacs do not agree.*)

A Month-by-Month Astrological Timetable for 1993

Herewith we provide the following yearlong chart, based on the Moon signs, showing the appropriate times each month for certain activities. BY CELESTE LONGACRE

	Jan.	Feb.	Mar.	Apr.	May	June	July	Aug.	Sept.	Oct.	Nov.	Dec.
Give up smoking	1,2, 18	19,20	13,14	10,11	1,2	1,2	27,28	12,13	3,4	1,2	1,2	3,4, 31
Begin diet to lose weight	1,2, 19,20	8,9, 14,15	14,15	8,9, 19,20	7,8, 12,13	8,9, 13,14	28,29	7,8, 12,13	3,4, 8,9	5,6, 10,11	8,9, 12	6,7, 10,11
Buy clothes	9,10, 13,14	6,7, 10,11	5,6, 9,10	2,3, 6,7	3,4, 26,27	22,23, 27,28	20,21	16,17, 20,21	13,14, 17,18	10,11, 14,15	6,7, 10,11	3,4, 8,9
Seek favors	24,25	24,25	28,29	29,30	26,27	22,23	26,27	27,28	19,20	16,17	17,18, 21	14,15
Dental care	5,6, 13,14	10,11	28,29	11,25, 26	24,25	20,29, 30	26,27	21,26	4,9, 18,22	19,28	25,30	8,9, 22,27
End old projects	20,21	20,21	21,22	19,20	19,20	18,19	16,17	15,16	14,15	13,14	11,12	11,12
Hair care	14,26, 27	7,10, 12	9,10	29,30	3,4, 27,28	22,23, 27,28	24,25	16,17, 20,21	13,14, 17,18	10,11, 14,15	6,7, 10,11	3,4, 8,9
Seek pleasures	16,17, 18	12,13	11,12	8,9, 29,30	5,6, 8	1,2, 29,30	26,27	22,23	10,11,12, 13,14	16,17, 20	17,18, 21,22	1,3, 8,9
Start a new project	28,29	24,25	24,25	24,25	26,27	21,22	28,29	18,19	17,18	16,17	21,22	14,15
Fishing	18,19	14,15	13,14	10,11	7,8	4,5	28,29	24,25	21,22	18,19	14,15	12,13
Breed	16,17	12,13	11,12	8,9	5,6	29,30	26,27	22,23	19,20	16,17	12,13	10,11, 19
Destroy pests/ weeds	28,29	24,25	23,24	19,20	17,18	13,14	10,11	7,8	3,4	1,2, 27,28	24,25	21,22
Graft or pollinate	16,17	4,5	30,31	27,28	14,15	29,30	8,9,26	5,6	1,2	16,17	21,22	19,20
Harvest above-ground crops	1,2, 28,29	27,28	30,31	27,28	28,29	1,24, 25	22,23	27,28	23,24	20,21	21,22, 26,27	24,25
Harvest root crops	11,12	8,9, 16,17	21,22	12,13	14,15	15,16	13,14	9,10	5,6	8,9	8,9	6,7
Begin logging	20,21	16,17	28,29	12,13	9,10	6,7	26,27	27,28	23,24	20,21	17,18	14,15
Prune or cut hay	29,30	24,25	28,29	24,25	7,8	13,14	11,12	7,8	3,4	1,2	24,25	21,22
Seed grain	7,8, 16,17	4,5	30,31	29,30	24,25	2,29, 30	26,27	22,23	19,20, 28,29	16,17, 25,26	21,22	19,20, 28,29
Set posts or pour concrete	20,21	16,17	28,29	12,13	9,10	6,7	30,31	27,28	23,24	21,22	17,18	14,15
Slaughter	20,21	12,13	11,12	8,9	5,6	1,2, 29,30	26,27	22,23	19,20	16,17	12,13	10,11
Wean	18,19	14,15	28,29	10,11	12,13	4,5	28,29	29,30	21,22	18,19	24,25	12,13
Castrate animals	23,24	19,20	18,19	14,15	12,13	8,9	5,6	29,30	25,26	22,23	19,20	16,17

THE ASTROLOGICAL SIGNS
by Celeste Longacre

ARIES MARCH 21-APRIL 20

Symbol: ♈ *The Ram.* Ruling planet: *Mars.* Element: *Fire.* Quality: *Assertiveness.* Ability: *Leadership.*

You are the initiators of the zodiac. Dashing hither and yon (you are always in a hurry), you rush fearlessly ahead with little regard for your own safety. You like to be first in all that you do, and you are happiest when sharing your new discoveries with your friends. Willing to begin conversations with total strangers, you usually have many friends.

Generally optimistic, you often possess a bright, cheery smile that warms the hearts of those around you. While sometimes tactless, you are without guile, and what comes into the head slips right out of the mouth (unless Scorpio predominates elsewhere in your chart).

You should work in a job or career that allows you to pioneer something new or encourages you to be independent. You are very capable and will aim for the top. Boundless energy is yours, and you should get up and move around frequently or spend your lunches at the gym if you are chained to a desk.

In love, Leo meets your strength, Gemini your wit, Sagittarius your energy, and Aquarius your love of the peculiar. Capricorn fascinates you (and you Capricorn), and you enjoy the way that Cancer makes you the center of the world (although you will have to work on tact here). Libra, as your polar opposite, can balance you out nicely or the two of you can create a battleground.

TAURUS APRIL 21-MAY 20

Symbol: ♉ *The Bull.* Ruling planet: *Venus.* Element: *Earth.* Quality: *Practical.* Ability: *Persistence.*

You are the most grounded members of the zodiac. Able to see the practical side of matters, you can be counted upon not only to do the job right, but to do it thoroughly as well. While it may sometimes take you a while to gain momentum, your gift is the determination and persistence that carries you along once you have begun. You have staying power.

Your most basic need is for security; this is why it is so important for you to have your name on the deed somewhere. You like to build upon that which has already been established, and a firm home life makes it possible for you to go out and accomplish much in the workplace. Fond of comfort, you prefer soft fabrics and easy designs in your living space.

Known for your ability to spot bargains, you nevertheless go for quality rather than quantity. Value is important to you, and shoddiness just won't do. Often possessing a green thumb, you have the ability to make things grow and a need to feel connected to the Earth. Walking barefoot or having somebody rub your feet can always bring you back to center when you begin to feel unbalanced.

In love, you seek monogamy. Capricorn shares your desire to live in the best of neighborhoods, and you enjoy Virgo's ability to help around the house. Pisces makes you feel strong and brings out your protective feelings, while Cancer understands your nesting instincts. Libra's good taste is attractive to you, but you will have to leave your easy chair often to make it work. Passion is available with a Scorpio as long as you both don't dig in.

GEMINI
MAY 21-JUNE 20

Symbol: ♊ *The Twins.* Ruling planet: *Mercury.* Element: *Air.* Quality: *The intellect.* Ability: *Writing and communications.*

You are the witty communicators of the zodiac. Words trip lightly off your tongue under any and all circumstances. You possess natural gifts for writing and speaking and are often drawn into fields where you can express your abilities.

Like your ruling planet, you are mercurial. You have a strong need for diversity and bore easily. In choosing a life path, you would do best to find an occupation that contains many different parts, as well as something that would allow you to move around. Many of you are found throughout journalism as this career satisfies your needs while allowing you also to emphasize your talents.

You love being part of your local community, and you can be counted upon to know and pass along most of the current gossip. Friends use you as a resource when seeking information about a particular service or product. Generally positive, you enjoy being cheerful, and you search for the lightness in all things.

In love, Aries captures your imagination and responds powerfully to your wit. Gemini can engage your brain cells like few others, while Leo warms your heart and soul. Virgo possesses a similar love of language, and Libra has a sense of style you find attractive. Sagittarius, your polar opposite, is more similar to you than you might suspect, while Aquarius understands your need for freedom. Most of all, you seek a partner with enough self-confidence to allow you to maintain some of your own interests and friends.

CANCER JUNE 21-JULY 22

Symbol: ♋ *The Crab.* Ruling planet: *Moon.* Element: *Water.* Quality: *Sensitivity.* Ability: *Nurturing.*

You are the shy, supportive members of the zodiac. Home and family are very important to you, and you are willing to submerge your own wants and desires for the good of your immediate group. Often quite ambitious, you seek to get ahead in order to provide the best for your loved ones.

Like your animal, the crab, your tough exterior hides a very soft interior. You take everything to heart; while you may not show it, you are easily wounded. You feel experiences intensely, and you bring this knowledge into your relationships with others. Gentle and caring, you are always ready to lend an ear or fix another a cup of tea.

You often possess extraordinary culinary abilities, and your meals, while delicious, are also quite nutritious. In choosing a profession, you would do well to pick an occupation that gives you an opportunity to express the compassion that you feel for others. You are loyal and patriotic, and employers can be sure of your personal devotion.

In love, Taurus can provide you with a great deal of security. Cancer understands your sensitive nature; Leo possesses a similar inner vulnerability although Leo is externally bolder. Libra's tactfulness allows you to relax, and Scorpio's passion gets your juices flowing. Pisces has an understanding nature and can match your kindness, but here (or with another Cancer), be especially careful to develop channels of communication.

LEO JULY 23-AUGUST 22

Symbol: ♌ *The Lion.* Ruling planet: *Sun.* Element: *Fire.* Quality: *Dramatic.* Ability: *Natural leadership.*

You are the naturals of the zodiac. Unusually talented, you possess inherent abilities for which even you can't account. Often dazzlingly charming, you light up a room with your presence, and all in attendance know where you are. Your broad smile and bright eyes make others feel warm and welcome.

You always play to the audience. With dramatic effect, you tell your stories, pausing at the right places, occasionally gesturing for emphasis. You need to see a response. Some form of acknowledgment such as a pat on the back is as important to you as the air you breathe. You need to be noticed.

As your personality is strong, you prefer friends who can meet your strength. You seek positions of leadership in employment, and you do well as the head of a department or in business for yourself. As you think big, bold, bright, and beautiful, your dreams can carry you far.

In love, Aries's strength melts your heart and warms your soul. Gemini's wit challenges your mind, while Cancer's sensitivity brings out your protective nature. Leo can help you to make your dreams come true as long as you can remain flexible. Libra is someone of whom you can be proud, and Sagittarius brings out your sense of humor. Aquarius, your polar opposite, can balance you out nicely or set up camp on the other side. Above all, you seek a mate who will acknowledge you.

VIRGO AUGUST 23-SEPTEMBER 22

Symbol: ♍ *The Virgin.* Ruling planet: *Mercury.* Element: *Earth.* Quality: *Logical.* Ability: *To reason.*

You are the organized thinkers of the zodiac. With a critical eye, you dissect and analyze all sorts of data. You seek perfection, and you are able to see instantly the flaw in any given situation. Loving information, you file and store it away for future retrieval. You understand computers intuitively, as your own brain functions in exactly the same manner.

You do well in all sorts of scientific pursuits. Able to memorize infinite amounts of information, you love the study of phylums and dictums. Your organizational ability is particularly strong, and while your home and office may not always be as neat as a pin, you are aware of the placement of each and every one of your belongings. You desire life at the top, and you are well aware of the steps involved in getting there.

Incorporating a sense of humor into your personality keeps you from becoming overly serious. Dependable and responsible, you must guard against taking on the accountability of others. Once you have truly learned how to have fun, yours is an enviable life.

In love, Taurus keeps your home fires burning, while Cancer makes it a cozy nest. Gemini can challenge and stimulate your intellect, and another Virgo provides complete understanding. Libra appeals to your aesthetic sense. Capricorn shares your desire to get ahead in the world and can help you to purchase that home in the suburbs. Pisces, your polar opposite, can balance you, but you must leave the critic at the office for this one to work.

LIBRA SEPTEMBER 23-OCTOBER 22

Symbol: ♎ *The Scales.* Ruling planet: *Venus.* Element: *Air.* Quality: *Relating.* Ability: *Diplomacy.*

You are the tactful diplomats of the zodiac. Ever concerned with the impact of your words and actions, you strive for harmony in all things. You weigh and balance with careful deliberation and thoroughly think through all your plans and activities. Good at seeing all sides of a situation, you are often drawn to fields dealing with the law or courts. Justice is your companion.

While balance is your watchword, you do not maintain center at all times, rather, continuously swing and sway back and forth, always striving for the central point. If you work too many hours one week, you will sleep in a lot during the next. You intuitively sense where to fulfill your needs.

Your sense of color and design is usually very high, and you possess a highly developed aesthetic sense. Because of this, many of you enjoy careers having to do with beauty: art, interior decorating, modeling, or design. You also do well in partnerships due to your need to relate, but you should guard against giving away your power for fear of loneliness.

In love, Taurus's sense of value appeals to your appreciation of beauty, but you must understand that this one will keep you too much at home. Gemini shares your love of socializing, while Leo really knows how to show you the town. Aquarius stimulates your intellect, but can also sometimes shock your sensibilities. Pisces brings out your protective nature and understands your soft inner side.

SCORPIO OCTOBER 23-NOVEMBER 22

Symbol: ♏ *The Scorpion or the Eagle.* Ruling planet: *Pluto.* Element: *Water.* Quality: *Willpower.* Ability: *To focus on goals.*

You are the strongest members of the zodiac. Because of this, there is no middle road for you: Choose the high road or the low road, but choose you must. Unlike the other astrological signs of strength, you don't waste it showing it off. You wait until you truly want something and then focus your will on your goals, drawing them in like a fisherman reels in his net. You have the capacity to get what you want.

You understand the intricacies and the innuendos of power. Using advantage, you always have a

plan and build upon those plans for an improved future. Intuitively, you sense ulterior motives and hidden agendas, and your shrewdness amazes and intrigues others. With your X-ray vision, nothing can be hidden from you.

Because of your strength, you often intimidate other people. As long as your own motivations remain pure, you needn't worry; the weak are always frightened by the strong. Choosing the low road, however, will always get you in the end. Spread your wings of protection over your brood and fly like the eagle, and there will be no stopping you.

In love, Aries meets your strength and looks you right in the eye. Cancer understands your depth of emotion and enjoys plumbing the limits with you. While Taurus's sensuality attracts you, the two of you can lock horns unless you both possess much mutability elsewhere in your natal charts. Capricorn will help you climb the corporate ladder, and Pisces brings out your softer nature.

SAGITTARIUS
NOVEMBER 23-DECEMBER 21

Symbol: ♐ *The Archer.* Ruling planet: *Jupiter.* Element: *Fire.* Quality: *Philosophical.* Ability: *To see the bigger picture.*

You are the philosophers of the zodiac. On a personal mission to discover Truth (with a capital "T"), you intuitively understand that there is more to life and living than what is apparent on the surface. You seek to know the inner causes of the outer manifestations, and yours is a spiritual quest.

Loving both the country and the city, your ideal would be to own two homes. You feel drawn to the wide expanses, but the hustle and bustle of town also excites you. Interested in just about everything, you are a wonderful conversationalist; so much so that you are often bored when speaking with signs other than your own. Your need for freedom is very strong and you quickly tire of jobs that keep you stationary.

As you quite literally need to move about, you can often be found in groups traveling to foreign countries and faraway places. Generally athletic, you enjoy safaris into the outback and hikes up the mountains. If you can't travel physically, you will travel intellectually, and your nose can often be found in a book.

In love, other Sagittarians are your favorite people. Aries's energy and enthusiasm capture your imagination while Leo's bold style and grand plans appeal to your sense of adventure. Aquarius completely understands your need for freedom. Gemini's versatility is attractive to you, but there is sometimes too much mutability for stability here.

CAPRICORN DECEMBER 22-JANUARY 19

Symbol: ♑ *The Mountain Goat.* Ruling planet: *Saturn.* Element: *Earth.* Quality: *Discipline.* Ability: *Working for goals.*

You are the hardest-working members of the zodiac. Able to organize your thoughts and create specific plans, you set goals and work toward them. You seek to prove to the world that you are capable and efficient, and you don't rest until you have either a title after your name or a business of your own.

Born old, you begin life with a serious start. Responsibility is often emphasized in your youth, and you are encouraged to make something of yourself. Once accomplishment becomes yours, however, look out! All of a sudden, the fun side of you becomes apparent, and your dry wit finds increasing opportunities for expression.

You not only want to partake of the best that life has to offer, but you are well aware of the steps involved in getting there. Preferring the penthouse, you can generally be found at the top. Your taste in clothing and furnishings tends toward the conservative, as you feel that there are rules to this game, so you may as well play by them.

In love, Taurus's innate sense of value warms your heart. Aries's youthful buoyancy also deeply attracts you, while Pisces's total understanding helps you to forget your troubles at the end of the day. Virgo can help you to achieve material success, and Scorpio shares your dream of power. A Cancer, your polar opposite, can fluff up your nest if you agree to balance one another.

AQUARIUS JANUARY 20-FEBRUARY 19

Symbol: ♒ *The Water Bearer.* Ruling planet: *Uranus.* Element: *Air.* Quality: *Inventiveness.* Ability: *To see the future.*

You are the enthusiastic inventors of the world. Able to see the world as it should be or could be rather than as it is, you have the capacity to set things in motion. Of course, there are a few of you out there who are more conservative, and if this

is you, go back and read the Capricorn section.

Detached and impersonally friendly to all, you have many acquaintances. You are a dedicated humanitarian and very tolerant — of everything but intolerance. You function well in groups and organizations as long as you can maintain your independence. Freedom is extremely important to you, and you need to be able to do your work your own way.

You are often politically involved as you see certain ordinary aspects of our culture and society as truly strange. Needing to be different, some aspect of your personality will be seen as eccentric by others.

In love, Aries's eagerness for new experience delights you, while Sagittarius's love of freedom feels like a kindred soul. Gemini's mental gymnastics keep you on your toes, and Libra's exquisite tact and diplomacy can help to smooth troubled waters. Leo, your polar opposite, can warm you up, but you must be willing to melt under the thaw; too much cool detachment will cause trouble here.

PISCES FEBRUARY 20-MARCH 20

Symbol: ♓ *The Fish.* Ruling planet: *Neptune.* Element: *Water.* Quality: *Creativity.* Ability: *Understanding.*

You are the romantic dreamers of the zodiac. As with Aquarius, some of you more go-getter types might prefer to go back and read the Capricorn section, but the sensitive ones can stay here (there are two distinct types of Pisces). You have the ability to visit the Muses and bring back a fine creativity.

Unlike the other signs of the zodiac, you possess no singular energy of your own; rather, you are a combination of all of the signs. Because you have an overwhelming desire to merge consciously or unconsciously, you intuit what others need from you and you act accordingly. The compassion and understanding that is your ultimate gift can sometimes be problematic until you have learned how to define yourself.

Because of your sensitivity, you should always have a room of your own. You need regularly scheduled "alone time" and should be encouraged to learn how to say "No." Your world is full of imagination and fantasy, so a creative outlet is also a must.

In love, Taurus provides a sense of security while Cancer's sensitivity makes you feel right at home. Leo's warmth and protective nature appeals to your heart, and Libra's artistic taste is right up your alley. Scorpio's depth intrigues your sense of the dramatic. Capricorn can take you places as long as you can handle a few nights home alone.

TIME CORRECTION TABLES

The times of sunrise, sunset, moonrise, moonset, and the rising and setting of the planets are given for Boston only on pages 56-82 and 42-43. Use the Key Letter shown there and this table to find the number of minutes that should be added to or subtracted from Boston time to give the correct time of your city. The answer will not be as precise as that for Boston, but will be within approximately 5 minutes. If your city is not listed, find the city closest to you in both latitude and longitude and use those figures. **Boston's latitude is 42° 22' and longitude is 71° 03'.** Canadian cities appear at the end of the list. For a more complete explanation see pages 34-35.

Time Zone Code: Atlantic Std. is -1; Eastern Std. is 0; Central Std. is 1; Mountain Std. is 2; Pacific Std. is 3; Alaska Std. is 4; Hawaii-Aleutian Std. is 5.

City	North Latitude ° '	West Longitude ° '	Time Zone Code	A min.	B min.	C min.	D min.	E min.
Aberdeen, SD	45 28	98 29	1	+37	+44	+49	+54	+59
Akron, OH	41 5	81 31	0	+46	+43	+41	+39	+37
Albany, NY	42 39	73 45	0	+ 9	+10	+10	+11	+11
Albert Lea, MN	43 39	93 22	1	+24	+26	+28	+31	+33
Albuquerque, NM	35 5	106 39	2	+45	+32	+22	+11	+ 2
Alexandria, LA	31 18	92 27	1	+58	+40	+26	+ 9	− 3
Allentown-Bethlehem, PA..	40 3	75 28	0	+25	+20	+17	+13	+10
Amarillo, TX	35 12	101 50	1	+85	+73	+63	+52	+43
Anchorage, AK	61 10	149 59	4	−46	+27	+71	+122	+171
Asheville, NC	35 36	82 33	0	+67	+55	+46	+35	+27
Atlanta, GA	33 45	84 24	0	+79	+65	+53	+40	+30
Atlantic City, NJ	39 22	74 26	0	+23	+17	+13	+ 8	+ 4
Augusta, GA	33 28	81 58	0	+70	+55	+44	+30	+19
Augusta, ME	44 19	69 46	0	−12	− 8	− 5	− 1	0
Austin, TX	30 16	97 45	1	+82	+62	+47	+29	+15
Bakersfield, CA	35 23	119 1	3	+33	+21	+12	+ 1	− 7
Baltimore, MD	39 17	76 37	0	+32	+26	+22	+17	+13
Bangor, ME	44 48	68 46	0	−18	−13	− 9	− 5	− 1
Barstow, CA	34 54	117 1	3	+27	+14	+ 4	− 7	−16
Baton Rouge, LA	30 27	91 11	1	+55	+36	+21	+ 3	−10
Beaumont, TX	30 5	94 6	1	+67	+48	+32	+14	0
Bellingham, WA	48 45	122 29	3	0	+13	+24	+37	+47
Bemidji, MN	47 28	94 53	1	+14	+26	+34	+44	+52
Berlin, NH	44 28	71 11	0	− 7	− 3	0	+ 3	+ 7
Billings, MT	45 47	108 30	2	+16	+23	+29	+35	+40
Biloxi, MS	30 24	88 53	1	+46	+27	+11	− 5	−19
Binghamton, NY	42 6	75 55	0	+20	+19	+19	+18	+18
Birmingham, AL	33 31	86 49	1	+30	+15	+ 3	−10	−20
Bismarck, ND	46 48	100 47	1	+41	+50	+58	+66	+73
Boise, ID	43 37	116 12	2	+55	+58	+60	+62	+64
Brattleboro, VT	42 51	72 34	0	+ 4	+ 5	+ 5	+ 6	+ 7
Bridgeport, CT	41 11	73 11	0	+12	+10	+ 8	+ 6	+ 4
Brockton, MA	42 5	71 1	0	0	0	0	0	− 1
Brownsville, TX	25 54	97 30	1	+91	+66	+46	+23	+ 5
Buffalo, NY	42 53	78 52	0	+29	+30	+30	+31	+32
Burlington, VT	44 29	73 13	0	0	+ 4	+ 8	+12	+15
Butte, MT	46 1	112 32	2	+31	+39	+45	+52	+57
Cairo, IL	37 0	89 11	1	+29	+20	+12	+ 4	− 2
Camden, NJ	39 57	75 7	0	+24	+19	+16	+12	+ 9
Canton, OH	40 48	81 23	0	+46	+43	+41	+38	+36
Cape May, NJ	38 56	74 56	0	+26	+20	+15	+ 9	+ 5
Carson City–Reno, NV	39 10	119 46	3	+25	+19	+14	+ 9	+ 5
Casper, WY	42 51	106 19	2	+19	+19	+20	+21	+22
Chadron, NE	42 50	103 0	2	+ 5	+ 6	+ 7	+ 8	+ 9
Charleston, SC	32 47	79 56	0	+64	+48	+36	+21	+10
Charleston, WV	38 21	81 38	0	+55	+48	+42	+35	+30
Charlotte, NC	35 14	80 51	0	+61	+49	+39	+28	+19
Charlottesville, VA	38 2	78 30	0	+43	+35	+29	+22	+17
Chattanooga, TN	35 3	85 19	0	+79	+67	+57	+45	+36
Cheboygan, MI	45 39	84 29	0	+40	+47	+53	+59	+64
Cheyenne, WY	41 8	104 49	2	+19	+16	+14	+12	+11

City	North Latitude ° '		West Longitude ° '		Time Zone Code	Key Letters				
						A min.	B min.	C min.	D min.	E min.
Chicago-Oak Park, IL...........	41	52	87	38	1	+ 7	+ 6	+ 6	+ 5	+ 4
Cincinnati-Hamilton, OH ...	39	6	84	31	0	+64	+58	+53	+48	+44
Cleveland-Lakewood, OH..	41	30	81	42	0	+45	+43	+42	+40	+39
Columbia, SC......................	34	0	81	2	0	+65	+51	+40	+27	+17
Columbus, OH.....................	39	57	83	1	0	+55	+51	+47	+43	+40
Cordova, AK	60	33	145	45	4	−55	+13	+55	+103	+149
Corpus Christi, TX..............	27	48	97	24	1	+86	+64	+46	+25	+ 9
Craig, CO	40	31	107	33	2	+32	+28	+25	+22	+20
Dallas-Fort Worth, TX	32	47	96	48	1	+71	+55	+43	+28	+17
Danville, IL.........................	40	8	87	37	1	+13	+ 9	+ 6	+ 2	0
Danville, VA	36	36	79	23	0	+51	+41	+33	+24	+17
Davenport, IA	41	32	90	35	1	+20	+19	+17	+16	+15
Dayton, OH	39	45	84	10	0	+61	+56	+52	+48	+44
Decatur, AL	34	36	86	59	1	+27	+14	+ 4	− 7	−17
Decatur, IL..........................	39	51	88	57	1	+19	+15	+11	+ 7	+ 4
Denver-Boulder, CO...........	39	44	104	59	2	+24	+19	+15	+11	+ 7
Des Moines, IA...................	41	35	93	37	1	+32	+31	+30	+28	+27
Detroit-Dearborn, MI	42	20	83	3	0	+47	+47	+47	+47	+47
Dubuque, IA........................	42	30	90	41	1	+17	+18	+18	+18	+18
Duluth, MN	46	47	92	6	1	+ 6	+16	+23	+31	+38
Durham, NC	36	0	78	55	0	+51	+40	+31	+21	+13
Eastport, ME	44	54	67	0	0	−26	−20	−16	−11	− 8
Eau Claire, WI....................	44	49	91	30	1	+12	+17	+21	+25	+29
El Paso, TX	31	45	106	29	2	+53	+35	+22	+ 6	− 6
Elko, NV	40	50	115	46	3	+ 3	0	− 1	− 3	− 5
Ellsworth, ME.....................	44	33	68	25	0	−18	−14	−10	− 6	− 3
Erie, PA	42	7	80	5	0	+36	+36	+35	+35	+35
Eugene, OR	44	3	123	6	3	+21	+24	+27	+30	+33
Fairbanks, AK	64	48	147	51	4	−127	+ 2	+61	+131	+205
Fall River– New Bedford, MA............	41	42	71	9	0	+ 2	+ 1	0	0	− 1
Fargo, ND	46	53	96	47	1	+24	+34	+42	+50	+57
Flagstaff, AZ.......................	35	12	111	39	2	+64	+52	+42	+31	+22
Flint, MI.............................	43	1	83	41	0	+47	+49	+50	+51	+52
Fort Randall, AK	55	10	162	47	4	+62	+99	+124	+153	+179
Fort Scott, KS	37	50	94	42	1	+49	+41	+34	+27	+21
Fort Smith, AR	35	23	94	25	1	+55	+43	+33	+22	+14
Fort Wayne, IN...................	41	4	85	9	0	+60	+58	+56	+54	+52
Fort Yukon, AK	66	34	145	16	4	+30	−18	+50	+131	+227
Fresno, CA	36	44	119	47	3	+32	+22	+15	+ 6	0
Gallup, NM	35	32	108	45	2	+52	+40	+31	+20	+11
Galveston, TX.....................	29	18	94	48	1	+72	+52	+35	+16	+ 1
Gary, IN	41	36	87	20	1	+ 7	+ 6	+ 4	+ 3	+ 2
Glasgow, MT.......................	48	12	106	38	2	− 1	+11	+21	+32	+42
Grand Forks, ND	47	55	97	3	1	+21	+33	+43	+53	+62
Grand Island, NE	40	55	98	21	1	+53	+51	+49	+46	+44
Grand Junction, CO............	39	4	108	33	2	+40	+34	+29	+24	+20
Great Falls, MT	47	30	111	17	2	+20	+31	+39	+49	+58
Green Bay, WI....................	44	31	88	0	1	0	+ 3	+ 7	+11	+14
Greensboro, NC..................	36	4	79	47	0	+54	+43	+35	+25	+17
Hagerstown, MD.................	39	39	77	43	0	+35	+30	+26	+22	+18
Harrisburg, PA....................	40	16	76	53	0	+30	+26	+23	+19	+16
Hartford-New Britain, CT ..	41	46	72	41	0	+ 8	+ 7	+ 6	+ 5	+ 4
Helena, MT	46	36	112	2	2	+27	+36	+43	+51	+57
Hilo, HI	19	44	155	5	5	+94	+62	+37	+ 7	−15
Honolulu, HI.......................	21	18	157	52	5	+102	+72	+48	+19	− 1
Houston, TX.......................	29	45	95	22	1	+73	+53	+37	+19	+ 5
Indianapolis, IN..................	39	46	86	10	0	+69	+64	+60	+56	+52
Ironwood, MI......................	46	27	90	9	1	0	+ 9	+15	+23	+29
Jackson, MI........................	42	15	84	24	0	+53	+53	+53	+52	+52
Jackson, MS	32	18	90	11	1	+46	+30	+17	+ 1	−10
Jacksonville, Fl...................	30	20	81	40	0	+77	+58	+43	+25	+11
Jefferson City, MO	38	34	92	10	1	+36	+29	+24	+18	+13
Joplin, MO	37	6	94	30	1	+50	+41	+33	+25	+18
Juneau, AK	58	18	134	25	4	−76	−23	+10	+49	+86
Kalamazoo, MI....................	42	17	85	35	0	+58	+57	+57	+57	+57
Kanab, UT...........................	37	3	112	32	2	+62	+53	+46	+37	+30

City	North Latitude ° '		West Longitude ° '		Time Zone Code	Key Letters				
						A min.	B min.	C min.	D min.	E min.
Kansas City, MO	39	1	94	20	1	+44	+37	+33	+27	+23
Keene, NH	42	56	72	17	0	+ 2	+ 3	+ 4	+ 5	+ 6
Ketchikan, AK	55	21	131	39	4	–62	–25	0	+29	+56
Knoxville, TN	35	58	83	55	0	+71	+60	+51	+41	+33
Kodiak, AK	57	47	152	24	4	0	+49	+82	+120	+154
LaCrosse, WI	43	48	91	15	1	+15	+18	+20	+22	+25
Lake Charles, LA	30	14	93	13	1	+64	+44	+29	+11	– 2
Lanai City, HI	20	50	156	55	5	+99	+69	+44	+15	– 6
Lancaster, PA	40	2	76	18	0	+28	+24	+20	+17	+13
Lansing, MI	42	44	84	33	0	+52	+53	+53	+54	+54
Las Cruces, NM	32	19	106	47	2	+53	+36	+23	+ 8	– 3
Las Vegas, NV	36	10	115	9	3	+16	+ 4	– 3	–13	–20
Lawrence-Lowell, MA	42	42	71	10	0	0	0	0	0	+ 1
Lewiston, ID	46	25	117	1	3	–12	– 3	+ 2	+10	+17
Lexington-Frankfort, KY	38	3	84	30	0	+67	+59	+53	+46	+41
Liberal, KS	37	3	100	55	1	+76	+66	+59	+51	+44
Lihue, HI	21	59	159	23	5	+107	+77	+54	+26	+ 5
Lincoln, NE	40	49	96	41	1	+47	+44	+42	+39	+37
Little Rock, AR	34	45	92	17	1	+48	+35	+25	+13	+ 4
Los Angeles incl. Pasadena and Santa Monica, CA	34	3	118	14	3	+34	+20	+ 9	– 3	–13
Louisville, KY	38	15	85	46	0	+72	+64	+58	+52	+46
Macon, GA	32	50	83	38	0	+79	+63	+50	+36	+24
Madison, WI	43	4	89	23	1	+10	+11	+12	+14	+15
Manchester-Concord, NH	42	59	71	28	0	0	0	+ 1	+ 2	+ 3
McAllen, TX	26	12	98	14	1	+93	+69	+49	+26	+9
McGrath, AK	62	58	155	36	4	–52	+42	+93	+152	+213
Memphis, TN	35	9	90	3	1	+38	+26	+16	+ 5	– 3
Meridian, MS	32	22	88	42	1	+40	+24	+11	– 4	–15
Miami, FL	25	47	80	12	0	+88	+57	+37	+14	– 3
Miles City, MT	46	25	105	51	2	+ 3	+11	+18	+26	+32
Milwaukee, WI	43	2	87	54	1	+ 4	+ 6	+ 7	+ 8	+ 9
Minneapolis-St. Paul, MN	44	59	93	16	1	+18	+24	+28	+33	+37
Minot, ND	48	14	101	18	1	+36	+50	+59	+71	+81
Moab, UT	38	35	109	33	2	+46	+39	+33	+27	+22
Mobile, AL	30	42	88	3	1	+42	+23	+ 8	– 8	–22
Monroe, LA	32	30	92	7	1	+53	+37	+24	+ 9	– 1
Montgomery, AL	32	23	86	19	1	+31	+14	+ 1	–13	–25
Muncie, IN	40	12	85	23	0	+64	+60	+57	+53	+50
Nashville, TN	36	10	86	47	1	+22	+11	+ 3	– 6	–14
New Haven, CT	41	18	72	56	0	+11	+ 8	+ 7	+ 5	+ 4
New London, CT	41	22	72	6	0	+ 7	+ 5	+ 4	+ 2	+ 1
New Orleans, LA	29	57	90	4	1	+52	+32	+16	– 1	–15
New York, NY	40	45	74	0	0	+17	+14	+11	+ 9	+ 6
Newark–Irvington–East Orange, NJ	40	44	74	10	0	+17	+14	+12	+ 9	+ 7
Nome, AK	64	30	165	25	4	–48	+74	+132	+199	+271
Norfolk, VA	36	51	76	17	0	+38	+28	+21	+12	+ 5
North Platte, NE	41	8	100	46	1	+62	+60	+58	+56	+54
Norwalk-Stamford, CT	41	7	73	22	0	+13	+10	+ 9	+ 7	+ 5
Oakley, KS	39	8	100	51	1	+69	+63	+59	+53	+49
Ogden, UT	41	13	111	58	2	+47	+45	+43	+41	+40
Ogdensburg, NY	44	42	75	30	0	+ 8	+13	+17	+21	+25
Oklahoma City, OK	35	28	97	31	1	+67	+55	+46	+35	+26
Omaha, NE	41	16	95	56	1	+43	+40	+39	+37	+36
Orlando, FL	28	32	81	22	0	+80	+59	+42	+22	+ 6
Ortonville, MN	45	19	96	27	1	+30	+36	+40	+46	+51
Oshkosh, WI	44	1	88	33	1	+ 3	+ 6	+ 9	+12	+15
Parkersburg, WV	39	16	81	34	0	+52	+46	+42	+36	+32
Paterson, NJ	40	55	74	10	0	+17	+14	+12	+ 9	+ 7
Pendleton, OR	45	40	118	47	3	– 1	+ 4	+10	+16	+21
Pensacola, FL	30	25	87	13	1	+39	+20	+ 5	–12	–26
Peoria, IL	40	42	89	36	1	+19	+16	+14	+11	+ 9
Philadelphia-Chester, PA	39	57	75	9	0	+24	+19	+16	+12	+ 9
Phoenix, AZ	33	27	112	4	2	+71	+56	+44	+30	+20
Pierre, SD	44	22	100	21	1	+49	+53	+56	+60	+63
Pittsburgh-McKeesport, PA	40	26	80	0	0	+42	+38	+35	+32	+29

City	North Latitude ° '		West Longitude ° '		Time Zone Code	Key Letters				
						A min.	B min.	C min.	D min.	E min.
Pittsfield, MA	42	27	73	15	0	+ 8	+ 8	+ 8	+ 8	+ 8
Pocatello, ID	42	52	112	27	2	+43	+44	+45	+46	+46
Poplar Bluff, MO	36	46	90	24	1	+35	+25	+17	+ 8	+ 1
Portland, ME	43	40	70	15	0	− 8	− 5	− 3	− 1	0
Portland, OR	45	31	122	41	3	+14	+20	+25	+31	+36
Portsmouth, NH	43	5	70	45	0	− 4	− 2	− 1	0	0
Presque Isle, ME	46	41	68	1	0	−29	−19	−12	− 4	+ 2
Providence, RI	41	50	71	25	0	+ 3	+ 2	+ 1	0	0
Pueblo, CO	38	16	104	37	2	+27	+20	+14	+ 7	+ 2
Raleigh, NC	35	47	78	38	0	+51	+39	+30	+20	+12
Rapid City, SD	44	5	103	14	2	+ 2	+ 5	+ 8	+11	+13
Reading, PA	40	20	75	56	0	+26	+22	+19	+16	+13
Redding, CA	40	35	122	24	3	+31	+27	+25	+22	+19
Richmond, VA	37	32	77	26	0	+41	+32	+25	+17	+11
Roanoke, VA	37	16	79	57	0	+51	+42	+35	+27	+21
Roswell, NM	33	24	104	32	2	+41	+26	+14	0	−10
Rutland, VT	43	37	72	58	0	+ 2	+ 5	+ 7	+ 9	+11
Sacramento, CA	38	35	121	30	3	+34	+27	+21	+15	+10
Salem, OR	44	57	123	1	3	+17	+23	+27	+31	+35
Salina, KS	38	50	97	37	1	+57	+51	+46	+40	+35
Salisbury, MD	38	22	75	36	0	+31	+23	+18	+11	+ 6
Salt Lake City, UT	40	45	111	53	2	+48	+45	+43	+40	+38
San Antonio, TX	29	25	98	30	1	+87	+66	+50	+31	+16
San Diego, CA	32	43	117	9	3	+33	+17	+ 4	− 9	−21
San Francisco incl. Oakland and San Jose, CA	37	47	122	25	3	+40	+31	+25	+18	+12
Santa Fe, NM	35	41	105	56	2	+40	+28	+19	+ 9	0
Savannah, GA	32	5	81	6	0	+70	+54	+40	+25	+13
Scranton–Wilkes Barre, PA.	41	25	75	40	0	+21	+19	+18	+16	+15
Seattle-Tacoma-Olympia, WA	47	37	122	20	3	+ 3	+15	+24	+34	+42
Sheridan, WY	44	48	106	58	2	+14	+19	+23	+27	+31
Shreveport, LA	32	31	93	45	1	+60	+44	+31	+16	+ 4
Sioux Falls, SD	43	33	96	44	1	+38	+40	+42	+44	+46
South Bend, IN	41	41	86	15	0	+62	+61	+60	+59	+58
Spartanburg, SC	34	56	81	57	0	+66	+53	+43	+32	+23
Spokane, WA	47	40	117	24	3	−16	− 4	+ 4	+14	+23
Springfield, IL	39	48	89	39	1	+22	+18	+14	+10	+ 6
Springfield-Holyoke, MA	42	6	72	36	0	+ 6	+ 6	+ 6	+ 5	+ 5
Springfield, MO	37	13	93	18	1	+45	+36	+29	+20	+14
St. Johnsbury, VT	44	25	72	1	0	− 4	0	+ 3	+ 7	+10
St. Joseph, MO	39	46	94	50	1	+43	+38	+35	+30	+27
St. Louis, MO	38	37	90	12	1	+28	+21	+16	+10	+ 5
St. Petersburg, FL	27	46	82	39	0	+87	+65	+47	+26	+10
Syracuse, NY	43	3	76	9	0	+17	+19	+20	+21	+22
Tallahassee, FL	30	27	84	17	0	+87	+68	+53	+35	+22
Tampa, FL	27	57	82	27	0	+86	+64	+46	+25	+ 9
Terre Haute, IN	39	28	87	24	0	+74	+69	+65	+60	+56
Texarkana, AR	33	26	94	3	1	+59	+44	+32	+18	+ 8
Toledo, OH	41	39	83	33	0	+52	+50	+49	+48	+47
Topeka, KS	39	3	95	40	1	+49	+43	+38	+32	+28
Traverse City, MI	44	46	85	38	0	+49	+54	+57	+62	+65
Trenton, NJ	40	13	74	46	0	+21	+17	+14	+11	+ 8
Trinidad, CO	37	10	104	31	2	+30	+21	+13	+ 5	0
Tucson, AZ	32	13	110	58	2	+70	+53	+40	+24	+12
Tulsa, OK	36	9	95	60	1	+59	+48	+40	+30	+22
Tupelo, MS	34	16	88	34	1	+35	+21	+10	− 2	−11
Vernal, UT	40	27	109	32	2	+40	+36	+33	+30	+28
Walla Walla, WA	46	4	118	20	3	− 5	+ 2	+ 8	+15	+21
Washington, DC	38	54	77	1	0	+35	+28	+23	+18	+13
Waterbury-Meriden, CT	41	33	73	3	0	+10	+ 9	+ 7	+ 6	+ 5
Waterloo, IA	42	30	92	20	1	+24	+24	+24	+25	+25
Wausau, WI	44	58	89	38	1	+ 4	+ 9	+13	+18	+22
West Palm Beach, FL	26	43	80	3	0	+79	+55	+36	+14	− 2
Wichita, KS	37	42	97	20	1	+60	+51	+45	+37	+31
Williston, ND	48	9	103	37	1	+46	+59	+69	+80	+90
Wilmington, DE	39	45	75	33	0	+26	+21	+18	+13	+10

City	North Latitude ° '	West Longitude ° '	Time Zone Code	Key Letters A min.	B min.	C min.	D min.	E min.
Wilmington, NC	34 14	77 55	0	+52	+38	+27	+15	+ 5
Winchester, VA	39 11	78 10	0	+38	+33	+28	+23	+19
Worcester, MA	42 16	71 48	0	+ 3	+ 2	+ 2	+ 2	+ 2
York, PA	39 58	76 43	0	+30	+26	+22	+18	+15
Youngstown, OH	41 6	80 39	0	+42	40	+38	+36	+34
Yuma, AZ	32 43	114 37	2	+83	+67	+54	+40	+28
CANADA								
Calgary, AB	51 5	114 5	2	+13	+35	+50	+68	+84
Edmonton, AB	53 34	113 25	2	− 3	+26	+47	+72	+93
Halifax, NS	44 38	63 35	− 1	+21	+26	+29	+33	+37
Montreal, PQ	45 28	73 39	0	− 1	+ 4	+ 9	+15	+20
Ottawa, ON	45 25	75 43	0	+ 6	+13	+18	+23	+28
Saint John, NB	45 16	66 3	− 1	+28	+34	+39	+44	+49
Saskatoon, SK	52 10	106 40	1	+37	+63	+80	+101	+119
Sydney, NS	46 10	60 10	− 1	+ 1	+ 9	+15	+23	+28
Thunder Bay, ON	48 27	89 12	0	+47	+61	+71	+83	+93
Toronto, ON	43 39	79 23	0	+28	+30	+32	+35	+37
Vancouver, BC	49 13	123 6	3	0	+15	+26	+40	+52
Winnipeg, MB	49 53	97 10	1	+12	+30	+43	+58	+71

KILLING FROSTS AND GROWING SEASONS

Courtesy of National Climatic Center

Dates given are averages; local weather and topography may cause considerable variation.

City	Growing Season (Days)	Last Frost Spring	First Frost Fall	City	Growing Season (Days)	Last Frost Spring	First Frost Fall
Montgomery, AL	279	Feb. 27	Dec. 3	St. Louis, MO	220	Apr. 2	Nov. 8
Little Rock, AR	244	Mar. 16	Nov. 15	Helena, MT	134	May 12	Sept. 23
Phoenix, AZ	318	Jan. 27	Dec. 11	Omaha, NE	189	Apr. 14	Oct. 20
Tucson, AZ	262	Mar. 6	Nov. 23	Reno, NV	141	May 14	Oct. 2
Eureka, CA	335	Jan. 24	Dec. 25	Concord, NH	142	May 11	Sept. 30
Los Angeles, CA	*	*	*	Trenton, NJ	211	Apr. 8	Nov. 5
Sacramento, CA	321	Jan. 24	Dec. 11	Albuquerque, NM	196	Apr. 16	Oct. 29
San Diego, CA	*	*	*	Albany, NY	169	Apr. 27	Oct. 13
San Francisco, CA	*	*	*	Raleigh, NC	237	Mar. 24	Nov. 16
Denver, CO	165	May 2	Oct. 14	Bismarck, ND	136	May 11	Sept. 24
Hartford, CT	180	Apr. 22	Oct. 19	Cincinnati, OH	203	Apr. 5	Oct. 25
Washington, DC	201	Apr. 10	Oct. 28	Toledo, OH	184	Apr. 24	Oct. 25
Miami, FL	*	*	*	Oklahoma City, OK	224	Mar. 28	Nov. 7
Macon, GA	252	Mar. 12	Nov. 19	Medford, OR	178	Apr. 25	Oct. 20
Pocatello, ID	145	May 8	Sept. 30	Portland, OR	279	Feb. 25	Dec. 1
Chicago, IL	192	Apr. 19	Oct. 28	Harrisburg, PA	201	Apr. 10	Oct. 28
Evansville, IN	217	Apr. 2	Nov. 4	Scranton, PA	173	Apr. 24	Oct. 14
Fort Wayne, IN	179	Apr. 24	Oct. 20	Columbia, SC	252	Mar. 14	Nov. 21
Des Moines, IA	182	Apr. 20	Oct. 19	Huron, SD	149	May 4	Sept. 30
Wichita, KS	210	Apr. 5	Nov. 1	Chattanooga, TN	229	Mar. 26	Nov. 10
Shreveport, LA	271	Mar. 1	Nov. 27	Del Rio, TX	300	Feb. 12	Dec. 9
New Orleans, LA	302	Feb. 13	Dec. 12	Midland, TX	217	Apr. 3	Nov. 6
Portland, ME	169	Apr. 29	Oct. 15	Salt Lake City, UT	203	Apr. 12	Nov. 1
Boston, MA	192	Apr. 16	Oct. 25	Burlington, VT	148	May 8	Oct. 3
Alpena, MI	156	May 6	Oct. 9	Richmond, VA	220	Apr. 2	Nov. 8
Detroit, MI	181	Apr. 25	Oct. 23	Spokane, WA	175	Apr. 20	Oct. 12
Marquette, MI	156	May 14	Oct. 17	Parkersburg, WV	188	Apr. 16	Oct. 21
Duluth, MN	125	May 22	Sept. 24	Green Bay, WI	160	May 6	Oct. 13
Minneapolis, MN	166	Apr. 30	Oct. 13	Madison, WI	176	Apr. 26	Oct. 19
Jackson, MS	248	Mar. 10	Nov. 13	Lander, WY	128	May 15	Sept. 20
Columbia, MO	198	Apr. 9	Oct. 24	*Frosts do not occur every year			

TIDE CORRECTIONS

Many factors affect the time and height of the tides: the coastal configuration, the time of the Moon's southing (crossing the meridian) at the place, and the phase of the Moon. This table of tidal corrections is a sufficiently accurate guide to the times and heights of the high water at the places shown. (Low tides occur approximately 6.25 hours before and after high tides.) No figures are shown for the West Coast or the Gulf of Mexico, since the method used in compiling this table does not apply there. For such places and elsewhere where precise accuracy is required, consult the Tide Tables published annually by the National Ocean Service, 6501 Lafayette Ave., Riverdale, MD 20840; telephone 301-436-6990.

The figures for Full Sea on the Left-Hand Calendar Pages 56-82 are the times of high tide at Commonwealth Pier in Boston Harbor. (Where a dash is shown under Full Sea, it indicates that time of high water has occurred after midnight and so is recorded on the next date.) The heights of these tides are given on the Right-Hand Calendar Pages 57-83. The heights are reckoned from Mean Lower Low Water, and each day listed has a set of figures — upper for the morning, lower for the evening. To obtain the time and height of high water at any of the following places, apply the time difference to the daily times of high water at Boston (pages 56-82) and the height difference to the heights at Boston (pages 57-83).

	Time Difference: Hr. Min.	Height Feet
MAINE		
Bar Harbor	−0 34	+0.9
Belfast	−0 20	+0.4
Boothbay Harbor	−0 18	−0.8
Chebeague Island	−0 16	−0.6
Eastport	−0 28	+8.4
Kennebunkport	+0 04	−1.0
Machias	−0 28	+2.8
Monhegan Island	−0 25	−0.8
Old Orchard	0 00	−0.8
Portland	−0 12	−0.6
Rockland	−0 28	+0.1
Stonington	−0 30	+0.1
York	−0 09	−1.0
NEW HAMPSHIRE		
Hampton	+0 02	−1.3
Portsmouth	+0 11	−1.5
Rye Beach	−0 09	−0.9
MASSACHUSETTS		
Annisquam	−0 02	−1.1
Beverly Farms	0 00	−0.5
Boston	0 00	0.0
Cape Cod Canal:		
East Entrance	−0 01	−0.8
West Entrance	−2 16	−5.9
Chatham Outer Coast	+0 30	−2.8
Inside	+1 54	*0.4

	Time Difference: Hr. Min.	Height Feet
Cohasset	+0 02	−0.07
Cotuit Highlands	+1 15	*0.3
Dennis Port	+1 01	*0.4
Duxbury (Gurnet Pt.)	+0 02	−0.3
Fall River	−3 03	−5.0
Gloucester	−0 03	−0.8
Hingham	+0 07	0.0
Hull	+0 03	−0.2
Hyannis Port	+1 01	*0.3
Magnolia (Manchester)	−0 02	−0.7
Marblehead	−0 02	−0.4
Marion	−3 22	−5.4
Monument Beach	−3 08	−5.4
Nahant	−0 01	−0.5
Nantasket	+0 04	−0.1
Nantucket	−0 56	*0.3
Nauset Beach	+0 30	*0.6
New Bedford	−3 24	−5.7
Newburyport	+0 19	−1.8
Oak Bluffs	+0 30	*0.2
Onset (R.R. Bridge)	−2 16	−5.9
Plymouth	+0 05	0.0
Provincetown	+0 14	−0.4
Revere Beach	−0 01	−0.3
Rockport	−0 08	−1.0
Salem	0 00	−0.5
Scituate	−0 05	−0.7
Wareham	−3 09	−5.3
Wellfleet	+0 12	+0.5
West Falmouth	−3 10	−5.4
Westport Harbor	−3 22	−6.4
Woods Hole Little Harbor	−2 50	*0.2
Oceanographic Institute	−3 07	*0.2
RHODE ISLAND		
Bristol	−3 24	−5.3
Sakonnet	−3 44	−5.6
Narrangansett Pier	−3 42	−6.2
Newport	−3 34	−5.9
Pt. Judith	−3 41	−6.3
Providence	−3 20	−4.8
Watch Hill	−2 50	−6.8
CONNECTICUT		
Bridgeport	+0 01	−2.6
Madison	−0 22	−2.3
New Haven	−0 11	−3.2
New London	−1 54	−6.7
Norwalk	+0 01	−2.2
Old Lyme (Highway Bridge)	−0 30	−6.2
Stamford	+0 01	−2.2
Stonington	−2 27	−6.6
NEW YORK		
Coney Island	−3 33	−4.9
Fire Island Lt	−2 43	*0.1
Long Beach	−3 11	−5.7
Montauk Harbor	−2 19	−7.4
New York City (Battery)	−2 43	−5.0
Oyster Bay	+0 04	−1.8
Port Chester	−0 09	−2.2
Port Washington	−0 01	−2.1
Sag Harbor	−0 55	−6.8
Southampton	−4 20	*0.2
(Shinnecock Inlet)		
Willets Point	0 00	−2.3

	Time	Height
Difference: Hr. Min.		**Feet**

NEW JERSEY

Asbury Park	−4 04	−5.3
Atlantic City	−3 56	−5.5
Bay Head (Sea Girt)	−4 04	−5.3
Beach Haven	−1 43	*0.24
Cape May	−3 28	−5.3
Ocean City	−3 06	−5.9
Sandy Hook	−3 30	−5.0
Seaside Park	−4 03	−5.4

PENNSYLVANIA

Philadelphia	+2 40	−3.5

DELAWARE

Cape Henlopen	−2 48	−5.3
Rehoboth Beach	−3 37	−5.7
Wilmington	+1 56	−3.8

MARYLAND

Annapolis	+6 23	−8.5
Baltimore	+7 59	−8.3
Cambridge	+5 05	−7.8
Havre de Grace	+11 21	−7.7
Point No Point	+2 28	−8.1
Prince Frederick	+4 25	−8.5
(Plum Point)		

VIRGINIA

Cape Charles	−2 20	−7.0
Hampton Roads	−2 02	−6.9
Norfolk	−2 06	−6.6
Virginia Beach	−4 00	−6.0
Yorktown	−2 13	−7.0

NORTH CAROLINA

Cape Fear	−3 55	−5.0
Cape Lookout	−4 28	−5.7
Currituck	−4 10	−5.8
Hatteras:		
Ocean	−4 26	−6.0
Inlet	−4 03	−7.4
Kitty Hawk	−4 14	−6.2

SOUTH CAROLINA

Charleston	−3 22	−4.3
Georgetown	−1 48	*0.36
Hilton Head	−3 22	−2.9
Myrtle Beach	−3 49	−4.4
St. Helena		
Harbor Entrance	−3 15	−3.4

GEORGIA

Jekyll Island	−3 46	−2.9
Saint Simon's Island	−2 50	−2.9
Savannah Beach:		
River Entrance	−3 14	−5.5
Tybee Light	−3 22	−2.7

FLORIDA

Cape Canaveral	−3 59	−6.0
Daytona Beach	−3 28	−5.3
Fort Lauderdale	−2 50	−7.2
Fort Pierce Inlet	−3 32	−6.9
Jacksonville		
Railroad Bridge	−6 55	*0.10
Miami Harbor Entrance	−3 18	−7.0
St. Augustine	−2 55	−4.9

CANADA

Alberton, P.E.I.	−5 45**	−7.0
Charlottetown, P.E.I.	−0 45**	−3.5
Halifax, N.S.	−3 23	−4.5
North Sydney, N.S.	−3 15	−6.5
Saint John, N.B.	+0 30	−8.0
St. John's, Nfld.	−4 00	−6.5
Yarmouth, N.S.	−0 40	+3.0

* Where the difference in the "Height/Feet" column is so marked, height at Boston should be multiplied by this ratio.
** Varies widely; accurate only within 1½ hours. Consult local tide tables for precise times and heights.

Example: The conversion of the times and heights of the tides at Boston to those of New Haven, Connecticut, is given below:

Sample tide calculation July 1, 1993:

High tide Boston (p. 72)	8:45 A.M., EST
Correction for New Haven	−0:11 hrs.
High tide New Haven	8:34 A.M., EST

Tide height Boston (p. 73)	9.4 ft.
Correction for New Haven	−3.2 ft.
Tide height New Haven	6.2 ft.

TIDAL GLOSSARY

Apogean tide: A monthly tide of decreased range that occurs when the Moon is farthest from the Earth (at apogee).

Diurnal: Applies to a location that normally experiences one high water and one low water during a tidal day of approximately 24 hours.

Mean Lower Low Water: The arithmetic mean of the lesser of a daily pair of low waters, observed over a specific 19-year cycle called the National Tidal Datum Epoch.

Neap tide: A tide of decreased range occurring twice a month when the Moon is in quadrature (during the First and Last Quarter Moons, when the Sun and Moon are at right angles to each other relative to the Earth).

Perigean tide: A monthly tide of increased range that occurs when the Moon is closest to the Earth (at perigee).

Semidiurnal: Having a period of half a tidal day. East Coast tides, for example, are semidiurnal, with two highs and two lows in approximately 24 hours.

Spring tide: Named not for the season of spring, but from the German *springen* (to leap up). This tide of increased range occurs at times of syzygy (q.v.) each month. A spring tide also brings a lower low water.

Syzygy: Occurs twice a month when the Sun and Moon are in conjunction (lined up on the same side of the Earth at the New Moon) and when they are in opposition (on opposite sides of the Earth at the Full Moon, though usually not so directly in line as to produce an eclipse). In either case, the gravitational effects of the Sun and Moon reinforce each other, and tidal range is increased.

Vanishing tide: A mixed tide of considerable inequality in the two highs or two lows, so that the "high low" may become indistinguishable from the "low high" or vice versa. The result is a vanishing tide, where no significant difference is apparent.

WEEDING IN THE DARK

Sounds crazy. But a recent test in Germany has shown that gardens cultivated on cloudy, moonless nights produce 78 percent fewer weeds!

BY JON VARA

Where do all those garden weeds come from? They come from seeds — seeds that, in most cases, are an integral part of the garden itself.

Microscopic scrutiny of a sample of fertile garden soil inevitably turns up a disheartening number of unwanted seeds — the product of generations of weeds that have grown, matured, died, and been incorporated into the soil. A single pigweed plant, for example, may produce several million seeds.

Moreover, buried weed seeds may remain viable for the better part of a century. During that time they lie dormant and await conditions that will allow them to germinate, grow to maturity, and produce seed of their own. Those conditions include relatively warm temperatures, adequate soil moisture, and — according to recent research by German botanists — exposure to light.

According to the German study — as reported in the journal *Naturwissenschaften* — the seeds of most common field

weeds contain chemical triggers called phyto-chromes, which induce germination only when stimulated by light. Very brief flashes of light — lasting only a few thousandths of a second — will cause germination, even if the briefly exposed seeds are immediately reburied (as is likely to be the case during plowing, harrowing, sowing, and other soil-disturbing activities).

That is not particularly startling news in itself. As every experienced gardener knows, tilling the soil before planting also promotes weed growth, and attacking the initial weed crop with a hoe, a few weeks later, lays the groundwork for a succes-sive crop of weeds.

What is intriguing about the German study is its suggestion of a novel approach to breaking the cycle of soil disturbance, light exposure, and weed growth. Rather than seeking to avoid disturb-ing the soil — as modern agribusiness does by replacing mechanical cultivation with chemical herbicide sprays or in some cases by no-till planting — the researchers tried eliminating the germination-inducing light. The results, they found, were "quite astonishing."

By performing all soil-disturbing operations af-ter dark, they discovered that weed germination

could be reduced by as much as 78 percent. Weeds typically covered only two percent of night-cultivated test strips, while adjacent strips cultivated during daylight hours were 80 percent covered with weeds.

For best results, the soil preparation before crops are planted should be performed near noon on a bright sunny day.

Apparently, even the odd twinkle of starlight can be enough to activate some seeds; the re-searchers found that weed suppression was most pro-nounced when cultivation took place on cloudy, moonless nights. Light from artificial sources — such as headlight beams — was also enough to stimu-late weed-seed germina-tion. To prevent such un-wanted exposure, tractor drivers participating in the study used sophisticated infrared night-vision equipment to maneuver across the fields in near-to-tal darkness.

Few home gardeners will want to go to such extremes. Still, significant reductions in weed growth may be obtained by

performing soil-disturbing operations on moonlit nights or at dawn or dusk.

For best results, the German researchers say, the soil preparation be-fore crops are planted — plowing, harrowing, or other tillage — should be performed near noon on a bright sunny day. That will help to draw down the so-called "seed bank" by stimulating a large initial flush of weeds. Four weeks later, the immature weeds may be destroyed by a night-time cultivation, followed by nighttime seeding of crops.

A Word of Caution:

The authors of the study suggest that it may be prudent to practice night cultivation only in alter-nate years. Although the vast majority of the mil-lions of weed seeds slum-bering in the soil will re-quire the stimulus of light to germinate, a few light-independent renegades are inevitably present. If these dark germinators are allowed to mature and produce seed of their own, the resulting progeny are likely to in-herit the trait as well. After a few generations of such unintentional — and unwanted — selective pressure, the seed bank could become permeated with light-independent weed seeds, robbing nighttime cultivation of its effectiveness. □ □

OUTDOOR PLANTING TABLE, 1993

The best time to plant flowers and vegetables that bear crops above the ground is during the LIGHT of the Moon; that is, between the day the Moon is new to the day it is full. Flowering bulbs and vegetables that bear crops below ground should be planted during the DARK of the Moon; that is, from the day after it is full to the day before it is new again.

These Moon days for 1993 are given in the "Moon Favorable" columns below. See pages 56-82 for the exact times and days of the new and full Moons.

The three columns below give planting dates for the Weather Regions listed. (See Map p. 129.) Consult page 202 for dates of killing frosts and length of growing season. Weather Regions 5 and the southern half of 16 are practically frost free.

Above-Ground Crops Marked(*)	Weather Regions 1, 6, 9, 10, North 13		Weather Regions 2, 3, 7, 11, South 13, 15		Weather Regions 4, 8, 12, 14, 16	
E means Early L means Late	Planting Dates	Moon Favorable	Planting Dates	Moon Favorable	Planting Dates	Moon Favorable
*Barley	5/15-6/21	5/21-6/4, 6/19-21	3/15-4/7	3/23-4/6	2/15-3/7	2/21-3/7
*Beans (E)	5/7-6/21	5/21-6/4, 6/19-21	4/15-30	4/21-30	3/15-4/7	3/23-4/6
(L)	6/15-7/15	6/19-7/3	7/1-21	7/1-3, 19-21	8/7-31	8/17-31
Beets (E)	5/1-15	5/6-15	3/15-4/3	3/15-22	2/7-28	2/7-20
(L)	7/15-8/15	7/15-18, 8/3-15	8/15-31	8/15-16	9/1-30	9/1-14
*Broccoli (E)	5/15-31	5/21-31	3/7-31	3/7-8, 23-31	2/15-3/15	2/21-3/8
Plants (L)	6/15-7/7	6/19-7/3	8/1-20	8/1-2, 17-20	9/7-30	9/15-30
*Brussels Sprouts	5/15-31	5/21-31	3/7-4/15	3/7-8, 3/23-4/6	2/11-3/20	2/21-3/8
*Cabbage Plants	5/15-31	5/21-31	3/7-4/15	3/7-8, 3/23-4/6	2/11-3/20	2/21-3/8
Carrots (E)	5/15-31	5/15-20	3/7-31	3/9-22	2/15-3/7	2/15-20
(L)	6/15-7/21	6/15-18, 7/4-18	7/7-31	7/7-18	8/1-9/7	8/3-16, 9/1-7
*Cauliflower (E)	5/15-31	5/21-31	3/15-4/7	3/23-4/6	2/15-3/7	2/21-3/7
Plants (L)	6/15-7/21	6/19-7/3, 7/19-21	7/1-8/7	7/1-3, 7/19-8/2	8/7-31	8/17-31
*Celery Plants (E)	5/15-6/30	5/21-6/4, 6/19-30	3/7-31	3/7-8, 23-31	2/15-28	2/21-28
(L)	7/15-8/15	7/19-8/2	8/15-9/7	8/17-31	9/15-30	9/15-30
*Corn, Sweet (E)	5/10-6/15	5/21-6/4	4/1-15	4/1-6	3/15-31	3/23-31
(L)	6/15-30	6/19-30	7/7-21	7/19-21	8/7-31	8/17-31
*Cucumber	5/7-6/20	5/21-6/4, 6/19-20	4/7-5/15	4/21-5/5	3/7-4/15	3/7-8, 3/23-4/6
*Eggplant Plants	6/1-30	6/1-4, 19-30	4/7-5/15	4/21-5/5	3/7-4/15	3/7-8, 3/23-4/6
*Endive (E)	5/15-31	5/21-31	4/7-5/15	4/21-5/5	2/15-3/20	2/21-3/8
(L)	6/7-30	6/19-30	7/15-8/15	7/19-8/2	8/15-9/7	8/17-31
*Flowers (All)	5/7-6/21	5/21-6/4, 6/19-21	4/15-30	4/21-30	3/15-4/7	3/23-4/6
*Kale (E)	5/15-31	5/21-31	3/7-4/7	3/7-8, 3/23-4/6	2/11-3/20	2/21-3/8
(L)	7/1-8/7	7/1-3, 7/19-8/2	8/15-31	8/17-31	9/7-30	9/15-30
Leek Plants	5/15-31	5/15-20	3/7-4/7	3/9-22, 4/7	2/15-4/15	2/15-20, 3/9-22, 4/7-15
*Lettuce	5/15-6/30	5/21-6/4, 6/19-30	3/1-31	3/1-8, 23-31	2/15-3/7	2/21-3/7
*Muskmelon	5/15-6/30	5/21-6/4, 6/19-30	4/15-5/7	4/21-5/5	3/15-4/7	3/23-4/6
Onion Sets	5/15-6/7	5/15-20, 6/5-7	3/1-31	3/9-22	2/1-28	2/7-20
*Parsley	5/15-31	5/21-31	3/1-31	3/1-8, 23-31	2/20-3/15	2/21-3/8
Parsnips	4/1-30	4/7-20	3/7-31	3/9-22	1/15-2/4	1/15-21
*Peas (E)	4/15-5/7	4/21-5/5	3/7-31	3/7-8, 23-31	1/15-2/7	1/22-2/6
(L)	7/15-31	7/19-31	8/7-31	8/17-31	9/15-30	9/15-30
*Pepper Plants	5/15-6/30	5/21-6/4, 6/19-30	4/1-30	4/1-6, 21-30	3/1-20	3/1-8
Potato	5/1-31	5/6-20	4/1-30	4/7-20	2/10-28	2/10-20
*Pumpkin	5/15-31	5/21-31	4/23-5/15	4/23-5/5	3/7-20	3/7-8
Radish (E)	4/15-30	4/15-20	3/7-31	3/9-22	1/21-3/1	1/21, 2/7-20
(L)	8/15-31	8/15-16	9/7-30	9/7-14	10/1-21	10/1-14
*Spinach (E)	5/15-31	5/21-31	3/15-4/20	3/23-4/6	2/7-3/15	2/21-3/8
(L)	7/15-9/7	7/19-8/2, 8/17-31	8/1-9/15	8/1-2, 17-31, 9/15	10/1-21	10/15-21
*Squash	5/15-6/15	5/21-6/4	4/15-30	4/21-30	3/15-4/15	3/23-4/6
*Swiss Chard	5/1-31	5/1-5, 21-31	3/15-4/15	3/23-4/6	2/7-3/15	2/21-3/8
*Tomato Plants	5/15-31	5/21-31	4/7-30	4/21-30	3/7-20	3/7-8
Turnips (E)	4/7-30	4/7-20	3/15-31	3/15-22	1/20-2/15	1/20-21, 2/7-15
(L)	7/1-8/15	7/4-18, 8/3-15	8/1-20	8/3-16	9/1-10/15	9/1-14, 10/1-14
*Wheat, Winter	8/11-9/15	8/17-31, 9/15	9/15-10/20	9/15-30, 10/15-20	10/15-12/7	10/15-30, 11/13-29
Spring	4/7-30	4/21-30	3/1-20	3/1-8	2/15-28	2/21-28

GARDENING BY THE MOON'S SIGN

Astrology is not the same science as astronomy. The actual sign placements of planets differ drastically between these two bodies of knowledge. For a fuller explanation of this phenomenon, see "Secrets of the Zodiac," page 192.

The *astrological* placement of the Moon, by sign, is given in the chart below. Gardeners who prefer to use this method should follow the chart.

For planting, the most fertile signs are the three water signs: Cancer, Scorpio, and Pisces. The astrological signs of Taurus, Virgo, and Capricorn would be good second choices for sowing. It should be noted that above-ground crops like to be planted between the new Moon and full Moon (waxing), whereas the root and below-ground crops prefer to be sown after the full Moon and before the new Moon (waning). The dates for the Moon's phases can be found on pages 56-82; the Outdoor Planting Table on the opposite page can also be used as a guide.

Weeding and plowing are best done when the Moon occupies the signs of Aries, Gemini, Leo, Sagittarius, or Aquarius. Insect pests can also be handled at those times. Transplanting and grafting are most successful when done under a Cancer, Scorpio, or Pisces Moon. Clean out the garden shed when the Moon occupies Virgo and the work will flow along extremely smoothly. Fences or permanent beds could be nicely built or mended when Capricorn predominates. Avoid indecision when under the Libra Moon.

MOON'S PLACE IN THE ASTROLOGICAL ZODIAC

	Nov. 92	Dec. 92	Jan. 93	Feb. 93	Mar. 93	Apr. 93	May 93	June 93	July 93	Aug. 93	Sept. 93	Oct. 93	Nov. 93	Dec. 93
1	AQU	PSC	ARI	GEM	GEM	CAN	VIR	SCO	SAG	CAP	PSC	ARI	GEM	CAN
2	AQU	PSC	ARI	GEM	GEM	LEO	VIR	SCO	SAG	AQU	PSC	ARI	GEM	CAN
3	AQU	PSC	TAU	GEM	CAN	LEO	LIB	SAG	CAP	AQU	ARI	TAU	GEM	LEO
4	PSC	ARI	TAU	CAN	CAN	VIR	LIB	SAG	CAP	PSC	ARI	TAU	CAN	LEO
5	PSC	ARI	GEM	CAN	LEO	VIR	SCO	SAG	AQU	PSC	TAU	GEM	CAN	VIR
6	ARI	TAU	GEM	LEO	LEO	LIB	SCO	CAP	AQU	ARI	TAU	GEM	LEO	VIR
7	ARI	TAU	CAN	LEO	VIR	LIB	SAG	CAP	AQU	ARI	TAU	CAN	LEO	VIR
8	ARI	TAU	CAN	VIR	VIR	SCO	SAG	AQU	PSC	ARI	GEM	CAN	VIR	LIB
9	TAU	GEM	LEO	VIR	LIB	SCO	CAP	AQU	PSC	TAU	GEM	CAN	VIR	LIB
10	TAU	GEM	LEO	LIB	LIB	SAG	CAP	PSC	ARI	TAU	CAN	LEO	LIB	SCO
11	GEM	CAN	VIR	LIB	SCO	SAG	CAP	PSC	ARI	GEM	CAN	LEO	LIB	SCO
12	GEM	CAN	VIR	SCO	SCO	CAP	AQU	PSC	ARI	GEM	LEO	VIR	SCO	SAG
13	CAN	LEO	LIB	SCO	SAG	CAP	AQU	ARI	TAU	GEM	LEO	VIR	SCO	SAG
14	CAN	LEO	LIB	SAG	SAG	AQU	PSC	ARI	TAU	CAN	VIR	LIB	SAG	CAP
15	CAN	VIR	SCO	SAG	CAP	AQU	PSC	TAU	GEM	CAN	VIR	LIB	SAG	CAP
16	LEO	VIR	SCO	CAP	CAP	AQU	PSC	TAU	GEM	LEO	LIB	SCO	CAP	AQU
17	LEO	LIB	SCO	CAP	CAP	PSC	ARI	TAU	CAN	LEO	LIB	SCO	CAP	AQU
18	VIR	LIB	SAG	CAP	AQU	PSC	ARI	GEM	CAN	VIR	SCO	SAG	CAP	PSC
19	VIR	SCO	SAG	AQU	AQU	ARI	TAU	GEM	CAN	VIR	SCO	SAG	AQU	PSC
20	LIB	SCO	CAP	AQU	PSC	ARI	TAU	CAN	LEO	LIB	SAG	CAP	AQU	PSC
21	LIB	SAG	CAP	PSC	PSC	ARI	GEM	CAN	LEO	LIB	SAG	CAP	PSC	ARI
22	SCO	SAG	AQU	PSC	PSC	TAU	GEM	LEO	VIR	SCO	SAG	AQU	PSC	ARI
23	SCO	SAG	AQU	PSC	ARI	TAU	GEM	LEO	VIR	SCO	CAP	AQU	PSC	TAU
24	SAG	CAP	AQU	ARI	ARI	GEM	CAN	VIR	LIB	SAG	CAP	AQU	ARI	TAU
25	SAG	CAP	PSC	ARI	TAU	GEM	CAN	VIR	LIB	SAG	AQU	PSC	ARI	TAU
26	CAP	AQU	PSC	TAU	TAU	GEM	LEO	LIB	SCO	CAP	AQU	PSC	TAU	GEM
27	CAP	AOU	ARI	TAU	TAU	CAN	LEO	LIB	SCO	CAP	PSC	ARI	TAU	GEM
28	CAP	AQU	ARI	TAU	GEM	CAN	VIR	LIB	SAG	CAP	PSC	ARI	TAU	CAN
29	AQU	PSC	ARI	—	GEM	LEO	VIR	SCO	SAG	AQU	PSC	ARI	GEM	CAN
30	AQU	PSC	TAU	—	CAN	LEO	LIB	SCO	CAP	AQU	ARI	TAU	GEM	CAN
31	—	ARI	TAU	—	CAN	—	LIB	—	CAP	PSC	—	TAU	—	LEO

WINTERING OVER

From a northern gardener, here are a few hard-won lessons on transplanting, drainage, and mulching for the cold-weather months.

☐ WE GARDENERS WHO LIVE IN THE northern parts of North America, especially those areas designated on USDA plant-hardiness maps as Zones 5 or 4, must exercise considerable ingenuity to bring marginally hardy plants safely through the winter. We tend to envy people who live on the West Coast or in England, but that envy is accompanied by the smug certainty that we deserve more credit for achieving beautiful gardens than they do. Who couldn't have a nice garden in Washington State, Victoria, or Kent? This consciousness of our own valor and worth is a comfort to us as we trudge about, devising schemes for minimizing the damage our winter weather can cause.

And it's not simply the cold weather — that's comparatively easy to prepare for. I know a woman who raises very fine heaths and heathers in Old Forge in the Adirondacks, the coldest spot in New York State, because Old Forge gets and keeps lots of snow. Here in Zone 5 by Lake Cayuga in western New York State, we can expect very cold weather to alternate fast and frequently with warmish weather that will melt the snow we've been blessed with, leaving our poor plants bare and unprepared for the next cold period. We do what we can to help them out.

HOW TO PROTECT THE LITTLE ONES

The first thing northern gardeners learn is not to set out any small plants, even very hardy ones, or to divide large plants late in the year. I used to think it was safe to do this until the first of October, but now I've moved the date to late August or the first ten days in September. Set out even that early in autumn, very small

by **Elisabeth Sheldon**
– illustrated by Sara Mintz Zwicker

plants are at risk and may be hurled out of the ground by alternate freezing and thawing. In February I've found little things I had set out at the end of August sitting on top of frozen 3" hummocks, their twisted half-dead roots dangling in the wind — a heartbreaking spectacle.

You can lessen the risk of this happening by covering the small plants with cloches in November. As cloches I use heavy glass meter covers discarded by the local gas and electric company, but you can use large jars or sawed-off gallon jugs almost as well. If the cloche doesn't succeed in keeping its small tenant from being heaved out of the ground, it will at least keep it out of the wind and remind the gardener to inspect it on his rounds. He (or, it goes without saying, she) can lift the cloche and either press the plant back into the mud or sift extra soil over its roots until the earth thaws enough to make it possible to do so. I've got so I keep a large container of loose soil in the garage all winter for this purpose.

Large perennials that have been separated in late summer will have had time before winter comes to put out strong new roots that can get a grip on the soil before the heaving-up and settling-down routine begins. Even so, they'll probably need to be firmed back into the ground in the spring. Larger hardy plants, undivided, can be lifted and deposited whole in large deep holes as late as October. I wouldn't dream, however, of moving shallow-rooted or tender plants such as astilbes, shasta daisies, nepetas, helianthemums, santolinas, lavenders, some of the cranesbills, or anemones any later than August. As for tall bearded and dwarf iris, never after July. No matter how early they have been moved, you're apt to find them on top of the ground after a particularly capricious winter. Not having any hairy roots seems to be a great disadvantage when it comes to hanging in there.

NO FOOD OR PRUNING BEFORE WINTER

No doubt everyone knows that it is unwise to administer chemical fertilizers late in the year, since plants should not be stimulated into putting out tender new growth just before their time of trial. But do you know that tender evergreen herbs and perennials should not have radical pruning in fall for the same reason? Heavy pruning in mild fall weather often causes these plants to put out new leaves, making them more vulnerable to the cold. One can — tidy gardeners feel they should — cut back the season's dead or dwindling growth from herbaceous perennials, but thymes, lavenders, santolinas, dwarf box — those evergreen or ever-gray subjects—should be left alone until spring. That goes for tender deciduous shrubs such as caryopteris (sometimes called blue mist) as well.

BEWARE OF WET FEET AND RICH LIVING

Another thing we gardeners learn is that drainage and appropriate soil have as much to do with winter survival as temperature. I discovered this for myself when, after growing lavender plants in the amended clay soil of my perennial border for many years, I planted one or two on top of a raised wall built around a dead elm stump. The ones in the border often died or lost branches during the winter, even though snugly covered with pine boughs. On the high wall the pine boughs usually blew off during winter storms, but the lavenders didn't appear to notice it; they throve, seeding themselves into all the interstices of the wall and even into the wood of the old stump. Ha! said I, swift drainage is the answer. I was more than half right. It's true that resinous plants such as lavender and thyme can, like pine trees, resist

Not having any hairy roots seems to be a great disadvantage when it comes to hanging in there.

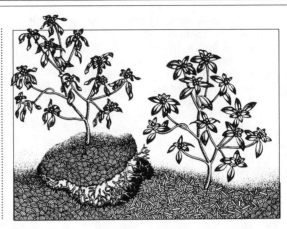

cold well if they aren't sitting in soggy ground, but the fact that the lavender on the wall was planted in light, gritty, limey soil rather than the richer, heavier border mixture was the rest of the explanation for its valiant winter performance.

The shrubby herbs from Mediterranean hills are used to living on a meager diet as they cling to their rocky ground, battered by all the winds. Rich soil not only keeps them and other shrubby herbs from producing as much volatile oil as they should, but also makes them more susceptible to winter damage. When they are protected and overfed, they become lush, less fragrant, and less cold resistant — weak from high living, like the ancient Romans. Thyme and winter savory on that same wall flourished as well as the lavender did, and neither of them is any more dependable than lavender on level ground in the border.

So it behooves us to find out where our plants come from and what their preferences are as to soil content, moisture, light, shade, and exposure, then come as close to duplicating these conditions as we can. Naturally, if a plant is in good health, it can better endure a trying season. Often we think that the cold weather killed an individual that actually died from a combination of cold and too much water on its roots.

Or it was a plant that needed lots of water it had been denied and so couldn't help dehydrating in the winter sun (this is often the case with evergreens). Or it was in weakened condition from not having had enough sunlight during the summer. Or too much. We should combine gardening with reading. Dedicated gardeners end up with quite a large library, as a rule. They will have several books on herbs, on shrubs and trees, and many on perennials.

MULCH ADO

In gardening books one often comes on the instruction, "Mulch for winter protection." But there are two kinds of mulch — which one do they mean? Mulch can be fine or chopped organic material (buckwheat hulls, sawdust, shredded bark, leaves, etc.) that is placed around a plant; or large stuff (such as salt hay or evergreen boughs) that is laid over it to cut the wind and trap snow. One is told to apply the latter after the ground freezes when it will tend to keep it frozen. Shallow-rooted plants will benefit from the first kind of mulch; and other, deep-rooted but tender plants, from the second. In the woodland garden I depend on the fallen leaves to protect most of the plants, figuring that's what they like, but from the

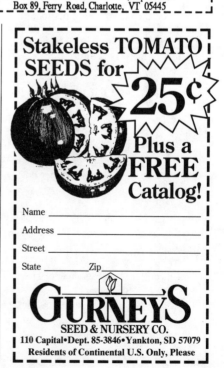

perennial border I remove the fallen (maple) leaves, which tend to pack and rot the crowns of the plants. I put old silage (obtained from a neighboring dairy farm) around astilbes, cardinal flowers, phlox, and delphiniums.

After Christmas my husband kindly stuffs our old Volvo station wagon and covers the top of it with discarded Christmas trees that he picks up along the streets in town and brings home to me. I lop off the branches and lay them, as thick as I can, over lavenders, helianthemums, flax, fancy thymes and silver horehound, Japanese anemones, santolinas, the tender cranesbills, the heaths and heathers, and any other doubtfully hardy plants I happen to be growing. I also pile them up around roses and caryopteris whose lower parts I have already covered with heaps of silage or soil swiped from the vegetable garden.

The one drawback to the evergreen bough mulch is that one can't easily check on the condition of plants under the branches. I have lifted them off in the spring to find that mice have established whole villages under my heathers, chopping up the roots and branches for bedding, making roads and tunnels, leaving me only a few miserable shreds to try to nurse back to health. I used to put orchard bait in mason jars under the pine boughs to prevent this, but now we have a cat, unfortunately a cat for whom hunting is a hobby rather than a profession. Occasionally he catches a mouse or a mole but not often enough to keep us vermin-free. Since I can't have him eating a poisoned mouse, I am caught between two stools . . .

Another problem with evergreen boughs is that they must be removed in spring when the weather turns hot or the plants huddled under them will turn to mush. Since, as I have said, our weather changes a lot, you have to leave them stacked up close by where you can grab and redistribute them when the radio tells you that the thermometer is going down to 15° F in a few hours. This sort of thing keeps us on our toes — it's a character-building exercise that gardeners in England and on the West Coast miss out on. □ □

ORIGINS OF OLD-TIME (PRE-METRIC) MEASURING UNITS

FOOT
The length of Charlemagne's foot, modified in 1305 to be 36 barleycorns laid end to end.

INCH
The width across the knuckle on King Edgar's thumb or, obviously, three barleycorns.

YARD
The reach from King Henry I's nose to his royal fingertips, a distance also twice as long as a cubit.

CUBIT
The length of the arm from elbow to fingertip.

MILE
1,000 double steps of a Roman legionary. Later, Queen Bess added more feet so the mile would equal eight furlongs.

FURLONG
The length of a furrow a team of oxen could plow before resting.

ACRE
The amount of land a yoke of oxen could plow in one day.

FATHOM
The span of a seaman's outstretched arms; 880 fathoms make a mile.

The metric system, on the other hand, uses the meter, defined precisely as 1,650,763.73 wavelengths of orange-red light emitted by the krypton-86 atom, or originally one-ten-millionth the length of the longitude from the North Pole to the equator. The meter is exactly 39.37 inches — or, that is, some 118 barleycorns.

– *Courtesy of the National Geographic News Service*

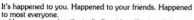

Rustic Garden Bench
BY JAMIE TROWBRIDGE

We assigned this specific task to an Almanac editor who'd never before built anything in his life. Thanks to the following directions, it came out beautifully!

"I n all mankind there is a certain longing for nature, a desire to be free from the bondage of the artificial and to come back to the real natural beauty found only in nature itself." So began the catalog of the Rustic Hickory Furniture Company in 1904, when Americans, in reaction to the Industrial Revolution and Victorianism, were getting back to basics. Successful city dwellers fled to wilderness retreats: lodges in the West, "camps" in the Adirondacks, summer resorts in northern New England, and rural cottages everywhere provided the harried urbanites a rustic respite.

Rustic furniture — furniture crafted out of unfinished logs, sticks, and twigs — had been made since the days of the caveman. But it was in this period that it gained wide popularity in the United States. Craftsmen of the time proved that such pieces need not be crude or uncomfortable. To the contrary, the comfort and quiet charm of the rustic furniture Americans found at summer resorts created a vast market for the affordable furniture. Soon no porch or backyard garden was complete without a piece.

Rustic furniture is back in style today for much the same reasons as at the turn of the century. It can be expensive and hard to find, but don't let that get in your way. You can make it very simply yourself.

You don't need much in the way of tools or woodworking skills. You don't even need an indoor workspace; you can use hand tools and work on your lawn. Materials couldn't be cheaper, assuming you have access to some trees. As furniture making goes, rustic furniture is entry level.

This plan for a rustic garden bench is a simple project for the be-

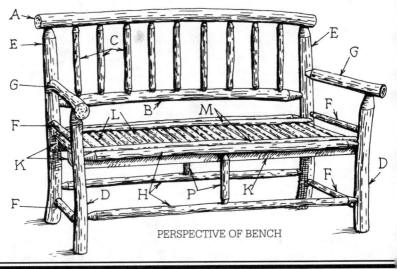

PERSPECTIVE OF BENCH

ginner. You can graduate later to more complex designs and construction procedures, such as the use of bent saplings and joints pegged with dowels. The very best thing about making rustic furniture is that your design options are unlimited. Bunk beds for your kids. A gazebo for the back lawn. A wood box for the fireside. A swing for your porch. Using your imagination and a little common sense, you can make any piece of furniture, for indoors or out, out of logs.

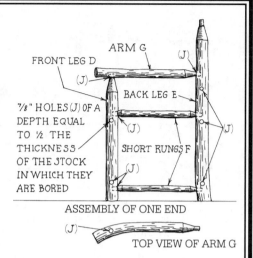

ASSEMBLY OF ONE END

TOP VIEW OF ARM G

The first step in making the rustic bench here illustrated is to review thoroughly the directions, materials list, and drawings. The next step is to head for the woods. The best lumber for rustic furniture is neither too hard nor too soft: hickory, yellow birch, cedar, willow, and sassafras are all popular choices. Stay away from pine and white birch; they rot easily. There's nothing wrong with hardwoods. They're just more difficult to work with.

Leaving the bark on or peeling it off is strictly a matter of personal taste. Fall and winter is the best time to cut your lumber if you wish to keep the bark on the logs, since the sap does not run in these seasons. (Conversely, spring and summer is the best time to cut your lumber if you want to peel the bark from the logs.) Before you wield your saw, consider how you will use a tree in your project. Look for trees with the correct contours and widths, as outlined in the lumber table below. (Note the curve in the top and bottom rail of the back and the flair in the arms and all four legs.) Knots and limbs aren't necessarily a problem; you can file them smooth. Cut your pieces a little longer than their required length to allow for shrinkage when drying.

Season the wood until it is dry. Allow about three months if you cut in the fall or winter and about six months if you cut in the spring or summer. Dry the wood slowly or it will crack or "check." Different woods dry at different rates at different times of the year. Your logs are dry if they make a ringing sound when you bang two of them together. A "thud" means they are still wet. The weight of a log is another indicator: Wet logs are heavier than dry ones.

When the timber is dry, cut it to the proper lengths as outlined in the lumber table. Do not cut any of the seat pieces until you are ready to assemble the seat. The next step is to prepare the mortise-and-tenon joints. The diagram (above) illustrates how the pieces fit together; joints are indicated with a "J." To create the tenons, taper the ends of the logs to a ⅞" diameter. You can use an ax or hatchet to accomplish this. Or put the piece in a vise and shape it with a drawknife. A chisel is handy for finishing touches. Do not make the tenon too small; it

The very best thing about making rustic furniture is that your design options are unlimited. Using your imagination and a little common sense, you can make any piece of furniture, for indoors or out, out of logs.

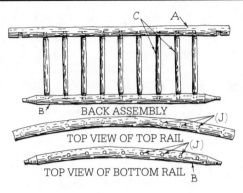

C   A

BACK ASSEMBLY

(J)

TOP VIEW OF TOP RAIL

(J)

TOP VIEW OF BOTTOM RAIL   B

B

should fit snugly in a ⅞" round mortise. Drill the ⅞" mortises to a depth half the thickness of the log.

Now you're ready to put your bench together.

Start with the back assembly (note diagram). Drill the mortises for the spindles (**C**) in the top (**A**) and bottom (**B**) rails. (Space the spindles evenly, starting in the center and working out.) Check to see that the joints all fit. With waterproof glue, fasten the joints and assemble the section loosely. Then lay it on the floor and align it so that all four ends touch the floor. Drive the parts together with a hammer until all the joints are tight, using a block of wood to protect your logs. Now drill a ³⁄₃₂" hole through the wood and into the end of each tenon. Hammer a 6-penny coated ribbed nail into these holes to complete the joint. It is important that you predrill all nail holes to avoid splitting the logs. Set the nail heads below the surface of the wood or bark.

Assemble the two end units according to the diagram on the previous page, using the same method of joinery. Drill mortises for the short rungs

Rustic Garden Bench Lumber Table

Piece	Letter	Quantity	Length	Width	Notes
BACK					
top rail	A	1	43"	1¾" to 2"	note curve
bottom rail	B	1	39"	1¾" to 2"	note curve
spindles	C	9	13"	1" to 1¼"	
ENDS					
front leg	D	2	24"	2½" to 3"	note flair
back leg	E	2	34"	2½" to 3"	note flair
rungs	F	4	17"	1½"+	
arms	G	2	22"	2"+	note flair
SEAT & BRACING *(Lengths are approximate. Do not cut to final length until back and end units are assembled.)*					
long rungs	H	4	44"	1½" to 1¾"	
seat support	K	2	44"	1" x 2½" finished lumber	
seat pieces	L	48	17"	¾" to 1"	
seat trim	M	2	44"	1½" to 1¾"	
rung supports	P	2	11"	1½"	

Hardware Required:

☞ 1 pound each of 4-, 6-, 8-, and 10-penny coated ribbed nails
☞ 4 bolts: 3" x ¼"
☞ Waterproof glue, preferably labeled "environmentally safe"

(**F**) in the front and back legs 3" and 16½" from the bottom of the legs. Stop to check the alignment of each unit before you drive all the pieces together and nail. Use your judgment to determine the proper nail size for each joint.

Once the back and two end units are assembled, it's time to fit those pieces together. Drill the mortises in the top rail (**A**) for the tenons of the back legs (**E**) directly in line with the tenons for the bottom rail (**B**). Hang the back in place on the end units (see diagram on page 219). This will show you where on the end units to drill the mortises for the bottom rail (**B**) of the back. Lay the end units down to bore the mortises. Also bore mortises in the front and back legs (**D** and **E**) for the long rungs (**H**) that will connect the two end units. Drill these 4" and 15" up from the bottom of each leg.

Fit together the back and end units, but do not glue. Set the front legs the same distance apart as the back legs so that the bench seat is rectangular. Now you can measure the length required for the long rungs (**H**) and cut them accordingly. Fit the rung supports (**P**) between the rungs (**H**) in the center of the bench before you connect the rungs to the end assemblies. Glue all the joints connecting the various components of the bench. Be sure that all four legs touch the floor evenly before driving the joints together once and for all. Predrill and nail each joint.

Now for the seat. Cut the two pieces of 1" x 2½" finished lumber (**K**) to the full width of the bench at seat height. Drill ¼" holes in the front and back legs (see diagram) and bolt on the pieces of finished lumber (**K**), the tops of which

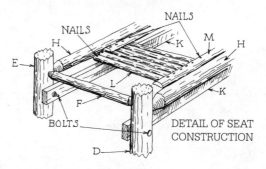

DETAIL OF SEAT CONSTRUCTION

should be about 14½" from the floor. Cut pieces of the seat (**L**) to fit, drill, and nail them to the finished lumber with 4-penny nails. (You can substitute finished lumber for the log seat pieces if you want.) Split a long piece of seat trim (**M**) in half and use it to cover the ends of the seat pieces. Predrill and nail it through to the seat supports with 8-penny nails.

If your bench is still a little shaky after you've finished assembling it, you can add some diagonal braces to strengthen it. Cut four saplings about the size of a broom handle. Predrill and nail two of the braces to the center back of the top rail (**A**) of the back assembly and to the bottoms of the rear legs (**E**). Nail the other two braces to the ends of the top rail (**A**) of the back assembly and to the bottoms of the front legs (**D**).

It's common to leave rustic furniture unfinished, allowing the wood to season with time. However, an application of linseed oil, tung oil, or wood preservative will extend the life of your piece, especially if you're planning to leave it outside. □ □

The plan for this garden bench was adapted from one published in HOW TO BUILD RUSTIC FURNITURE by Ed Smith. The 64-page book includes old plans for everything from gazebos to bookends. Send $7.95 plus $1 postage and handling to Smith Brook Press, R.R. 1 Box 217D, Diamond Point, NY 12824.

My Father's Gardens

A Special Country Memory

Five days a week my father wore a suit and wingtips and commuted 20 miles to his office in Bangor, Maine. Two days a week he wore baggy shorts and a disreputable pair of moccasins and commuted the few steps to his gardens. After he retired and could afford the luxury of being a full-time "character," he would supplement this weekend wardrobe with knee pads and T-shirts emblazoned with rock-band logos or liberal slogans. This regalia, when worn to the local grocery store or post office, did much to convince the natives that they were justified in never completely accepting him, despite 30-odd years of residence in their midst — a result that was as amusing to him as it was satisfying to them. I don't mean to imply by this that he was disliked or, worse, avoided by his neighbors. They just thought him odd. Had they had occasion to examine his flower beds closely, they would have found nothing to allay their suspicions.

From the street, only one garden could be seen in detail, and it was wholly conventional. In the spring it sprouted crocuses and snowdrops,

by
James A. B.
Patterson

– illustrated by Carolyn Croll

bluets, daffodils, and grape hyacinths. A blanket of tulips gave way to Siberian iris that, in season, were followed by masses of daylilies and true lilies. These were my father's pride and joy. Several times a year he would cross the Penobscot to Monroe and visit with his old friend, Phillip White, an octogenarian with a high-pitched cackle, an encyclopedic knowledge of all things floral, and a small greenhouse from which he sold lilies and lesser creations. He wore knee pads, too, and claimed to have three thousand distinct daylily hybrids in his garden. My father claimed as many as he could fit into his much smaller plot, and as a result, July and August provided a forest of bladelike leaves and trumpet-shaped blooms ranging in color from palest yellow to deepest magenta.

Despite this profusion, few found their way into vases for my mother to admire. She felt they were too gaudy, or too foreign, and preferred gladioli. In late summer there was always a huge arrangement of glads in the house, and Mother would mark the passing days by pulling off the wilted blooms from the bottom of the stalks. The shortened stems would be moved to successively smaller vases until only the topmost blooms were left to float in a shallow cut-glass bowl. Then this curious calendar would be repeated with a new bouquet.

He was never comfortable in discussions of sex or other quite normal bodily functions [so] he constructed a parable in plants . . .

The gardens at the back of the house offered a much wider scope for Dad's constant diggings and odd bent. His favorite was the sex education garden. Having been reared in an age that still gave more than a passing nod to the sensibilities of Queen Victoria, he was never comfortable in discussions of sex or other quite normal bodily functions. However, being blessed with three daughters and two sons (and a wife who shared his reticence), such conversation couldn't be entirely avoided. For the purpose of passing on such wisdom as he felt necessary, he constructed a parable in plants. In the garden he laid down two paths. The first meandered aimlessly and was bordered by heavy-scented, almost decadent blooms. At the end was bleeding heart. The second, straight and narrow and hemmed in by primroses, led to a jack-in-the-pulpit. The message, not lost on his children, was that if we needed more information, we had best visit the local library.

This was not the only garden to feature walkways. Another began as a straightforward grid pattern framing mixed annuals and perennials, but evolved over the years as mood and whimsy dictated. He would work for days moving slabs of slate into spirals, checkerboards, or free-form swirls, planting and transplanting until he had the desired effect. At the height of the war in Vietnam he constructed a peace sign and occasionally resorted to short-lettered messages such as ERA NOW or GARDEN. Unfortunately these products of his wry humor could be viewed properly only from an upstairs porch accessible via a window. It didn't seem to matter — he knew they were there. Recently, while going through some of Dad's papers, I came across a file marked, simply, "gardens." It contained plans on graph paper for most of his gardens, drawn to scale and with each plant meticulously labeled. These, the product of winter weekends, allowed him to get dirt under his fingernails, at least figuratively, all 12 months of the year. He carried this passion for order outside as well, and most plantings sported small wire tags inserted in the soil should any casual observer need to know the Latin nomenclature of the blooms. Few did, but he carried on. These markers provided a certain challenge for autumn raking, and on more than one occasion whole congregations of perennials were unnamed in a single swipe.

A previous owner of the house had planted a fence of bamboo to lend privacy to the backyard. The removal of this obnoxious stand became Dad's first and, as it turned out, longest gardening project. He cut it down — it grew back thicker than before. He pulled it up by its roots — it snickered greenly and shot up on the lawn. It became a personal matter with him. He wanted to grow asparagus and alium, Chinese lanterns and top onions, and other exotic or interesting things. The garden wanted to grow bamboo. After one particularly contentious session with his machete, he emerged from the jungle with a bamboo splinter in his eye. Forced to wear an eye patch for several weeks, he found himself at a dinner with the president of the Hathaway shirt company. The gentleman was much amused to see Dad sporting the firm's unofficial logo, and the next week he received two shirts in the mail — presumably a modeling fee. This was not enough to reconcile him to the foreign invasion. Finally, after 30 years of constant battle — including the judicious use of gasoline on the remaining roots — new plantings finally seemed to edge out the interloper.

One of the beneficiaries of this apparent victory was his crop of honesty, or money plant, the first seeds of which had come to him through the good offices of Phillip White. "The Crop," as it was always referred to in our family, was remarkably ugly in the garden and revealed its true worth only after harvest. In ritual autumn sessions we would strip the withered, podlike coverings from the branchlets of the dried stalks, revealing coin-shaped panels of translucent fiber that looked like miniature isinglass windows. The seeds were gathered up for resowing and the branches decorated the house until the next crop came in. Once, when visiting me at college in Cambridge, Dad saw a street vendor selling honesty sprays for two dollars each. For a while the family feared that avocation would become vocation, and it well might have had I not objected to dropping out in order to act as the distribution system.

Before disease arrived to claim the giant elms that lined the streets and cooled the summers of our town, there were five that ringed the property, so massive that their crowns cast dappled shadow over house and yard. One of them sheltered what was, for us, the truest harbinger of spring. When the small patch of trilliums first appeared each year, Dad would herd the entire family out to admire the blooms and ritually sniff the pungent scent of these "stinking benjamins." When the elms disappeared, so did they. Dad dug up the stumps of four of the elms and planted maples and birch. The fifth he made into what he called the wedding cake garden by creating terraces around and atop the stump, each level varying by color. It was a private memorial to a public disaster.

*M*y brother lives in the house now, and although he is not as avid a gardener as was Dad, he keeps the lawns mowed and the gardens presentable. Last week, however, I saw a bamboo stalk that was five feet high and noticed that the straight and narrow path is overgrown. This would be cause for concern unless one knew that Robby has a seven-year-old daughter who will have to be told certain things. Eventually the primroses will be thinned. I can almost hear the slates shifting. ☐☐

Shine On, Harvest Moon

The Harvest Moon is not just the full Moon that occurs at the time of harvest.

It is the full Moon that actually helps the harvest by providing more light at the right time than other full Moons do.

Here's the explanation . . .

(Warning: It's almost incomprehensible.)

BY FRED SCHAAF

Traditional sources usually define Harvest Moon as the full Moon nearest the autumnal equinox (the beginning of autumn). Less commonly, it is called the first full Moon after the autumnal equinox or simply the full Moon of either September or October. But astronomers would support the first definition, for the notable behavior of the Harvest Moon is dependent on its closeness to the autumnal equinox.

The usual behavior of the Moon is to rise distinctly later each night — an average of about 50 minutes later. This is because the Moon's orbital motion (combined with the larger orbit of the Earth around the Sun) carries it farther eastward among the constellations of the zodiac from night to night. At any one moonrise, the Moon occupies a particular place on the celestial sphere (the great dome of the heavens), but when the Earth turns toward that point 24 hours later, the Moon has moved off to the east about 12 degrees, and it takes an average of 50 minutes longer for the Earth to rotate toward the Moon and for the Moon thus to "rise." Think of it as a giant Slinky in which each loop, representing one lunar orbit of the Earth, advances the orbit a bit farther along the spiral path.

The shallower angle of the zodiac band around the time of the autumnal equinox allows the Moon to be already above the horizon (rising) on the second night only 30 minutes after sunset.

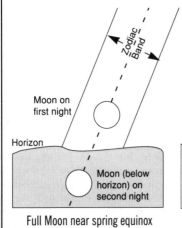

Full Moon near spring equinox

Full Moon near autumnal equinox (Harvest Moon)

But around the date of the Harvest Moon, the Moon rises at almost the same time for a number of nights in our intermediate northern latitudes. Why is the Harvest Moon different? Well, remember that the zodiac is the band of constellations through which the Moon travels from night to night. The section of the zodiac band in which the full Moon travels around the start of autumn is the section that forms the most shallow angle with the eastern horizon (see diagram). Because the Moon's orbit on successive nights is more nearly parallel to the horizon at that time, its relationship to the eastern horizon does not change appreciably, and the Earth does not have to turn as far to bring up the Moon. Thus, for several nights near the full Harvest Moon (September 11 in 1992; September 30 in 1993), the Moon may rise as little as 23 minutes later on successive nights (at about 42 degrees north latitude), and there is an abundance of bright moonlight early in the evening, a traditional aid to harvest crews. By the time the Moon has reached last quarter, however, the typical 50-minute delay has returned.

By contrast, the full Moon near the start of spring is in the section of the zodiac that has the steepest angle with respect to the eastern horizon, and the opposite applies. For several days bracketing the full Moon nearest the vernal equinox, the delay in moonrise is as much as 75 minutes (at 42 degrees north latitude).

Here is another way of expressing what happens with the Harvest Moon: It is in this part of the zodiac that the Moon's eastward (orbital) motion has its largest northward component. For observers in Earth's Northern Hemisphere, the farther north an object is in the heavens, the longer an arc it makes across the sky, and the longer a time it is visible above the horizon. Thus, to say that the Moon is getting rapidly farther north each night around the time of the Harvest Moon is to say that, for northern latitudes on Earth, it will keep rising distinctly earlier than would otherwise be expected — nearly the same time as the night before.

How nearly the same is "almost the same time" each night? This varies with latitude, for the farther north you are, the shallower the angle of the zodiac is with respect to your horizon. In most of the United States and southern Canada, the Harvest Moon rises 25 to 30 minutes later each night. The effect is less noticeable the farther south you go. But going north makes the Harvest Moon more extreme. According to astronomy author Guy Ottewell, the idea of the Harvest Moon originated in Europe (average latitude about 50 degrees north), where the Harvest Moon rises only ten to 20 minutes later each night. It must have seemed a boon that just when days were getting rapidly shorter and the Sun seemed to go down all too soon, the Harvest Moon arrived to extend the hours that harvesting could be done.

As a final note, I should add that it is not just western civilization that has given special importance to the Harvest Moon. This Moon is for Chinese people everywhere the occasion for the Festival of the August Moon (the "August" is through a calendar discrepancy) or Mid-Autumn Festival (in some cultures, the equinoxes and solstices have been considered the middle of the seasons). This festival is celebrated with joyful games and the eating of "Mooncakes." I remember vividly being invited to one such celebration and singing songs and playing my guitar to a circle of friendly faces in the light of the rising Harvest Moon. □□

Think of it as a giant Slinky in which each loop, representing one lunar orbit of the Earth, advances the orbit a bit farther along the spiral path.

ONIONS TO THE FEET

and Other Remedies from a Midwife's Diary

From 1785 to 1812, Martha Ballard of Maine attended to 814 women giving birth and hundreds of other people in need of medical help. What's more, she kept a record of what she did in nearly every case . . .

by Laurel Thatcher Ulrich

hen a Maine woodsman of the 1780s got frostbite, he consulted a midwife, not a doctor. Midwives in early New England not only delivered babies, but they also handled most of the medical care in their towns. Doctors existed, but they were too expensive for ordinary use. Besides, there was little a doctor could do that a good midwife couldn't do just as well, if not better.

The most important midwife in Augusta, Maine, in the years after the American Revolution was Martha Ballard. The diary she kept from 1785 to 1812 lists the 814 births she attended (with great success) and hundreds of medical remedies. Some of her remedies seem very strange today. When Mr. Davis was suffering from the shingles, she "bled a Cat & applied the Blood which gave him Relief." Most of her remedies were as ordinary as a cup of chamomile tea.

Martha Ballard administered herbs internally as teas, decoctions, syrups, pills, enemas, vapors, and smoke; externally in poultices, plasters, blisters, cataplasms, baths, ointments, and salves. "Find Dolly lame. Poulticed her foot with sorril roasted," she wrote on October 11, 1787. When Theophilus Hamlin came to the house feeling ill, she "made a bed by the fire & gave him some catnip tea." When George Brown visited on November 28, 1786, an "exceeding Cold & windy" day, she found he had "froos Both his Ears." She put some salve on them, perhaps her melilot ointment made with hog grease and a kind of sweet clover.

Martha wilted burdock leaves in alcohol to apply to sore muscles, crushed comfrey for a poultice, added licorice to urine for cough medicine, boiled agrimony, plantain, and Solomon's seal into syrups. She also used homely garden vegetables in surprising ways. "Elisa very unwell," she wrote on August 4, 1810. "We applied Turnip poultice to her bowels which gave relief soon." On October 14, 1790, called in haste to Mrs. Hamlin "who was in a fitt," she "applied Vinegar to her Lips, temples, and hands, & onions to her feet & shee revived."

If the woman's fit was caused by a high fever, the application of cool vinegar may have helped bring her temperature down. Onions, applied raw to the feet, may also

- illustrated by John Edens / represented by Creative Freelancers

have contributed to cooling, though we cannot be certain Martha used them for that purpose. Traditional herbals classified the onion as a "hot and dry" plant, though they credited it with the power of drawing forth corruption and opening up stopped passages. Whatever her reason, Martha consistently used onions in treating the fever

ister is very unwell," she wrote on April 18, 1810. "I sent for flies to draw a blister."

and all-over achiness we might associate with the "flu." On September 5, 1786, for example, when her son Jonathan was "siesed with fever and universally pained," she "put him to bed, applied onions to his feet, [and] gave him teas to promote sweating."

Martha didn't simply prescribe medicine. She often stayed around to see that it worked. In October 1785 she spent most of a week caring for Mrs. Howard and her five children. "Took a sleep forepart of the night," she wrote on October 13. "Sat up after two in Mrs. Howard's chamber." She went home the next evening and got a good night's sleep, but was back again the next day. After sitting up another night, she "helped move the sick, dress their Blisters, etc."

The blisters weren't symptoms of the disease but part of the cure. Like the laxatives and "sweats," they helped the body expel excessive or troublesome "humors." The technique was simple: A small patch of an irritating substance was placed on the skin until it raised a watery welt. The greater the discharge, the more effective the cure, or so contemporaries believed. Blisters could be made from local plants like mustard, but the favorite blistering agent was an imported powder made from cantharides, or "Spanish flies" (dried beetles).

Martha purchased cantharides and other exotic ingredients from a local physician-importer. "Sister is very unwell," she wrote on April 18, 1810. "I sent for flies to draw a blister." But most of the medicines she used were available

in the earth around her. During a scarlet fever epidemic, she "went to the field and got some Cold water root, then Called to Mr. Kenydays to see Polly very ill with the Canker. Gave her some of the root." Cold water root, a form of wild aster, was supposedly introduced to English settlers by an Indian named Nathan Hope during a diphtheria epidemic in 1754. Martha knew something about diphtheria. Three of her nine children died in the Oxford, Massachusetts, epidemic of 1769 shortly before she and her family moved to Maine.

Although a few of Martha's remedies were native to America, three-quarters of the herbs mentioned in the diary can be found in Nicholas Culpeper's *The Complete Herbal,* published in London in 1649 and reprinted many times in America. Almost all can be found in E. Smith, *The Compleat Housewife: Or, Accomplish'd Gentlewoman's Companion,* an early 18th-century English recipe book. Martha didn't get her cures directly from these books, however, but from the oral traditions the books helped to preserve. When she used feverfew to treat a newly delivered mother, she followed Culpeper whether she knew it or not. When she used saffron to treat jaundice in newborn children, she followed the ancient doctrine of "signatures," the yellow plant being the obvious cure for yellow skin.

She may also have been influenced by early almanacs. (She ruled the pages of her homemade diary in the almanac form, using the dominical letter for Sunday.) "Dog Days begin this day," she wrote on July 26, 1788. Since antiquity, the period in late summer when the Dog Star became visible in the heavens had been linked with illness. In fact, Martha consistently made more medical calls in August and September than in any other time of the year. Whether her neighbors were actually more sickly during dog days or simply more disposed to ask for help, we do not know.

It would be a mistake to imagine Martha Ballard as a fringe practitioner preserving ideas lost to male physicians. Quite the contrary. Most of the therapies we now associate with folk medicine were still a part of academic practice in Martha's time. One of Maine's best educated physicians, Dr. Moses Appleton of Waterville, left a manuscript collection of recipes that included cures compounded of parsley roots, horseradish, and mustard seed and a treatment for sore throat that called for applying carded black wool soaked in vinegar, ear to ear.

Eighteenth- and early 19th-century physicians had few tools that weren't also available to women. The stethoscope had not yet been invented. Watches with second hands were so rare that pulse taking was unknown, nor did the clinical thermometer exist. Amputation was one of the few surgical procedures available. No one had yet thought of the germ theory of disease.

Doctors, like midwives, were part-time practitioners. In the Colonial period many of them had been ministers. In Martha's time they were often merchants or judges, gentlemen with some reputation for learning but with little interest in getting involved in the day-to-day care of the sick. They were less professionals in the modern sense than learned gentlemen or what passed for learned gentlemen in rural villages. Their prestige allowed them to charge more for doing less, treating desperate cases surgically, by bleeding, or through the administration of strong drugs like opium, calomel, digitalis, or quinine.

Quinine, for example, was not only used for "intermittent fevers," or what we know as malaria, but also as a general stimulant or "astringent." Contemporaries usually referred to it as "the Peruvian bark" or the "Jesuit's bark" because it had been discovered in the early 1600s by missionaries in South America. Martha Ballard was skeptical about its value, preferring local remedies. Whether it was a physician or some member of the patient's family who recommended quinine for Mrs. Pillsbury, we do not know, but when Martha found her "in a kind of delirium" she concluded "the use of the Bark was in some measure the Cause." Fortunately, "Old Mrs. Kenny Came and advised to give her a syrup of vinegar & onions and a decoction of Gold thread and shumake Berries. It was done and she seemed revived."

By contemporary standards, neither Martha's herbs nor the doctors' imported medicines had much impact on the infectious diseases that were the major causes of death in the period. Even in the 18th century, however, illnesses cured themselves often enough to give people faith in the remedies they had available. Just as important, Martha's gentle ministrations made her patients feel better while nature did its work. "I gargled her throat which gave her great ease," Martha wrote after preparing cold water root tincture for little Polly Kenydays. Beyond the physical comfort of a fragrant tea or a soothing syrup was the comfort of an idea. Remedies for illness could be found in the earth, in the animal world, or in the human body itself. Even the common onion, if one had the power to see it, held the secret of healing. □ □

To learn more about Martha Ballard, see Laurel Thatcher Ulrich's Pulitzer Prize-winning book, A Midwife's Tale: The Life of Martha Ballard Based on Her Diary, 1785-1812, *Alfred A. Knopf, 1990; Vintage Paperback, 1991. The author is a professor of history at the University of New Hampshire.*

The OLD FARMER'S GENERAL STORE

A special section featuring unique mail order products for all our readers who shop by mail.

 # THE OLD FARMER'S GENERAL STORE

CLASSIFIED ADVERTISING

ANTIQUES/ART

NAVAJO, ZUNI. Jewelry, sand paintings, kachinas, more! Wholesale catalog $3. Distant Drums, Box 54422-A, Phoenix AZ 85078

DRAW, PAINT FOR LOVE OR MONEY? Children's story about a goose has space for over 20 illustrations. An artist's dummy book to showcase talent to publishers or your gift to an artist or child? 8½ x 11, GBC bound so heavy stock pages lie flat. Media test sheets included. Send payment of $19.95 to Unicorn Press, 892 W. Street Rd., Suite 103, Warminster PA 18974

ASTROLOGY/OCCULT

MOTHER FIXER. Affordable. Emergencies. Drugs, business, love, luck, court, health, justice, anything. 616-382-5759. Anytime. Guaranteed.

GENTLE SURVIVALIST. Harmonic ecology digest validates environmental truths, Native preparedness, wisdom/prophecies. Spirited, motivating monthly. $16. 482 East 300 South, St. George UT 84770

LEARN WITCHCRAFT for protection, success, and serenity. Gavin and Yvonne Frost, world's foremost witches, now accepting students. Box 1502-0, Newbern NC 28563

BIORHYTHMS. Your physical, emotional, intellectual cycles charted in color. Interpretation guide. Six months ($10). Twelve months ($14). Send name, birthdate. CYCLES, Dept. FAB, 2251 Berkley Ave., Schenectady NY 12309.

WITCHCRAFT COURSE. Send self-addressed, stamped envelope for full details. Mac, Box 51943, San Jose CA 95151

WITCHCRAFT POWERS bring success, protection, love. World's foremost occult school offers home study and on-campus classes. Free information. Box 1366, Nashua NH 03061. 603-880-7237

ONE MAGIC SPELL! No charge! Tell me what you need! B.Zenor, 18533 Roscoe, Northridge CA 91324-4632

FREE LUCK NUMBERS. Send birthdate, self-addressed stamped envelope. Mystic, Box 2009-R, Jamestown NC 27282

BE A WINNER! Our oils, perfumes, bath, incense can help. Free 1993 new catalog. Asturo, Box North, Miami Beach FL 33160

CAST YOUR OWN SPELLS. Fast, sure, and easy. Learn from a real master of the mystic arts. Save money by learning how. Send $2 with your problems to Dr. Deprince Co, 69033 Metro Station, Brooklyn NY 11369

OCCULT CATALOG: Large, Informative. Herbs, oils, incense, etc. $2. Joan Teresa Power Products, P.O. Box 442-F, Mars Hill NC 28754

VOODOO, OLDEST ORGANIZATION. Catalog $8. Ritual work by request. T.O.T.S., Suite 310, 1317 North San Fernando Blvd., Dept OFA, Burbank CA 91504

ASTROLOGY.

ASTROLOGY. Personalized, comprehensive Natal Chart ($10). Progressed chart for current year ($10). Both ($14). Send name, birthdate, birthtime, birthplace. CYCLES, Dept FAA, 2251 Berkley Avenue, Schenectady NY 12309

YESTERDAY & TODAY. Any month from 1920 thru today. Filled with history, economics, news, and events. Great gift idea! Include name, month, year and $5: J. Glocksien, Box 86086, Phoenix AZ 85080. Include birthdate for personalized bonus.

AUTOMOTIVE

AUTOMOBILE LITERATURE WANTED: 1900-1975. I buy automobile sales brochures, manuals, etc. Walter Miller, 6710 Brooklawn, Syracuse NY 13211. 315-432-8282.

BEER & WINE MAKING

WINEMAKERS-BEERMAKERS. Free illustrated catalog. Fast service. Large selection. Kraus, Box 7850-YB, Independence MO 64054. 816-254-0242

BEERMAKERS. Free Catalog of supplies, featuring great beginners' kits. Brewery, 1310 Quincey, Minneapolis MN 55413-1541, 800-347-4042.

POWERFUL WINE WITHOUT FRUIT. Easy recipe. $3. International Concepts, 60 Martin Creek Ct., Stockbridge GA 30281

BOAT KITS & PLANS

BOAT KITS & PLANS. Boatbuilding supplies. 250 designs. Catalog only $3. Clarkcraft, 16-29 Aqualane, Tonawanda NY 14150

BOOKS/MAGAZINES

PUBLISH YOUR BOOK! Join our successful authors. All subjects invited. Publicity, advertising, beautiful books. Send for fact-filled booklet and free manuscript report. Carlton Press, Dept. OA, 11 West 32 Street, New York NY 10001

"HOW TO" books and videos on self-reliance, practical survival, and dozens of other subjects! 50-page catalog describes over 300 titles. Send $1 to: Paladin Press, P.O. Box 1307-3AZ, Boulder CO 80306

THE BEST BOOKS on country living, cooking, gardening, fishing, camping, nature, sports. Free catalog. Lyons & Burford, 31 W. 21 St., New York NY 10010

DEBT RELIEF made easy! Lawyer writes simple manual about federal laws that wipe out debt. $9.95 to Atty. Tolliver, 316 N. Michigan, Toledo OH 43624. Money-back guarantee.

WE PRINT COOKBOOKS, fund-raising, family. Details: Calico Kitchen Press, Drawer 606, Hartwell GA 30643. 1-800-RECIPES, 706-376-5711 GA

COMFORT TO THE SICK. HERBAL BOOK. 448 pages of herbal information and recipes used to cure at the turn of century. Backyard plants come in handy. MC/V/CHECKS, $19.95 plus $3 postage to Samuel Weiser, Box 612, York Beach ME 03910 or 800-423-7087

HERBS/SPICES TO FOODS

HERBS/SPICES TO FOODS cross-reference book. A must for anyone who cooks! $6 plus $1.50 S&H to Eastwyck, Rte. 3 Box 44, Boyd TX 76023. Allow 2-3 weeks.

POWER! SUCCESS! Asian strategy used by millions! $11.50. ATLI, Box 7768, Chicago IL 60680

BUSINESS OPPORTUNITY

MLM PROGRAM. 2000+ people build your downline. Send #10 SASE. Builders, Box 1701-FA, Fairborn OH 45324. 800-982-6692. 2A0369WZ

HOMEWORKERS: EARN $60 per 10 units making "Cuddly Bunnies". Send SASE or call: Kerray Products, Inc., P.O. Box 1347, Holly Hill FL 32117-1347. 904-258-3966.

MAKE $300 WEEKLY! Mail our "List" advertisements . . . from home! Universal-ALM, Box 558027, Chicago IL 60655

GOOD WEEKLY INCOME processing mail for national company. No experience necessary! No selling. Bonuses! Start immediately. Genuine opportunity! Rush stamped envelope: GSECO, 11220 W. Florissant-FA, Florissant MO 63033

GUIDE TO HOME EMPLOYMENT! Rush $1 and SASE for information: Mirrora Enterprises, 1828 Stadium Place 11F, Ann Arbor MI 48103-5234

READ BOOKS FOR PAY. $95 each. Free report! Send LSASE: B.E.S., Box 8187-MF, Pittsburg CA 94565-8187

LET THE GOVERNMENT FINANCE your small business. Grants/loans to $500,000 yearly. Free recorded message: 707-448-0270. (KE1)

FREE INFORMATION. Unbelievable money-making opportunities. Send LSASE. Almon Senechal, 669 Bennington Road, Hancock NH 03449

HOMEWORKERS EARN $60 per 10 units making "Buddy Bears". For details send SASE or call Jo-El Enterprises, Inc., P.O. Box 2937, DeLand FL 32723-2937. 904-736-4114

HOME ASSEMBLY WORK Available! Guaranteed easy money! Free details! Homework-FA, Box 520, Danville NH 03819

$600/WEEK AT HOME. Legitimate. We need you. Send SASE: Box 336A, Geneseo NY 14454

STEADY INCOME WORKING from your home! $1,000's weekly possible processing mail. For details send long self-addressed stamped envelope to: DLP Enterprises, PO Box 75, Havana IL 62644-0075

RECORD VIDEOTAPES . . . at home. $5,000 monthly possible. No pornography. Free details. Write: CMS Video Company, 210 Lorna Square - #163FA, Birmingham AL 35216

WE BUY newspaper clippings. $574.83 weekly. Send stamped envelope. Edwards, Box 467159-FA, Atlanta GA 30346

$27,000 IN BACKYARD! Growing new specialty plants. Start with $100. Free information. Growers, Box 1058-OFA, Bellingham WA 98227

$20,000 FROM 1/4 ACRE! Grow ginseng. $60/pound. Free information. 5712-FB, Cooper Road, Indianapolis IN 46208

GET CASH from manufacturers' coupons. Detail-pak only $3: Pyramid, 144 Village Landing, #254-BC4, Fairport NY 14450-1804

STUFF ENVELOPES for $140/100. Write: William Daas, Box 8720-F, Toledo OH 43537

FREE LIST — "legitimate" companies offering home employment. (Many choices!) Free! Write: Joblist - FA93, Alexandria Bay NY 13607-0250

AMAZING HOME MAILING PROGRAMS. Send $1, LSASE to: Almon Senechal, 669 Bennington Road, Hancock NH 03449

LEARN GUNSMITHING. Rifles, shotguns, pistols. Professional level home study. Free Career Literature. 800-362-7070 Dept. GL554.

$25/POUND PAID for your scrap aluminum? (Yes . . . Free Details!) Write: Ameriscrap-FA93, Alexandria Bay NY 13607-0127

WE'LL PAY YOU to type names and addresses from home. $500 per 1000. Call 900-896-1666 ($1.49 min/18yrs.+) or Write: PASSE - XOF992, 161 S. Lincolnway, N. Aurora, IL 60542

OVER $150,000 PAID TO DATE! Have fun solving puzzles for cash. Free details. Write: Unique, Box 3501-J, Mankato MN 56002

PUBLIC NOTICE! Wanted! Your Quality arts/crafts, from California to New York. To display/sell year-round in exclusive gift shop to millions Zion National Park visitors. Information $2. Zion's Handicrafts, Box 27OFA, LaVerkin UT 84745-0270

STUFF ENVELOPES for average $140/100. Send SASE to: Taylor's, Green Acres Road #18, Jacksonville AR 72076

$329.84 WEEKLY assembling our products at home. Free report! LSASE: Sparetime, Box 8145-FM, Pittsburg CA 94565-8145

MAKE MONEY AT HOME 10 ways. Report shows how. $3. MW Bookstore, 313 Fairview Road, Ellenwood GA 30049

HOME TYPING. Hand addressing. $500 weekly possible! Details free: National, Box 104-FA, Island Park NY 11558

CARNIVOROUS PLANTS

CARNIVOROUS (INSECT-EATING) plants, seeds, supplies, and books. Peter Paul's Nurseries, Canandaigua NY 14424

CATALOGS

NATIONAL COMPREHENSIVE Wholesale Directory. "Wholesalers' Yellow Pages." 1,000,000 Products. Prime Sources! $9.95. Rajotte's, 85(F) Vanderbilt, Central Islip NY 11722

64-PAGE DIRECTORY listing over 1,001 free items. For directory and free gift, send $4 P/H to: Simmons Publishing Co., PO Box 12691, New Bern NC 28562

FREE! WORLD'S most unusual novelty catalog. 2000 things you never knew existed. Johnson-Smith, F-520, Bradenton FL 34206

MASON SHOES; Quality made in America. Many formal, casual, and work styles from 5AA to 16EEEE. For a free catalog send SASE to David Horman, 2113 N. 39th Street, Seattle WA 98103-8334

CRAFTS

LEARN FLOWER arranging at home. Fascinating hobby or business. Brochure. Lifetime Career Schools, Dept. OB0213, 101 Harrison Street, Archbald PA 18403.

INDIAN CRAFTS. Free brochure showing materials used. Recommended to Indian guides, scout troops, etc. Cleveland Leather, 2629 Lorain Ave., Cleveland OH 44113

144 YARDS BETTER LACE trims $13.50, twelve delightful patterns. Oppenheims's, Dept. 550, North Manchester IN 46962-0052

DO IT YOURSELF

INSTALL IT YOURSELF! Free Details. Complete systems, upgrades. Orbitek Satellite Communications, Box 264A, Bohemia NY 11716-0264. 516-589-1292

ARROWHEAD MAKING. Modern method. Information $1. VHS $29.95. S/H $3.50. Commons, Box 5012-A, Central Point OR 97502

NO-STITCH CURTAIN CREATIONS, 26 pages how to make your own beautiful curtains using only an iron & board! Three basic curtain designs, swag, balloon and café. Book includes decorating tips, tieback section and bonus bed overhang design. Send $3.95 plus $1.75 shipping/handling to: P.O. Box 767474, Roswell GA 30076

EDUCATION/INSTRUCTION

BECOME A VETERINARY Assistant/Animal care specialist. Home study. Free career literature. 800-362-7070 Dept. CL554.

COLLEGE DEGREE/HOME STUDY. Catalog $1. CBC, Station Square, Suite 227, Rocky Mount NC 27804. 919-442-1211. Accredited.

UNIVERSITY DEGREES without classes! Accredited Bachelor's, Master's, Doctorates. Free revealing facts. Thorson-FA, Box 470886, Tulsa OK 74147

HIGH SCHOOL AT HOME. No classes. Low monthly payments. Information free. Our 96th year. Call 1-800-228-5600 or write American School, Dept #348, 850 E. 58th St., Chicago IL 60637

VIDEO - COMPLETE RUG BRAIDING instructions. Student tested, $39.95, S&H $3. Cox Enterprises, RR #2 Box 245, Bucksport ME 04416

BECOME A PARALEGAL. Work with attorneys. Lawyer-instructed home study. Free catalog. 800-362-7070 Dept. LL554.

UNIVERSITY DEGREES BY MAIL. Free money grants. Free information. Hido, 33227 Bainbridge, Cleveland OH 44139

FARM AND GARDEN

FREE CATALOG. Unusual seed varieties — Giant Belgium, Evergreen, Pineapple tomatoes, and more. We make gardening fun. Glecker Seedman, Metamora OH 43540

GREENHOUSES. Redwood/fiberglass kits, hobby/commercial sizes. Free brochure. Gothic Arch Greenhouse, Box 1564-OLD, Mobile AL 36633. 800-628-4974

EVERGREEN TREE SEEDLINGS. Direct from grower. Free catalog. Carino Nurseries, Box 538, Dept. AL, Indiana PA 15701

PVC GREENHOUSE PLANS. Blueprints. Extended season. $12.95. Art Lewis, 101 N. Summit St., Greenville NC 27858

LEARN LANDSCAPING at home. Free brochure. Lifetime Career Schools, Dept OB0113, 101 Harrison Street, Archbald PA 18403

LLAMAS. Wonderful pets and breeding stock, Takemmy Farm, Mary and Frank Bailey, RFD 521, Vineyard Haven MA 02568

DEALERS NEEDED! "Pet lovers only" T-shirts and sweatshirts. Mapp's, 169-TOA Williamsburg Lane, Athens GA 30605

FREE GARDEN CATALOG. 4,000 items! Seeds, plants, trees, supplies. Mellinger's, Dept. 720G Range Rd., North Lima OH 44452-9731

ALL ABOUT RABBITS. Learn more about more than 40 breeds of rabbit, the care, feeding, and training of your pet with "A Practical Beginning to Successful Rabbit Raising." $1. A 250-page cookbook filled with rabbit recipes, $5. Send check or money order to ARBA, Dept. LAS2, 1925 S. Main, Box 426, Bloomington IL 61704

TWO DWARF INDIAN BLOOD clingstone peach trees for $15 postpaid. Price list free. Ponzer Nursery, HCR 33 Box 18, Rolla MO 65401

FREE BROCHURE – Vermiculite, Perlite, starting mixes, pots, hand tools, labels. SASE. Maplewood Garden Supply, PO Box 141, Wilmington MA 01887

RARE SEEDS. Catalog and free sample. Send SASE. E.T. Seeds, Rte.3 Box 1894, Retreat TX 75110

BIG MONEY RAISING REDWORMS! 5,000 – $22.50, 10,000 – $37.95. Postpaid. Instructions. Bronwood Worm Farms, OF, Bronwood GA 31726

RARE HILARIOUS PETER. Female and Squash Pepper Seeds. $3 per pkg. Any two $5. All three $7.50, and over 100 more rare peppers, etc. SEEDS, Rte. 2 Box 246, Atmore AL 36502

THE COUNTRY BOY Incubator Specialists. We build the finest incubators for you. Eight models, all fully automatic. Full see-thru, and wood cabinets. When you see how different we are, you'll know why we're better! The Country Boy Incubators, 3428 Beret Lane, Dept OG, Wheaton MD 20906

PURPLE MARTIN HOUSE kits. Easy. Inexpensive. Biodegradable. Free information. Erie Bay Co., P.O. Box 568-FA, Erie PA 16512-0568

GREENHOUSE KITS & SUPPLIES. Texas Greenhouse Company, 2524 White Settlement Road, Dept. FA, Fort Worth TX 76107. Color Catalogs $4. Visa, M/C & check accepted. 800-227-5447.

DON'T LOSE YOUR CROPS TO FROST! Amarillo wind machines protect citrus fruit, tree fruit, and vegetables from frost damage. New and used. Gas, diesel and electric. Complete sales, service, parts and installation. Phone 209-592-4256, FAX 209-592-4194.

DYNAMIC DAYLILY SALE. Beautiful color catalog $2. (deductible). Goravani Growers, 1730-A Keane, Naples FL 33964

PERSONALS

NEW AGE contacts, occultists, circles, wicca, companionship, love, etc. America/worldwide. Dollar bill: Dion, Golden Wheel, Liverpool LI5 3HT, England

FREE DATING SERVICE OFFER! Singles 18-88. (Local/nationwide) Brochure: Compatible-OF, Box 2592, Lakeland FL 33806. 813-682-8744

LATIN AND ORIENTAL ladies seek friendship, marriage. Free photo brochure. "Latins," Box 1716-FR, Chula Vista CA 91912

FREE LIST of discreet, adventurous ladies, local/nationwide. Mailed discreetly. Lori, Box 20001-FA, Columbus OH 43320

MEET CHRISTIAN SINGLES the sensible way! Local, worldwide, phone. Mail Introductions test. Love, dating, marriage, meaningful companionship can change your life today! Free brochure, samples, 800-323-8113 X-433

NICE SINGLES with Christian values wish to meet others. Free magazine. Send age, interests. Singles, Box 310-OFA, Allardt TN 38504

ASIAN WOMEN DESIRE ROMANCE! Overseas, sincere, attractive. Free details, photos! Sunshine International Correspondence, Box 5500-YH, Kailua-Kona, HI 96745. 808-325-7707

NEED HELP DESPERATELY? Mrs. Stevens, Astrologer. Lonely? Unlucky? Unhappy? Helps all. Marriage, love, business, health, stress. I will give you options you never considered, never dreamed of. Immediate results. Call or write now. 803-682-9889. Mrs. Stevens, P.O. Box 207, Laurens SC 29360

SISTER HOPE SOLVES ALL problems. Are you sick? Have bad luck? Bothered by evil spells? Are you having love problems? Call today, 706-548-8598, or send $5, SASE to: 4502 Atlanta Hwy., Bogart GA 30622

REVEREND PASTOR LEWIS, reader and advisor on all problems. Love, business, health, marriage, lost nature. Will help solve your problems in your home. Send $5 with SASE to: 1214 Gordon Street, Atlanta GA 30310. 404-755-1301

MOTHER DOROTHY, reader and advisor. Advice on all problems — love, marriage, health, business, and nature. Gifted healer, she will remove your sickness, sorrow, pain, bad luck. ESP. Results in 3 days. Write or call about your problems. 404-755-1301. 1214 Gordon Street, Atlanta GA 30310

UNMARRIED CATHOLICS, unlimited selections. Singles magazines, world directory. State choices. Sparks, Box 872, Troy NY 12181

SHORTCUT TO romance; unique, new, never-before-offered service brings happiness, exciting news, yours free: Council Introductions, Dept. FA, 307 East 44th St., Suite PH-1, New York NY 10017

SISTER ADAMS, Spiritual healer, will solve problems in love, marriage, business, health, evil influences. 8287 Spanish Fort Blvd., Spanish Fort AL 36527. Immediate results. 205-626-7997

SPIRITUAL ADVISOR, Sister Mary. Thirty years experience in removing bad luck, sickness, pain, and sorrow. Tells past, present, future. I can and will help in marriage, love, nature, money, job, lawsuits, drug and alcohol problems. For fast help call: Sister Mary, 6019 South U.S. 1, Fort Pierce FL 34982. 407-466-0589

PSYCHIC CRYSTAL. She will help you with all your problems. Call today for help. 205-265-2112.

POSTCARDS

OLD PICTURE POSTCARDS. Free information on buying, selling, collecting, plus large directory of more than 300 dealers. Send large SASE with two stamps to Postcard Federation, Box 1765, Manassas VA 22110

POULTRY

FREE CATALOG! Goslings, ducklings, chicks, turkeys, guineas, gamebirds, bantams, swans, peafowl. Books, equipment. Hoffman Hatchery, Gratz PA 17030

GOSLINGS, DUCKLINGS, CHICKS, turkeys, guineas. Illustrated catalog, book list $1, deductible. Visa/MC. Pilgrim Goose Hatchery, OF-93, Williamsfield OH 44093

REAL ESTATE

ARKANSAS LAND – FREE LISTS!!! Farms, ranches, homes, recreational acreages. Gatlin Farm Agency, Box 790, Waldron AR 72958. 800-562-9078 X/OFA

OZARK MOUNTAIN or lake acreages. From $30 a month, nothing down, environmental protection codes, huge selection. Free catalog. Wood & Waters, Box 1-FA, Willow Springs MO 65793. 417-469-3187

ARKANSAS – FREE CATALOG. Natural beauty. Low taxes. The good life for families and retirement. Fitzgerald-Olsen Realtors, P.O. Box 237-A, Booneville AR 72927. Call toll free 800-432-4595, ext. 641A.

FLORIDA. NEW HOMES, $58,000 & up, land-country, city-commercial, write: Palm West Home Realty, 1 Florida Pk. Dr. N. Suite 107, Palm Coast FL 32137. Call 800-552-9879, ask for Frank M.

GOVERNMENT LANDS from $10. Repossessed homes, $1. Drug/tax seizures. Surplus recreational, agricultural, commercial properties. Nationwide Directory, $3. Lands, Box 5730-JM, Lighthouse Point FL 33074

FOR SALE. 500-acre walnut & oak Forest Reserve. Deer & turkey paradise. All fenced. So. Iowa. Raymond W. Howard, Rte.9, Bloomfield IA 52537

NORTHERN VERMONT. Land, homes, farms, waterfront, businesses. Free brochure. Peter Watson Agency, Greensboro VT 05841-0158. 800-732-4999

UPSTATE N.Y. Catskills, Adirondacks-Vacation land, houses. For list & packet, send $2 + #10 SASE to: G.M.C., Box 326, Highmount NY 12441. Buyers Broker.

GOVERNMENT LAND NOW AVAILABLE for claim. Up to 160 acres/person. Free recorded message: 707-448-1887. (4KE1)

RECIPES

CHOCOLATE FUDGE – No fat. No cholesterol. Recipe $1. Mrs Teeny, 1213A St. John, Monroe LA 71202

THREE DELICIOUS CATFISH/one eel recipe. $2 plus SASE to: S&W, P.O. Box 9191, N. Fay. Sta., Fayetteville NC 28311

GUARANTEED FOOLPROOF Homemade Bread. Send SASE, $5. Farmgirl Recipes, 1913 Stampede Avenue, Cody WY 82414. 307-587-3313.

GEORGIA PECANS! Wholesale-Retail. Grower direct year-round. Shelled/in shell, pecan candies, peanuts, free recipes with order. Merritt Pecans, P.O. Box 39, Weston GA 31832. 912-828-6610

RELIGION

BIBLE CALENDAR unveiled at last! Learn dates of Mosaic law, the Flood, Jesus' life and ministry, all Bible dates on our Gregorian calendar. Inspiration Research Publications. Write DAYS, P.O. Box 3344, Frankfort KY 40603

BIBLE TRUTHS really helpful every day. Expect revealing information. 32 pp. Free. Hopebooks, Box 15324, San Diego CA 92175

"DISTRESS OF NATIONS with perplexity" (Luke 21:25). Free booklet "What is this world coming to?" Clearwater Bible Students, P.O. Box 8216, Clearwater FL 34618

FREE ADULT OR CHILDREN'S bible study courses. Project Philip, Box 35A, Muskegon MI 49443

IMPROVE YOUR LIFE with the perfect prayer personalized just for you. Send $3.95 and prayer request to: Myron's, Box 141, Rochibucto, New Brunswick, Canada E0A 2M0

FREE BOOKLETS. On Life, Death, Soul, resurrection, pollution crisis, hell, judgment day, restitution. Bible Standard (OF), P.O. Box 679, Chester Springs PA 19425

BECOME an Ordained Minister. Free ministerial credentials legalize your right to the title "Reverend." Write: Ministry of Salvation Church, P.O. Box 5206, Chula Vista CA 91912

FREE BIBLE COURSE. Zion Faith College, P.O. Box 804, Caldwell ID 83606-0804

REVEREND MOON'S MESSAGE to America. Find out about the man and the message. Send SASE to: Mike and Sue, P.O. Box 27, Croton NY 10520-0027

STAMPS

1,000 STAMPS, $2.95. Guaranteed worth over $30 at International Catalog prices! All different; 55 countries! Money back. Other stamps to buy or return. Kenmore, OM-624, Milford NH 03055

WANTED

WANTED: WILD ROOTS AND HERBS. For free price list write to: Wilcox Natural Products, P.O. Box 37, Eolia MO 63344. 314-485-2400. Send your full correct address.

AUTOGRAPHS, LETTERS, SIGNED photos of famous people wanted. Herb Gray, P.O. Box 5084, Cochituate MA 01778. 617-426-4912

BUYING OLD FISHING LURES, FROGS. Send descriptions, photos, prices, SASE. Campbell, Box 891, Montebello CA 90640

WORK CLOTHES

WORK CLOTHES. Save 80%. Shirts, pants, coveralls. Free folder. Write: Galco, 4004 East 71st St., Dept. OF-9, Cleveland OH 44105

ANECDOTES AND PLEASANTRIES

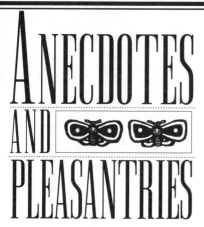

A motley collection of amazing (if sometimes useless) facts, strange stories, and questionable advice kindly sent to us during 1992 by readers of this 201-year-old publication.

ESSENTIAL COUNTRY WISDOM FOR CURRENT-DAY POLITICAL CANDIDATES

During the 1992 New Hampshire primary campaign, U.S. presidential candidate, philosopher, and poet Eugene J. McCarthy visited our Almanac office in Dublin and shared with us much food for thought, including the following ...

THE SIGNIFICANCE OF PRIME NUMBERS:

A knowledge of the significance of prime numbers by a presidential candidate is considered desirable. The principal advocate of this qualification is Lyt Woods, formerly the county forester in Rappahannock County, Virginia. Lyt explains the importance of such numbers relative to the life cycle of the 13- and 17-year locusts, noting that the eggs of locusts with a life cycle measurable in prime numbers are not likely to hatch in the same year in which their natural predators are present in force. Thus he notes that the 13-year locust might avoid potential enemies having a two-year cycle since those enemies, if the cycles were properly adjusted, would appear in the 12th or 14th years and miss the 13th. Enemies with a three-year cycle, in the 12th and 15th years; those with a four-year cycle, in the 12th and 16th; those with a five-year cycle, in the 10th and 15th, thus giving the locust a chance of surviving in numbers. The relevance of this to politics is that a president who understands prime numbers should seek to arrange his election, or his dealing with controversial issues, in such a way that his natural political enemies, principally the House of Representatives and the Senate, might not be present or, if present, be in a weakened condition. Thus a single seven-year presidential term might be better than the two four-year terms now allowed.

READING THE ECONOMIC SIGNS:

A significant indicator, signaling both long- and short-term economic trends in Rappahannock County, is, according to country storekeepers, the change in the sales of blueberry muffin mix. In periods of rising optimism and expectations and prosperity, blueberry muffin mix sales are high. A downturn in the economy is indicated by generally falling sales. According to

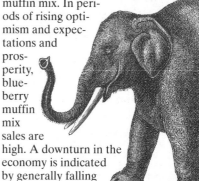

these same storekeepers, oatmeal sales are useless as an indicator and remain relatively constant throughout the whole cycle of business and economic change. During recession, it appears, the poor eat less and therefore buy less oatmeal; but those losses are offset by increased purchases of oatmeal by persons whose income is declining and who therefore are cutting down on blueberry muffin mix purchases.

AND DEALING WITH CONGRESS:

Possibly the most important thing for political candidates to know is that pigs and cattle have to be handled differently. If one is attempting to drive cows, he or she must start them slowly, sing to them, and gradually speed up the drive to stampede level as one gets them near where one wants them. The House of Representatives is best handled by this method. It was the favorite, almost the only, method used by President Johnson. Pigs, on the other hand, must be started into action under near-panic conditions through shouting at them, preferably in Latin *(Sui, Sui)*, beating on the pig troughs and fences, giving them no time to think. They can be allowed to slow down gradually so that they arrive at the appointed place at a slow walk, believing that they have made choices all along the way. Pig techniques are preferred and are most effective in moving the Senate to action. A candidate should also know that in very cold weather a pig will do almost anything to keep its nose warm. The remains of five prehistoric pigs were once discovered in a glacier frozen to death in a circle.

Editor's note: For more gems from Eugene McCarthy in book form, write E. P. M. Publications, Inc., 1003 Turkey Run Road, McLean, VA 22101.

....

And speaking of politics . . .

GEORGE WASHINGTON'S SECOND INAUGURAL ADDRESS *(In Full)*

MARCH 4, 1793

"Fellow-Citizens: I am again called upon by the voice of my Country to execute the functions of its Chief Magistrate. When the occasion proper for it shall arrive, I shall endeavor to express the high sense I entertain of this distinguished honor and of the confidence which has been reposed in me by the people of United America.

"Previous to the execution of any official act of the President, the Constitution requires an Oath of Office. This Oath I am now about to take, and in your presence, that if it shall be found during my administration of the Government I have in any instance violated willingly, or knowingly, the injunction thereof, I may (besides incurring Constitutional punishment) be subject to the upbraidings of all who are now witnesses of the present solemn Ceremony."

That is it, complete. It remains the briefest speech in the history of America's presidential inaugurations.

Immediately at the end of Washington's words, Vice President John Adams, acting in his capacity as president of the Senate, walked to Washington and said: "Sir, one of the judges of the Supreme Court of the United States is now present and ready to administer to you the oath required by the Constitution to be taken by the President of the United States." Then Supreme Court Justice William

Cushing administered the oath of office. Washington took no further time; he exited the room as promptly as he had arrived, went back to his home, and picked up with the documents he had been working on. The whole thing, travel and all, took less than half an hour; by 12:30 P.M. George Washington was actively performing the functions of a second-term president.

Excerpted from The Age of Washington *by George W. Nordham (Adams Press, Chicago)*

Does Anyone Care to Know the Origin of "Hello"?

In order to be even slightly interested in this question, you have to realize that the word "hello," as used today, didn't really exist back in the 19th century. They did call out "halloo" to incite hounds to chase or to hail someone from a long distance away. Like "Halloo! You up there on the roof." And the English had been saying "hullo" but not as a greeting. They used it as an expression of surprise as in "Hullo, what have we here?"

So how and when did "hello" begin as a simple greeting? Well, in a *New York Times* article by William Grimes, sent to us by no less than four readers last March, the "hello" mystery seems finally to have been, if not totally solved, somewhat clarified. It now seems likely it originated with Thomas Edison and his telephone. Alexander Graham Bell is credited with inventing the telephone, of course, but Edison also developed one,

which he envisioned as exclusively a business device with open lines at both ends.

"Are you there?" and "Are you ready to talk?" were suggested methods, initially, of starting a conversation on Edison's phones. His rival, Bell, however, was insisting on "Ahoy!" as the preferred initial greeting.

The reason we can now credit Edison with "hello" is due to a letter discovered recently by Allen Koenigsberg, a classics professor at Brooklyn College, New York. It had been stored away for over a hundred years in the American Telephone and Telegraph Company archives in lower Manhattan. Dated August 15, 1877, it is addressed to one T. B. A. David who was preparing to introduce Edison's version of the telephone to the city of Pittsburgh, Pennsylvania. "Dear David," Edison began, "I don't think we shall need a call bell as 'hello' can be heard 10 to 20 feet away. What do you think?" Signed, "Edison."

From then on, according to Professor Koenigsberg, "hello" became the

recommended greeting in telephone operating manuals. It also became something of a social liberator and leveler, too, in that it cut through 19th-century etiquette that said you don't speak directly to someone unless you've been introduced.

For us this solves yet another mystery. We've always wondered why, when he first spotted Livingston in the jungle, Stanley said, "Dr. Livingston, I presume." Why not a simple "hello"? Well, as we now know, the word did not as yet exist.

How to Have a Real Star Named After You

It'll cost you $40, but it's not hard to do. There are still millions of unnamed stars out there, most of them invisible to the naked eye. If you want one to be named for you — or for someone you wish to impress mightily — just call the toll-free number of International Star Registry of Ingleside, Illinois: 800-282-3333. They claim to have sold over 400,000 stars since the company began in 1979 — to the likes of Fred Astaire, Johnny Carson, Mick Jagger, Dolly Parton, Elvis Presley, Prince Charles, Frank Sinatra, Oprah Winfrey, and Bob Smith. (Bob Smith?)

You don't have to be a big star yourself, however. Just call, as we did, and they'll send an application form and brochure explaining that for your $40 they'll put a name of your choice (up to 35 characters) on a specific unnamed star and include it in the star registry. They'll also send you some other stuff, including a colorful certificate of ownership with the precise coordinates of your star so that future generations can, with the help of a telescope, actually locate it in the sky.

Stellar idea. Wish we'd thought of it.

Court Conversations Just Never Go Away

The reason all court exchanges are with us forever is because during courtroom trials there exists an army of court reporters whose job it is to take down and preserve every statement made during the proceedings. The following samples of verbatim conversations from real court trials, excerpted from a Zenith Forum *feature a couple of years ago, was sent to us last winter by Virginia Kidd via Larry Ashmead of New York. We couldn't resist . . .*

Satchel Paige's Six Guidelines for Good Health and Long Life

As everyone knows, Satchel Paige was one of baseball's great pitchers. Even more remarkable than his pitching, however, was that he was able to pitch effectively at such an advanced age. No one's sure what that age was except that it was a lot older than anyone in the game today, including Nolan Ryan. Here then, for posterity, are Satchel's six lifelong guidelines . . .

RULE #1: "Avoid fried meats, which angry up the blood."

RULE #2: "If your stomach disputes you, lie down and pacify it with cool thoughts."

RULE #3: "Keep the juices flowing by jangling around gently as you move."

RULE #4: "Go very light on the vices, such as carrying on in society. The social ramble ain't restful."

RULE #5: "Avoid running at all times."

RULE #6: "Don't look back. Something might be gaining on you."

Courtesy of Ira Truckine
Tampa, Florida

Q: What is your brother-in-law's name?
A: Borofkin.
Q: What is his first name?
A: I can't remember.
Q: He's been your brother-in-law for 45 years, and you can't remember his first name?
A: No. I tell you I'm too excited. [Rising from the witness chair and pointing to Mr. Borofkin] Nathan, for God's sake, tell them your first name!

Q: Did you stay all night with this man

in New York?
A: I refuse to answer that question.
Q: Did you stay all night with this man in Chicago?
A: I refuse to answer that question.
Q: Did you stay all night with this man in Miami?
A: No.

Q: James stood back and shot Tommy Lee?
A: Yes.
Q: And then Tommy Lee pulled out his gun and shot James in the fracas?
A: [After hesitation] No sir, just above it.

Q: Doctor, did you say he was shot in the woods?
A: No, I said he was shot in the lumbar region.

Q: Now, Mrs. Johnson, how was your first marriage terminated?
A: By death.
Q: And by whose death was it terminated?

Q: Are you married?
A: No, I'm divorced.
Q: What did your husband do before you divorced him?
A: A lot of things that I didn't know about.

Q: How did you happen to go to Dr. Cheney?
A: Well, a gal down by the road had had several of her children by Dr. Cheney and said he was really good.

Q: Do you know how far pregnant you are right now?
A: I will be three months November 8th.
Q: Apparently then, the date of conception was August 8th?
A: Yes.
Q: What were you and your husband doing at that time?

Q: You say you're innocent, yet five people swore they saw you steal a watch.
A: Your Honor, I can produce 500 people who didn't see me steal it.

Q: Did the lady standing in the driveway subsequently identify herself to you?
A: Yes, she did.
Q: Who did she say she was?
A: She said she was the owner of the dog's wife.

Q: And lastly, Gary, all your responses must be oral, OK?
A: Oral?
Q: How old are you?
A: Oral.

A FARMER'S LAST WILL

The following was sent to us by Arthur Morris, a pecan farmer from Broken Arrow, Oklahoma. We decided to include it here because (1) it made us laugh and (2) it made us cry . . .

I leave:

To my wife, my overdraft at the bank — maybe she can explain it.

To my banker, my soul — he has the mortgage on it anyway.

To my neighbor, my clown suit — he'll need it if he continues to farm as he has in the past.

To the ASCA, my grain bin — I was planning to let them take it away next year anyway.

To the county agent, 50 bushels of corn to see if he can hit the market — I never could.

To the junk man, all my machinery — he's had his eye on it for years.

To my undertaker, a special request — I want six implement and fertilizer dealers for my pallbearers. They're all used to carrying me.

To the weatherman, rain and sleet and snow for the funeral, please — no sense having good weather now.

To the grave-digger — don't bother. The hole I'm in should be big enough.

MODERATELY GOOD NEWS

Everyone complains that there's nothing but horrible news on television and in the papers these days. "Why doesn't anyone report good news?" they ask. Well, OK. We had to search through mounds of clippings sent to us over this past year, but we found some . . .

 ☞ Kissing is not a health hazard. According to Dr. Timothy Sankary, a West Coast specialist in infectious diseases, it is "a common assumption that kissing spreads colds. But some interesting studies have been done where cold-free people kissed people with colds, and the bug just didn't spread." *(Courtesy of Richard O'Donnell)*

☞ Cattle and sheep are now willing to help out with waste problems. Dr. Paul Walker, animal scientist at Illinois State University, has developed an experimental feed mixture that includes 61.1 percent grass clippings, 24.9 percent shredded newsprint, and 14 percent corn — to which is added 1 percent molasses. "The sheep ate it just fine," Walker said, "and if sheep will eat it, cattle will." Walker also plans to study a mixture of cafeteria food waste, corn, and paper. (Paper accounts for 34 percent of municipal solid waste; lawn waste, 10 percent.)

☞ Rose-colored glasses help headaches. Ophthalmic specialists at Birmingham University in England found that after four months of using rose-colored lenses, the average number of migraine attacks among a group of children ages 8 to 14 who had suffered from them frequently fell from 6.2 to 1.6 headaches a month.

☞ Eating chocolate doesn't cause pimples. Recent studies indicate there is no evidence to link chocolate with pimples. Instead pimples are probably linked with increased levels of sex hormones. And genetics may well play a part.

☞ If you're a sports fan, you're not necessarily a knucklehead. According to a survey by Lieberman Research for *Sports Illustrated* magazine, sports fans generally are younger, more affluent, better educated, and in better physical condition than nonfans. Also, they are more likely to eat out at expensive restaurants, rent movie cassettes, entertain at home, buy paperback books, work on crossword puzzles, and say they're interested in sex, politics, music, and religion. (In fact, it seems the only subject that nonfans are more interested in is reading. Oh, well.)

A SHAGGY SHEEP STORY

Seems a certain Maine farmer was apprehensive about shearing his big old ram, Euclid. He'd experienced a severe butting the last time and the time before that, too. So he spent the day shearing the ewes and then decided he'd tackle Euclid in the morning.

The next day he found Euclid lying dead in the doorway of the lean-to, both lambs and ewes leaping gracefully over his remains on their way to the trough. Too bad, he thought. But then he'd been pretty old. Might's well shear him, however, before he buried him. Why waste the wool? So he dug a five-foot trench and was commencing the shearing operation when a car pulled into the driveway. The driver only wanted directions to the local campground but, upon seeing the performance in progress, lingered to watch. The shearing being completed, the farmer proceeded with the burial before the onlooker voiced his curiosity. "Makes you appreciate the wool more," he said. The farmer nodded his assent while widening the bottom of the hole to accommodate Euclid's stiffened legs. "I've never seen that done before," the observer continued as the farmer finally dumped Euclid into the pit. "I didn't realize they had to be dead first."

The farmer paused at this, considered Euclid a bit, and then replied, "I don't know about the others, but I'd have never been able to get him in the hole if he wasn't, let alone keep him there while I covered him up!"

Courtesy of Ian B. Ormon
Leeds, Maine

FINALLY, SOMETHING TO THINK ABOUT

Cynics have always scoffed at so-called miracle cures. If it can't be proved to have a scientific basis, then it's just so much hysterical poppycock. So when the following article (excerpted here) by Boyce Rensberger for the Washington Post *was sent to us by R. S. Hayes of Glen Ridge, New Jersey, we felt it seemed worthy of contemplation ...*

"The word placebo in Latin means 'I shall please.' It was adopted long before the era of scientific medicine by physicians who knew they had little to offer patients except hope and the sense that something was being done for them, even if it was only the laying on of hands or the administration of an impressively prepared potion. But scientists now know that there really is a placebo force — a power, or probably several powers, in the brain that can heal the body of many different (though definitely not all) ailments — from warts and battle wounds to infections and headaches. The power must, however, be invoked in the right way.

It does not matter what form the placebo takes. It can be a country doctor's sugar pill or a Navajo medicine man's five days of chanting and sand painting inside the sacred hogan. It can be a thwack upside the head from a tent revivalist faith healer (even one of the variety shown to be outright frauds), or it can be a mother's kiss. The one paramount factor that matters, scientific experiments show, is that the patient truly believes the method can work. "Faith healing" turns out to be an apt name, though faith in a specific religion is not necessary. Faith is.

If that faith is present, messages go out from the believing brain to communicate with many different physiological mechanisms throughout the body. Researchers believe the messages start out as ordinary nerve impulses transmitted from the brain through the nervous system to the afflicted part of the body. There the nerves release certain chemicals that act on the cells to correct the problem."

Where, we might ask now, does that leave miracles? Well, perhaps right where they've always been. Because surely all of life remains nothing less than a miracle.

On that note, we'll leave you until next year. And, as the philosopher said, "Be kind, for everyone you meet is fighting a hard battle." ☐☐

CONCERNING

Thomas Jefferson

BY CASTLE FREEMAN JR.

He is the only American
president who was an
authentic and undoubted
genius. And 250 years after
his birth, we still want to
preserve his idea of America.

homas Jefferson, third
president of the United
States, who was born 250
years ago in what is today
Albemarle County, Virginia, disliked dogs,
Great Britain, cold weather, and kings. For
virtually all the rest of the wealth of experience that his long life and extraordinary
mind brought his way, he seems to have had
the largest and most welcoming affection.
Flowers, trees, music, any and every kind of
useful device from the hot-air balloon to a
handy table cruet for salad dressing, good
wine, handsome buildings, thrifty farms,
well-tended gardens, France and the French

people, songbirds — these he loved, enjoyed,
and studied all his life.

Jefferson lived in a time — near the end
of the time, really — when one man could
gain a competent knowledge of everything
that belonged to civilization. What the West
knew of history, the sciences, the arts, math-
ematics, geography, government, philosophy, and every other subject could be acquired by one student. Jefferson was that
student. For him, education wasn't
something that could be finished; it was a
way of life. His mind was, above all, active,
capacious, passionate, insatiable for knowledge. Yet in his life Jefferson found time as

well to learn at least five languages and to become a first-rate horseman, an accomplished violinist, a skilled draftsman, a lavish host, a generous friend, and a fond parent. He is the only American president who was an authentic and undoubted genius.

Jefferson was not an especially handsome man, but he must have been striking. He stood about six-feet-two, unusually tall for a man of his time. He had red hair and the pink complexion that often goes with it, green or hazel eyes, and somewhat sharp features. In all, he might have looked a little like an enormous fox, a comparison that would have given his legion of distinguished enemies no trouble at all.

He was born the third of ten children of a substantial landowner and planter who died young. The Virginia piedmont, on the western fringe of settlement in Jefferson's childhood, had no school system; he was tutored privately, later attending a couple of the tiny one-teacher schools of the day, where the master was an Anglican clergyman and the subject matter was the three Rs plus Latin and Greek. At 16 he entered the College of William and Mary in Williamsburg, the Colonial capital of Virginia.

In Jefferson's time a young man of his station and abilities would be expected to train for the law and eventually to enter the Colonial government. This Jefferson did following two years at William and Mary and a legal apprenticeship in Williamsburg. His first election to the Virginia legislature came when he was 26. As it happened, though, a tranquil career of uneventful officeholding was not in Jefferson's future. He joined in the growing radical movement to demand from England fairer treatment for the American colonies and, because he was a quick and forceful writer, soon became one of the united colonies' most useful spokesmen. When the Continental Congress organized in 1775, Jefferson was a delegate from Virginia, and for the next 35 years he was — reluctantly, he said — a public man.

All his life Jefferson complained of the burdens of a public career and deplored the nastiness of politics. He despised both, he protested; he far preferred the retired, innocent life of his mountain farm, Monticello, near Charlottesville. "I am to be liberated from the hated occupations of politics," he wrote his friend Angelica Church in 1793, "and to remain in the bosom of my family, my farm, and my books." It was his constant theme: the evil and ugliness of the world of affairs, the peace and contentment of private life among his mountains.

Even one who loves Jefferson may find it hard to believe wholly in his eagerness for rustic retirement. No man who hates public life compiles a resumé like his: Jefferson was, successively, delegate to the Continental Congress (and author of the Declaration of Independence), Revolutionary War governor of Virginia, the United States' minister to France, secretary of state, vice president, and president for two terms. His periods out of office in that astonishing career were less often voluntary than they were forced upon him by political reverses. Jefferson is hardly believable as a reluctant hero. Clearly, he sought office because he loved the fight, the struggle that was the history of his time: to establish and protect a free, democratic society demonstrating that men can govern themselves by reason rather than submit to government by force.

Nevertheless, if Jefferson was never quite the unambitious, bookish farmer he sometimes pretended to be, neither did his public career ever come close to filling his attention. On the contrary, for anyone today who studies his life, Jefferson appears as a remarkably casual statesman. The presidency of the United States he seems to have regarded as about a half-time job, the vice presidency and the office of secretary of state as rather less than that. Founding the American republic was, for Jefferson, one occupation among the others, many others, that went to make up an

We know the geography of Mars today more accurately than Jefferson's contemporaries knew the upper Missouri River country.

enlightened life. It was the conduct of life that was important, and right conduct of life meant life put to the work of inquiry, reflection, improvement. He wrote to his daughter: "A mind always employed is always happy. This is the true secret, the grand recipe for felicity. The idle are the only wretched."

North America in Jefferson's lifetime was the most perfect setting imaginable for one who believed man was put on Earth to learn and be busy. Here was a whole continent to be learned; vast lands to be explored, new plants and animals to be described, farms to be settled and towns laid out, wise laws to be passed. Jefferson couldn't get enough of America.

The country has never had a more intelligent and untiring celebrator. For several years Jefferson carried on a debate with the great French naturalist Buffon, who claimed that the wild animals of Europe were larger and stronger than those of the New World. Jefferson would have none of that. He wrote and researched at great length to refute Buffon. In 1787 he went so far as to arrange the shipment to Buffon in Paris of a dead moose from New Hampshire, which ought to have been conclusive.

Nothing in America could fail to claim Jefferson's interest and allegiance. He regarded Philadelphia as a finer city than either London or Paris and declared the American climate with its clear, warm sun more healthful by far than the fogs of Europe. In a letter from France, he assured Abigail Adams that, having "heard the Nightingale in all its perfection, I do not hesitate to pronounce that in America it would be deemed a bird of the third rank only, our mockingbird being unquestionably superior to it." So fond was Jefferson of the mockingbird, in fact, that he kept one on a perch in the presidential office during his administration.

The cardinal act of Jefferson's presidency was the Louisiana Purchase, in which the United States in a single stroke increased its territory by something more than double. We know the geography of Mars today more accurately than Jefferson's contemporaries knew the upper Missouri River country. He lost no time in organizing a party to explore the new lands. Jefferson's instructions to the expedition's leader, his secretary Meriwether Lewis, an army captain, are among the most characteristic products of his mind. Lewis was to measure latitude and longitude; map rivers and mountains; fix all "interesting points" of land; describe all animals and useful plants; observe soil, climate, and minerals; learn all he could of the western Indian tribes and their histories, languages, laws, and customs. Jefferson wanted to know everything. And he wanted to know it for sure. "Your observations are to be taken with great pains and accuracy," he warned Lewis, "to be entered distinctly, & intelligibly . . . to comprehend all the elements necessary. . . ."

Jefferson's passion for exact observation of nature was lifelong. From his early manhood, when he began keeping a record of the first flowers to appear each spring at Monticello, to the end of his life, Jefferson amassed observations, took notes, filled up tables of information. Wherever he happened to be living, he measured and recorded the temperature twice a day. He also noted the wind's direction and humidity, the date each year on which his garden first produced peas, the appearance of various vegetables in the Washington markets, the first bloom on his fruit trees, the dates of arrival of the first spring birds. Traveling up the Rhine during his embassy to France, he listed crops, inspected vineyards, sketched bridges and buildings, inquired tirelessly into prices and products — and wrote it all down.

Minute observation and recording were obviously fun for Jefferson. He loved looking about him, noticing, and keeping track. But his devotion to careful observation was more than a quirk of his personality and education. It had a plan: better agriculture. And that plan had a purpose: better politics. Jefferson believed that democratic self-government was only possible among farming people who were pretty widely dispersed over the ground. He also believed that farms, to support democracy, must produce wealth. There-

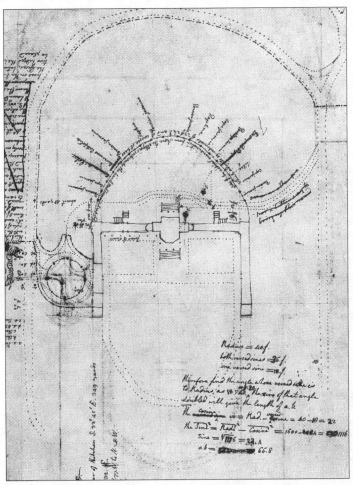

When Jefferson moved to his beloved mountaintop home, Monticello, in 1770, his attention turned immediately to designing the landscape. This 1772 plan for house and gardens, in Jefferson's hand, has later notations and revisions.

Jefferson wasn't the country's first "improving" farmer, but he was certainly among its most ambitious.

fore agriculture must be improved, made more productive, more efficient, by its being subjected to the most up-to-date scientific methods.

Jefferson wasn't the country's first "improving" farmer, but he was certainly among its most ambitious. His land holdings around Monticello at one time covered 10,000 acres, and he was constantly at work about them, experimenting with new crops, new seeds, new livestock, new methods of cultivation. He invented an improved plow and was keenly interested in ways of working land to minimize erosion. He developed an elaborate sevenfold system of crop rotation intended to improve the soil on his farms. He had a large and meticulously ordered collection of seeds and exchanged seeds, bulbs, and nursery stock with like-minded agriculturists all over the United States, Europe, and England.

Jefferson was also a joyful flower and landscape gardener, although his idea of a garden for Monticello was a spread that in New England would have made a considerable upland farm all by itself. Like many a gardener since, Jefferson planned bigger than he planted, but he laid out the flower beds at Monticello himself, many of them after his retirement from the presidency in 1809 and with the help of one or another of his seven granddaughters.

In his seventies Jefferson began, he said, to contemplate the onset of senile decline. In his letters he observes with regret that "reduced mental activity" obliges him to pass over some topic more quickly than he would like. Fortunately Jefferson's senility was of a piece with his unwillingness to en-

ter public life. Well into his seventies he rode up to 30 miles a day, and his correspondence in his declining years includes scores of brilliant letters to James Madison, John Adams, Madame de Staël, Lafayette, and a hundred others on topics ranging from the ancient language of the Anglo-Saxons and the philosophy of Plato to the classification of animals, the creation of the University of Virginia, and the history of the potato. He ascribed his good health to luck, moderation in food and drink, and "the habit of bathing my feet in cold water every morning for sixty years past."

Among the Founding Fathers, Jefferson is the only one whose name we still conjure with in the political world of 1993. No one any longer claims to be a Washingtonian, a Hamiltonian — few can even be certain what those terms might mean. Many claim to be Jeffersonians. In what is a neat trick indeed, both major political parties today eagerly acknowledge Jefferson's parenthood.

It is not at all the case that Jefferson's own political principles have always prevailed in our history. The rural republic of enlightened farmer-democrats governing themselves with wisdom and restraint and reading Homer (in Greek) after dinner is long gone, if it ever existed in the first place. Nevertheless, even when it has departed from Jefferson's order of things, the country has wanted to preserve Jefferson's idea of America. This most *educated* of our forefathers has given us the most courageous, optimistic, and exciting image that we have of ourselves:

No experiment can be more interesting than that we are now trying, and which we trust will end in establishing the fact, that man may be governed by reason and truth.

Jefferson died at Monticello in 1826, on the Fourth of July. □□

1992

JANUARY
S	M	T	W	T	F	S
—	—	—	1	2	3	4
5	6	7	8	9	10	11
12	13	14	15	16	17	18
19	20	21	22	23	24	25
26	27	28	29	30	31	—

FEBRUARY
S	M	T	W	T	F	S
—	—	—	—	—	—	1
2	3	4	5	6	7	8
9	10	11	12	13	14	15
16	17	18	19	20	21	22
23	24	25	26	27	28	29

MARCH
S	M	T	W	T	F	S
1	2	3	4	5	6	7
8	9	10	11	12	13	14
15	16	17	18	19	20	21
22	23	24	25	26	27	28
29	30	31	—	—	—	—

APRIL
S	M	T	W	T	F	S
—	—	—	1	2	3	4
5	6	7	8	9	10	11
12	13	14	15	16	17	18
19	20	21	22	23	24	25
26	27	28	29	30	—	—

MAY
S	M	T	W	T	F	S
—	—	—	—	—	1	2
3	4	5	6	7	8	9
10	11	12	13	14	15	16
17	18	19	20	21	22	23
24	25	26	27	28	29	30
31						

JUNE
S	M	T	W	T	F	S
—	1	2	3	4	5	6
7	8	9	10	11	12	13
14	15	16	17	18	19	20
21	22	23	24	25	26	27
28	29	30				

JULY
S	M	T	W	T	F	S
—	—	—	1	2	3	4
5	6	7	8	9	10	11
12	13	14	15	16	17	18
19	20	21	22	23	24	25
26	27	28	29	30	31	—

AUGUST
S	M	T	W	T	F	S
—	—	—	—	—	—	1
2	3	4	5	6	7	8
9	10	11	12	13	14	15
16	17	18	19	20	21	22
23	24	25	26	27	28	29
30	31					

SEPTEMBER
S	M	T	W	T	F	S
—	—	1	2	3	4	5
6	7	8	9	10	11	12
13	14	15	16	17	18	19
20	21	22	23	24	25	26
27	28	29	30	—	—	—

OCTOBER
S	M	T	W	T	F	S
—	—	—	—	1	2	3
4	5	6	7	8	9	10
11	12	13	14	15	16	17
18	19	20	21	22	23	24
25	26	27	28	29	30	31

NOVEMBER
S	M	T	W	T	F	S
1	2	3	4	5	6	7
8	9	10	11	12	13	14
15	16	17	18	19	20	21
22	23	24	25	26	27	28
29	30					

DECEMBER
S	M	T	W	T	F	S
—	—	1	2	3	4	5
6	7	8	9	10	11	12
13	14	15	16	17	18	19
20	21	22	23	24	25	26
27	28	29	30	31	—	—

1993

JANUARY
S	M	T	W	T	F	S
—	—	—	—	—	1	2
3	4	5	6	7	8	9
10	11	12	13	14	15	16
17	18	19	20	21	22	23
24	25	26	27	28	29	30
31						

FEBRUARY
S	M	T	W	T	F	S
—	1	2	3	4	5	6
7	8	9	10	11	12	13
14	15	16	17	18	19	20
21	22	23	24	25	26	27
28	—	—	—	—	—	—

MARCH
S	M	T	W	T	F	S
—	1	2	3	4	5	6
7	8	9	10	11	12	13
14	15	16	17	18	19	20
21	22	23	24	25	26	27
28	29	30	31	—	—	—

APRIL
S	M	T	W	T	F	S
—	—	—	—	1	2	3
4	5	6	7	8	9	10
11	12	13	14	15	16	17
18	19	20	21	22	23	24
25	26	27	28	29	30	—

MAY
S	M	T	W	T	F	S
—	—	—	—	—	—	1
2	3	4	5	6	7	8
9	10	11	12	13	14	15
16	17	18	19	20	21	22
23	24	25	26	27	28	29
30	31					

JUNE
S	M	T	W	T	F	S
—	—	1	2	3	4	5
6	7	8	9	10	11	12
13	14	15	16	17	18	19
20	21	22	23	24	25	26
27	28	29	30	—	—	—

JULY
S	M	T	W	T	F	S
—	—	—	—	1	2	3
4	5	6	7	8	9	10
11	12	13	14	15	16	17
18	19	20	21	22	23	24
25	26	27	28	29	30	31

AUGUST
S	M	T	W	T	F	S
1	2	3	4	5	6	7
8	9	10	11	12	13	14
15	16	17	18	19	20	21
22	23	24	25	26	27	28
29	30	31	—	—	—	—

SEPTEMBER
S	M	T	W	T	F	S
—	—	1	2	3	4	5
5	6	7	8	9	10	11
12	13	14	15	16	17	18
19	20	21	22	23	24	25
26	27	28	29	30	—	—

OCTOBER
S	M	T	W	T	F	S
—	—	—	—	—	1	2
3	4	5	6	7	8	9
10	11	12	13	14	15	16
17	18	19	20	21	22	23
24	25	26	27	28	29	30
31						

NOVEMBER
S	M	T	W	T	F	S
—	1	2	3	4	5	6
7	8	9	10	11	12	13
14	15	16	17	18	19	20
21	22	23	24	25	26	27
28	29	30	—	—	—	—

DECEMBER
S	M	T	W	T	F	S
—	—	—	1	2	3	4
5	6	7	8	9	10	11
12	13	14	15	16	17	18
19	20	21	22	23	24	25
26	27	28	29	30	31	—

1994

JANUARY
S	M	T	W	T	F	S
—	—	—	—	—	—	1
2	3	4	5	6	7	8
9	10	11	12	13	14	15
16	17	18	19	20	21	22
23	24	25	26	27	28	29
30	31					

FEBRUARY
S	M	T	W	T	F	S
—	—	1	2	3	4	5
6	7	8	9	10	11	12
13	14	15	16	17	18	19
20	21	22	23	24	25	26
27	28	—	—	—	—	—

MARCH
S	M	T	W	T	F	S
—	—	1	2	3	4	5
6	7	8	9	10	11	12
13	14	15	16	17	18	19
20	21	22	23	24	25	26
27	28	29	30	31	—	—

APRIL
S	M	T	W	T	F	S
—	—	—	—	—	1	2
3	4	5	6	7	8	9
10	11	12	13	14	15	16
17	18	19	20	21	22	23
24	25	26	27	28	29	30

MAY
S	M	T	W	T	F	S
1	2	3	4	5	6	7
8	9	10	11	12	13	14
15	16	17	18	19	20	21
22	23	24	25	26	27	28
29	30	31	—	—	—	—

JUNE
S	M	T	W	T	F	S
—	—	—	1	2	3	4
5	6	7	8	9	10	11
12	13	14	15	16	17	18
19	20	21	22	23	24	25
26	27	28	29	30	—	—

JULY
S	M	T	W	T	F	S
—	—	—	—	—	1	2
3	4	5	6	7	8	9
10	11	12	13	14	15	16
17	18	19	20	21	22	23
24	25	26	27	28	29	30
31						

AUGUST
S	M	T	W	T	F	S
—	1	2	3	4	5	6
7	8	9	10	11	12	13
14	15	16	17	18	19	20
21	22	23	24	25	26	27
28	29	30	31	—	—	—

SEPTEMBER
S	M	T	W	T	F	S
—	—	—	—	1	2	3
4	5	6	7	8	9	10
11	12	13	14	15	16	17
18	19	20	21	22	23	24
25	26	27	28	29	30	—

OCTOBER
S	M	T	W	T	F	S
—	—	—	—	—	—	1
2	3	4	5	6	7	8
9	10	11	12	13	14	15
16	17	18	19	20	21	22
23	24	25	26	27	28	29
30	31					

NOVEMBER
S	M	T	W	T	F	S
—	—	1	2	3	4	5
6	7	8	9	10	11	12
13	14	15	16	17	18	19
20	21	22	23	24	25	26
27	28	29	30	—	—	—

DECEMBER
S	M	T	W	T	F	S
—	—	—	—	1	2	3
4	5	6	7	8	9	10
11	12	13	14	15	16	17
18	19	20	21	22	23	24
25	26	27	28	29	30	31

The Old Farmer's Almanac

GREAT★AMERICANS
HALL OF FAME

A dozen people whose lives changed all our lives since this Almanac
was first published 201 years ago.

....

T he people whose lives are described herein (like those written
about in the 1992 Special Bookstore Supplement) include men
and women whose hard work, courage, and genius helped to
shape and reshape the everyday lives of Americans over the past
201 years. Their impact was not always the stuff of headlines; few of them
ever had anything to do with politics or celebrity except to rebel against
it. Some names are fairly well known: plant breeder Luther Burbank, poet
John Greenleaf Whittier, photographer Mathew Brady. Some, like George
Mowbray, whose expertise with explosives made oil gushers and railroad
tunnels possible, are unsung heroes. But the accomplishments of each one
are an integral part of our culture, from labor unions (Mother Jones) and
the Pill (Margaret Sanger) to college football (Knute Rockne) and "Mood
Indigo" (Duke Ellington).

From time to time the editors of this Almanac will nominate other
American men and women to *The Old Farmer's Almanac* Great Americans
Hall of Fame.

Written by Lawrence Doorley

MOTHER JONES (1830-1930): HELL-RAISER

The grand old warhorse was dying. It seemed certain that the long-planned birthday celebration would be a memorial service in the local cemetery instead. The rank and file, for whom she had fought so valiantly, had little hope that Mother Jones, labor's indomitable champion, would make it to her 100th birthday.

But when the great day dawned, she was not only still alive, she was also having the time of her life. On the gorgeous spring day of May 1, 1930, she basked happily amid people, gifts, flowers, and telegrams. They honored the woman whom a governor of Arizona had praised as "unquestionably the greatest woman America has ever produced."

"I was born in revolution," Mother Jones always boasted; a true statement, for when she, Mary Harris, was born on May 1, 1830, in a one-room thatched cottage in County Cork, Ireland, the impoverished "cotters" (cottage tenants) were being evicted by the wealthy absentee landowners, who had decided that it was more profitable to raise sheep and cows than to collect rents from cantankerous peasants. Blood flowed over the rolling green hills of County Cork. Hundreds of cotters were hanged, including Mary's grandfather. Her father, Richard, escaped the noose by fleeing to America in a fishing boat, vowing to send for his family as soon as he earned the money. Although it took 11 years, he was true to his word.

By then Richard had found work on a Toronto railroad, and there in icy Canada, the family found a sliver of paradise. Best of all, Toronto had a free public school system, including a normal school for training teachers, from which Mary graduated with honors. But when she applied for a teaching certificate, she was turned down. Roman Catholics were not permitted to teach in the public schools.

Hand-to-mouth years followed. Learning that the Memphis, Tennessee, school system was in need of teachers, she took the first train south. She arrived in July 1860, was hired in August, fell in love in September, married in October, and was fired in November.

But she was happy in her marriage to a tall, thin, compassionate ironmolder named George Jones who, on his Sundays off, was an organizer for the outlawed Knights of Labor. After the birth of their fourth child, Mary began to accompany him on his secret organizing trips with the four tots tagging along.

It was too good to last, and it didn't. In the summer of 1867, a yellow-fever epidemic swept Memphis. In one terrible week Mary lost her husband and four children. "I sat alone through nights of grief," she wrote in her autobiography. "No one came. No one could. Other homes were stricken, just as mine."

Mary Jones emerged from that crucifying experience forever scornful of death and burning with a fierce determination to spend the remainder of her life working ceaselessly for the exploited class. It was a formidable challenge. Labor had no rights; owners dictated wages, hours of work, and working conditions. Child labor was a mainstay of industry. Little girls, some as young as seven, made up a large percentage of the textile work force. In the anthracite coalfields of eastern Pennsylvania, breaker boys ("sad, gray, old men," Mother Jones wrote) spent their childhoods

Mary began to accompany him on his secret organizing trips with the four tots tagging along.

hunched over coal chutes, picking slate from the cascading coal.

Childless now, 37-year-old Mary Harris Jones began a 60-year career as mother to labor. She became an organizer for the Knights of Labor, then for the United Mine Workers of America. She organized miners' unions in many states, but her longest struggles took place in West Virginia, where conditions were most deplorable. She participated in the great strikes of the 19th and early 20th centuries, and there were many. She led the strikes against the railroad barons, the meat packers, the steel magnates, the textile oligarchs, but most of all, against the lairds of coal.

She was at Homestead in 1892 when the Carnegie Steel Corporation broke the steelworkers' strike by sending 300 armed Pinkerton guards against them. She was in Colorado in 1914 directing the strike against the Rockefellers' Colorado Fuel and Iron when the National Guard fired on the marchers, resulting in the infamous Ludlow Massacre. In 1903 Mother Jones led a small army of children, many mutilated from mill accidents, to New York City. Her plan was to bring the parade to the summer home of President Theodore Roosevelt on Oyster Bay, Long Island. The president refused to receive them, but her well-publicized march helped develop popular support for national child-labor laws.

Industry attacked her with every weapon it possessed. She was denounced as "a vulgar, heartless creature who inflames the ignorant workers to bite the hand that feeds them." She was spat at, kicked, and clubbed. Jail became routine for Mother Jones; she was 86 when she was jailed for the last time. She didn't quit her efforts until late in her nineties.

Mother Jones died six months after reaching 100 and was buried in a union-owned cemetery in an Illinois coal-mining town. She fought countless battles, lost most, but left a legacy that became the foundation of the American labor movement.

A stranger once asked the little grandmotherly looking lady if she was a housewife. "Hell, no," Mother Jones retorted, "I'm a hell-raiser and proud of it."

A more fitting epitaph would be hard to find.

Small of stature but powerful in her ideals, Mother Jones fought a lifelong crusade for laborers.

– Culver Pictures

MATHEW B. BRADY
(1823-1896): PIONEER PHOTOGRAPHER

The picnic hampers were stuffed; every carriage and gig had been rented; there wasn't a saddle horse to be found. The young ladies were giddy with excitement — how often did one have the opportunity to witness a real battle? It was July 1861, and Confederate and Union troops were massing near Centreville, Virginia. The Battle of Bull Run was about to begin, and official Washington wanted a front seat.

From studio portraits to battlefield scenes, Mathew Brady documented life in mid-19th-century America.

Mathew Brady, America's fashionable photographer, had left Washington at midnight en route to Centreville. Brady saw himself as the recorder of history, and it was his determination to make a complete pictorial record of the war and its campaigns for all the world to see.

Although he would be noted for an art that revealed every detail, Mathew Brady's life remains something of a mystery. He was born in Warren County, New York, either in 1823 or 1824. Little is known of his background. There is no evidence that he ever went to school; in fact, many biographers have held that he was illiterate. Illiterate or not, Brady was a brilliant man, a pioneer in a new technology, whose accomplishments remain unparalleled.

Brady left home when he was 16 and moved to New York City. There, at the same time, was Samuel F. B. Morse, a trained scientist and inventor of the telegraph, from which he had yet to make a penny. Hard up for funds, Morse opened the first school of photography in America, teaching the process recently invented by Frenchman Louis J. M. Daguerre. A box camera was used to take the pictures, but instead of using paper, Daguerre used silver plates coated with silver iodide. The results, called daguerreotypes, were amazingly lifelike pictures.

The tuition was $50, a fortune back then, but Brady paid it, graduated, and became a photographer. He opened Brady's Daguerrian Miniature Gallery on Broadway, a block from Astor House, the city's best hotel. It was a perfect location to snare the elite. No dumbbell, Brady made himself conspicuous. Only 5'6", lean and wiry, he sported a mass of bushy hair, a large moustache, and a neat goatee. He wore bright scarves and a trademark Parisian artist's flat-topped, broad-brimmed hat.

Brady prospered as the famous and the infamous flocked to his studio. From the beginning, it was his passion for photographing "history" that made his collection so unique. From 1844 on, practically every famous American had his or her picture taken by Brady, including Dolley Madison, then in her eighties. He photographed American presidents from John Quincy Adams to William McKinley; he took pictures of Abraham Lincoln, Henry Clay, Daniel Webster, even a young Prince of Wales.

Honors multiplied, money flowed in. Brady decided to open a studio in Washington, D.C., and again, as in New York, everyone came to have portraits made. Then in 1861, as war talk abounded and a battle seemed imminent, a grandiose plan began brewing in Brady's head. Why not be the first to photograph a battle? He made an appointment to see the newly inaugurated president, Abraham Lincoln. Lincoln said he had no objection as long as Brady didn't get in the way and paid his own

– Culver Pictures

expenses. Armed with his official "Pass Brady" from Lincoln, he rushed about getting the equipment he would need and made arrangements with illustrated journals, such as *Harper's Weekly*, to publish the photographs.

By July 19 Brady was ready. He moved south with his black photographic wagon, dubbed "Brady's what's-it" by the troops, and prepared to photograph the Battle of Bull Run. At sunset, July 21, the stampede of the Union troops was in full force, and the horrified spectators had fled back to Washington. Mathew Brady limped into the city three days after the battle, his wagon destroyed and his horse dead, but he had managed to salvage a dozen or so plates and carried them back in a wooden box. Brady's Bull Run photographs sold hundreds of copies. For the first time, Americans saw the true horror of war, up close, in amazingly clear pictures.

> For the first time, Americans saw the horror of war, up close, in amazingly clear pictures.

Before the war ended, Brady would have his photographic wagon in every theater of the war. He said later he spent over $100,000 and "had men in all parts of the army, just like a rich newspaper." The job of photographing the war was unbelievably difficult, and there are few examples of "action shots"; one of the few was taken at the Battle of Antietam by Brady's camera. At first the pictures commanded premium prices, but competition arose, the market became saturated, and Brady was forced to store his plates in warehouses.

By the end of the war, Brady was hopelessly in debt. His dream was that the priceless collection he had gathered would be bought by the government and displayed in a national gallery. But the government wasn't interested; the public was sick of the war and had no interest in perpetuating painful memories. Brady was forced to file for bankruptcy, and his precious plates were sold at auction. Brady's eyesight, never good, was rapidly worsening, and now in the prime of his life, the man who had brought a new vision to America was himself nearly blind.

"Brady of Broadway" died in a New York hospital alms ward on January 15, 1896, and he was laid to rest in Arlington National Cemetery among the Civil War dead. His presidential pictures, his battlefield photographs, still stand as a stunning testimony to his greatness. Mathew Brady's contribution remains timeless, a documentary of the 19th century.

JOHN GREENLEAF WHITTIER
(1807-1892): ABOLITIONIST'S BARD

There are better poets than John Greenleaf Whittier. Even he admitted that, saying: "I am not one of the master singers and don't pose as one. By the grace of God I am only what I am and don't wish to pass for more." Although dismissed by a majority of today's critics as a mere barnyard poet, the "Quaker poet" had a tremendous following among the common folk of New England.

His themes were farm themes — the spring mud, the smell of new-mown hay, the falling leaves, the husking bee. His religion was one of faith, not intellect. Farm boys and girls, drawn to the textile mills of the cities, loved Whittier. He brought back memories of clean air and deep silences, birds and trees, fields and flowers.

John Greenleaf Whittier was born on an isolated farm near Haverhill, Massachusetts, on December 17, 1807. His only companions were his brothers and sisters. When in later years he rhapsodized about the simple pleasures of farm life, he must have felt more than a few twinges of conscience, for it had been a hard life. Overwork in inclement weather brought on a number of chronic ailments. Cash money was as rare as corn on the Fourth of July. But the sweet memories — the wild grapes, the woods covered with new-fallen snow — were too precious to remain buried.

GREAT·AMERICANS

HALL
OF
FAME

Whittier had little formal schooling, but when he was 14 an itinerant peddler gave him a battered copy of Robert Burns's poetry, and he was enthralled. He began to write crude verse whose themes were a love of nature and the need for social equality. When he was 19, his sister sent

one of his poems to the Newburyport *Free Press,* whose young editor, William Lloyd Garrison, was just beginning his stormy career as an abolitionist. Garrison printed the poem and asked for more. When none appeared, he rode out to the farm and found Whittier, in tattered overalls, under the barn looking for eggs. Garrison told Whittier's father that his son was a "genius of a high order" and persuaded him to enroll the young man in the recently opened Haverhill Academy.

Two years at the academy improved Whittier's education enormously and enabled him to compare his verse with that of the great masters. He worked at odd jobs to pay his tuition, devoting his meagre spare time to writing poetry and "sparking" the town girls. He struck out on both counts. His collected poems were rejected by publishers, and he was turned down by at least two town beauties with such cruel finality that he came close to suicide.

John Greenleaf Whittier, the "Quaker poet," was fierce in his devotion to abolitionism and poetry.

But he survived. He found a job as a teacher, read Byron, Wordsworth, and Shelley, and wrote letters to editors deploring slavery and cruelty to animals, felons, and Indians. His impassioned writing led to an offer of the position of editor with the *New England Weekly Review,* a highly regarded Hartford, Connecticut, publication.

Whittier spoke of the 18 months in Hartford as the happiest of his life. He was a rising star and was fawned upon by the girls. Sickness forced him to resign his editorship, and he crept back to the farm, feeling a dismal failure. But he was a Quaker, and Quakers frowned on quitters; adversity should be regarded as a blessing, the means by which one hones his character. So he plunged into farm life, wrote poems by candlelight — by 1833 he had written over 300 — and supported the abolitionist cause.

Garrison, now editing the *Liberator* in Boston, was in the process of founding the New England Antislavery Society. He wrote to Whittier in 1833 exhorting him to apply his talents to the cause. Whittier was galvanized into publishing, at his own expense, a pamphlet arguing for emancipation. He so infuriated the antiabolitionists that he was placed on the blacklist of many publications that had previously published his poetry.

The Rubicon crossed, Whittier left the farm in charge of a brother and devoted his time to antislavery agitation. He traveled New England, preaching abolitionism and promoting antislavery candidates, and served

– Culver Pictures

for a time in the Massachusetts legislature. He became a marked man, nearly losing his life in Pennsylvania when he escaped an armed mob that was shouting, "Hang Whittier! Hang Whittier!"

For 20 years he pleaded, in poetry and prose, for nonviolent action in freeing the slaves, breaking with Garrison who had grown ever more belligerent. As the nation stumbled closer to armed conflict, Whittier argued that disunion was better than war. Finally, worn out by years of fighting, he withdrew and moved to Amesbury. Always proud of his "nature poetry," he settled down to writing ballads of rural life, idylls of village and farm — "The Barefoot Boy," "Telling the Bees," "The Old Burying-Ground."

He became a celebrity. America rushed to buy his poems, women swooned over him. He who had once yearned for female approbation now wanted to be left alone; he fled, spending many afternoons roaming the countryside in disguise. John Greenleaf Whittier died on September 7, 1892. He, who once said he didn't expect to live to the age of 40, was 84 years old. By then his abolitionist poetry was long forgotten, but his "Yankee pastorals" endured.

GEORGE MOWBRAY
(1814-1891): PRACTICAL SCIENTIST

Born in England, George Mowbray became a key figure in America's fledgling oil industry.

It was somewhere around midnight on Saturday, August 27, 1859, near Titusville in northwestern Pennsylvania. History was about to be made. Drake's Folly, the first well drilled with the specific aim of finding oil, was ready to release its black gold. There was no one around to witness the momentous event, but a farmer living near the derrick heard what he described as "a buncha hiccupin' fer a minute or two, then a kinda burp like."

That's how the mammoth petroleum industry arrived. Not with a bang but with a burp.

George Mowbray joined in the rush to the well the next day. The oil rained down in misty clouds and flowed into nearby ditches. It was a wonderful, hideous, awful, beautiful mess.

Mowbray was 45 years old. He had reached Titusville the long way around. Born in Brighton, England, on May 5, 1814, he had received an excellent education, then took advanced courses in medicine, chemistry, and engineering. He became a prosperous drug manufacturer, but after suffering a breakdown in 1854, followed his doctor's advice to take a long sea voyage and booked passage on a clipper bound for California.

Mowbray was a brilliant man with an inquisitive mind, and he had been keeping up-to-date with scientific developments. Thus, when he read that a consortium was drilling for oil in northwestern Pennsylvania, he went to Titusville. He watched the drilling, took a sample of the oil, and came to the conclusion that an enormous opportunity beckoned. In the space of four months he built a small refinery, and when Drake's well came in, Mowbray was ready. He refined the world's first crude oil and produced clear, clean kerosene, several lubricants, and a number of other by-products.

By then, the stampede was on. Towns sprang up overnight, derricks became as plentiful as chestnut trees, other refineries were built. Overnight kerosene became the illuminant in America's lamps, and petroleum lubricants replaced whale blubber in machinery. But by 1865 many wells had run dry or dwindled to a trickle. The problem was twofold: paraffin clogging the pipes, and loss of pressure. The boom seemed doomed.

George Mowbray thought he had the solution. He planned to use a powerful liquid explosive called nitroglycerin, which had been discovered by an Italian chemist, Ascanio Sobrero, and which was enormously more powerful than black powder. Nitroglycerin had been too unstable to be manufactured commercially, until Alfred Nobel of the Swedish family of munitions makers had discovered accidentally that when mixed with saw-dust, diatomaceous earth, and ground walnut shells, it became a much safer explosive. (This became dynamite and made the Nobels rich.)

A contract was signed and the first shot was made early in 1868. It was a stunning success.

Mowbray built a small factory in an isolated area and produced several gallons of the milky-looking liquid. But by the time he was ready to offer his solution to the gloomy well owners, a fellow named Colonel A. L. Roberts arrived on the scene with a four-foot-long tin torpedo containing four pounds of black powder. Roberts shot one test well, increasing the flow from a trickle to a rousing 30 barrels a day. Somewhat chagrined, Mowbray explained to Roberts that nitroglycerin would be easier to detonate and generate more energy; Roberts agreed to a test.

By then, dozens of owners were eager to pay from $300 to $1,000 to have their becalmed wells shot. Three quarts of Mowbray's nitroglycerin brought the next test well back to life. That did it. Mowbray's nitroglycerin was henceforth used in all Roberts's torpedoes; the two men had a monopoly. But, as usual, moonlighters sprang up, undercutting Mowbray and Roberts with nitroglycerin shipped in by Nobel. Overproduction and Wall Street speculation in oil shares brought on a panic, and wells shut down. But Mowbray, constantly improving both safety and efficiency in his nitroglycerin factory, had great faith in the explosive.

He put an ad in the *Scientific American* of December 8, 1866, inviting "parties requiring nitroglycerin in quantity to correspond with the subscriber." The commissioners of the Troy and Greenfield Railway in Massachusetts responded. They were in terrible trouble, the railroad having made little progress in trying to blast a 2,500-foot tunnel through Hoosac Mountain, near North Adams, Massachusetts.

A contract was signed and the first shot was made early in 1868. It was a stunning success, shattering tons of rock that black powder had barely dented. Mowbray manufactured over one million pounds of nitroglycerin at North Adams. The tunnel, still in use, is a tribute to a brilliant scientist.

After completion of the Hoosac Tunnel in 1875, Mowbray delivered tons of nitroglycerin for tunnel work to the Canadian Pacific Railroad, deliberately freezing the explosive to lessen its sensitivity in transport. He later did valuable work in celluloid, smokeless powder, and dynamite and wrote the first work on high explosives to be published in America.

George Mowbray died on June 22, 1891, in North Adams. One of his obituaries praised him as "a practical man who devoted his talents in a practical way to the solution of problems in line with the demands of the time."

CHIEF JOSEPH (1840-1904): RELUCTANT WARRIOR

It was General Philip Sheridan, hero of the Union Army, who purportedly insisted, "The only good Indians I ever saw were dead Indians." Sheridan, in charge of the Army in Indian Territory in 1869, was expressing the majority opinion back then. As the population surged westward, it was felt that "no pack of filthy, lying heathen" should stand in the way. A minority of citizens decried the federal government's policy of forcing the Indian to cede rich ancestral land in return for worthless reservation land, but following Custer's defeat at Little Bighorn in 1876, antagonism against all Indians intensified, and Sheridan's remark became the rallying cry for all those who insisted that their total extermination was long overdue.

Then, far out in the lush Wallowa Valley where the present states of Idaho, Oregon, and Washington join, there strode center stage, wearing the ceremonial robes of a royal personage, a tall, ruggedly built, handsome, 36-year-old Nez Percé chief named Inmuttooyahlatlat ("Thunder Rolling in the Mountains"): Chief Joseph to the white man.

Chief Joseph might have been just another faceless, defamed Indian had it not been for two scientific developments: the telegraph and photography. For over three months during the summer of 1877, an amazed nation followed the day-by-day war of the U.S. Army against Chief Joseph and his small band of Nez Percés. Outnumbered ten to one, Chief Joseph, a man of peace despite his thunderous Indian name, fought a brilliant retreat of nearly 1,300 miles before finally being trapped 30 miles south of the Canadian border, almost within sight of freedom.

The opening act of the tragedy took place in late September 1805. The Lewis and Clark expedition, after enjoying incredible success, encountered harsh weather conditions at the Bitterroot Range, between Montana and Idaho. Half-frozen and starving, they staggered down onto an "emence Plain and leavel Country," the homeland of the Nez Percé, a tribe that had never seen a white man. There their epic journey might have ended had not the Nez Percés ("Chearfull people with apparent sincerity") cared for the explorers with great tenderness. When the expedition resumed its journey, outfitted with fine horses and canoes, both sides pledged eternal friendship.

Eternity lasted for about 30 years. Then came the missionaries and mis-

Chief Joseph, tenacious defender of his people, the Nez Percé, unwittingly led them into tragedy.

sion schools. Chief Joseph's father, also called Joseph, was educated in such a school. With the increased use of the Oregon Trail in the 1840s, settlers appeared in the Wallowa Valley and began to pressure the tribe to give up some of its territory in return for smaller reservation land. Old Chief Joseph, imbued with his new religion, signed the treaty in 1855. Then gold was discovered on the reservation; the old chief refused to renegotiate the treaty, but through bribery and chicanery some of the land was lost.

Before his death, the chief summoned his son and warned him never to give away the tribal land. But more settlers moved in, tensions mounted, and President Grant issued an edict giving the entire Wallowa valley to the whites, moving the Nez Percés to Oklahoma.

This was the last straw to the young braves. They demanded a war, but Chief Joseph counseled patience, believing the president would rescind his order once he learned the truth. He wrote many messages to Washington, but following the death of an Indian, the young warriors went on the warpath, killing four of the attackers and providing the government with an excuse for all-out war.

The young braves demanded a war, but Chief Joseph counseled patience.

Broken-hearted, Chief Joseph determined to fight a rearguard action while leading his people to safety in Canada. By the middle of June during that summer of 1877, Joseph had organized his warriors (never more than 250), ferried the cattle, the old, and the young across the swollen Salmon River, and was ready to begin the long trek to freedom. But General O. O. Howard, in charge of the Military Department of the Columbia, sent an advance contingent of cavalrymen that was sighted before the warriors could cross the river. Chief Joseph planned a successful ambush in White Bird Canyon, killing 36 cavalrymen and losing only two of his men. Howard gathered up 300 regulars and took charge himself, but by then the Nez Percés had moved to the mountains, and Howard's unit was repulsed again with heavy losses.

Now the newspapers and photographers took over. For the next 113 days Chief Joseph outmaneuvered and outfought forces far superior in manpower and firepower. Impressed by his brilliant tactics, his concern for the members of his tribe, and his humane treatment of enemy prisoners and wounded, the press worked overtime to provide their papers with accounts of his accomplishments and his bravery. A mesmerized nation watched in mounting admiration as Joseph and his Nez Percés eluded everything the U.S. Army could throw at them. They fought through Idaho, Montana, Oregon, Washington — in the Bitterroots, where their ancestors had nursed the Lewis and Clark expedition back to life.

By late September the army had over 3,000 troops in the field, armed with howitzers, Gatling machine guns, and the latest Winchester rifles. Finally on October 5, with only 80 able-bodied warriors plus 184 women and 117 children, the latter two groups barely alive, Chief Joseph surrendered near the Bear Paw Mountains just south of the Canadian border.

His speech would ring through the decades. "I am tired of fighting," he said. "Our chiefs are killed. Our old men are all dead. It is cold and we have no blankets. The little children are freezing to death. . . . Hear me, I am tired; my heart is sick and sad. From where the sun now stands, I will fight no more ever."

No mercy was shown. The Nez Percés were shipped in boxcars to bleak Indian Territory, where many died. Agitation back east finally forced the government to transfer the remnants of the tribe to Washington State, and it was there Chief Joseph died. He had wanted above all to be a man of peace; necessity made him the greatest tactician the northern Indian tribes ever produced.

LUTHER BURBANK (1849-1926): PLANT WIZARD

Luther Burbank maintained that he disliked being labeled a plant wizard, but the name and the publicity it generated helped him sell plants and seeds. He needed all his wizardry in the late 1880s when a large cannery asked him if he could develop a pea that would rival the dainty French petit pois: uniform in size, sweet, all pods maturing at the same time. By then canneries and seed companies expected the plant wizard to create new plants to order, as one might give an architect specifications for a new castle with a drawbridge.

Plant breeder Luther Burbank revolutionized horticulture – and gave us the Burbank potato and the Shasta daisy.

Burbank took the order, but said it would take six years, for he was busy trying to develop a mammoth pea for another cannery. It took only three years, not six, and a mere 200,000 plantings to come up with the perfect petit pois; unfortunately, the large-pea project never made it.

Still, one out of two was cause for rejoicing, for 75 percent of his experiments ended in failure. Burbank's supposed wizardry can be attributed to the multiplication table, the law of averages, and above all, hard work. Until he came along, hybridization — the breeding of plants of different varieties or species to produce a more beautiful or productive strain — was the province of university-trained horticulturists who usually worked with one or two varieties, all allowed to grow at nature's pace. Burbank quadrupled the number of plantings, matings, and graftings, and forced his specimens to grow much faster than nature intended.

– Culver Pictures

Luther Burbank was born on a farm in Lancaster, Massachusetts, on March 7, 1849. He received a good education, studying the classics and sciences and reading the works of the great naturalists. "When I was about nineteen," he wrote, "I borrowed Darwin's *Variation of Animals and Plants Under Domestication* from the local library. It was the most inspiring book I have ever read . . . it has been the main influence on my life."

At 21 Luther used his share of his deceased father's estate to buy 17 acres in nearby Lunenburg and became a market gardener. He began to experiment with "new creations," mating various varieties of the same vegetable. His efforts produced nothing until he accidentally came upon an Early Rose potato plant bearing a seed ball. Taking a chance, Burbank planted each of the 23 seeds contained in the ball. One seed produced a well-shaped potato with a white skin. This became the famous "Burbank potato," superb for baking.

From the one potato, he raised several dozen tubers and sent them to established New England seedsmen. One merchant sold $3,000 worth of potatoes for seed that first year, advertising it as the "Burbank seedling potato" — the first recognition accorded the eventual wizard. In the meantime, three of Luther's brothers had settled in California, and they sent back glowing reports. Convinced that California offered excellent possibilities, in 1875 Luther sold his farm and took a train out to Santa Rosa, 50 miles north of San Francisco. He immediately wrote back home, "I firmly believe from what I have seen that it is the chosen spot on earth as far as Nature is concerned."

It may well have been paradise, but manna had not yet begun to drop from heaven. Luther had to take a series of odd jobs in order to support himself, but busy as he was, he managed to rent a few acres and plant nursery stock. The business grew. Luther had arrived in California at the right time; with the gold mines depleted, people had begun to realize the enormous potential for agricultural wealth. Large orchards sprang up, and Luther worked long hours to supply plants and trees.

He was doing moderately well by the spring of 1882, when a banker, lured by the "prune fever" sweeping the country, offered to pay $5,000 plus expenses if Burbank could deliver 20,000 plum trees by December. Burbank took the challenge. He couldn't take the time to plant plum seedlings, because plums grow too slowly; instead he bought 20,000 almond nuts, which belong to the genus *Prunus* and which sprout much faster. He sprouted them, grafted on 20,000 plum buds, and completed the order by December 1. Enthralled, the banker gave him a bonus of $3,500.

That feat brought Burbank national publicity in farm and home journals and newspapers. Luther Burbank was on his way. He sold his nursery, bought 18 acres, and committed himself exclusively to the development of new varieties of plants, using the mass production method of the plum-tree project.

Over the next 44 years, Burbank created anywhere from 125 to 800 new species (depending on whose figures, his or his detractors, are used). Every year a new Burbank creation appeared in the seed catalogs. Schoolchildren wrote him; presidents issued proclamations on his birthdays.

All was not perfection. As the years went by and Burbank frantically kept turning out dozens of new varieties, nature gradually caught up with him. His spineless cactus, trumpeted as the perfect food for cattle in drought areas, needed prodigious amounts of water to stay alive. His "winter rhubarb" froze to death in New England. His "sunberry" perished in the North Dakota summer.

When he died at Santa Rosa in 1926, he was eulogized as the man who revolutionized horticulture, but time has dimmed his name. Only a few of his creations — the Shasta daisy, the Burbank potato — are listed in seed catalogs. Perhaps his fame lies more in the intangible results of his work. He popularized horticulture among millions of amateur gardeners, and he gave a great impetus to the study of plant breeding.

Over the next 44 years, Burbank created anywhere from 125 to 800 new species.

EMILY DICKINSON (1830-1886): RHAPSODIST

The poor little reclusive "Maid of Amherst." She has been dissected, explicated, probed, and analyzed by everyone from famous psycho-biographers to the offspring of her family's household maids. The inquiry has been going on for over a hundred years. The verdict: a hung jury. She was either mad or not mad. She was either a shrewd, canny, narcissistic publicity seeker whose plan to go into temporary seclusion in order to attract attention backfired and doomed her to permanent reclusion; or she was a dedicated poet who shut herself off from the outside world to be free to pursue her chosen craft.

Emily Dickinson was born in the college town of Amherst, Massachusetts, on December 10, 1830, the second child of Edward and Emily Norcross Dickinson. Her father was a lawyer, treasurer of Amherst College, and later a representative to the United States Congress. While not rich, the family lived well. Emily had a happy childhood with many close girlfriends. They gossiped and giggled, played jokes on each other, went on huckleberry excursions and sleigh rides. She attended Amherst Academy and spent a year at Mount Holyoke, excelling in the difficult courses and being named the Belle of the Class.

Back home in Amherst, she began to evidence little peculiarities. Unlike other girls of her station, she felt no desire to visit the sick, aid the poor, choose a religion. Her parents had little influence over her. When she was 16 and her father decided it was time the family joined a church, Emily locked herself in the basement with a mind-jostling book. Decades of exhaustive digging have failed to unearth irrefutable proof that she ever had a lover. Her younger sister Lavinia always maintained there just wasn't one.

She was an authentic agnostic. She made a gallant effort to embrace atheism, but always turned back at the last moment, unable to concede that the subjects of her verse — the grass ("A sphere of simple green"), the bee ("His feet are shod with gauze, his helmet is of gold") — all came about accidentally.

She began writing seriously in 1853, gradually becoming more reclusive. All biographers agree that she underwent a deep emotional trauma in 1862 that ignited a frenzied explosion of poetry, as many as 350 poems that year alone. If so, perhaps Thomas Wentworth Higginson, literary editor of the *Atlantic Monthly*, must bear the blame — or credit.

Higginson was Emily's first preceptor, to whom she sent samples of her work, and it was he who responded with such cruel phrases as "spasmodic metres" and "uncontrolled lyrics." He seemed more interested in how old she was and what she looked like than in her poetry. He may have been the unwitting instrument that galvanized poor Emily — who had "panged" for praise — into gritting her teeth and vowing never to stop writing her verse.

Higginson wasn't alone. None of the seven or eight critics to whom Emily had sent samples of her verses gave her the slightest wisp of en-

Emily Dickinson described herself as "small like the Wren, and my Hair is bold, like the Chestnut Burr ..."

— Culver Pictures

couragement. She violated all the rules of ladylike poetry by dwelling on such subjects as "The Snake," "Joy in Death," and "The Lovers." Most heinous was the manner in which she made fun of God ("The White Frost," "Papa up There") and such blasphemies as:

> *Of God we ask one favor*
> *That we may be forgiven —*
> *For what, he is presumed to know —*
> *The Crime, from us, is hidden.*

Emily replied to Higginson's letter, thanking him "for the surgery" and describing herself: ". . . small like the Wren, and my Hair is bold, like the Chestnut Burr and my eyes like Sherry in the Glass." She corresponded with him and the other preceptors for nearly 30 years. All failed to recognize her genius. Although Emily Dickinson had acquired a localized notoriety as an eccentric during her lifetime, she was thought to be little different from the "normal peculiar" New England spinster poet.

Emily died of Bright's disease on May 15, 1886, having published only seven poems, all anonymously, most attributed to Emerson. After her death, Lavinia found hundreds of poems in her bedroom and badgered Higginson into getting them published. They fell on a stunned world. More were published; finally, in 1955 the Thomas E. Johnson edition appeared, containing all 1,775 poems.

Emily Dickinson was an original. In all her lifetime she was away from Amherst only a few times, but in her poetry she roamed the cosmos. One of her last requests:

> *If I shouldn't be alive*
> *When the robins come,*
> *Give the one in red cravat*
> *A memorial crumb.*

MARY McLEOD BETHUNE
(1875-1955): EDUCATOR, CIVIL RIGHTS LEADER

Mary McLeod Bethune, a black woman born of freed slaves, always gave the Lord credit for helping her overcome the obstacles in her life. "Nothing in life has ever come without faith and prayer," she often said. She always hastened to add, "But nothing in my life has ever come without sweat, too."

She was born Mary Jane McLeod on July 10, 1875, in a log cabin near Mayesville, South Carolina, the 13th of 17 children. Her parents had managed to buy a few acres of land, and her father tilled his farm and hired out to plantations while her mother worked as a maid and laundress. All the children worked; when Mary was barely eight years old, she picked 200 pounds of cotton a day. In those days black people in the South had little chance of being educated or even learning to read. That fact was impressed upon Mary at a young age. While waiting on the veranda of a plantation mansion for her mother to finish work, she picked up a colorful book on a nearby table. Immediately a little white girl rushed over and grabbed the book from her. "That's not for such as you," she snapped.

Mary determined she would learn to read. When she was 11, a mission school opened, and Mary, the brightest of the McLeods, was chosen by the family to attend; their meagre resources were pooled to buy her clothes and school supplies. It was a proud day for them when 12-year-old Mary received her certificate of graduation, but there was no opportunity to use her education, and she returned to work on the farm, reading constantly and praying for an opportunity to continue her formal education.

Her prayers were answered. A Miss Chrissman, a white Quaker teacher in far-off Denver, Colorado, wrote to the Board of Missions for Freemen, offering a scholarship to a "deserving young Negro girl worthy of further education." Mary was chosen and spent seven years at Scotia Seminary, a school for black girls in North Carolina. Upon graduation, and determined to become a foreign missionary, Mary was accepted at the Moody Bible Institute in Chicago, her fees paid again by Miss Chrissman. Mary graduated with honors and eagerly awaited her appointment to "somewhere in Africa." But the Mission Board of the Presbyterian Church turned her down, claiming that "there were no openings for Negro missionaries in Africa." Or anywhere else. Mary remembered the incident as "the greatest disappointment in my life."

– courtesy Lawrence Doorley

She returned to Mayesville to teach, then moved to the Haines Normal Institute in Atlanta, Georgia, and on to two other schools in the South. In Sumter, North Carolina, she joined the church choir and fell in love with a fellow choir member, Albertus Bethune. They were married and in time a son was born. As Mary's reputation as a teacher grew, she felt ever more constricted by the inequalities and the inferior education offered to black children. She determined to do something about it.

She moved to Daytona, where many Negroes had settled to work on the Florida East Coast Railway, and in 1904 opened her school, the Daytona Educational and Industrial Training School for Negro Girls, in a ramshackle frame house near the railroad tracks. Her assets, she reported, were "Five little girls, a dollar and a half ... and faith in God." The news spread, parents dug deep for tuition, and soon the school outgrew its precarious location. Mary Bethune, never doubting that "God will provide," went begging. Her targets were the northern millionaires who, following the establishment of the railroad, had built winter homes in Florida. Mary got substantial contributions from the likes of James Gamble of Procter & Gamble, and John D. Rockefeller, and managed to purchase 20 acres in the former city dump. Buildings were erected, more teachers were hired, and the school was expanded to include boys.

Mary McLeod Bethune, a formidable figure, lived to see racial segregation outlawed.

Mary did not confine herself to running her school. She established the Tomoka Mission schools for the children of workers in the "turpentine camps," infamous hovels in the pine forests where workers lived in deplorable conditions. As no hospitals were available for Negroes, she raised $5,000 to build McLeod Hospital in Daytona. The 20-bed institution was run by her school, the Daytona Institute, for 20 years until the town finally agreed to build a facility.

Mary Bethune became a national celebrity. Honors descended on her. The Coolidge administration, perhaps seeking to improve its standing among blacks, sought to "adopt" her, but Mary would have none of it. She stormed up to Washington and demanded — and got — a commission devoted exclusively to minority affairs, with herself in charge. Herbert Hoover gave her even more authority, which she used to get more black men into supervisory positions and more money allocated to black schools. Eleanor Roosevelt became a friend and admirer, and when Franklin Roosevelt became president, he made Mary director of Negro Affairs in the National Youth Organization.

Her constant theme was to protect and exercise the right to vote.

Mary gave generously of her time to every organization devoted to the promotion of racial understanding. In 1920 she was elected to the board of the National Urban League, and in the 1930s she created the National Council of Negro Women. She was in demand as a lecturer to black groups, and her constant theme was to protect and exercise the right to vote. She supervised a merger between her Daytona school and a nearby boys' academy. Now known as Bethune-Cookman College, it is a fully accredited institution.

Mary McLeod Bethune died in her home on the campus on May 18, 1955. Born in an era when blacks had almost no rights, this valiant descendant of slaves had lived to see the Supreme Court of the United States declare that segregation according to color was unconstitutional.

CLARENCE BIRDSEYE
(1886-1956): JACK-OF-ALL-TRADES

Clarence Birdseye, an eccentric, adventurous maverick, raced through life full sail to the wind: curious, daring, indefatigable, an outspoken admirer of free enterprise. In his late years, when asked to summarize his life, he smiled and replied, "Well, I was just a jack-of-all-trades who went around asking a lot of damn fool questions and taking chances."

Born in Brooklyn, New York, on December 9, 1886, Clarence was one of eight children of an affluent lawyer and his wife. In high school he excelled in science, but during this period the family fortunes declined and college seemed out of the question. However, Clarence held a series of summer jobs until by the fall of 1908, he was able to enroll at Amherst College, Massachusetts, his father's alma mater. His studies included entomology, ornithology, mammology, and other science courses. He waited on tables to help pay his fees, and during what time was left, he roamed the fields, "Nature's bountiful garden."

On a cold spring day he stumbled on an open spring hole where thousands of hibernating frogs had congregated. Excited and knowing that snakes regard frogs as a supreme delicacy, he wrote the Bronx Zoo of his find and eventually netted $115 from the sale of hundreds of sleeping frogs, collected and shipped in wet burlap bags.

His efforts with a mail-order taxidermy business were less successful, but undaunted, he got into the black rat trade, his source being a mother lode of rats housed in a shed behind an Amherst butcher's shop. Once more his active mind shifted into high gear. He wrote Columbia University laboratories, which offered to take every rodent he could find. The deal not only earned Birdseye $135, but may have forestalled a bubonic plague in lovely Amherst.

Emboldened by his success, he left college at the end of his sophomore year and found a job as an assistant naturalist with the Biological Survey in the U. S. Department of Agriculture. His assignment was New Mexico and Arizona. Birdseye began cataloging birds and mammals and discovered that Indian traders were paying only 25¢ apiece for bobcat and coyote skins. He contacted furriers in New York City and was elated to learn they would pay $1 for a pelt. A telegram to several traders offering 50¢ for each skin eventually netted him a profit of $600.

Things were going great. He was only 26, had a fine position with the government, and a bright future lay ahead of him; however, he felt his scientific knowledge should be put to better use. Learning that the famous medical missionary Sir Wilfred Grenfell was about to embark for Labrador for a summer's work ministering to the Eskimos, Birdseye resigned his government job and joined the hospital ship in 1912.

It was a great and exciting summer; there was even an opportunity for an enterprising young fellow to make some money. Birdseye discovered that the fur traders had not considered shipping live silver foxes, abundant in the region, to American breeders. Telegrams to the United States convinced him there was a fortune to be made in exporting the beautiful animals.

Over the next two years Birdseye mushed over 5,000 miles with his dog teams, buying, feeding, and shipping foxes. He went broke when the Labrador government passed a law prohibiting export of the live animals, but soon found that no such restriction applied to the pelts. World War I had started by then, igniting a roaring prosperity in the United States, and Birdseye was able to obtain financial backing. After another year he was able to pay back the loan and realize a profit of $6,000.

Inveterate explorer and innovator Clarence Birdseye first froze vegetables in his baby's bathtub.

Meantime, love had blossomed. Birdseye returned to the States and proposed to Eleanor Gannett, daughter of a founder of the National Geographic Society. One can only imagine the feelings of the parents as they watched their daughter embark for a land where winter temperatures plummeted to 50 degrees below zero, where home was a three-room shack, the nearest doctor was 250 miles away, and life was dependent upon a 75-mile trapline. The couple, eventually with a child, lived happily in Labrador for two years.

All the while, Birdseye had been experimenting with the fish he caught through holes chopped in the ice. His curiosity had been aroused by the fact that the fish, frozen instantly in the subzero temperatures, when thawed much later "were juicier and more flavorful than similar foods frozen in relatively mild weather." He and Eleanor began to experiment in weather 45 degrees below zero, using the baby's bathtub to freeze fresh cabbage; when cooked it was as delicious as if freshly harvested.

Returning to the United States, Birdseye worked for a company involved in shipping iced fish coast to coast. Horrified at the spoilage and remembering the Labrador experiments, he moved to Gloucester, Massachusetts, founded a company called General Seafoods, and began an eight-year struggle to perfect a commercially practical method of quick-freezing fish. This turned out to be the easy part; selling the grocers and housewives of America on frozen fish was the hard part.

Clarence and Eleanor, with four children and on the verge of bankruptcy, never flinched. Finally, in 1926, Lady Luck, in the person of heiress Marjorie Merriweather Post, hove into view. While her yacht was in harbor, her chef had gone ashore and bought both frozen fish and frozen goose at Birdseye's retail store. Mrs. Post was so impressed by the tenderness and delicacy of both foods that she persuaded her husband, Wall Street broker E. F. Hutton, to go ashore with her and interview Birdseye. Hutton invested immediately and prevailed upon several of his associates to do so. The project was saved, and three years later the Postum Company (which Mrs. Post inherited) paid $22,000,000 for General Seafoods. On March 6, 1930, the first packages of Birds Eye frozen food appeared in grocery stores in Springfield, Massachusetts. Birdseye, who already held over 100 patents, spent the last 20 years of his life perfecting another hundred inventions.

Clarence Birdseye wasn't the first person to freeze food. He did perfect the process, and in doing so he invented a $500 billion industry — quite commendable for a self-styled "jack-of-all-trades."

MARGARET SANGER
(1883-1966): BIRTH-CONTROL PIONEER

Not every heroine goes into battle as confident as Joan of Arc was when she led the French against the mighty English army in 1429. Another heroine, whose valiant fight against ignorance and intolerance made an even more lasting impression on the world, began her fight in a little meeting room on the Lower East Side of New York City in 1911.

"I was frightened," she later wrote, "Shaking and quaking, I faced the little handful of women. . . ."

Margaret Sanger was 28 years old that momentous evening; a slim, somewhat frail-looking woman with masses of red hair piled atop her head. Margaret had a high school education, a brilliant mind, and was also a trained nurse. The subject that evening was women's reproductive organs. As a public health nurse in the tenement districts, Margaret was appalled at the number of young women who were dying at a young age, worn out from constant childbearing. Even worse was the terrible number dying from self-inflicted abortions. Someone, she felt, had to speak out against this frightening inhumanity.

Margaret started that night. Hesitantly, her voice quivering, she began to talk about "the simple facts of sex and reproduction." The nine women present, many of them mothers of five or six children and fated to have many more, sat engrossed, hearing for the first time in their lives the kind of information they desperately needed and that was always denied them.

Margaret was appalled at the number of women dying at a young age...

The meeting was an enormous success. The next week 70 eager women pushed their way into the hall; the following week a hundred came. By the third week Margaret, becoming more confident and more exhilarated, changed the sessions to questions and answers. *The Call,* a Socialist paper, asked her to put them in a weekly column, "What Every Mother Should Know." In it she discussed the beauty, wonder, and sacredness of sex. A follow-up column, "What Every Girl Should Know," was an equal success.

She was born Margaret Higgins on September 14, 1883 (some sources say 1879), in Corning, New York, the sixth of 11 children. The flower of the fold, the one for whom great expectations were held, she excelled at nearby Claverack College, becoming a student leader and an outspoken advocate of feminism. Following college, she came to New York to study nursing and met and married William Sanger, an architect; the marriage produced three children. The Sangers became part of a Socialist group that included Eugene Debs, Max Eastman, Emma Goldman, and Alexander Berkman. Those were heady days; they were going to change the world.

Margaret Sanger (shown here in 1945) fought for women's rights, especially reproductive freedom.

But Margaret's initial effort to change the world was temporarily thwarted by one Anthony Comstock of the Boston Watch and Ward Society, secretary of the New York Society for the Suppression of Vice, and United States Postal Inspector charged with keeping the mails free of obscene matter. Comstock had functioned as America's censor for almost 50 years, and he appeared at *The Call* with an order canceling the paper's mailing privileges. That was the beginning of Sanger's lifelong battle with "Comstockery," for though he died in 1915, the laws he had pushed through were still in existence.

Following Comstock's death, *The Call* hurriedly issued "What Every Girl Should Know" in pamphlet form; it would go through more than 50 printings, bringing the most elementary facts of life to girls and young women. Emboldened, Margaret began publishing *The Woman Rebel,* a journal devoted to radical feminism, advocating "birth control" (she originated the term), sexual autonomy, and equal rights. Outraged, Comstockery went to court, and she was arrested and jailed. Friends made bail, and Margaret fled to England.

Friends in New York had managed to have the charges against her dropped, and she returned. By then her cause had aroused enormous enthusiasm among women, and she determined to proceed, come what may. In 1916 she opened the first birth-control clinic in the United States in the squalid Brownsville section of Brooklyn. It was a dismal, gray October morning when the clinic opened, and Margaret and her helpers were full of anxiety, uncertain if any women would appear.

They need not have worried. By opening time, the line stretched around the block; over 150 women came, "some shawled, some hatless, their red hands clasping the cold, chapped, smaller ones of the children."

For nine joyous days Margaret and her followers were ecstatic. Then Comstockery struck again in the person of a member of the vice squad. Everyone was arrested, and the clinic's records were confiscated. Public interest mounted, and a huge rally was held at Carnegie Hall. Margaret was arrested and jailed, but her conviction was overturned by the New York State Court of Appeals, which ruled that physicians could give "contraceptive advice for the protection of health and prevention of disease."

By opening time, the line stretched around the block; over 150 women came.

With that victory events accelerated. In 1920 she published *Woman and the New Race*, which sold more than 300,000 copies. In 1921 she became president of the American Birth Control League, whose aim was to influence public opinion and lobby for the elimination of the Comstock laws.

Margaret divorced her husband in 1921 and married J. Noah Slee, a wealthy owner of Three-in-One-Oil. His money financed the birth-control movement from then on. She established a new clinic but stayed within the law, dispensing contraceptives only to those women whose medical history ruled out any more pregnancies; other women were referred to physicians who believed in the cause.

By then an international celebrity, Margaret toured the world lecturing on birth control, women's rights, and population control. She became president of the Planned Parenthood Federation of America, initiated funding for the development of the oral birth-control pill, and never ceased proclaiming that "women must demand the right to exercise ultimate control over their own bodies." She spent her last years in retirement in Tucson, Arizona, dying there on September 6, 1966. The tremulous crusade that she began with nine women on the dingy Lower East Side had grown to a massive movement still affecting the entire world.

Someone else would have eventually begun the birth-control movement once the Comstock laws were repealed in the 1930s, but Margaret Sanger took up the banner when the cause seemed hopeless. As Joan of Arc was urged on by "voices from above," Margaret Sanger once wrote, "All my life I have acted on an inner voice, and when it speaks to me, it speaks wisely and never fails me."

KNUTE ROCKNE (1888-1931): GRIDIRON GENIUS

At the turn of the century it was a struggling, unknown Catholic college in northern Indiana. The small campus was dominated by the main building with its golden dome topped by the statue of the Blessed Virgin. The enrollment was 400.

It is now the most prestigious Catholic university in America, if not in the whole world. Its endowment of $600 million exceeds that of more prominent schools. The enrollment is 9,500, and 90 percent of last year's freshmen were in the top ten percent of their high school class.

The golden dome and Our Mother (Notre Dame) would no doubt still be there anyway, but without a Protestant Norwegian named Knute Rockne, Notre Dame would still be one of dozens of fine, small Catholic colleges barely known beyond their geographical boundaries.

Knute Rockne was born in Voss, Norway, on March 4, 1888. After his father, a carriage maker, won second prize for one of his carriages at the World's Columbian Exposition in Chicago in 1893, the family emigrated and settled in a predominantly Swedish neighborhood in Chicago. Rockne would always remain a Swede to his Notre Dame classmates.

Knute was an all-around high school athlete and after graduation worked to accumulate enough money to enter the University of Illinois. But friends prevailed upon him to enter Notre Dame, only 85 miles away. Knute arrived with a suitcase, $1,000, and a determination to excel in the classroom. He was 22, older than his classmates, going bald, and he talked in a rapid-fire, staccato bark; all that, coupled with his jug ears and smashed nose, made him a standout on the campus.

He went out for football and became the varsity right end. At this time a new coach, Jesse Harper, had taken over to infuse more life and enthusiasm into the athletic program. The president of Notre Dame, Father John Cavanaugh, regarded varsity sports as too expensive for the cash-poor college, but Harper had other ideas. When mighty Army, the scourge of collegiate football, needed a breather in its 1913 schedule, it offered Notre Dame $600 to come to West Point and play the cadets. Harper held out for $1,000.

Harper's ace-in-the-hole was the forward pass. He had Rockne and quarterback Gus Dorais practice, practice, practice all through the summer. Every football fan knows what the outcome was on that gray November afternoon in 1913. The outweighed, ill-equipped Notre Dame team trounced mighty Army 35-13. Dorais threw an unheard-of 17 passes and Rockne caught nine of them.

As player and coach, Knute Rockne brought college football – and especially Notre Dame – to unprecedented heights.

Rockne was a second team all-American in his senior year and graduated magna cum laude. He accepted a position as a graduate assistant in chemistry with the provision that he be allowed to help Harper coach football, and when Harper retired in 1918, Rockne became coach.

Knute Rockne coached Notre Dame's football team for 13 years. His teams won 105 games, lost 12, tied 5, a winning percentage still at the top of the list of college football. He was an innovator. His teams were quick, and they had to be. Jack Elder, a star halfback of the late 1920s, said, "Rock was a severe taskmaster, demanding perfection in all his assignments. He hesitated to pass out compliments . . . they came begrudgingly."

Genius notwithstanding, Rockne had an enormous amount of star material to work with. As the college's fame spread, the high school stars of Catholic parochial schools descended on Notre Dame in numbers that taxed the equipment department. One of those small-town heroes appeared on the campus in the fall of 1916. His name was George Gipp, and he was the most famous athlete in the history of Calumet High in Laurium, Michigan. Gipp was actually at the school on a baseball scholarship, but he never did play baseball for Notre Dame. Rockne saw him kicking punts on the field one day, and the next day he was on the freshman squad.

Gipp played four years for Notre Dame. On the field he was a terror to opposing players; off the field he caused Rockne almost as much trouble. No saint, he was twice expelled and only readmitted on Rockne's plea that redemption was possible. On December 14, 1920, George Gipp lay dying of pneumonia in the hospital in South Bend. Rockne was with him when he received the final rites of the Roman Catholic church. When the lights dimmed in the Oliver hotel, his favorite hangout, everyone knew the Gipp was gone.

When the lights dimmed in the Oliver hotel, everyone knew the Gipp was gone.

It was at the 1928 game against Army in Yankee Stadium, before 78,188 rabid spectators, that Rockne used his famous "Win One for the Gipper" speech. Jack Elder claimed that no one ever doubted what Gipp's last words had been: "Someday, Rock, when the going gets tough . . . the boys are up against it . . . tell them to win one for the Gipper . . . I'll know about it." It worked. Notre Dame beat Army that day 12-6.

Notre Dame kept winning. It was Grantland Rice, a famous sportswriter of the era, who christened the 1924 backfield of Stuhldreher, Miller, Crowley, and Layden, the "Four Horsemen." Rockne was better known than many movie stars, and Notre Dame became the best-advertised college in the country.

By the beginning of 1931, Rockne and the school were riding the crest of an unprecedented wave of publicity, and he was earning large fees speaking at public gatherings. The *Chicago Tribune* described him as "looking like a beaten-up tin can"; Grantland Rice wrote, "He has a magnetism, an indefinable champion's touch . . . Rockne of Notre Dame is unique . . . he has no equal."

Hollywood beckoned. A series of football documentaries was in the works, but Rockne never reached Hollywood. He died in a plane crash in eastern Kansas on March 31, 1931.

Given today's lack of real heroes, it is impossible to comprehend what Knute Rockne meant to America. One current Notre Dame rooter remembers his father bowing his head when the news came over the radio. "He was a saint," the father whispered. "If the Pope doesn't declare Knute Rockne a saint, then the church better get out of the business."

The prime requisite for Catholic sainthood is two authentic, well-documented miracles. Knute Rockne performed at least two every season before thousands of spectators.

DUKE ELLINGTON (1899-1974): CROWN PRINCE OF JAZZ

Edward Kennedy Ellington was born in Washington, D. C., on April 29, 1899. He reached his teens as a cherished boy, growing up in a well-regulated, middle-class household, where good behavior was expected and confidence in oneself an accepted virtue. Always the best dressed of his teenage group, he is supposed to have been dubbed "Duke" by one of them, not only for his elegant clothes but also for his grace and polish.

His mother, Daisy, had him take piano lessons at age 7, but because young

Edward seldomed practiced, they came to a stop. However, when he was 14, he became fascinated with a pianist he heard playing in a restaurant, impressed by the musician's "tremendous left hand" and his ability to "swing through the keys." To his mother's delight, he resumed lessons. A job as a soda jerk inspired his first composition, "Soda Fountain Rag" (1915).

Duke won an art scholarship to New York's Pratt Institute, but he turned it down. By then, smitten with ragtime, he had formed a small orchestra and was playing at parties and dances. Following graduation, he began gaining a reputation with his orchestra, moving from high school gyms to night clubs. Marriage and fatherhood forced him to seek a steadier income, so he took out the most expensive ad in the "orchestra" section of Washington's classified telephone directory. It paid off. He formed a larger band, bookings increased, the future seemed assured.

Fats Waller was so impressed with Duke and his orchestra that he induced him to give New York a try. The stage of the Kentucky Club, at 49th Street and Broadway, was where Duke launched his half-century career as a composer and bandleader.

The Kentucky Club was Big Time. Paul Whiteman was at the nearby Palais Royale, as many as 70 or 80 new plays and musicals were featured on Broadway every season, and though Prohibition was the law of the land, it had little effect on the Kentucky Club. "Duke Ellington and his Washingtonians" pushed out the parameters of popular dance music. He composed blues pieces — slow blues, fast blues — that became famous among musicians; he added new instrumentalists. His piano playing, influenced by some of the "greats" he heard in New York, developed a distinctive voice that became an integral part of the orchestral sound.

In 1927 the orchestra was booked into Harlem's famous Cotton Club,

His career in full swing, Duke Ellington rehearsed with trombonist Tommy Dorsey at a recording session.

where they stayed for five years. Gangster-owned, the club was operated as a tourist attraction for out-of-towners and rich New York "slummers," and it had a strict policy of whites only. Negro orchestras and lavish Negro revues entertained up to 500 customers nightly.

All of the bands of that era strove for an identifiable style, and since the Cotton Club featured scantily clad girls performing "shaking and shimmying jungle-type gyrations," Ellington came up with what was dubbed "jungle music" — tense rhythms, piercing tones. This was not so much a choice as a necessity, since he had to provide the background music for the constantly changing revues, but it did allow him to explore territory not open to other dance bands and enabled him to feature brass musicians whose innovative use of the mute provided the wailing, readily identifiable "Ellington sound."

By then powerful radio stations and the expanding networks were sending night-club music all over the nation in late-night broadcasts, and Duke's fame spread beyond Harlem and New York. The worldwide success of Ellington's "Mood Indigo" (1930) and "Sophisticated Lady" (1933) solidified both the personnel and structure (six brasses, four reeds, and four rhythms) of the band. Ellington's soloists of this period — Cootie Williams, Barney Bigard, Johnny Hodges, Ben Webster — were artists who became legends in the jazz world. Magazines such as *Variety, Billboard,* and *Orchestra World* ran stories on Duke and the band and the new, exciting music they were producing.

In the early 1930s, they began the first of many cross-country tours, their fame ensuring sold-out crowds at every stop though the Depression was at its height. They toured England and Europe in 1933 and again in 1939, overwhelmed at the adulation. For several years Duke topped the list as most popular recording artist in the country.

In 1943 the band played its first Carnegie Hall concert, and it was in this period when everything came together for Duke and his orchestra. He had been composing steadily for years and had dozens of hit tunes — "Solitude," "Echoes of Harlem," "Black and Tan Fantasy," "Ko Ko," "Bojangles," to name but a few — but now he began writing more ambitious compositions that pushed beyond the standard three-minute record: chamber jazz for small groups; extended works like "Harlem Suite," and the sacred concerts performed before people of all creeds.

Metronome, the magazine of the Swing Era, said: "Though pressed to cater to popular tastes, Duke's forte is the kind of stuff he *likes* to play. For sheer originality, interest, and structure, his orchestrations have yet to be equalled. . . ." To Duke Ellington, the word "jazz" was too restrictive. He loosely defined it as "music with an African foundation which came out of an American environment," adding that what it primarily stood for was "freedom of expression." That freedom is the key to understanding the breadth of his music.

For the music poured out. It is estimated that he composed, arranged, or collaborated on more than 2,000 works during his career. He was well served by his orchestra. The matchless group of musicians he had assembled stayed with him for decades. Together they became a smooth, seamless whole. Duke, a tall, commanding figure, always impeccably dressed, presided over it all with wit and style.

The fame continued, but there came a time when critics complained that the spark and originality were gone, and Duke was simply rehashing his old triumphs. To which charges he responded, "I am more concerned with *who's* playing the music rather than the style of music itself. I *always* write for the men in the band." No one needed to tell Duke Ellington the fine line between commercialism and "art."

Edward Kennedy Ellington died in New York City on May 24, 1974. He was a man of singular grace; he had charm, flair, charisma; he was a showman. But he was more than that: he was an all-time jazz genius. Count Basie once said of him, "Duke Ellington is definitely a statue in American music. He doesn't have to move an inch; he's great as he is."

□□

Writer Lawrence Doorley (Notre Dame '33) lives in Florida.

He loosely defined jazz as "music with an African foundation which came out of an American environment."